Specialty Competencies in Couple and Family Psychology

Series in Specialty Competencies in Professional Psychology

TITLES IN THE SERIES

Specialty Competencies in School Psychology
Rosemary Flanagan and Jeffrey A. Miller

Specialty Competencies in Organizational and Business Consulting Psychology
Jay C. Thomas

Specialty Competencies in Geropsychology
Victor Molinari (Ed.)

Specialty Competencies in Forensic Psychology
Ira K. Packer and Thomas Grisso

Specialty Competencies in Couple and Family Psychology
Mark Stanton and Robert Welsh

MARK STANTON
ROBERT WELSH

Specialty Competencies in
Couple and Family Psychology

OXFORD
UNIVERSITY PRESS

Oxford University Press, Inc., publishes works that further
Oxford University's objective of excellence
in research, scholarship, and education.

Oxford New York

Auckland   Cape Town   Dar es Salaam   Hong Kong   Karachi
Kuala Lumpur   Madrid   Melbourne   Mexico City   Nairobi
New Delhi   Shanghai   Taipei   Toronto

With offices in
Argentina   Austria   Brazil   Chile   Czech Republic   France   Greece
Guatemala   Hungary   Italy   Japan   Poland   Portugal   Singapore
South Korea   Switzerland   Thailand   Turkey   Ukraine   Vietnam

Copyright © 2011 by Oxford University Press, Inc.

Published by Oxford University Press, Inc.
198 Madison Avenue, New York, New York 10016
www.oup.com

Oxford is a registered trademark of Oxford University Press

ISBN-13: 978-0-19-538787-2 (Paper)

Cataloging-in-Publication data is on file with the Library of Congress

9 8 7 6 5 4 3 2 1

Printed in the United States of America
on acid-free paper

ABOUT THE SERIES IN SPECIALTY COMPETENCIES IN PROFESSIONAL PSYCHOLOGY

This series is intended to describe state-of-the-art functional and foundational competencies in professional psychology across extant and emerging specialty areas. Each book in this series provides a guide to best practices across both core and specialty competencies as defined by a given professional psychology specialty.

The impetus for this series was created by various growing movements in professional psychology during the past 15 years. First, as an applied discipline, psychology is increasingly recognizing the unique and distinct nature among a variety of orientations, modalities, and approaches with regard to professional practice. These specialty areas represent distinct ways of practicing one's profession across various domains of activities that are based on distinct bodies of literature and often addressing differing populations or problems. For example, the American Psychological Association (APA) in 1995 established the Commission on the Recognition of Specialties and Proficiencies in Professional Psychology (CRSPPP) in order to define criteria by which a given specialty could be recognized. The Council of Credentialing Organizations in Professional Psychology (CCOPP), an interorganizational entity, was formed in reaction to the need to establish criteria and principles regarding the types of training programs related to the education, training, and professional development of individuals seeking such specialization. In addition, the Council on Specialties in Professional Psychology (COS) was formed in 1997, independent of the APA, to foster communication among the established specialties, in order to offer a unified position to the pubic regarding specialty education and training, credentialing, and practice standards across specialty areas.

Simultaneously, efforts to actually define professional competence regarding psychological practice have also been growing significantly. For example, the APA-sponsored Task Force on Assessment of Competence in Professional Psychology put forth a series of guiding principles for the assessment of competence within professional psychology, based, in part, on a review of competency assessment models developed both within (e.g., Assessment of Competence Workgroup from Competencies Conference [Roberts, Borden, Christiansen, & Lopez, 2005]) and outside (e.g., Accreditation Council for Graduate Medical Education and American Board of Medical Specialties, 2000) the profession of psychology (N. J. Kaslow et al., 2007).

Moreover, additional professional organizations in psychology have provided valuable input into this discussion, including various associations primarily interested in the credentialing of professional psychologists, such as the American Board of Professional Psychology (ABPP), the Association of State and Provincial Psychology Boards (ASPBB), and the National Register of Health Service Providers in Psychology. This widespread interest and importance of the issue of competency in professional psychology can be especially appreciated given the attention and collaboration afforded to this effort by international groups, including the Canadian Psychological Association and the International Congress on Licensure, Certification, and Credentialing in Professional Psychology.

Each volume in the series is devoted to a specific specialty and provides a definition, description, and development timeline of that specialty, including its essential and characteristic pattern of activities, as well as its distinctive and unique features. Each set of authors, long-term experts and veterans of a given specialty, were asked to describe that specialty along the lines of both functional and foundational competencies. *Functional competencies* are those common practice activities provided at the specialty level of practice that include, for example, the application of its science base, assessment, intervention, consultation, and, where relevant, supervision, management, and teaching. *Foundational competencies* represent core knowledge areas that are integrated and cut across all functional competencies to varying degrees, and dependent upon the specialty, in various ways. These include ethical and legal issues, individual and cultural diversity considerations, interpersonal interactions, and professional identification.

Whereas we realize that each specialty is likely to undergo changes in the future, we wanted to establish a baseline of basic knowledge and principles that comprise a specialty highlighting both its commonalities with other areas of professional psychology and its distinctiveness. We look forward to seeing the dynamics of such changes, as well as the emergence of new specialties in the future.

Couple and family psychology is a broad and general specialty in professional psychology that is founded on an understanding of the human experience in a systems context. For the public, the terms *couples* and *family* provide a user-friendly translation but underestimate the multifaceted perspectives required of the specialty. Specialists in couple and family psychology have developed unique assessment and treatment methods that impact behavioral and dynamic factors across individuals, couples, families, and larger social systems. In this volume, Drs. Mark Stanton and Robert Welsh provide a comprehensive explanation of the competencies involved in the specialty and illustrate how complexity, reciprocity, interdependence, adaptation, and self-organization are important aspects of the epistemology of a couples and family approach. As the authors underscore for the reader, the specialty of couple and family psychology is not confined to marital or family therapy but encompasses a broad orientation to human behavior that occurs in the context of relationships as well as larger macrosystemic dynamics. The conceptualization and application of systemic concepts to human behavior include a body of knowledge and evidence-based interventions that require specialty training and competence.

The historical background and careful attention the authors provide regarding illustration of defined practice areas, as well as the breadth of formal models of treatment with specific techniques, provide the definitive text for the way in which specialists begin with a strong systemic framework, even when influenced by additional theoretic frameworks.

Arthur M. Nezu
Christine Maguth Nezu

CONTENTS

AUTHOR PREFACE

We would like to thank the couple and family psychologists who reviewed preliminary materials or chapters of this book. These include: James H. Bray, Joy Bustrum, Cindy Carlson, Marianne Celano, Marv Erisman, Frank R. Ezzo, Michele Harway, George Hong, Florence Kaslow, Nadine Kaslow, John Northman, A. Rodney Nurse, Roberta L. Nutt, Terence Patterson, Sheryn Scott, Thomas L. Sexton, Melton Strozier, Keren Chansky Suberri, John Thoburn, and Nathan Turner. The reviews were very helpful in shaping the content of the text. Any errors or omissions remain our responsibility. The couple and family psychology community is itself a type of family and we appreciate the interest and support we have received.

Dr. Stanton would like to thank his executive assistant, Candi Adermatt, for her assistance in various aspects of the production process. As is appropriate in a couple and family text, he would like to recognize the support and encouragement of his wife, Kathleen, and his children, April, Erin, Chelse, and Sean, throughout the writing process. Dr. Welsh would like to thank his wife Elizabeth for her unwavering encouragement and many cups of tea when writing did not come easily.

PART I

Introduction to Couple and Family Psychology

ONE

Introduction to Couple and Family Psychology

Couple and family psychology (CFP) is a broad and general orientation to the science and practice of professional psychology that is based on a systemic epistemology (Nutt & Stanton, 2008; Stanton, 2009b). CFP understands human behavior within a systemic paradigm that recognizes the reciprocal interaction between individual, interpersonal, and environmental or macrosystemic factors over time (see Chapter 2; Liddle, Santisteban, Levant, & Bray, 2002; Stanton, 2009b). CFP is distinct from psychological orientations that focus primarily on the individual because CFP practitioners treat individuals, couples, families, social groups, and organizations from this systemic perspective (Council of Specialties in Professional Psychology, 2009).

CFP is recognized as a specialty by the American Board of Professional Psychology (ABPP; American Board of Professional Psychology, 2008), the Council of Specialties in Professional Psychology (CoS; Council of Specialties in Professional Psychology, 2009), and, under the general rubric of family psychology, by the Commission for the Recognition of Specialties and Proficiencies in Professional Psychology (CRSPPP; Commission for the Recognition of Specialties and Proficiencies in Professional Psychology, n.d.). Until 2008 the specialty was known exclusively as family psychology, but it is now known primarily as CFP after a name change was approved by ABPP and CoS.

This chapter defines the specialty of CFP, identifies the populations served by the specialty, specifies defined practice areas, and describes the evolution of CFP from early family therapy models espoused by charismatic leaders to a broad competency-based specialty that utilizes clinically-informed evidence-based practices.

Definition of the Specialty

There are several official definitions of the specialty, each originating in one of the organizations constituting the specialty (Table 1.1). A review of these definitions finds several key elements and common themes that define CFP.

FOUNDED ON SYSTEMS THEORY

There is consistent agreement that CFP is founded on *systems theory* and that the specialty incorporates concepts and applications from systems theory into treatment case conceptualization, assessment, and intervention (Stanton, 2009b). The official definitions all explicitly or implicitly identify this foundation and evidence its influence.

The key element is the adoption of an overarching systemic epistemology (see Chapter 2) that informs the understanding and treatment of human behavior. Systemic concepts, such as complexity, reciprocity, interdependence, adaptation, and self-organization, are important aspects of that epistemology. The official definitions refer to these principles and incorporate terms such as *interdependent, reciprocal, environment, context,* and *interaction* (see Table 1.1). See Chapter 2 for a more complete description of the conceptual foundations of CFP, critiques, and recent variations.

The specialty focus is often on the family system (e.g., couple and dyadic interaction, family relationships), and it is understood that the family system can only be understood and assisted within the matrix of individual, interpersonal, and environmental or macrosystemic factors (Stanton, 2009b). Individual psychological functioning is influenced by family dynamics and vice versa (Commission for the Recognition of Specialties and Proficiencies in Professional Psychology, n.d.). Sometimes the primary focus is on the larger system, including such concrete entities as business organizations or abstract macrosystems like culture.

CONTEXTUAL CONCEPTUALIZATION

One element of systemic conceptualization is the recognition of the role of context in understanding individual and interpersonal dynamics. The definitions regularly refer to the environmental context in which individual, couple, and family behavior exists. Bronfenbrenner (1979) raised awareness of the importance of the context for human development, comparing

TABLE 1.1 **Official Definitions of Couple and Family Psychology**

2009 CRSPPP Petition

"Family Psychology is an approach to understanding human functioning and treating problems that is based on general systems theory. The systems perspective assumes that the emotional functioning of individuals within a group is interdependent so that the feelings and behavior of one person can only be understood within the context of other group members. A Family Psychologist addresses both the internal psychology of individuals and the reciprocal relationship process that takes place between family members, with family being broadly defined. Family Psychologists also use the systems approach to understand and intervene with other human systems such as schools, healthcare clinics, businesses, etc. Family Psychology is sometimes thought to be synonymous with family therapy, a subcategory of Family Psychology; Family Psychology uses a broad, developmental perspective to understand health and illness or problems" (Family Psychology Specialty Council, 2009, p. 15).

CRSPPP Website: Brief Characterization

"Family Psychology is a specialty in professional psychology that is focused on the emotions, thoughts, and behavior of individuals, couples, and families in relationships and in the broader environment in which they function. It is a specialty founded on principles of systems theory, with the family as a system being of most central focus. The premise of practice in this specialty is that family dynamics play a vital role in the psychological functioning of family members. This applies to extended families as well as nuclear families. The practice of family psychology takes into consideration as well the family's history and current environment (e.g., family history, ethnic culture, community, school, health care system, and other relevant sources of support or difficulty)" (Commission for the Recognition of Specialties and Proficiencies in Professional Psychology, n.d.).

CoS: Formal Specialty Definition

"Family Psychology focuses on relationships in families, couples, groups and organizations and the larger settings and contexts in which those relationships exist. Family psychologists teach, supervise, do research and engage in practice via consultation and treatment in a variety of settings" (Council of Specialties in Professional Psychology, 2009).

Society for Family Psychology

"Family Psychology integrates the understanding of individuals, couples, families and their wider contexts" (Society for Family Psychology, 2008).

"The Society's mission is to expand both the study and practice of Family Psychology through education, research and clinical practice. The Society goes about fulfilling its mission through the application of systems theory to the ever-changing family unit. The Society places emphasis on diversity and inclusion, both among its membership and in its practical application of theory" (Society for Family Psychology, 2009)

American Board of Couple and Family Psychology

"The specialty of Couple and Family psychology is not confined to 'Couple and Family therapy,' but is a comprehensive application of the science and profession of psychology with families, Couple and Family subsystems, and individual Couple and Family members. Couple and Family psychologists stress the centrality of understanding and constructively changing the Couple and Family unit or subsystems, as well as the individual. Couple and Family psychologists consider the individual, Couple and Family, and human relationships from a perspective that includes systemic interactions and developmental processes over the life span and takes into account the context in which they are embedded" (American Board of Professional Psychology, 2008).

1989 Original Application for Identification as a Specialty by the American Board of Professional Psychology (as recorded in Weeks & Nixon, 1991)

"Family Psychology represents a significant conceptual leap in the field of psychology. Traditionally, psychologists have focused on the individual as the unit of study. Family psychologists focus on the individual in the context of intimate others. They see the individual within a social system which means their thinking and interventions are relational and contextual in nature. In this respect, the family psychologist is a system thinker. The individual system (the individual), the interactional system (the couple), and the intergenerational system (family-of-origin) are all related and exert reciprocal influences on each other. Viewing the individual within the interlocking nature of these systems results in a more holistic, comprehensive, and multi-determined theory of human functioning" (Weeks & Nixon, 1991, p. 10).

the relationship between systems to a set of Russian nested dolls, and CFP definitions consistently use the term *context* to note the importance larger settings play in individual and interpersonal behavior, as understood by the specialty.

Several of the definitions identify specific contexts, such as groups (e.g., neighborhoods, ethnic subcultures), organizations (e.g., schools, health care clinics, businesses), or the macrosystemic context (e.g., culture; this could also include religion or socioeconomic status). CFP has consistently identified ethnic and cultural diversity as an important aspect of the specialty and expects specialists to demonstrate the competency to practice across elements of diversity.

DEVELOPMENTAL PROGRESSION

CFP includes an awareness of time and developmental progression that interacts with individual, interpersonal, and environmental factors (see Chapter 2; Stanton, 2009b). The specialty definitions note that our understanding of problems and healthy behavior needs to include a developmental perspective, including awareness of family history, changing social definitions of the family unit, life span issues, and current personal, family, or environmental circumstances.

One way this is commonly manifest in CFP is through the use of the *multigeneration genogram* (McGoldrick, Gerson, & Petry, 2008) during the assessment phase in treatment. This tool allows the CFP psychologist to gather pertinent historical and developmental information that informs case conceptualization and intervention. CFP specialists also consider individual factors (e.g., life span development-in-context), and they are cognizant of macrosystemic issues (e.g., changing norms, social structures, and societal influences) that may impact treatment.

BROAD DEFINITION OF FAMILY

The term *family* is defined in a broad manner in the specialty definitions. Patterson (2009) notes that CRSPPP originally recommended that CFP be labeled *systems psychology* to more accurately denote the broad focus on systems in the specialty, but the term *family psychology* was adopted because it seemed to translate better to the general public. The systemic epistemology was explained in the definition and continues to be the CFP orientation; the specialty intends to center on human behavior in the context of relationships (i.e., in couples, dyads, families, groups, organizations, and larger settings) and to recognize the reciprocal interaction that occurs in these relationships.

This broad focus is evident in the official definitions, but it may be the most common misunderstanding regarding CFP. Even among psychologists in the American Psychological Association, it appears that some understand CFP not as a broad and general orientation to psychology (i.e., systems psychology) but as merely the practice of couple and family therapy by psychologists (Nutt & Stanton, 2008). The official definitions attempt to correct this misunderstanding: "Family Psychology is sometimes thought to be synonymous with family therapy, a subcategory of Family Psychology" (Family Psychology Specialty Council, 2009, p. 15) and "The specialty of Couple and Family Psychology is not confined to 'Couple and Family therapy' but is a comprehensive application of the science and profession of psychology" (American Board of Professional Psychology, 2008, n.p.). CFP uses the terms *couple* and *family* to denote a broad orientation to human behavior that occurs in the context of relationships and larger macrosystemic dynamics.

In addition, the term *family* was intended to recognize various forms of family and to extend beyond the nuclear family to incorporate the extended family. The definitions recognize that our understanding of family changes over time as we recognize cultural and cohort variations.

COMPREHENSIVE TREATMENT ISSUES

As a broad and general specialty, CFP applies a systemic and developmental understanding to the comprehensive realm of psychological health and pathology. Affective, cognitive, and behavioral factors across individuals, couples, families, groups, organizations, and larger social systems fall within the domain of the specialty and are noted in the official specialty definitions (Commission for the Recognition of Specialties and Proficiencies in Professional Psychology, n.d.). A systemic epistemology facilitates a comprehensive assessment, conceptualization, and intervention process that takes into account the variety of factors that may need to be included to address real-world issues. So, for instance, CFP specialists may treat individual issues (e.g., depression, anxiety), but they will do so within the context of the system (Whisman, Whiffen, & Whiteford, 2009). Or, CFP specialists may work in an organization to facilitate teamwork using knowledge and interventions from CFP. Of course, an individual CFP specialist may function only in the areas where he or she has education and experience, and defined practice areas have developed to address particular issues that require extensive knowledge and supervised experience (see below). Finally, the CFP specialist will take into consideration systemic interactions that surround particular issues and seek to intervene in the system in a holistic fashion.

VARIETY OF FUNCTIONS

CFP specialists are involved in a variety of psychological functions, including professional practice, supervision, consultation, education, and research in an assortment of settings (see below). CFP board certification by ABPP considers these functions in the review of qualification credentials and tests one's professional practice in these functions thoroughly as part of the certification process (American Board of Couple and Family Psychology, 2008).

SUMMARY DEFINITION

CFP is a broad and general specialty in professional psychology that is founded on a systemic epistemology, including explicit awareness of the importance of context, diversity, and developmental perspectives, to understand, assess, and treat the comprehensive issues of psychological health and pathology, including affective, cognitive, behavioral, and dynamic factors across individuals, couples, families, and larger social systems. The crucial element of the specialty is a thorough systemic conceptualization and the application of systemic concepts to human behavior. CFP includes a body of knowledge and *evidence-based interventions* that require specialty competence.

Populations Served and Practice Settings

CFP specialists

> work with individuals, couples, families, and broader environmental systems, such as schools, medical clinics, and business organizations. Even when an individual is the client, the Family Psychologist conceptualizes treatment and interventions from an interpersonal, systems perspective. In working with families, the entire family is viewed as a single emotional unit, and the client is the family, not the identified patient. (Family Psychology Specialty Council, 2009, p. 15)

Because CFP is a broad specialty, it may not be characterized narrowly by particular populations served or "the number of people in the consulting room. Rather, it is defined by its systems perspective from which problems and developmental issues are addressed" (Family Psychology Specialty Council, 2009, p. 15). Although some understand the specialty as serving only couples and families, this is an inaccurate perception of the specialty.

CFP specialists work in a variety of contexts and conduct a variety of roles and interventions, as noted in descriptions of the specialty.

> Professional settings may include hospitals, clinics, independent practice, schools, colleges and universities, businesses, government and other organizations. Within these environments family psychologists may perform a variety of tasks, including interventions with individuals and their families, testing and evaluation, conducting workshops, advocating and impacting policies that affect families, teaching, consulting, and conducting research related to families and other social systems. (Council of Specialties in Professional Psychology, 2009)

Nutt and Stanton (2008) note that CFP specialists work in school settings to increase collaboration between families and schools and in primary health care to enhance systemic functioning and patient care. See Chapter 6 for detailed information about CFP specialists' provision of consultation to schools, health care, and business organizations.

Defined Practice Areas and Subspecializations

There are currently no subspecialties in CFP formally recognized by ABPP. However, there are several defined practice areas that require significant knowledge and experience beyond the generalist level for competent practice. Board-certified specialists in CFP should have fundamental knowledge and initial experience in these domains; active practice in each of these areas requires substantial additional education and experience beyond that required for general board certification as a CFP specialist. Formal identification of any of these defined practice areas as a subspecialty will entail establishment of qualification criteria, procedures for examination of practice competencies, and ABPP approval. Some practice areas may overlap with other identified specialties (e.g., clinical child and adolescent, school psychology, forensic psychology), and CFP specialists may pursue board certification in both specialties to demonstrate competence if they are working actively in that practice area. Systemic sex therapy, family forensic psychology, family business consultation, and systemic substance abuse treatment are among the current specialty defined practice areas.

SYSTEMIC SEX THERAPY

Sex therapy has been an integral aspect of the specialty from the beginning. In fact, when the precursor to the current American Board of Couple and

Family Psychology (ABCFP) was formed at the 1958 annual convention of the American Psychological Association, it was named the Academy of Psychologists in Marital, Sex, and Family Therapy (American Board of Couple and Family Psychology, 2008). Issues of intimacy and sexuality are part of the expected knowledge base for specialists, and there are developed models of sex therapy based on systems theory, often under the rubric of systemic sex therapy (Adams, 2006; Hertlein, Weeks, & Sendak, 2009).

It is possible that the ABCFP will petition ABPP for recognition of systemic sex therapy as a formal subspecialty to CFP. Efforts are under way to formalize systemic sex therapy as a practice area and establish qualification criteria and competency standards.

FAMILY FORENSIC PSYCHOLOGY

CFP specialists often provide professional services to children, couples, and families who are engaged with the legal system (Grossman & Okun, 2003; F. W. Kaslow, 2000). Welsh, Greenberg, and Graham-Howard (2009) distinguish between the roles of the "forensically informed family psychologist" and the "family forensic psychologist" (p. 703), suggesting that all psychologists who treat individuals, couples, or families involved with the legal system need to understand the level of competency required to provide the specific services performed and that some roles clearly call for expertise beyond the scope of normal clinical practice. According to this preliminary distinction (currently not formally delineated in any ethics code), responsible practice requires the psychologist to stay within the scope of her or his education, training, and experience. All CFP specialists need to be informed sufficiently about forensic issues when treating anyone involved in legal action; only those with advanced education, training, and experience that establish competency may represent themselves as family forensic psychologists and/or provide services that require expert status.

Some CFP specialists pursue the necessary education and supervised experience to practice at the advanced level of family forensic psychologist. CFP board certification requires competency at the forensically informed level unless the psychologist works primarily in forensic arenas, in which case the examination would focus on forensic issues and include committee members with this advanced competency. These individuals may also pursue board certification by the American Board of Forensic Psychology, another ABPP constituent board, in order to demonstrate competency in the overlapping domains.

There is an active Special Interest Group in Family Forensic Psychology within the APA Society for Family Psychology (see details regarding

membership at http://www.apa.org/divisions/div43/Forensic1_files/
Forensic/Forensic1.htm). This group publishes regularly in *The Family Psychologist* and presents programming within the Division 43 APA convention schedule. See Chapter 7 for more information regarding family forensic psychology.

FAMILY BUSINESS CONSULTATION

Consultation to organizations is an extension of the systemic epistemology and clinical competencies of the CFP specialist to a larger social unit (see Chapter 6). One subset of consultation that particularly matches the specialty focus is family business consultation (F. W. Kaslow, 2006b). Family business consultation addresses the unique characteristics of businesses owned and operated by family members with close ties that complicate the business dynamics. Treatment goals may include enhancing cross-generational understanding and appreciation, addressing issues of psychological indebtedness or entitlement, succession planning and transition management (F. W. Kaslow, 2005). See Chapter 6 for more coverage of family business consultation.

SUBSTANCE ABUSE TREATMENT

CFP conceives substance abuse treatment from a systemic perspective (Stanton, 2009c). CFP recommends treatment that actively incorporates the individuals within the social system of the substance-abusing person and that recognizes the salience of environmental or macrosystemic factors in the etiology, progression, and treatment of the disorder, unlike many of the approaches that focus primarily on the individual misusing substances and/or provide treatment that largely removes the individual from his or her environment for treatment.

A number of CFP models have been developed that address adolescent or adult substance use disorders. Some programs target adolescent substance abuse (often concurrently with other behavioral and psychological issues), such as Multidimensional Family Therapy (Liddle, 2009), Multisystemic Therapy (Henggeler, Sheidow, & Lee, 2009), and Functional Family Therapy (Sexton, 2009). These models address the individual issue(s) within the reciprocal interactive context of other individuals, interpersonal relations (e.g., peers, parents, family members), and the larger environment (e.g., schools, juvenile justice organizations, culture, and geographic area). Other models target adult substance abuse through systemic interventions that include partners or significant others, such as Behavioral Couples Therapy (Fals-Stewart, Birchler, O'Farrell, & Lam, 2009). These models demonstrate significant evidence for their success, often more than individual approaches (Fals-Stewart et al., 2009) and are part of an increased reliance on evidence-based interventions in CFP.

Evolution Toward Specialty Competencies and Evidence-Based Interventions

CFP has evolved over time from a family therapy orientation driven by charismatic personalities to one characterized by defined specialty competencies and evidence-based interventions (Goldenberg & Goldenberg, 2009; N. J. Kaslow, Celano, & Stanton, 2005). CFP recognizes the strengths of families, as well as the need for interventions that facilitate healthy functioning.

HISTORICAL BACKGROUND

Goldenberg and Goldenberg (2009) note the origins of CFP among pioneers in the 1950s (e.g., Bateson, Bowen, Lidz, & Wynne), who were primarily researchers, to clinicians who adopted systemic concepts in the 1960s and created therapeutic models (e.g., Jackson, Satir, Haley, Ackerman, Bell, Whitaker, & Minuchin).

They suggest that the 1970s and 1980s were the pinnacle of initial influence, as training institutes and professional organizations (e.g., APA Division of Family Psychology) came into existence and the initial treatment approaches developed into formal models of practice with specified techniques: Transgenerational, Systemic Psychodynamic, Experiential, Structural, Strategic, and Systemic Behavioral/Cognitive-Behavioral (Goldenberg & Goldenberg, 2009). These models were critiqued from a feminist perspective (Avis, 1985, 1987; Hare-Mustin, 1988, 1989; Wheeler, Avis, Miller, & Chaney, 1985) and informed by increased awareness of cultural diversity. Postmodernism and social constructionism, focused on language and learning in social context, provided an alternative approach to therapy in the late 1980s and 1990s (Gergen, 1985).

Across this timeline, systemic thinking has influenced psychology in general, and it has been incorporated into the general landscape, albeit generally as one approach among many rather than as an overarching epistemology (Stanton, 2009b). The early models that were identified with particular pioneers have lost their distinctiveness, and many CFP specialists select from them to create integrated models that address a variety of treatment problems (Lebow, 2003). "Integrative models require considerable skill in decision making and differ from eclectic models in that they rely on principles for integration that consider the benefits and potential pitfalls of integration"

(Nutt & Stanton, 2008, p. 524). CFP specialists begin with a strong systemic framework and add interventions that are consistent with the paradigm and applicable to the case according to the principles for integration (Lebow, 2002). Integration efforts require broad and general education and training in CFP that includes the general content and competencies of professional psychology. This background set the stage for the movements toward competency and evidence-based practice in the 1990s and 2000s.

SPECIALTY COMPETENCIES

Professional psychology has moved progressively in recent years to an increased focus on the competencies required for the ethical practice of psychology (Rubin et al., 2007). "*Competencies* are complex and dynamically interactive clusters of integrated knowledge of concepts and procedures; skills and abilities; behaviors and strategies; attitudes, beliefs, and values; dispositions and personal characteristics; self-perceptions; and motivations" (Rubin et al., 2007, p. 453) that contribute an individual's competence to suitably practice psychology. Professional competence may be defined as "the habitual and judicious use of communication, knowledge, technical skills, clinical reasoning, emotions, values, and reflection in daily practice for the benefit of the individual and community being served" (Epstein & Hundert, 2002, p. 226). This definition is increasingly recognized in psychology because it highlights the need for reflective practice that incorporates critical thinking and the evaluation and modification of decisions (N. J. Kaslow & Ingram, 2009).

CFP is part of this movement to emphasize professional competence. The original CRSPPP petition in 2002 aligned CFP with a focus on competencies, and the initial framework for generic competencies in professional psychology was extended to delineate competencies required for CFP specialists (N. J. Kaslow et al., 2005). In each of the competency domains, CFP requires specific or additional knowledge, skills, and attitudes not required by professional psychology.

The competency framework has now been reconceptualized into foundational and functional competencies, and additional competencies have been delineated to ensure full coverage of essential aspects of professional practice (Rodolfa et al., 2005). There has been strong interest in the assessment of competencies, including guiding principles for assessment (N. J. Kaslow et al., 2007) and effective assessment strategies (Leigh et al., 2007; Roberts, Borden, Christiansen, & Lopez, 2005).

ABPP board certification emphasizes competency assessment in all specialty domains and includes examination of specialty-specific versions of all foundational and functional competencies (N. J. Kaslow & Ingram, 2009). This text is intended to provide an overview of these competencies for CFP.

EVIDENCE-BASED INTERVENTIONS

The interventions created by the early pioneers in systemic approaches, in general, did not provide significant research evidence for their models (Goldenberg & Goldenberg, 2009). However, as CFP evolved, more emphasis has been placed on demonstrating the effectiveness of intervention models through clinical research as part of the general trend in professional psychology (Goodheart, Kazdin, & Sternberg, 2006). Recognition as a specialty by CRSPPP required demonstration of the effectiveness of CFP services through research-based outcome studies (Criterion IX. Effectiveness; Family Psychology Specialty Council, 2009). CFP also recognizes the importance of evidence-based relationships (Norcross, 2002) and the importance of including clinical judgment in a review of effectiveness (see Chapter 5 for a thorough review of the role of science and clinical judgment in evidence-based interventions).

CFP specialists seek to bridge the gap between science and practice in the specialty (Liddle et al., 2002; Pinsof & Lebow, 2005). Active steps to join research and practice have been the focus of presidential initiatives in the Society for Family Psychology (Lebow, 2004; Sexton, 2009), including conference presentations and committee action (see Chapter 2 for a description of the scientific foundations of the specialty).

The Society for Family Psychology appointed a task force on evidence-based practice in 2004 to consider how clinical experience, practice theory, and clinical research might be integrated to improve CFP practice (Nutt & Stanton, 2008; Sexton & Coop-Gordon, 2009). This task force considered the definition of the APA Task Force on Evidence-Based Practice that advanced to official APA policy: "*Evidence-based practice in psychology* (EBPP) is the integration of the best available research with clinical expertise in the context of patient characteristics, culture, and preferences" (APA Presidential Task Force on Evidence-Based Practices, 2006, p. 273). The Society task force considered the evolution of evidence-based practices and the conclusions of other specialties and controversies in the field (e.g., the challenges of extending the outcomes of laboratory or strictly controlled studies to normal professional practice; Levant, 2004), as well as a "levels of evidence" approach that considers the varied nature of evidence and the need to match research strategy with the clinical issue (Sexton, Kinser, & Hanes, 2008) in order to develop guidelines for the review of

CFP literature to determine practices with the most potential to assist treatment recipients (Sexton & Coop-Gordon, 2009). They proposed three levels that denote increasing evidence of model effectiveness: (a) Level I: evidence-informed interventions/treatments, built on an evidence base; (b) Level II: promising interventions/treatments, initial research support; and (c) Level III: evidence-based treatments, substantial evidence that the intervention does what it was designed to do (Sexton & Coop-Gordon, 2009). This approach recognizes different types of evidence and the value of clinical expertise (Wampold, Goodheart, & Levant, 2007). See Chapter 5 for a thorough review of specialty intervention practices.

A number of CFP models demonstrate support within these levels, including Emotionally Focused Couple Therapy (S. Johnson & Bradley, 2009; S. M. Johnson & Greenman, 2006); Behavioral Couples Therapy (Fals-Stewart et al., 2009; O'Farrell & Fals-Stewart, 2006); Brief Strategic Family Therapy™ (Robbins, Szapocznik, & Horigian, 2009; Santisteban, Suarez-Morales, Robbins, & Szapocznik, 2006); Multidimensional Family Therapy (Hogue, Dauber, Samuolis, & Liddle, 2006; Liddle, 2009); Multisystemic Therapy (Henggeler et al., 2009); and Functional Family Therapy (Alexander & Parsons, 1982; Sexton, 2009b), and psychoeducational relationship enhancement programs, such as the Prevention and Relationship Enhancement Program (Ragan, Einhorn, Rhoades, Markman, & Stanley, 2009).

Finally, CFP recognizes the growing importance of process variables in practice and the need to monitor change during the intervention process by receiving frequent feedback from therapy participants. Progress research allows the CFP specialist to adapt treatment to the changing circumstances in order to enhance effectiveness (Friedlander, Escudero, & Heatherington, 2006; Pinsof & Chambers, 2009).

Conclusion

CFP is a recognized specialty within professional psychology that provides a broad and general orientation to psychology. CFP specialists utilize a systemic framework to conceptualize human behavior, and they practice in a wide variety of practice settings based on demonstrated competency in the specialty and experience in defined practice areas. CFP specialists use evidence-based interventions, defined according to APA policy, to inform assessment and intervention.

TWO

Conceptual and Scientific Foundations

The specialty of couple and family psychology (CFP) is founded on a systemic epistemology that recognizes the complex, reflexive interaction between individual, interpersonal, and macrosystemic-environmental factors over time (Stanton, 2009b). Inculcation and use of a systemic epistemology is the hallmark of the specialty. CFP specialists ground their practice in the conceptual and scientific foundations of the discipline and evidence that underpinning as they demonstrate specialty competence across the foundational and functional competencies.

This chapter describes the knowledge, skills, and attitudes related to CFP competency in conceptual and scientific foundations. CFP specialists enhance specialty practice through systemic conceptualization and the application of systemic research to case conceptualization, professional assessment, intervention, and monitoring of treatment progress. Scientific methods consistent with a systemic epistemology enable specialty research that advances the field. Table 2.1 specifies the competency domains, behavioral anchors, and assessment methods for this competency.

Conceptual and Scientific Knowledge

The CFP specialist has acquired a command of the specialty epistemology, scientific knowledge, and scientific methods that provides a foundation for the development of specialty skills. This section describes the foundation of knowledge necessary to capably articulate a systemic epistemology, demonstrate advanced scientific knowledge in the specialty, and display an understanding regarding the application of the CFP epistemology and scientific methods to specialty practice.

TABLE 2.1 Conceptual and Scientific Foundations: Developmental Level—Specialty Competence in Couple and Family Psychology

COMPETENCY DOMAIN AND ESSENTIAL COMPONENT	BEHAVIORAL ANCHOR	ASSESSMENT METHODS
Knowledge (A) Scientific foundation of CFP (A.1) Command of specialty epistemology, scientific knowledge, and scientific methods	(A.1.1) Demonstrates advanced knowledge and capably articulates a systemic epistemology, including a systemic paradigm and key concepts, as well as the critiques and contemporary variations on a systemic orientation (A.1.2) Demonstrates advanced level of CFP scientific knowledge and scientific methods (A.1.3) Demonstrates advanced level of understanding regarding application of CFP epistemology and science to specialty practice	1. ABPP Examination 2. Ongoing status for practice through licensure 3. Self-evaluation 4. Client feedback 5. Peer review and consultation 6. Continuing education 7. Consultation or supervision feedback 8. Publication and presentation in scholarly venues
Skills (B) Scientific foundation of CFP practice (B.1) Intentional inclusion of CFP concepts, scientific knowledge, and scientific methods in all aspects of specialty activity	(B.1.1) Ability to think systemically and demonstrate systemic mental habits (B.1.2) Ability to apply systemic orientation to all CFP competencies (B.1.3) Ability to apply specialty scientific knowledge and scientific methods to all CFP competencies	
Attitudes (C) Scientific mindedness (C.1) Independently values and applies CFP theory and scientific methods to specialty practice	(C.1.1) Aware of epistemological options and ability to transition between paradigms in specialty practice (C.1.2) Independent attitudes that demonstrate scientific mindedness related to specialty practice (C.1.3) Conducts self-evaluation and invites peer review of specialty practice	

Note. Adapted from the format and content of the Assessment of Competency Benchmarks Work Group (2007). This table assumes that the specialist has achieved competence in professional psychology at the three previous developmental levels, as specified in the benchmarks. The competency domains and behavioral anchors serve as the primary organizing structure for this chapter; content explaining each domain and anchor is provided in the chapter.

KNOWLEDGE OF SYSTEMIC EPISTEMOLOGY

The CFP specialist demonstrates advanced knowledge of a systemic epistemology, including understanding of a systemic paradigm to categorize and
coordinate system information and properties, knowledge of key concepts
and ideas, and understanding of critiques and contemporary variations on
a systemic orientation.

Systemic Epistemology

An *epistemology* refers to an encompassing set of rules used in thought
processes by a group of people to define reality (Auerswald, 1990; Bateson,
1972; Stanton, 2009b). These rules govern the perception and use of information. Most people give little thought to the way they think or to the
fact that they have been educated to think in particular ways, or according to particular rules about thinking. We simply think, assuming that the
way we think is the way everyone thinks, or should think. In fact, we are
socialized to think according to particular rules, and there are significant
differences between people educated in Eastern versus Western thought
methods (Nisbett, 2007).

For example, many people, especially in the United States and Europe,
have been educated in the scientific method originated by René Descartes
in 1637 (Capra, 2002). The Cartesian method emphasized scientific doubt,
dividing problems into parts in order to solve them, commencing problem
solving with the easiest aspects of the problem despite the natural relationship between the parts, and conducting thorough analyses (Descartes,
1999). These rules were the foundation for significant scientific progress, but they also resulted in several errors when taken too far, including extreme individualism ("the tendency to frame reality through the
lens of the individual rather than the collective whole"; Stanton, 2009b,
p. 7), reductionism ("the idea that a complex system is only the sum of its
parts" used to the point that the complexity of the whole is lost; Stanton,
2009b, p. 7); linear thinking ("the idea that there is a simple cause-and-
effect mechanism that may explain most acts as one explores them using
logical, rational analysis"; Stanton, 2009b, p. 8); and extreme objectivism
(the limitation of knowledge to only that which may be known through a
narrow interpretation of the scientific method; see Stanton, 2009b, for an
explanation of these errors).

The CFP specialist adopts a systemic epistemology as a means of avoiding these errors by balancing the rules of Descartes with methods that recognize context, complexity, and reciprocity (Stanton, 2009b). This involves
a primary paradigm shift from a Cartesian individualism to an inclusive

systemic mind-set (Stanton, 2005). The process of change involved in such an epistemological transformation is described in Chapter 9. A systemic epistemology recognizes the whole *and* its parts by balancing individual, interpersonal, and macrosystemic factors. As Harway (2003) notes, "The systemic thinker has made a paradigm shift to considering all aspects of human behavior within the multiplicity of contexts within which they occur. This provides a more expansive view than traditional psychological approaches" (p. 4). The adoption of a systemic epistemology is a hallmark of the CFP specialty because it impacts each of the specialty competencies (see the competency chapters in this volume).

Systemic Paradigm

The adoption and use of a systemic epistemology are facilitated by a systemic framework for the understanding and organization of knowledge. Barton and Haslett (2007) refer to the importance of a systemic paradigm as a cognitive construct that enables us to make sense of complexity and organize knowledge. Figure 2.1 depicts human behavior within the dynamic interaction between individual, interpersonal, and environmental-macrosystemic factors over time.

This model is a significant shift from the hierarchical and linear models often used to describe social systems in the United States. The interactive arrows depict the complexity and reciprocity of the system (Robbins, Mayorga, & Szapocznik, 2003). This simple paradigm allows the CFP specialist to conceptualize and categorize complex social systems that present in clinical practice, as long as it is not reified or reduced too far. It is a representation of the system for purposes of understanding and ordering

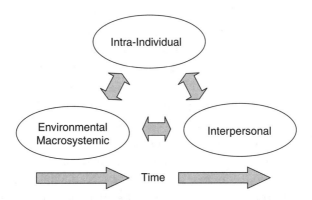

FIGURE 2.1 **Systemic Paradigm of Family Psychology**

Reprinted with permission by Wiley-Blackwell from M. Stanton (2009b), The systemic epistemology of family psychology, in J. Bray & M. Stanton (Eds.), *Wiley-Blackwell handbook of family psychology* (Oxford, UK: Wiley-Blackwell).

our interaction with the system. It must remain a dynamic framework that simply serves to assist the specialist in mentally conceptualizing the system factors and the manner in which those factors interact within the system.

There is strong research support for the mutual influence between individual and family behavior and increasing support for the role of environmental factors with both individual and family behavior (Lebow, 2005a). Marsella (1998) describes the linkage between global conditions (macrosystemic factors) and individual well-being. These interactions involve the provision and use of resources and support, as well as the possibility of negative interactions that create or increase problems.

Individual factors refer to intraindividual features that play a role in a person's social and environmental behavior (e.g., IQ, age, gender, developmental progression, personality, biological bases) as they interplay with system components (Andersen, Thorpe, & Kooij, 2007). Interpersonal factors refer to social dynamics that reveal patterns and processes. Macrosystemic-or environmental factors refer to the larger context and the role of economic, cultural, political, and environmental forces in interaction with individual and interpersonal processes. See Chapter 2 for examples of each category of factors. Time plays a role across the three categories. All exist within a sequence of time and are influenced by individual life progression, generational transmission and family life span development, as well as macrosystemic trends and changes.

Key Concepts

Knowledge of a systemic epistemology includes advanced understanding of several key concepts. However, it should be noted that simply understanding the concepts is insufficient for competency; knowledge is the foundation for the ability to apply the concepts to professional practice (see the "Skills" section later in the chapter for description of habitual use of systemic thinking in applied settings). Typically, awareness of basic concepts progresses to the ability to recognize or apply them in real situations. Sweeney and Sterman (2007) refer to this as "systems intelligence" in that it combines conceptual knowledge with reasoning skills (p. 286). This type of systems intelligence is needed to facilitate case conceptualization, assessment, and intervention for complex presenting issues in CFP practice.

A number of concepts are central to a systemic epistemology. Table 2.2 presents a list of concepts that are important to understanding systemic properties and processes. Definitions and explanations of these concepts may be located in the source citations. CFP specialists understand these terms and know how to think according to them.

TABLE 2.2 **Systemic Concepts**

Adaptation	Homology, patterns
Ambiguity	Inputs-outputs
Ascendency	Interdependence/mutual interdependence
Autopoesis	Linear vs. nonlinear causality
Boundaries	Living, open systems
Change	Mind-process of cognition
Chaos	Networks
Closed systems	Nonsummativity
Complexity	Reciprocity
Connection	Reification
Constructivism	Reductionism
Diversity-components	Resilience
Ecological succession	Self-correcting communication
Entrophy	Self-organization
Equifinality	Social construction of knowledge
Equilibrium-disequilibrium	Stocks and flows-accumulation
Far from equilibrium	Subsystems
Feedback loops or dynamics	Time-temporal factors
Hierarchical-nonhierarchical	Turbulence
Homeostasis	Wholes

Note. List draws from Capra, 1983, 1996, 2002; Stanton, 2009a; Sweeney & Sterman, 2007; Wadsworth, 2008. Definitions and explanations of the terms and concepts may be located in these source citations.

Critiques

What is systemic thinking?   One persistent concern expressed regarding systems thinking has to do with its definition. Cabrera, Colosi, and Lobdell (2008) note that it has been used synonymously with systems sciences, understood as a taxonomy of systemic approaches, and described as an emergent property of conceptual rules. They suggest that learning to apply basic rules may inform psychological practice. We take a more comprehensive approach. We suggest in this chapter and throughout this text that systemic competency involves an epistemological transformation, adoption and use of a systemic paradigm for categorizing and organizing information, knowledge of key systemic concepts, habitual systemic thinking, and application of that thought process to professional practice. The absence of any of these elements reduces systemic thinking to an abstract theory, reifies it into knowledge alone, or produces techniques apart from conceptual understanding. Systemic thinking involves all the features.

Feminist concerns.   Perhaps the most prominent critique of systems thinking came from feminist psychologists who suggested that some systemic interpretations of intimate partner violence (IPV) were problematic.

For example, Goldner (1998) was involved in the Gender and Violence Project at the Ackerman Institute, which studied domestic violence from a feminist-informed perspective. She was an early advocate for feminist perspectives and criticism of the "standard systemic couples therapy approach to violence" that may blame the victim (Goldner, 1998, p. 264). However, she proposed a means to "capitalize on the strengths of the systemic approach while minimizing its dangers" by positing an approach that is grounded in concerns for justice and safety, yet responds to couple desires for conjoint treatment and the need to treat the "extraordinarily intense, mutual reactivity" of their relationship (Goldner, 1998, p. 264). She concludes, "To argue that partners mutually *participate* in an interactional process does not mean they are mutually *responsible* for it, or for its catastrophic outcome" (Goldner, 1998, p. 264). Lebow (2005a) builds on Goldner's argument and notes that more complex systemic thinking (i.e., a shift away from simple reflexive or circular causation) may allow recognition that "one person's influence is greater than another's on their mutual process, even though the action of each has some impact….patterns of couple violence may show circular arcs of influence, but typically the individual personality of the abuser has much more impact on the initiation and continuation of abuse than that of the abused partner" (p. 2).

The underlying concern of the feminist critique is that systems concepts do not hold individuals responsible for their actions. Fuqua and Newman (2002) turn the argument on its head when they state:

> Too often, systems theory has become an excuse for personal failures, leading some to believe that people are simply products of their environment. The opposite conclusion, in fact, applies. The greatest potential of systems theory is to empower individuals to singularly and collectively take responsibility for the systems in which they work and live, to the end of building and rebuilding human systems to become increasingly responsive to human needs. (p. 79)

Core critique.   The feminist critique may provide the basis for understanding the core concerns that have arisen against systemic conceptualization. That is, these critiques may reflect more on older ideas related to systems that distorted, reified, or simplified dynamic systems ideas in a manner that eliminated the theoretical space to modify and adapt the ideas to the reality of the lived experience (Lebow, 2005a). These models were based more on cybernetic ideas and inanimate systems than on dynamic living systems. Contemporary variations on systemic thinking move away from that rigidity.

Contemporary Systems Thinking

Contemporary systems thinking is no longer the mechanistic and authoritarian model of the past. Some aspects of systems thinking formerly accentuated the structure of systems and posited a positivist approach to understanding human behavior that implied a simple deterministic circular causality. They suggested that systems seek equilibrium and avoid change. Contemporary dynamic systems theory moves away from elements of that older model (Wadsworth, 2008).

Lebow (2005a) rehearses the historical progression of systemic thinking and concludes that the twenty-first-century version of systems theory is less deterministic and provides more room for complex understandings of causal processes. The current version allows "for the differential impact of different individuals on the mutual systemic process, for influences on the system that reside within the inner selves of individuals, and for the impact of the larger system on the family" (p. 6). Lebow notes a shift away from the avoidance of individual problems and the idea of "identified patients" who are symptom bearers for the family to nonjudgmental recognition and diagnosis of individual difficulties firmly embedded in their context and a greatly enhanced understanding of the complex interaction between factors in problem development, maintenance, and progression toward improvement or deterioration. CFP specialists are not stuck in the past but progress with the field to recognize new developments.

Because systemic thinking was, in part, a reaction to the individual focus of Western psychology, it is interesting to note the current incorporation of systemic ideas into psychoanalysis and psychodynamic schools. Stephen Seligman (2005) notes that systemic thinking and psychoanalysis share an interest in ambiguity, change, patterns, chaos, and complexity. He suggests that dynamic systems models provide insights regarding the process of psychoanalysis. Bustrum (2007) suggests that dynamic systems theory impacts an understanding of contemporary psychoanalysis in the areas of theoretical understanding (i.e., the unconscious is dynamic and contains intolerable affective states vs. functioning like a locked vault), conceptualization of the analytic relationship (i.e., a shift from being an objective listener to an organizing perceiver), and consideration of therapeutic responses (i.e., a greater sense of the possibility of unique therapeutic relations and engagement vs. projective identification alone).

KNOWLEDGE OF SCIENTIFIC FOUNDATIONS

The 2002 Competencies Conference Work Group on Scientific Foundations and Research Competencies determined several shared assumptions about the role of science in professional psychology that underlie efforts to define the competency and its subcomponents. The group agreed that the scientific approach is the distinctive feature of the profession, that there is a scientific foundation for professional practice, that good science includes attention to sociocultural context and generalizability, and that science-practice integration is important (Bieschke, Fouad, Collins, & Halonen, 2004). These general assumptions that apply across psychology apply to the CFP specialty as well. In this section, we describe elements of the scientific knowledge and scientific methods needed for specialty competence.

The holistic approach of a systemic epistemology argues for a broad definition of data and a range of methods to accumulate those data. CFP researchers avoid reductionism in order to examine the complexity of human experiences (Stanton, 2009b). This is in accord with the report of the APA Presidential Task Force on Evidence-Based Practice, which noted the importance of an empirical foundation but "did not dictate the method used to collect data that would form the basis of evidence, nor did it privilege certain types of evidence" (Wampold, Goodheart, & Levant, 2007, p. 617). Sexton, Hanes, and Kinser (2010) focus on the definition of research as a "systematic, inquiry-based, and knowledge-producing set of methods and skills" (p. 166) in order to set aside the common tendency to distinguish or disparage quantitative or qualitative methods into separate camps. They suggest that the choice of method depends most on the research question; Wampold et al. (2007) agree, stating that "some methods are better suited for some purposes than for others" (p. 617). CFP research incorporates multiple methods to achieve relevant data to inform the specialty. Snyder and Kazak (2005) refer to this as "methodological pluralism" (p. 4) and argue that the specialty must value competing and complementary research paradigms.

Black and Lebow (2009) suggest that empirical research is valuable to CFP clinicians, noting that it helps justify the use of specialty treatments for client and third-party payers and avoids the use of ineffective or harmful treatments. However, they state that it is important to remain open to objective and subjective forms of knowledge.

A range of methods can be used effectively within a systemic epistemology, including methods that examine multiple aspects of complex systems; "because the science of family psychology is richly complex, so too must be the methods for examining couple and family phenomena be equally diverse" (Snyder & Kazak, 2005, p. 3). Snyder and Kazak, introducing a special issue of the *Journal of Family Psychology* on research methods (Vol. 19, No. 1, 2005), indicate that new methods now extend beyond description and covariation to capture the complexity of real problems. The special issue features articles that describe the evaluation of CFP intervention process, outcomes, and cost-benefit ratios; strategies for analysis of data regarding CFP subjective experiences; multilevel modeling techniques; and specific methods of data analysis relevant to complex couple and family processes. The quantitative models described extend far beyond earlier, more limited models that were unable to capture some of the systemic complexities of couples and families (Atkins, 2005).

Silverstein, Auerbach, and Levant (2006) suggest that qualitative methods are well suited to clinical practice and that they facilitate the goal of constructing knowledge of the experience of the participants. Gilgun (2009) notes that qualitative methods are "useful for theory construction and testing, for the development of descriptions of lived experiences, model and concept development, the delineation of social processes, the development of typologies, and the creation of items for surveys, assessment instruments, and evaluation tools" (p. 85). Qualitative methods pay attention to the role of the social context in human behavior (Bieschke et al., 2004), and they are particularly well suited to inclusion of multicultural dimensions in an ethical and appropriate manner (Bieschke et al., 2004; Silverstein & Auerbach, 2009). Attention to diversity is an important aspect of the CFP specialty (see Chapter 11), so methods that avoid reductionistic means of attempting to address cultural diversity in treatment and provide the means to understand the multiplicity of different ethnic and cultural groups that present for CFP treatment are crucial (Silverstein & Auerbach, 2009). Gilgun (2005, 2009) provides an overview of various qualitative methods in the specialty. Narrative methods that tell the story of family life routines and rituals are increasingly helpful (Fiese & Spagnola, 2005; Fiese & Winter, 2009).

Finally, Lebow (2005a) notes "the emergence of a true science of couple and family relationships" and cites 11 research sources that provide "vital implications for practice" (p. 6). These include: (a) increased volume of CFP research; (b) increased research on both specific problems and broad aspects of couple and family functioning; (c) established evidence for the circular relationship between individual and family functioning; (d) increased consideration of the system beyond the family; (e) significantly improved scientific methods and measures; (f) multimethod research; (g) longitudinal research findings now available; (h) treatment–family process linkage; (i) theory-research linkage; (j) increased awareness and inclusion of diversity in research; and (j) emergence of prevention research. The CFP specialist remains competent in the scientific foundations of the specialty by remaining current with scientific advances in order to be a knowledgeable consumer of specialty research.

KNOWLEDGE OF THE APPLICATION OF SYSTEMIC EPISTEMOLOGY AND SCIENCE TO PRACTICE

CFP specialists demonstrate advanced understanding of the application of specialty theory and psychological science to practice. There is a widely recognized historical disconnect between science and practice in psychology (Kazdin, 2008). Some note that "observation of clinician behaviors suggests that most clinicians do not use the best known evidence to influence clinical decision making" (Bieschke et al., 2004, p. 717). On the other hand, for some clinicians "the science of psychology is seen as oversimplified, clinically irrelevant, and unable to account for the unique nature of clinical practice" (Sexton, 2009b, p. 1). Kazdin (2008) describes many of the concerns regarding science and practice that perpetuate the disconnect. However, there have been a number of recent efforts to demonstrate how science and practice relate. Kazdin (2008) suggests that "there are opportunities for a rapprochement between research and practice that will not only foster improved clinical care but will also develop and strengthen the knowledge base" (p. 147). The importance of the connection between science and practice was central to the decision by the 2002 Competencies Conference Work Group on Scientific Foundations and Research Competencies' decision to "focus exclusively on how the practice of psychology maintains a scientific basis" (Bieschke et al., 2004, p. 714). CFP specialists recognize the challenges but share this commitment and actively seek to apply science to professional practice.

Sexton et al. (2010) move beyond existing research or practice competency definitions to provide a framework for the "translation" of psychological science and research into professional practice. They suggest that "few previous efforts have focused on the specific components required to successfully 'translate' science into practice. Attention to the 'translation' between science and practice is important, given the central role of scientific research in the understanding and practice of the wide range of activities that fall under the umbrella of professional psychology" (Sexton et al., 2010, p. 154). They proceed to describe competencies that "move the knowledge of science into the daily clinical practice of psychologists"

(p. 154). The knowledge competencies they delineate include understanding long-established domains, recently established arenas, and emerging ideas: (a) scientific methods (see above); (b) clinical intervention research; (c) evidence-based practice; and (d) specification of clinical practices (Sexton et al., 2010).

BRIDGES BETWEEN SCIENCE AND PRACTICE

There have been a number of efforts within the CFP specialty to "bridge" between science and practice. Two recent presidents of the Society for Family Psychology (2004 and 2009) made this issue a primary presidential initiative because it is considered crucial to the future of the specialty. Lebow (2004) initiated the theme "Bridging Research and Practice in Family Psychology" in hope that his efforts "to raise consciousness about this issue can help us move a few steps closer toward the integration of science and practice in our work" (p. 1). He notes that those who research and those who practice often work in separate silos and interface with dissimilar constituencies; this is evidenced by publications and presentations that focus on one element or the other and leave the field divided. He argues for a rapprochement in which research begins with clinically relevant questions and clinicians incorporate research findings into practice. Lebow appointed a task force to consider evidence-based practice in the specialty (see below). Sexton (2009b) suggests that increased ability to assist CFP clients relies on a "real" connection between science and practice, and he argues for a genuine partnership that facilitates interaction and discussion around theory-based and specified treatments that "give us a common language—help us *talk across* the walls of our offices and laboratories" (p. 26).

Skills

The CFP specialist has the ability to apply the knowledge of a systemic epistemology and specialty research methods to the specialty competencies. This is an important issue, for it highlights that all the CFP competencies are founded on a systemic conceptualization and specialty science. The specialty competencies are not simply skills or techniques that may be learned apart from their theoretical and scientific underpinnings. The CFP specialist has inculcated systemic concepts to the point where systemic thinking is habitual. The hallmark of psychology and of psychology specialties is thorough reliance on psychological theory and science (Bieschke et al., 2004). Overall CFP specialty competency requires an advanced level of knowledge in the specialty theory and science and the ability to apply it to all competencies. This suggests that an overarching specialist skill is to remain current in the knowledge of CFP theory and science by accessing and applying that knowledge habitually and appropriately (Bieschke et al., 2004).

In this section, we briefly identify the skills involved in habitual systemic thinking and the application of the CFP conceptual and scientific competency to the remaining CFP competencies. A more complete description of the conceptual and scientific foundations for each particular competency is provided in the subsequent chapters of this text.

HABITUAL SYSTEMIC THINKING

CFP specialists have inculcated a systemic epistemology to the point where they think systemically and articulate that process of perceiving, structuring ideas, and thinking about life situations. A number of aspects of systems thinking characterize those who adopt a systemic epistemology (Benson, 2007; Stanton, 2009b). Termed *habits of mind* (Sweeney, n.d.), they are perceptual practices and cognitive structuring processes that reflect key systemic concepts and principles that are adopted and used intentionally to address real-life issues or problems. The CFP manifests these habits in understanding human behavior, conceptualizing clinical cases, assessing strengths and problems, and conducting interventions. Our list of habits (Table 2.3) is adapted from Sweeney (n.d.), Stanton (2009b), and Benson (2007).

Challenge Mental Models

Systems thinking requires the willingness to reconsider one's own mental models. However, it is a challenge to recognize the need to examine mental

TABLE 2.3 **Systemic Thinking Habits**

Challenge mental models
See the system
Comprehend complexity
Recognize reciprocity
Consider connections
Accept ambiguity
Conceptualize change
Observe patterns and trends
Consider unintended consequences
Shift perspective
Factor in time

models and select modes of thinking most appropriate to the situation at hand when rules into which we were socialized are unconsciously followed. This type of mental flexibility is at the heart of systems thinking. Bateson (1972) called this "learning to learn" or "deutero-learning" and suggested that it requires an epistemological transformation. It also requires the humility to allow others to question your epistemological assumptions and conclusions and openness to new ideas, models, or methods. Don Michael calls this "error-embracing" and suggests that it is the "condition for learning. It means seeking and using—and sharing—information about what went wrong with what you expected or hoped would go right" (personal communication cited in Meadows, 2008, p. 181). CFP specialists think about their own thinking processes and confront epistemological bias in order to think in more complex ways about their work.

See the System

Perhaps the most crucial habit is the ability to picture the system relevant to the person(s) presenting for CFP services. Seeing the system is an abstract process that looks beyond the concrete person(s) or issue(s) to conceptualize the dynamic factors in the context around the presenting person(s) or issue(s). Seeing the system means first considering the whole system, then focusing on the constituent parts. This is important because it counters the tendency toward reductionism by many people educated in European American arenas that look first at the parts and may miss the whole, including the interaction or connection between parts of the system. A variety of concepts are related to this habit, including the function of boundaries around subsystems and systems and the idea of self-organization in systems (i.e., systems organize and reorganize according to demands).

Various metaphors have been used to describe the nature of systems. One of the most well known was posited by Bronfenbrenner (1979) when he described the system as similar to a set of nested Russian dolls, with each system containing subsystems that all rest within it and itself nesting in larger systems. Such metaphors enable the CFP specialist to picture the system and to describe it to the client(s). Other common metaphors that readily convey systemic dynamics are the human body, an orchestra, or an automobile. Each has its limits, but each helps explain some aspects of a system.

One substantive way to see the system is through the inculcation of a systemic paradigm that provides a structure or framework for system factors and systemic dynamics (Stanton, 2009b; see Figure 2.1). This figure may help make the system visible. Part of the ability to see the system involves active use of the paradigm in treatment conceptualization, assessment, and intervention. In professional practice, this habit means that the CFP specialist regularly uses the paradigm to conceptualize behavior and process. The questions that inform the process of conceptualization are: How do individual factors, interpersonal factors, and environmental or macrosystemic factors interact in this situation? Which specific factors in each category are salient? How have these factors interacted over time, or how do we predict they will interact over time? In this manner, the CFP specialist sees the system throughout the process and progress of treatment.

Comprehend Complexity

This habit recognizes the complex, interactive relationship between system levels and subsystem components that goes beyond linear cause-effect conceptualization. "Most systems thinking advocates agree that much of the art of systems thinking involves the ability to represent and assess dynamic complexity (e.g., behavior that arises from the interaction of a system's agents over time)" (Benson, 2007, p. 2). When thinking in this way, the CFP specialist looks for multifaceted understanding of presenting issues; it is not reasonable or helpful to facilitate or accept quick solutions that are reductionistic. For example, the idea that if the husband stops drinking alcohol the marriage will be fine is probably shortsighted, ignoring multiple factors that contributed to the etiology and progression of the marital problems (i.e., alcohol consumption is one factor that interacts with others in the complexity of the situation). Complexity is allied with chaos theory (i.e., the idea that dynamic systems evidence discontinuous change at random times); this suggests that interventions or changes in the system may lead to unexpected or unpredicted results (McBride, 2005).

It is a challenge to hold multiple factors in one's awareness throughout the process of psychotherapy. Some CFP specialists feel overwhelmed, especially early in their career, by the range of factors they need to consider in order to provide thorough treatment. One key aspect of comprehending complexity is to increase the range of factors when considering a problem (Sweeny & Sterman, 2007). Research suggests that individuals tend not to include factors that are outside the immediate boundary when presented with problem scenarios (Sweeney & Sterman, 2007). The systemic paradigm (see Figure 2.1) may assist the CFP specialist in organizing ideas and information. Ultimately, we suggest that it is better to struggle with complexity than to settle for reductionistic "solutions" that do not actually prove helpful over time.

Recognize Reciprocity

CFP specialists recognize the "mutual, interactive, non-sequential effects that occur between persons or circumstances" (Stanton, 2009b, p. 15). This is a significant shift away from reductionistic and linear cause-effect thinking that conceptualizes each action as distinct and sequential in relation to other actions. Capra (1983) notes that social transactions demonstrate a "simultaneous and mutually interdependent interaction between multiple components" (p. 267). For example, it is reductionistic to think in couple therapy that one partner speaks, then the other, in an orderly and sequential manner. In fact, the husband may laugh or ignore the wife while she is sharing her feelings, or the wife may roll her eyes as the husband expresses his opinion. The reciprocal effects in the interaction are often a roadblock to the achievement of effective communication. Substantially more complex reciprocity occurs in larger systems.

Even reciprocity must not be considered in a reductionistic fashion. It would be problematic to think that members of the system contribute equally to interactions (i.e., there are often power dynamics that modulate the relative influence and power of one person over another in a situation; see the feminist critique noted above in the knowledge section). Interdependence is not evenly distributed; rather, it is complex and variable over time and situation. It is sometimes difficult to parse out the specific contributions and the patterns (see below) of reciprocity that may constitute interaction and communication in a system, but recognition of the concept of reciprocity may allow the specialist to more regularly detect it and address it in psychotherapy and consultation.

Consider Connections

A core aspect of a system is the connection between the parts of the system. CFP specialists actively consider connections as they work with individual members, dyads, or subsystems. Capra (1996) refers to the interdependence and interrelatedness of systems as the "web of life" and suggests that all systems are networks of individual organisms that organize and nest within each other as "networks within networks" (p. 35). In the social sciences, this means adopting a fundamental shift from looking at individuals to looking at the connections between individuals. Humans in relationships, whether they are intimate, biological, or organizational, affect and impact each other in a dynamic process of interdependence. For example, is there an interrelationship between a parent's perception of a child and the child's self-perception? In addition, humans interact within a context that includes natural, political, cultural, economic, and other macroscopic or environmental elements. Once the CFP specialist comes to the habit of actively considering connections, it is possible to use a systemic paradigm (see Figure 2.1) to facilitate recognition and inclusion of the connections that exist in a particular situation or case.

Connections in social systems are often manifested and operate through the transmission of information and ideas (Meadows, 2008). The flow of communication helps coordinate interaction and interdependence. Ultimately, connection is centered on the purpose of the system, which may be determined from observation of system behavior (e.g., is the purpose of a particular marriage about relationship, partnership, control, sex?). The specialist may recognize power dynamics, cultural beliefs or restrictions, religious or spiritual convictions, and so forth, that are part of the systemic communication process and inform the connection. CFP specialists assume connections, look for them regularly, and factor them into interventions in individual, couple, family, and organizational dynamics.

Accept Ambiguity

Dynamic systems thinking recognizes that situations and circumstances are often unclear or uncertain. This counters the common desire for easy answers to complex situations. Systems thinking suggests that interdependence, complexity, and reciprocity alone create significant ambiguity in most situations. Therefore, a systemic habit would involve questioning solutions or answers that seem too certain or too absolute. Instead, the systems thinker recognizes the shades of gray present in most situations and seeks to include them in the therapeutic process. This requires that the CFP specialist accept ambiguity (or enjoy and embrace it) even while many people run from it. "Tolerance for ambiguity implies that one is able to deal with uncertainty and/or multideterminacy.... Ambiguity-tolerant people are comfortable with the shades of gray in life" (Beitel, Ferrer, & Cecero, 2004, p. 569). Acceptance of ambiguity allows the specialist to hold ambiguity in mind while considering complex problems or multiple perspectives. Constructivism suggests that many people, when faced with ambiguous situations, feedforward what they have already learned in the past in situations that seem similar or have comparable elements (Mahoney, 1991). This may reduce uncertainty and ambiguity, but it may also disallow new learning, new ideas, or change by disallowing novelty in experience (it may also perpetuate bias and prejudice). CFP interventions may require that the client(s) stretch beyond an existing comfort zone to perceive and understand the shades of gray in the life; Gelatt (1989) suggests that it is possible to be comfortable with the ambiguity we face in interpersonal relations today, calling for "positive uncertainty" (p. 252). The CFP specialist needs to embrace ambiguity and facilitate tolerance for it in others.

Conceptualize Change

CFP specialists understand systemic change processes. Self-organization is the ability of a system to change itself by creating new responses or new behaviors to cope with presenting challenges. It is a form of resilience that allows a system to adjust and adapt over time. For example, consider how the human immune system may evolve in response to new infections (Meadows, 2008). Equifinality, "the notion that there are multiple possible paths to a given outcome" (Fuqua & Newman, 2002, p. 84), is an aspect of self-organization. It means that individuals, couples, families, and organizations, when faced with daunting challenges, may create totally new pathways to face those issues. However, there are limits to resilience, and systems may not always reorganize effectively. The CFP specialist must conceptualize change in a manner that allows the system to manifest equifinality and self-organization, even if it means that the person(s) move in a direction the CFP specialist did not anticipate.

One mechanism of change involves the identification of leverage points ("places in the system where a small change could lead to a large shift in behavior"; Meadows, 2008, p. 145). Leverage points are not easily identified, but they can facilitate change. For instance, it is our experience in couple therapy that helping troubled couples solve one small issue that is part of a relationship pattern can have an exponential effect on their ability to solve future issues. This may be due, in part, to the restoration of hope for the relationship or the sense that they can collaborate effectively, but the first solution provides a lot more leverage than the second or third, so the specialist must identify the problem most likely to be resolved successfully.

Many of the evidence-based intervention models in CFP have specific change mechanisms embedded in the model. Often these are identified and tested leverage points. Model designers created change hypotheses, operationalized them in treatment, and conducted research to determine the actions, behaviors, and mechanism of change most likely to result in the intended outcomes. The CFP specialist studies evidence-based models, understands the mechanisms of change, and implements them in a manner consistent with the research findings (Sexton, 2007).

Observe Patterns and Trends

The recognition of patterns and trends in systems is an important habit of systemic thinking. Homologies are "recurring patterns that exist within a wide variety of systems" (Sweeney & Sterman, 2007, p. 286). Homologies look different on the surface and may manifest in very different areas of life, but they reflect the same feedback processes at a fundamental level. The ability to recognize these patterns enables the CFP specialist to move beyond addressing individual issues toward resolution of patterns of interaction that reveal themselves in various circumstances. For example, it is possible in couple therapy to focus successively on a series of disagreements and problems that exist or evolve between the couple over several sessions in a manner that suggests that each issue is entirely separate and distinct (e.g., arguments over finances, sexual relations, decision making). Many people focus on the content of the issue and think it is discrete because of that content. On the other hand, the CFP specialist who observes patterns will recognize underlying dynamics that are parallel across the various issues and seek to change that pattern of interaction, knowing that improvement in the pattern will impact diverse future relationship issues. The sequence of this process first requires CFP specialist recognition of the pattern, then facilitation of client(s)' recognition of the pattern, in order to consider possible pattern interrupts that are acceptable to both parties. The CFP specialist may identify one particular problem to illustrate the pattern and use that problem as the point of entry to pattern change, but the key result is the couple's ability to transfer the insights learned to other content domains.

Another type of pattern is that observed when considering events as part of a sequence that occurs over time. This may be done through mental analysis or by using a graph or equation to track systemic behavior, but this process involves ascending to a metalevel to consider a class of events rather than focusing on a single event. This analysis allows the systems thinker to recognize trends, movement toward a goal, and timing of that movement (e.g., the couple is making more mutual decisions in the last 3 months; the family recently shows less hierarchical control and more affective support). This type of trend recognition allows evaluation of treatment process and outcomes.

Consider Unintended Consequences

Because systems thinking incorporates elements of chaos theory, it is reasonable to recognize that interventions in the system may lead to unintended consequences (McBride, 2005). Linear thinking suggests that there are direct and proportionate reactions to every action (i.e., A leads to B), so that more A will result in more B. Systems thinking understands that we cannot always predict the exact response to an action (e.g., a little A may lead to more B, but a lot of A may result in less B; a little alcohol may reduce social anxiety, but more alcohol may increase social tension) and that many other factors may be associated with the A–B interaction, so an intervention with A–B may end up involving C, D, E, and F (or more). Unintended consequences can have beneficial effect (the windfall that occurs when an intervention to address one issue results in positive change in other problems) or negative effects (the intervention that was intended to create a win-win situation results in a lose-lose outcome). Senge (2006) calls the latter "fixes that fail" because although the fix is "effective in the short term, [it] has unforeseen long-term consequences" (p. 399). For example, consider the apparently simple goal of reducing the incidence of drivers running red lights.[1] Some cities installed cameras to monitor intersections and issue tickets. They expected that the ticket fines would bring revenue to the city and result in fewer accidents. However, there are reports that some cities shortened the time for yellow lights in order to increase ticket revenue and that increasing yellow-light time by one second might both reduce red-light violations and accidents and lower ticket revenue. In fact, some studies found an increase in rear-end accidents (perhaps due to sudden stops to avoid the camera ticket). Some cities have deactivated cameras due to reduced revenue. This problem and the various attempts to address it demonstrate the complexity of interactive factors and the possibility of unintended results for potential "solutions." Similar unexpected and unintended consequences may result from psychological interventions with individuals, couples, families, and social organizations. Key specialist abilities in this habit involve avoiding reductionistic assumptions about outcomes and remaining flexible to respond to unintended consequences.

Shift Perspective

It is possible to perceive situations differently if one assumes a new perspective or vantage point. For example, simply reversing the route of a morning walk may lead to new perspectives and discoveries. Many people lose perspective because they perceive circumstances only from their own location. Accurate empathy, or the ability to enter and take another's

---

[1] This apparently simple problem is actually a complicated situation, impacted by various interests and perspectives. A report of increased rear-end accidents by the Virginia Transportation Research Council may be found at http://www.virginiadot.org/vtrc/main/online_reports/pdf/07-r2.pdf. The city of Dallas, Texas, found that after initial periods, revenue fell significantly below projections, and it idled some cameras (http://www.dallasnews.com/sharedcontent/dws/news/localnews/stories/DN-redlights_15met.ART.North.Edition1.468120d.html). Other reports suggest that some cities have significantly lowered the time for yellow lights, perhaps to increase revenue from tickets, but increasing the danger of accidents (http://www.motorists.org/blog/6-cities-that-were-caught-shortening-yellow-light-times-for-profit/). Camera companies, which collect a percentage of the fines, make arguments in favor of the cameras, on the other hand.

perspective in a thorough manner, is an important mechanism of change in many CFP interventions.

Understanding system dynamics depends on one's place in the system. This requires the ability to recognize multiple levels of perspective (e.g., the microsystem level, the mesosystem level, the macrosystem level; Bronfenbrenner, 1986) and to "locate situations in wider contexts" (Sweeney & Sterman, 2007, p. 286). In addition, CFP specialists recognize that it is possible to perceive the same situation in very different ways. Necker's Cube is a famous example of human mental ability to look at the same object and perceive it in very different ways in the three-dimensional environment (Einhäuser, Martin, & König, 2004). The ability to shift perspective is a crucial CFP habit in order to work effectively with more than one person at a time (e.g., couples, families, or organizations). However, we would suggest that individual psychotherapy also benefits from the ability of the CFP specialist to shift perspectives as the client describes interaction with other people in order to assist the client in understanding her or his social environment.

CFP specialists facilitate empathy and mutual understanding because they regularly take the perspective of others and attempt to see what is occurring through new eyes. For example, in couple therapy the specialist must constantly shift between the partners to understand and accurately empathize with the different perspectives each person brings into the room; family psychotherapy requires even more agility in shifting perspectives. In organizational consultation, the CFP specialist needs to assess and understand the presenting consultation problem from multiples perspectives during the needs assessment.

Factor in Time

Dynamic systems thinking recognizes the role of time in systemic functioning. Systems arise from their history and manifest historical influences at the individual, interpersonal, and macrosystemic levels (e.g., life span development; intergenerational transmissions of values and traits; evolution of societal norms). Some research indicates that people vary in their recognition and reference to time when seeking to understand life situations from little or no reference to nonspecific reference (time in general) to specific reference (intervals or known categories of time) to a more complete awareness of the role of time (Sweeney & Sterman, 2007). CFP specialists include time in case conceptualization, assess for time-related factors (e.g., complete a multigenerational genogram; McGoldrick, Gerson, & Petry, 2008), and consider the impact of time on interventions.

Timing is one aspect of time; systems members may be in sync or out of sync in the course of CFP interventions. It is not uncommon to experience roadblocks or failed initiatives because one person is ready to institute interpersonal change but another is not (e.g., one partner is willing to work on the relationship, but the other does not recognize that there is a real problem). Some individuals make decisions quickly, while others need time to process their thoughts and come to a conclusion. Sometimes the same idea that failed to work earlier will work now because members of the system are ready for it (or vice versa). One person in a relationship may become exhausted waiting for the other person to engage in the change process, so that by the time the other finally responds it is too late to achieve the desired goals. "Delays are pervasive in systems, and they are strong determinates of behavior" (Meadows, 2008, p. 57). Conversely, the partner who is too anxious to satisfy the other does not delay enough, creating an overresponsive pattern that may irritate or annoy their partner (e.g., under threat of divorce, a previously unresponsive partner may suddenly become overresponsive in a manner that is not believable). The CFP specialist pays attention to timing and adjusts interventions to maximize the potential to bring systems members in sync.

APPLY SYSTEMIC ORIENTATION TO CFP COMPETENCIES

A hallmark of the CFP specialty is the ability of the specialist to apply the systemic epistemology consistently and thoroughly across all the specialty foundational and functional competencies. The CFP specialist has thought deeply about the systemic orientation and inculcated habits of systemic thinking. For example, the specialist approaches assessment informed by a systemic epistemology and systemic paradigm. This means that the specialist will consider the broad range of factors that may be salient to the presenting case and conduct an assessment that evaluates those factors deemed relevant. Please see the competency chapters in this text for descriptions of the application of a systemic epistemology to the specialty competencies.

APPLY SPECIALTY SCIENCE TO CFP COMPETENCIES

The CFP specialist also demonstrates the ability to apply specialty scientific knowledge and scientific methods to the specialty foundational and functional competencies. Knowledge and application of science are a hallmark of professional psychology practice, including specialty practice (Bieschke et al., 2004). This means that the CFP specialist has developed a solid foundation of specialty scientific knowledge and the ability to apply it in practice. For instance, the CFP specialist demonstrates competency in interpersonal interaction through awareness of the research findings regarding the establishment and maintenance of the therapeutic alliance with the client(s). The specialist has learned the common and specific factors that facilitate the therapeutic alliance, in general, and the particular factors that are important to working with specific models or particular client populations. Please see the competency chapters in this text for description of the application of CFP science to the specialty competencies.

Attitudes

The CFP specialist evidences scientific mindedness in which the specialist independently values and applies CFP theory and science to specialty practice. This overarching attitude toward the relationship of theory and science to practice involves wholehearted and enthusiastic espousal of the role of each element as they interact to inform the specialist. There is general recognition in psychology that a scientific approach to practice is a crucial discipline distinctive (Bieschke, 2006; Bieschke et al., 2004). A work group from the 2002 Competencies Conference suggested that scientific mindedness includes commitment to obtain and apply research knowledge to practice, contribute to knowledge, evaluate interventions and outcomes, recognize the role of sociocultural factors in practice, and invite peer and public review of practice (Bieschke et al., 2004). Sue (1998, 2006) suggests that scientific mindedness refers to the tendency to "form hypotheses rather than make premature conclusions" (Sue, 2006, p. 239) and indicates that this is especially important in multicultural treatment. He notes that scientifically minded clinicians do not make naive assumptions, perhaps based on one's own culture, but test hypotheses and act using acquired data. Sexton et al. (2010) agree that the scientifically minded psychologist must "set aside biases and preconceptions, avoid the temptation of superficial answers, and consider what the theories and research say" (p. 160). They recommend asking oneself *what* and *how* questions regularly to fully consider treatment processes.

We suggest that scientific mindedness also includes recognition that one's theoretical orientation may limit conceptualization. Too narrow an orientation or too rigid adherence to a model may hinder one's thinking and limit one's development of hypotheses. Evidence may be screened out if it does not fit the existing orientation. The benefit of a broad, systemic epistemology (see "Knowledge" section above; see Figure 2.1) is that it is capable of the inclusion of particular orientations or treatment models that fit under its umbrella. For instance, the CFP specialist may reasonably incorporate individual treatment approaches (e.g., personality-based perspectives) that evidence systemic characteristics that make them amenable with the overarching epistemology into interpersonal therapy (Magnavita, 2005). Scientific mindedness is best served by the willingness of the CFP specialist to recognize a comprehensive epistemology and to hold several treatment models that may be accessed as needed to address the treatment goals of a particular case.

INDICATORS

Scientific mindedness is demonstrated by key indicators. Sexton et al. (2010) identify four attitudinal markers: (a) scientific mindedness; (b) curiosity and openness (careful inquiry and nondefensive response to findings, even if they challenge existing knowledge); (c) recognition of ambiguity and the evolution of knowledge (knowledge is complex and dynamic, so clinicians must recognize the limits of current scientific knowledge while respecting and applying it); and (d) willingness to embrace the dialectical nature of science and practice (refusal to side with practice or science alone, but active pursuit of means for each to inform the other). Sexton et al. (2010) describe important elements of each dimension.

For the purposes of this text and consistent with the Competencies Conference consensus (Bieschke et al., 2004), we frame all indicators under the umbrella of scientific mindedness and add to the Sexton et al. list the indicator of CFP specialist self-evaluation and the willingness to invite peer and public review of practice. This indicator reveals an underlying attitude that values ongoing appraisal of professional practice ("subject work routinely to the scrutiny of colleagues, stakeholders, and the public"; Bieschke et al., 2004, p. 716). It requires efforts to remain current in the specialty and the inclination to set aside the presumption of final knowledge or expert status that disallows new learning. It is consistent with pursuit of board certification in the specialty (i.e., the willingness to pursue examination and evaluation of one's practice through the submission of a paper detailing one's theoretical orientation and a practice sample). CFP specialist participation in peer consultation groups or processes provides one means of habitual scrutiny. Psychotherapy progress research that regularly invites feedback from the client(s) about treatment during the progression of treatment provides a structured mechanism for inviting client review (Friedlander et al., 2006; Pinsof & Chambers, 2009). Methods to ensure continuing specialist competency are under consideration by ABPP in 2009–2010; CFP specialists should embrace these opportunities for practice assessment as part of continuing formative development.

Conclusion

CFP specialists recognize the importance of integrating theory, science, and practice. Specialty practice is built on the foundation of conceptual and scientific knowledge, skills, and attitudes. CFP specialists have become what Benson (2007) terms "systems citizens" who "view themselves as members of a global community. They understand the complexities of today's worldly systems and have the capability to face into problems with knowledge and skill" (p. 5). The knowledge, skills, and attitudes of the specialty conceptual and scientific competency create the foundation for the CFP specialist to provide effective specialty services.

PART II

Functional Competency—
Assessment

THREE

Case Conceptualization Competency

Case conceptualization is a separate competency that may be characterized as development of the overarching framework for contextualizing assessment, diagnosis, problem description, case formulation, and treatment planning. This is an expansion of the definition of case conceptualization at the entry level to practice, where it was identified more narrowly as one of six major domains of the assessment competency focused on activity that "independently and accurately conceptualizes the multiple dimensions of the case based on the results of the assessment" (Assessment of Competencies Work Group, 2007, p. 18). We believe that case conceptualization is a broader pursuit than assessment and includes more than making sense of assessment data. Case conceptualization provides a framework for systemic practice with individuals, couples, families, and larger social systems. To our knowledge, there is not a transtheoretical model that accommodates the range of systemic theoretical orientations. In this chapter we identify the knowledge, skills, and attitudes that the CFP specialist must demonstrate in case conceptualization to function competently at the specialist level (Table 3.1).

Knowledge

The knowledge domain of the case conceptualization competency is organized around understanding the two essential elements of case conceptualization: First, CFP specialists understand case conceptualization in the overall context of CFP service delivery. Second, CFP specialists possess knowledge of a model for producing a case conceptualization. In this section we describe these two components of knowledge.

TABLE 3.1 Conceptualization Competency: Developmental Level—Specialty Competence in Couple and Family Psychology

COMPETENCY DOMAIN AND ESSENTIAL COMPONENT	BEHAVIORAL ANCHOR	ASSESSMENT METHODS
Knowledge	(A.1.1) Understands the concept, purpose, and components of case conceptualization in the context of CFP service delivery	1. ABPP Examination
(A) Foundational case conceptualization knowledge	(A.1.2) Understands the benefits of conducting a client-centered case conceptualization	2. Exemplary work products
(A.1) Understands case conceptualization in the context of CFP service delivery	(A.2.1) Understands the steps in developing a problem formation	3. Evidence that case conceptualization guides treatment
(A.2) Knowledge of model for producing a case conceptualization	(A.2.2) Understands the steps in developing a case formulation	4. Self-evaluation
	(A.2.3) Understands the steps in developing a treatment formulation.	5. Ongoing supervision and consultation
Skills	(B.1.1) Able to establish a collaborative problem-solving frame	6. Peer consultation
(B) Able to produce a case conceptualization	(B.1.2) Able to clarify the couple/family's presenting complaint and generate initial hypotheses through preliminary data-gathering functions	7. Continuing education
(B.1) Demonstrates the ability to construct a client-centered problem formulation	(B.1.3) Ability to conduct an assessment and arrive at a clear description or diagnosis of the problem	8. Client feedback and evaluation of CFP
(B.2) Demonstrates the ability to construct a client-centered case formulation	(B.2.1) Demonstrates the ability to identify pertinent information and organize the case information	9. Supervision feedback
(B.3) Demonstrates the ability to construct a client-centered treatment formulation	(B.2.2) Demonstrates the ability to apply systemic principles to explain the problem formulation data in light of the presenting problem	10. Publication and presentation in scholarly venues
	(B.2.3) Able to identify and prioritize target areas	
	(B.3.1) Demonstrates the ability to provide therapeutic feedback to and consensually set goals with the couple/family	
	(B.3.2) Able to identify interventions and a plan for service delivery	
	(B.3.3) Able to monitor couple/family progress and barriers to goal attainment	
Attitudes	(C.1.1) Demonstrates a client-centered perspective when identifying the presenting problem, conducting the assessment, describing the problem, and giving feedback.	
(C) Assessment perspective	(C.1.2) Collaborates with couple/family when developing a treatment formulation	
(C.1) Demonstrates a client-centered perspective in the case conceptualization process		

Note. Adapted from the format and content of the Assessment of Competency Benchmarks Work Group (2007). This table assumes that the specialist has achieved competence in professional psychology at the three previous developmental levels, as specified in the benchmarks. The competency domains and behavioral anchors serve as the primary organizing structure for this chapter; content explaining each domain and anchor is provided in the chapter.

UNDERSTANDS THE CONTEXT FOR CASE CONCEPTUALIZATION

The first essential component of knowledge in the competency involves understanding case conceptualization within the context of the services provided by the CFP specialist. This component contains two behavioral anchors. First, CFP specialists understand the concept and purpose of case conceptualization in the context of service delivery. This includes understanding the three component features of case conceptualization. Second, CFP specialists understand the benefits of conducting a client-centered case conceptualization. These two behavioral anchors are described in some detail in the following sections.

The CFP specialist understands the concept and purpose of case conceptualization in the context of CFP service delivery. Case conceptualization is frequently limited to the functions of organizing and interpreting assessment data and is seen as a component feature of the assessment process. As noted, this description is consistent with the way the Assessment of Competencies Work Group (2007) characterized case conceptualization. We believe that case conceptualization is a broader framework and encompasses a series of tasks organized into three phases that occur prior to the implementation of treatment. We adapt our presentation of case conceptualization from the work of Sperry and colleagues (Sperry, 2005; Sperry, Blackwell, Gudeman, & Faulkner, 1992) and define case conceptualization as containing three distinct phases: (a) problem formulation, (b) case formulation, and (c) treatment formulation. Problem formulation is the first phase of tasks that is organized around therapeutically *describing* couple/family problems. The case formulation phase is organized around *explaining* the assessment results in light of a particular theory of human functioning. Finally, treatment formulation is the process of *prescribing* the plan for helping the couple/family solve their problem (Sperry, 2005).

The process of case conceptualization out into three distinct phases of tasks has several advantages. First, it provides a stepwise model for teaching and supervising students in the various phases of case conceptualization. Each phase contains a series of teachable activities that flow logically from one step to the next. Second, by distilling the process of case conceptualization into tasks, it is easier for researchers to study the process of arriving at clinical conclusions. Finally, a stepwise model for case conceptualization lends itself to teaching and evaluating competencies.

The CFP specialist also understands the benefits of conducting a client-centered case conceptualization. A client-centered perspective affirms the dignity and worth of all persons, demonstrates respect and kindness in professional interactions, and uses client strengths and resources to help couples and families achieve their goals. We believe that this therapeutic frame should be applied to all activities conducted by a CFP specialist and therefore also applies to case conceptualization. This perspective is not new. In psychological assessment there has been a movement toward therapeutic assessment (Finn, 2007) that focuses on the collaborative nature of the assessment and evaluation process and views assessment as a short-term intervention (Finn & Tonsager, 1997). Maintaining a client-centered perspective throughout the problem formulation, case formulation, and treatment formulation phases will improve the quality of the assessment, help establish a therapeutic alliance, and aid in setting goals for treatment (Friedlander et al., 2006; Sprenkle & Blow, 2007).

KNOWLEDGE OF MODEL FOR PRODUCING A CASE CONCEPTUALIZATION

The second essential component in the knowledge domain of the case conceptualization competency involves understanding a model for producing a case conceptualization. In this section we present a model for case conceptualization that builds on the work of several authors who have written on various aspects of the case conceptualization process (Adams & Grieder, 2005; Eells, 2006; Sperry, 2005; Stanton, 2009b). Accordingly, CFP

TABLE 3.2 **Steps in Case Conceptualization**

Problem Formulation	**Descriptive**
1. Set a therapeutic frame	
2. Preliminary interview with couple/family	
3. Formulate testable hypotheses	
4. Conduct assessment	
5. Diagnose or describe problem	
Case Formulation	**Explanatory**
6. Organize case information (Six Ps)	
7. Provide systemic explanation	
8. Identify and prioritize target areas	
Treatment Formulation	**Prescriptive**
9. Provide feedback to couple/family	
10. Consensual goal setting with couple/family	
11. Identify interventions for target areas	
12. Format for delivery	
13. Plan for monitoring	

Note. References used to construct the model: Adams & Grieder 2005; Eells 2007; Sperry 2005

specialists should be familiar with the stepwise progression toward case conceptualization organized around three phases as listed in Table 3.2: problem formulation, case formulation, and treatment formulation.

Problem Formulation

The CFP specialist understands the steps necessary in developing a problem formulation and is knowledgeable about the information that is required at each step of the problem formulation task. The goal of the problem formulation is to collaboratively collect pertinent data about the couple/family's presenting problem(s) and to clearly describe the problem(s). The problem formulation includes five tasks:

1. Set a therapeutic frame.
2. Conduct a preliminary interview.
3. Form testable hypotheses.
4. Conduct assessment.
5. Diagnose the problem.

The knowledge required for each of these tasks is covered in the sections that follow.

Establish a Therapeutic Frame   Many couples and families are not familiar with CFP services and may not know what to expect when they call for an appointment. The CFP specialist understands how to structure the first contacts and understands informed consent as it applies to the process of case conceptualization. A lot happens during the first contact with the couple or family, including allaying fears, developing rapport, receiving the initial description of the presenting problem, reviewing office policies, discussing fees, and obtaining informed consent. Most important, the initial alliance is formed during the first contacts, and the frame for the problem formulation phase is set from the beginning. The CFP specialist understands the nature of developing a therapeutic alliance and has knowledge of individual and cultural diversity factors that influence the development of a therapeutic alliance (see Chapter 12, "Interpersonal Interaction," and Chapter 11, "Diversity Competency").

Conduct the Clinical Interview   The second task is conducting the clinical interview. Although we list this as a separate step for clarity, the initial interview often overlaps with the discussion of presenting problem, informed consent, and other components involved in the first session. There is no easy way to discuss the vast amount of knowledge that a CFP specialist must have to conduct an efficient yet comprehensive clinical interview. At a minimum, CFP specialists must have a basic frame for conducting an interview and solicit information concerning individual, interpersonal, and contextual factors. A sample of important areas of inquiry is listed in Table 3.3. CFP specialists also have a command of DSM-IV-TR diagnostic nomenclature, common symptom presentations, and historical indicators of mental illness. Relatedly, CFP specialists must have knowledge of relational diagnoses (Lawrence, Beach, & Doss, 2009) and cultural formulations of psychiatric problems.

Formulate Testable Hypotheses and Conduct an Assessment   In this section we combine the third and fourth tasks of problem formulation, since the knowledge base required is similar. Following the initial interview, the CFP specialist has a better understanding of the client(s)' problem. The third step in problem formulation is to determine which information needs to be ruled out or further clarified through CFP assessment methods. The CFP specialist must understand which factors are amenable to assessment and have a working knowledge of which methods to utilize in order to collect the most useful data about the couple or family problem. CFP specialists must have knowledge of the individual, interpersonal, and contextual

TABLE 3.3 **Individual, Interpersonal, and Contextual Assessment**

INDIVIDUAL FACTORS	INTERPERSONAL FACTORS	CONTEXTUAL FACTORS
Individual development in context	Family development	Socioeconomic status
Cognitive process and intelligence	Family life-cycle stage	Work
Attachment and/or intrapsychic structures	Couple relations	Cultural differences
Personality	Parent-child relations	Politics – political forces
Gender, age, sexual orientation, physical Factors	Sibling relations	Medicine, healthcare, health insurance
Psychobiology	Family process	Physical environment Safety: crime, terrorism
Neuropsychology	Family strengths	Community organizations
Personal strengths	Family constructs	Religion – religious organizations
Psychopathology	Social network relations (including social support)	Media (internet, TV/cable, newspapers, magazines)
Personal beliefs, values, or Convictions	Family diversity	National ideology
	Communication style	
	Sexual relationship	

Adapted from Stanton (2009)

factors that are important to consider in a CFP assessment and be familiar with the various assessment methods for evaluating all three systemic domains. In this section we briefly review constructs that should be evaluated in the individual, interpersonal, and contextual domains, and the broad class of evaluation methods for each domain.

Individual factors need to be assessed as part of case conceptualization (Stanton, 2009b). As noted in Table 3.3, individual factors include, but are not limited to, cognitive and psychological characteristics, personality, genetic and biological factors, attachment patterns, intrapsychic structures, psychobiology, medical history, multicultural identity, and developmental social history, including trauma, immigration, losses, failures, and successes (Stanton, 2009b; see Chapter 12 this volume). Individual factors may be assessed through a variety of standardized or nonstandardized methods. The benefit of standardized testing is that the CFP evaluator can compare individuals with a similarly situated normal population. Standardized tests include intellectual, cognitive, and neuropsychological instruments, psychological and personality instruments, and self-report measures that operationalize a particular psychological construct such as depression. Nonstandardized assessment affords the ability to probe deeper into the individual's idiographic factors but does not have the benefit of being norm-referenced. Examples of nonstandardized assessments include qualitative or semistructured interviews, informal behavioral observation, mental status examination, and idiographic psychological assessment techniques such as projective drawings. Finally, individual records (e.g., medical, school, employment) should be obtained, and relevant collateral informants (e.g., teacher, clergy, friends) interviewed.

Interpersonal factors should also be considered when conducting an assessment. Depending on the nature of the presenting complaint, the CFP evaluator needs to identify the relational constructs that will be assessed and which family members should participate in the assessment. In the CFP assessment literature, there is a great deal of theoretical variance about which constructs are core features of relational assessment. Some methods are idiosyncratic to their particular school. For example, the Beavers Systems Model of assessment is organized around a structural theory of health and dysfunction (Beavers, 2003). In the Beavers model, prominence is given to structural constructs such as family competence (i.e., how well a family organizes and manages itself) and family style (i.e., the extent to which family members seek satisfaction inside or outside the family; Beavers & Hampson, 2003). Relatedly, the Circumplex Model of Marital and Family Systems organizes assessment around three dimensions: family cohesion, flexibility, and communication (Olson & Gorall, 2002). The McMaster Model of Family Functioning is another major theoretical effort to classify the constructs for evaluation in family assessment (Epstein, Bishop, & Levin, 1978). The McMaster Model organizes assessment around the following six dimensions: problem solving, communication, roles, affective responsiveness, affective involvement, and behavioral control (Epstein, Ryan, Bishop, Miller, & Keitner, 2003).

The problem with conducting an evaluation within a particular theory is that it may miss important dimensions and commits the evaluator to treatment planning within that perspective. Because we do not want to limit this discussion to a particular model, we have adopted an integrative stance that draws from the key contributions to the field of CFP. Several authors have organized family constructs around higher-ordered categories and represent a more flexible approach (Bray, 1995a; Carlson, 1995). Bray (2009) identifies six domains of interest in family assessment: family structure and composition, family process, relationship patterns, family affect, family organization, and family diversity. Family structure and composition include family membership (e.g., single-parent family) and family structure (e.g., divorced family). A related feature of assessing the *family composition and structure* construct is to understand which family members are central to the assessment and which are nonessential. This obviously will be based on the presenting problem of the couple or family (Bray, 2004). The *family process* construct captures the interactions and exchanges with an emphasis on form and not content. This construct encompasses communication styles, conflict, problem solving, and the system-maintaining function of the interactions and exchanges. The *relationship pattern* construct evaluates sequences over time as they are related to outcome. Gottman's (1994) marital research exemplifies the nature of this construct. *Family affect* encompasses the nature and pattern of affective expression. This construct includes the range, intensity, consistency, and appropriateness of emotional expression in the family. The *family organization* construct examines the implicitly and explicitly stated roles and rules that govern the family. Evaluation of family organization will include observations about family hierarchy, boundaries, division of labor, emotional support, values, and taboos. Finally, the *family diversity* construct contextualizes the family within their own idiographic characteristics. These include ethnic and racial identity, sexual orientation, mental and physical disability, religion, acculturation, socioeconomic status, education, immigration history, and phase of family life cycle. Evaluating the family diversity construct is central to accurately conceptualizing the case.

CFP assessment methodologies are varied and flexible (see Chapter 4, "Assessment Competency"). The CFP evaluator may choose from a range of structured self-report instruments, formal observational tasks, and microanalytic coding schemes. The evaluator may also select less structured interviews or observational tasks. The characteristics of the family (openness, psychological mindedness, motivation, multicultural factors) will largely dictate which methods are selected. For example, a CFP evaluator may select a variety of self-report measures if the couple/family is relatively motivated, forthcoming, and from an ethnic/racial group similar to the reference sample. Conversely, if a couple/family is defensive, in high conflict, members are openly hostile to the assessment process, or there is no instrument normed on their ethnic/racial group, then a more loosely structured interview might yield the most usable information.

Another common approach to the assessment of couples and families is the use of individual psychological instruments with separate batteries given to individual family members and then interpreted both individually and within a systemic framework (Nurse, 1999). Many couple and family problems result from maladaptive personality styles in one or more members; however, most of the traditional CFP instruments do not assess individual personality functioning. Accordingly, an assessment that involves examination of each partner's personality functioning can provide important insights into the nature of the relational problems and provide a clear direction for intervention (Nurse & Stanton, 2008; Stanton & Nurse, 2009).

Finally, CFP evaluators take *contextual factors* into account when assessing couple and family problems. Since individuals, couples, and families are situated within meso-, exo-, and macrosystems (Bronfenbrenner, 1977, 1979), the CFP evaluator must consider the impact that each of these social ecological levels has on the presenting problems and overall functioning of the family. *Mesosystemic factors* comprise "the interrelations among two or more settings in which the [couple/family] participates" (Bronfenbrenner, 1979, p. 25). These factors include the local community, school, religious group, neighborhood milieu, and local ethnocultural aspects in which the couple/family is situated. For example, an otherwise functional family may begin having problems if their teenage son is being harassed by a neighborhood gang. *Exosystemic factors* refer "to one or more settings that do not involve the developing person [couple/family] as an active participant, but in which events occur that affect, or are affected by, what happens in the setting containing the [couple/family]" (Bronfenbrenner, 1979, p. 25). Examples of exosystemic factors might include the work environment of one of the parents or the passing of one of the parents of the family babysitter. Finally, *macrosystemic factors* refer "to consistencies, in the form and content of lower-order systems (micro-, meso, and exo-) that exist, or could exist, at the level of the subculture or the culture as a whole, along with any belief systems or ideology underlying such consistencies" (Bronfenbrenner, 1979, p. 26). Macrosystemic factors include a political climate, cultural views toward members of a minority group, or broader cultural values such as meritocracy (i.e., the belief that anyone can succeed if they work hard enough).

Assessment of contextual factors is not as straightforward as individual and interpersonal factors, but it is equally important. Information about a couple/family's meso- and exosystem is gathered from the self-report of a client unless the CFP specialist is directly familiar with the client's local environment. Information about the social ecology of a client can come from the CFP specialist's own self-study, consultation, and supervision or from directly asking the client (see Chapter 11, "Diversity Competency"). Macrosystemic factors are harder to assess than some of the other levels. Most often, the assessment of macrosystemic factors occurs as a result of CFP specialists being aware of the macrosystemic climate in which they are situated.

Describe or Diagnose the Problem   The end point of the problem formulation is to arrive at a clear description of the problem or diagnosis. With the information that is obtained from the assessment, CFP evaluators arrive at a diagnosis of the individual or relationship when one is warranted. The DSM-IV-TR (American Psychiatric Association, 2000) offers a categorical taxonomy for classifying individual psychiatric disorders that may be appropriate for use with individuals within a couple/family. It is also important to consider relational diagnoses when developing the case formulation and treatment plan. Relational diagnoses include relational syndromes, central relational processes, and relational specifiers (Lawrence et al., 2009) (see Chapter 4 for more information). In many cases it may be appropriate to identify both individual and relational diagnoses. For example, if one of the partners in a marriage has a severe anxiety disorder, then it would be important for case formulation and treatment planning to single out the individual disorder, while being sensitive to relational specifiers that may be perpetuating the disorder.

Case Formulation

Case formulation is the often neglected step that lies between assessment and treatment planning. A CFP case formulation applies systemic principles to provide an *explanatory* framework for understanding the client's problems. The explanatory framework of case formulation contains three tasks that will eventually dictate treatment formulation:

1. Organize data into central components.
2. Explain the problem.
3. Identify and prioritize targets for intervention.

The knowledge necessary to complete a case formulation is briefly described in the sections that follow.

Organize Data   The first task in CFP case formulation is to organize the data into factors that are central to understanding the couple/family's problem in context. Because of the large amount of data available for consideration, the CFP specialist must be knowledgeable of methods to arrange case information. Adams and Grieder (2005) propose a model called the *Six Ps*, which has been adopted by the State of California Department of Mental Health as the guiding paradigm for case formulation (Table 3.4).

In the previous section on diagnostic formulation we discussed clarifying the *presenting problem(s).* As a step toward organizing case information, it is important to restate the problem after the assessment has been conducted. Often the problem statement is seen differently in retrospect. The CFP examiner will likely be able to be more specific about the presenting problem after the assessment. For example, instead of stating that the couple has communication problems, the examiner may have isolated the problem as associated with a particular type of communication (e.g., problem solving) under certain conditions (e.g., when talking about the in-laws immediately after work). Further clarifying the presenting problem(s) can often be therapeutic in and of itself.

Pertinent history includes information from individual, interpersonal, and contextual sources. Pertinent history may be sampled from individual domains, including educational history, medical history, legal history,

TABLE 3.4 **Organizing Case Formulation "Six Ps"**

Presenting problems
Pertinent history
Predisposing factors
Precipitating factors
Perpetuating factors
Previous treatment and response

Source: Adapted from Adams & Grieder 2005.

family of origin, psychiatric history, occupational history, and marital history. It may also be gathered from interpersonal contexts such as history of domestic violence in a relationship, sexual history, family life-cycle history, parenting history, and financial history. Finally, information can be obtained from contextual sources such as cultural history, immigration history, and socioeconomic history. It is important to document a history that draws from all levels of the social ecology because history can often explain individual and relational proclivities.

Predisposing factors are events or individual characteristics that enhance the likelihood that an individual, couple, or family will develop problems given the right precipitating stressors. Sperry (2005) defines a predisposition as "all the intrapersonal, interpersonal, and systemic factors, including attachment style and trauma, which render a client vulnerable to maladaptive functioning" (p. 359). Predisposing characteristics might include a particular personality or attachment style, intelligence, coping resources, strengths, skills, previous successes and important failures, genetic or biological predispositions to problems, racism, acculturation, and exposure to violence. Interpersonal factors might include prior marital infidelities, previous domestic violence, or conjoint substance abuse. Predisposing contextual factors might include experiences with institutional racism, neighborhood drug culture, or an unsupportive community.

Precipitating factors often explain why a couple or family has sought treatment and usually represents a decline in functioning from previous baseline levels. There are often identifiable stressors that exceed the couple or family's typical coping resources and are usually situational in nature. Precipitating factors might include individual features such as unemployment, onset of medical or psychiatric illness, legal troubles, or substance abuse. Interpersonal precipitating factors might include normal family life-cycle transitions such as the birth of a child, an empty nest, or retirement. Other interpersonal stressors might include infidelity, divorce and remarriage, and sexual problems. Finally, contextual factors may include the national economy, war, terrorism, change in national ideology, or local natural disaster.

Perpetuating factors are defined as "processes by which a client's pattern is reinforced and confirmed by both the client and the client environment" (Sperry, 2005, p. 359). Once a couple or family is in crisis, certain perpetuating factors keep them from successfully solving the problem and returning to their baseline level of functioning. Perpetuating factors are those system-maintaining elements that keep a family stuck and unable to grow without some type of intervention. Examples of individual perpetuating factors might include a chronic illness, frequent psychiatric or substance abuse relapse, compulsive behavior, or an inflexible problem-solving style. Interpersonal perpetuating factors might include couple communication styles, parenting patterns, or relational syndromes. Contextual perpetuating factors might include chronic poverty, the national housing market, or inadequate access to health care.

The final section of organizing the case formulation has to do with documenting any *previous treatment* that the couple or family has received and their responses to the treatment. In this section it is important to note the types of services received, interventions attempted, and barriers to success.

The amount of information that a CFP specialist needs to consider in order to separate data relevant to a presenting problem from peripheral data is indeed large. A case formulation model is simply a way to organize pertinent information prior to explaining how the data collected account for the etiology and persistence of the couple or family problem(s). The Six Ps model provides a comprehensive method for collecting and organizing case information. Organizing case material is a necessary preliminary step before linking all the information together within a systemic framework, which we will discuss later in the chapter. However, central to a systemic assessment and conceptualization is deciding which information is important to consider. Historically, individual factors have been considered most important, whereas CFP specialists consider the entire social ecology as equally important. Accordingly, information gathered about an individual, couple, or family will be collected from individual, interpersonal, and contextual sources.

Explain the Presenting Problem   The second task in CFP case formulation is to explain the presenting problem from a systemic perspective. The heart of a systemic case formulation is providing a theory-based explanation that makes sense of the case material. The explanation is the "inferred mechanism" that ties together all the information that was gathered during the assessment into an understandable whole (Kendjelic & Eells, 2007, p. 68). Up to this point the CFP specialist has organized information into cells without specifically explaining the relationship between the information in the cells and the presenting problem(s). At this step in the case formulation, the CFP specialist will use systemic concepts to infer relationships between the information that was organized across the two dimensions illustrated in Table 3.4 (*Six Ps* and *Tripartite System*) and the presenting problem. We illustrate the application of a systemic paradigm in Figure 3.1

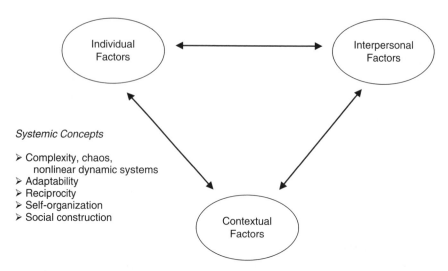

FIGURE 3.1 **Systemic Case Formulation**

A systemic inference will minimally consider the following concepts: (a) complexity, chaos, and nonlinear dynamic systems, (b) reciprocity, (c) adaptability, (d) self-organization, and (e) social constructivism (Nutt & Stanton, 2008; Stanton, 2009b). When applied to case material, a systemic explanation recognizes the multifaceted nature of human behavior (complexity), is aware that individual and couple and family behavior is a product of a reciprocal interaction between the client(s) and the environment (reciprocity), and understands that individuals, couples, and families exhibit flexibility to adjust to the demands of the environment (adaptability). Self-organization refers to the capability to spontaneously change one's behavioral repertoire when increasingly complex and sophisticated responses to the environment are required. Finally, social construction considers the individual and couple/family situated in a unique life story and a particular place in history. Applying a systemic paradigm to case material is covered in more detail in Chapter 5 ("Intervention Competency").

Identify and Prioritize Target Areas Third, CFP specialists identify and prioritize areas suitable for intervention. At this point in the case formulation, the CFP specialist has formed a tentative explanation of the case material as it relates to the presenting problem(s). In the face of a dizzying array of systemic problems, the CFP specialist needs to decide on a manageable number of targets that appear to be causing the problem. The CFP specialist needs to be able to distill a very complex system into a parsimonious set of prominent issues.

Treatment Formulation

The treatment formulation is the final process in the case conceptualization prior to implementing treatment. The treatment formulation is a *prescriptive* process where the CFP specialist produces a blueprint for treatment (Sperry, 2005). We have identified five tasks in the treatment formulation:

1. Provide feedback to the couple or family.
2. Collaboratively set treatment goals with the couple or family.
3. Identify interventions for target areas after considering client goals.
4. Specify format for delivery.
5. Develop a plan for monitoring treatment progress.

Provide Feedback   A person-centered assessment process should set the frame for delivering feedback to clients in a manner that immediately helps them (Adams & Grieder, 2005). In this sense, assessment is seen as a therapeutic enterprise (Finn & Tonsager, 1997). Conceptualizing the treatment planning process as a person-centered approach is a paradigm shift from the disembodied doctor providing expert feedback about an interesting case and dictating the course of treatment to the patient. Although the process is prescriptive, it should be seen as deeply respectful of client autonomy, dignity, and worth. Because of the therapeutic manner in which the CFP specialist has conducted the assessment, the couple/family will likely not be surprised by the feedback and recommendations, since they have been involved in a collaborative discovery process from the beginning.

Collaborative Goal Setting   Involving the couple or family in the assessment and feedback process invites them to "buy in" to the intervention strategy. The next step in the treatment planning process is to collaboratively arrive at treatment goals that seem reasonable to both the CFP specialist and the couple or family. In addition to the significant therapeutic contribution of involving couples and families in establishing goals, it is quickly becoming a standard of care. Adams and Grieder (2005) note that the Joint Commission on Accreditation of Healthcare Organizations' (JCAHO) "standards on treatment planning require that individuals be encouraged to participate in developing their treatment care, or service plans, and such involvement is documented" (p. 41). Involving the couple or family in goal setting communicates regard for their needs and preferences and will likely prevent working at cross-purposes.

Select Interventions   Once the CFP specialist and the couple or family have set goals, an intervention strategy is selected. When selecting strategies, the intervention should be based on the best science available and individualized for the unique needs and preferences of the couple or family (Adams & Grieder, 2005). The current state of the intervention literature in CFP has failed to demonstrate superiority of one treatment over another (relative efficacy), nor has it successfully identified specific ingredients, leading some to believe that the CFP modality is a common factor (Sprenkle & Blow, 2004; see Chapter 12, "Interpersonal Interactions"). When selecting an intervention, the CFP should be mindful of the skills and resources of the couple or family, participant motivation levels, members who are likely to attend, multicultural factors, and expectations. The CFP specialist should also work with the couple or family to decide on the intervention format. Would it be more appropriate to see the couple or family conjointly, in a mixed change of format setting, or with the entire family present? Relatedly, CFP specialists should consider if it may be appropriate to involve important community leaders or culturally recognized healers in the intervention. CFP interventions are discussed in more detail in Chapter 5 ("Intervention Competency").

Develop an Outcome Assessment Strategy   The last step in the treatment planning process is to determine how treatment response will be scientifically measured. Outcome measurement is frequently conducted by employing a single-subject (case) repeated measures format where the couple or family regularly fills out self-report instruments to document treatment progress. In the CFP field, there are two exemplar instruments that may be used in outcome assessment. First, the System for Observing Family Therapy Alliances (SOFTA) is an observer-rated measure (also available in self-report format) that focuses on therapist-client behaviors that indicate strength of therapeutic alliance (Friedlander et al., 2006). The second instrument for outcome assessment is the Systemic Inventory of Change (STIC®), which quantitatively tracks progress in individual, couples, and families (Pinsoff & Chambers, 2009). Both of these instruments are discussed in more detail later in the book (Chapter 12, "Interpersonal Interactions").

Skills

The skills domain in the case conceptualization competency involves the application of knowledge to create a case conceptualization. The CFP specialist evidences this competency by demonstrating the attendant skill required to construct a diagnostic formulation, construct a case formulation, and construct a treatment formulation from a systemic perspective.

PROBLEM FORMULATION SKILLS

The CFP specialist demonstrates the ability to construct a client-centered case formulation. Skills are organized across three behavioral anchors: First, the CFP specialist is able to establish a collaborative problem-solving frame, which includes managing the initial contacts, setting administrative and ethical parameters, and conducting the interview. Second, the CFP specialist is able to formulate testable hypotheses and conduct an assessment. Third, the CFP specialist is able to adequately describe the problem and provide a diagnosis if applicable.

The CFP specialist possesses the skills required to establish a strong therapeutic alliance at the beginning of the problem formulation process. Couples and families are frequently tentative about sharing their problems openly and divulging family secrets to a professional. The CFP specialist must be able to quickly establish rapport and create an environment that is conducive to openness, mutual collaboration, and empathic inquiry. The CFP specialist must be able to balance the administrative tasks of reviewing office practices, reviewing ethical and legal aspects of practice, and collecting preliminary interview information. The CFP specialist is skilled at communicating to couples and families the need to conduct a comprehensive assessment of the problem prior to beginning treatment. Many couples and families are eager to start working to solve their problem; therefore, it is important for the CFP specialist to skillfully frame the assessment process as a part of the treatment process. Oftentimes the thoroughness with which the CFP specialist goes about the assessment process can communicate confidence and provides the clients with hope that their seemingly intractable problem can be solved.

After setting the therapeutic evaluation frame and putting the clients at ease, the CFP specialist must first determine the problem(s) of interest and frame the interview in terms of questions that need to be answered. Oftentimes the evaluation will be in the context of a couple or family seeking treatment for a loosely defined complaint. For example, a couple may explain that they are unhappy together and want to figure out what went wrong in their relationship. Conversely, family complaints may be more focused on a particular individual, such as a child who is having behavior problems at home and school. Depending on the presenting complaint, the clinical interview provides the necessary historical and observational information that will later be used to explain and interpret the findings of the assessment. The clinical interview is perhaps the most important therapeutic assessment instrument, since it provides the CFP specialist an opportunity to meaningfully interact with the couple or family about their problem, while simultaneously improving the therapeutic alliance if conducted skillfully. The importance of the clinical interview should not be underestimated. Morrison (2008) noted that in a survey of practicing and teaching clinicians, comprehensive interviewing was listed as the most important skill from a list of 32 available options that mental health clinicians need.

The goal of the clinical interview is to collect as much information as necessary to contextualize the assessment in the most efficient manner. Frequently novice interviewers solicit information about detail that is unrelated or only peripherally related to the presenting problem, thereby unnecessarily burdening the couple or family with interview fatigue. The skillful CFP evaluator is able to quickly identify the most pertinent information without getting sidetracked. Relatedly, the CFP evaluator will control the interview in a manner that keeps the couple or family engaged in the process without appearing uninterested in aspects of the client's life. The CFP specialist needs to be attuned to subtle cues that warrant further explanation. Knowing which information to pursue only comes with time and experience.

After conducting the interview, the CFP specialist identifies areas that need further explanation. In many cases, a clinical interview is sufficient to proceed with the case formulation, and psychological testing is not required. At times, however, a more comprehensive assessment process needs to occur, either to rule out ambiguous factors or to corroborate interview information. Following the interview, the CFP specialist needs to decide if more assessment is necessary, and if it is, to identify the hypotheses that need to be tested through the assessment process. Once a problem is clearly framed in a manner that is answerable by the available CFP assessment procedures, the CFP specialist begins collaboratively gathering information about the couple or family. Information should be obtained from more "objective" methods such as functionally and structurally sound instruments, collection of collateral information (e.g., medical, legal, and educational records), and observations of behavior. More "subjective" measures are also important to consider, such as qualitative interviews, solicitation of a family's nuclear and multigenerational history, and individual perceptions of the presenting problem (e.g., circular questioning, 360-degree evaluation). The skills required to conduct a comprehensive CFP assessment are discussed in significant detail in Chapter 4.

Following the assessment, the CFP specialist will have enough information to formulate a working description or diagnosis of the problem.

The problem formulation can always be revisited after working with the couple/family in treatment and revised as necessary. The skills required to arrive at a problem formulation involve using the assessment information to describe the problem.

CASE FORMULATION SKILLS

The second essential element in the skills domain involves the ability to conduct a client-centered case formulation. Three behavioral anchors constitute this essential element: First, the CFP specialist demonstrates the ability to identify pertinent information from the assessment and meaningfully organize the information. Second, the CFP specialist is able to apply systemic principles to explain the problem formulation data in light of the presenting problem. Third, the CFP specialist is able to identify and prioritize target areas for intervention.

Throughout the process of case organization, the CFP evaluator should search for "meaningful data," with the presenting problem guiding the decision to include it or not. Inexperienced examiners typically take a "shotgun" approach to data collection and include all information that was gathered in the case formulation. Not all information is meaningful, and the presenting problem serves a similar focusing function that a research question does in qualitative data analysis. The examiner should ask two questions before deciding to include it in the formulation: First, what relationship does this information have to the presenting problem? Second, does including it help understand the problem? From this point forward, the CFP evaluator should have a clear rationale for including information in the case formulation.

Table 3.5 illustrates how the CFP evaluator may organize pertinent information to a family treatment case. In this hypothetical example we present a multiproblem family that is seeking treatment because the husband has recently engaged in acts of domestic violence toward his wife (e.g., pushing) and is having frequent conflict with his teenage son. In addition, the husband recently initiated contact with his former girlfriend, has been using substances sporadically, and was recently fired from his job. In a case like this, the amount of information to consider could be overwhelming, and the case organization model previously presented can help to make sense of the information. In the example shown here, we fill every cell with information to illustrate the type of content that would be relevant to consider. There may be many instances when a particular cell does not warrant any data.

The CFP specialist demonstrates the ability to apply systemic principles to explain the problem formulation data in light of the presenting problem. The

TABLE 3.5 **Case Organization Example (Six Ps by Tripartite System)**

	INDIVIDUAL FACTORS	INTERPERSONAL FACTORS	CONTEXTUAL FACTORS
Pertinent history	Family history of divorce; ex-military; many childhood conduct problems	Poor adjustment in life-cycle transitions	Raised in a misogynistic culture
Predisposing factors	Antisocial personality disorder; substance abuse	Domestic violence; two previous affairs	Living in a neighborhood with easy access to substances
Precipitating factors	Recently fired; reinitiated contact with former girlfriend	Minor acts of domestic violence (pushing); father has frequent conflict with teenage son	High unemployment rate in local area; stopped going to Catholic church
Perpetuating factors	Not committed to stopping contact with former girlfriend; does not think periodic drug use is a problem	Pursuer-distancer relational dynamic	Unable to refinance their house
Previous treatment and response	Three prior admissions to an inpatient drug treatment facility; relapsed after 3 months	Wife became overinvolved with husband's treatment	Husband has lost his insurance benefits

most important skill for this task is the ability to think systemically about complex problems and to recognize the difference between linear and recursive thinking. Other skills required for this behavioral anchor include the ability to recognize connections and interactions between data, and linking the pattern of data to ideas about why the problem exists and what keeps the couple/family from moving on. There is obviously a great deal of latitude with this task depending on the CFP specialist's theoretical proclivities.

The final skill set that the CFP specialist possesses in developing a case formulation involves the ability to identify and prioritize target areas for intervention. CFP specialists are able to recognize the individual, interpersonal, and contextual factors that cause and maintain a couple or family's problem(s) and identify which factors contribute most significantly to the presenting complaint. The CFP specialist also needs to be able to determine which elements are amenable to change and those that need to be accepted and managed accordingly. For example, direct encounters with racism cannot be changed; however, the couple or family can learn different ways of reacting to or coping with the affronts.

TREATMENT FORMULATION SKILLS

The final essential component in the skills domain involves the ability to construct a client-centered treatment formulation. This skill set includes three behavioral anchors: First, CFP specialists are able to provide therapeutic feedback and to consensually set goals with the couple or family. Second, the CFP specialist is able to identify interventions that have the highest probability of helping the couple or family and to create a plan for service delivery. Finally, the CFP specialist monitors treatment progress and outcomes and adjusts the interventions and goals as necessary.

CFP specialists skillfully provide therapeutic feedback and engage the couple or family in the goal-setting process. Delivering feedback to couples and families in distress takes considerable skill to communicate sometimes difficult information, while still keeping them therapeutically engaged and motivated. CFP specialists need to be able to explain complicated information about individual, interpersonal, and contextual problems in a manner that facilitates hope and understanding. If feedback is successfully therapeutic, then the couple or family is likely to be more engaged in the treatment goal setting. In order to involve the couple or family in goal setting, CFP specialists need to clearly lay out the treatment options and solicit client feedback about their wishes and expectations for help. When the client's expectations are not consistent with the prognosis, the CFP specialist clarifies expectations and educates the couple or family about the treatment process.

CFP specialists are also able to identify interventions and develop a plan for service delivery. After targeting areas for intervention, the CFP specialist considers which treatments would best suit the client's characteristics and problems. Because there is no perfect choice for intervention, the CFP specialist is able to weigh the pros and cons of various alternatives. In addition, the CFP specialist determines who will be seen in treatment, how frequently, and for how long. Finally, CFP specialists are able to monitor couple and family progress, through either formal or informal means, and are able to successfully identify barriers that keep couple/families from achieving their goals.

Attitudes

The CFP specialist demonstrates a client-centered perspective throughout the case conceptualization process. The CFP specialist views case conceptualization as a therapeutic process and actively collaborates with the couple or family in a manner that is respectful, strength-based, and empowering. Adams and Grieder (2005) propose that a person-centered approach offers the opportunity to think creatively with clients to help them solve their problems; it serves as a mechanism for "acknowledging the hopes and dreams as well as the strengths and resources of each individual and family" (p. 11) and a process for collaboratively developing a "guide for the journey to recovery of each individual and family" (p. 11). In addition, Adams and Grieder argue that a person-centered approach involves evidence-based interventions that are individually tailored to meet the needs and wishes of the client.

Finn and Tonsager (1997) articulate a model for therapeutic assessment as a paradigm shift away from an information-gathering approach to assessment. They suggest the goals of assessment include helping the clients think and feel differently about themselves and others, helping them explore new understandings about self and others, and applying the new perspective to help them solve their problems. Finn and Tonsager advocate developing empathic connections during the evaluation process, working collaboratively with clients, and sharing and exploring information with the clients throughout the assessment process. Both perspectives presented here highlight the importance of a client-centered approach to the case conceptualization process.

Conclusion

In this chapter we have presented the knowledge, skills, and attitudes that a CFP specialist must possess for the case conceptualization competency. We presented a 13-step transtheoretical model for case conceptualization consisting of three distinct phases: diagnostic formulation, case formulation, and treatment formulation. Conceptualizing a case in this manner will assist the CFP specialist in conducting assessment, providing treatment, and conducting research.

FOUR

Assessment Competency

Psychological assessment is a defining feature of the identity of a professional psychologist and central to CFP specialty practice. CFP assessment, along with case conceptualization and intervention, is a keystone feature of the specialty. Systemic assessment requires evaluation of the client's individual, interpersonal, and macrosystemic factors and is used to identify and clarify presenting problems, formulate a diagnosis and working hypotheses about the case, guide intervention, and assess treatment progress and outcomes (Nutt & Stanton, 2008; Sperry, 2004). In this chapter we introduce the specialty competency of CFP assessment under the domains of knowledge, skills, and attitudes.

Assessment Competency

At the 2002 Competencies Conference, the assessment work group identified eight core subcompetencies of psychological assessment that encompass knowledge, skills, values, and attitudes (Krishnamurthy et al., 2004). Assessment knowledge includes an understanding of basic psychometric theory; the theoretical and empirical bases of psychological assessment; the psychological domains of individuals and systems; and the relationship between assessment, intervention, and treatment planning. The requisite skills and abilities identified by the work group include the ability to assess the various dimensions of human experience (i.e., cognitive, affective, behavioral, and personality); the knowledge and skill to evaluate outcomes of psychotherapy interventions; the ability to assess relationships, contexts, and multiple roles; and the ability to initiate and maintain a collaborative working relationship with all parties involved in the assessment context (Kaslow, 2004). Technical skills include problem identification, case conceptualization, selection of appropriate instruments and methods, systematic data gathering, and integration to effectively communicate findings and recommendations. Assessment attitudes include psychological mindedness; rapport building; respect for persons; appreciation of diversity; and attention to accuracy, detail, and effective communication.

Definition of CFP Assessment

Professional psychology had its roots in the assessment of individual differences, and as such, assessment has always been a prominent feature of individually based psychology. In contrast, CFP assessment has received less attention and often does not play the same role in CFP treatment (Carlson, 1995).

Several differences may be noted between the traditional assessment of individuals and CFP assessment. The most prominent difference is the philosophy of science that underlies both approaches to assessment. Because of the revolutionary nature of family systems theory and the tenuous history with individually based psychology, some early family therapists and subsequent CFP specialists have been reluctant to introduce a positivistic form of assessment into systemically oriented family interventions. Individual assessment was understood to be based on a linear Cartesian philosophy of science, and couple and family assessment was based on nonlinear systems theory. In addition, consistent with systems theory, CFP specialists viewed evaluation and treatment as a reciprocal, nonlinear, and ongoing process. Family evaluation did not necessarily occur during the first interview and end prior to the commencement of treatment.

Because we believe that the bifurcation between these two philosophies of science has stunted the growth of CFP assessment, we offer a definition of CFP assessment that draws on the strengths of both systemic and linear epistemologies, while being mindful of the limitations of both. For this chapter, we define CFP assessment as the application of individual, couple, and family psychological assessment methods to identify the assets and liabilities of individuals, couples, and families for the purpose of problem identification, treatment planning, and intervention, or to answer a focused question related to couple or family functioning.

Knowledge

As listed in Table 4.1, CFP assessment knowledge begins with understanding the nature of CFP assessment and the ways in which it is distinct from other types of psychological assessment. Second, the CFP specialist

TABLE 4.1 Assessment Competency: Developmental Level—Specialty Competence in Couple and Family Psychology

COMPETENCY DOMAIN AND ESSENTIAL COMPONENT	BEHAVIORAL ANCHOR	ASSESSMENT METHODS
Knowledge **(A) Foundational assessment knowledge** (A.1) Understands nature of CFP assessment methodology (A.2) Understands the scope of CFP evaluation methods (A.3) Understands measurement and psychometrics of CFP assessment instruments	(A.1.1) Applies a systemic paradigm to CFP assessment and understands the distinction between CFP assessment and traditional psychological assessment (A.2.1) Understands the range of CFP assessment methods (A.2.2) Demonstrates knowledge of the appropriate uses and misuses of CFP assessment methods (A.3.1) Awareness of psychometrics that constitute the various CFP assessment instruments, including strengths and weaknesses of using the tools in diverse contexts	1. ABPP Examination 2. Coursework or continuing education 3. Self-evaluation 4. Peer consultation 5. Client feedback 6. Publication and presentation in scholarly venues 7. Peer review and consultation 8. Consultation or supervision feedback
Skills **(B) Application of Methods** (B.1) Ability to competently use multiple methods of assessment procedures appropriate to CFP (B.2) Demonstrates the ability to apply assessment methods to case conceptualization	(B.1.1) Demonstrates the ability to select and use common CFP measurement instruments appropriate to the client's sociocultural context (B.1.2) Demonstrates the ability to apply individual assessment instruments to CFP context (B.2.1) Demonstrates the ability to use CFP assessment methods to arrive at a description and explanation of individual and systemic problems that informs treatment planning. (B.3.1) Demonstrates the ability to communicate assessment findings in verbal and written feedback	
Attitudes **(C) Assessment Perspective** (B.1) Has a client-centered assessment perspective	(B.1.1) Values assessment as part of the therapeutic process (B.1.2) Values critical thinking, integration of information, and clear presentation of results (B.1.3) Committed to lifelong learning in the area of assessment	

Note. Adapted from the format and content of the Assessment of Competency Benchmarks Work Group (2007). This table assumes that the specialist has achieved competence in professional psychology at the three previous developmental levels, as specified in the benchmarks. The competency domains and behavioral anchors serve as the primary organizing structure for this chapter; content explaining each domain and anchor is provided in the chapter.

understands the scope and methodology of couple and family assessment. Finally, the CFP specialist understands the psychometric foundation and concomitant strengths and weaknesses of CFP assessment methods.

KNOWLEDGE OF CFP ASSESSMENT METHODOLOGY

This section discusses the three knowledge-based anchors necessary for understanding the nature of the CFP assessment methodology. The first anchor in CFP assessment includes knowledge of applying a systemic paradigm to psychological assessment. Second, the CFP evaluator will understand how CFP assessment is distinct from other types of psychological assessment. Third, the CFP specialist needs to understand the constructs that are evaluated in CFP assessment.

Application of Systemic Case Conceptualization to CFP Assessment

The CFP specialist understands how to apply a systemic paradigm to the assessment of couples and families and understands the distinction between CFP assessment and traditional psychological assessment (see Chapter 3, "Case Conceptualization"). A systemic epistemology, as described in Chapter 2, involves appraisal of an individual, couple, family, or larger social system's circumstances in light of personal characteristics, interpersonal relationships, and macrosystemic contextual factors. The epistemology of family psychology involves understanding the complex interaction between interpersonal factors, intraindividual dynamics, and macrosystemic contexts (Liddle, Santisteban, Levant, & Bray, 2002; Stanton, 2009b).

CFP specialists understand the distinction between CFP assessment and other types of psychological assessments. CFP assessments capture a broader range of psychological phenomena and are more complex because of the multiple persons being evaluated. There are many overlaps between a systemic approach to couple and family assessment and psychological assessment as usual, including the use of clinical interviews, observational assessments, and standardized psychological tests and collecting collateral data. Individual assessment has historically been focused on a positivist philosophy of science and is still the dominant methodology for individual psychological assessment. Positivism pursues quantitative description of latent constructs. Once constructs are operationalized, linear analytic methods are used to describe differences, explain and predict relationships, predict group membership, and identify latent structures (Tabachnik & Fidell, 2006). In contrast, CFP assessment is based on a systemic epistemology. The philosophy of science that characterizes CFP assessment is based on general systems theory. Elements of systems theory include circular causality (focus on holistic patterns of interaction rather than linear causality), nonsummativity (the whole is greater than the sum of its parts), and equifinality and multifinality (outcomes do not follow a linear or predictable course; Bray, 1995a).

Another significant difference between individual and CFP assessment is the scope of knowledge that the evaluator must have. The CFP specialist not only needs the knowledge base that encompasses the individual assessment competency but also must possess a solid knowledge base of important couple and family elements. These would include, but are not limited to, knowledge of systems theory, family life-cycle development, normal and pathological family processes, child development, parenting, effects of divorce, ethical and legal applications to CFP assessment, and the broad range of CFP assessment methods. Many of the aforementioned will be discussed later in the chapter.

In addition to the differences already mentioned, Snyder, Cavell, Heffer, and Mangrum (1995) note four differences between individual and CFP assessment. First, in contrast to those seeking individual therapy who believe that personal change is necessary, CFP clients tend to believe that other family members need to change. Accordingly, CFP evaluators must be mindful that individuals within the system may not be entirely forthcoming with their own individual struggles. Second, the CFP context allows the examiner to directly observe problematic behavior. In contrast to the individual assessment where examinees explain their relationship with third parties, the CFP assessment context allows the examiner to directly observe the interactions and validate the consistency of individual self-reports with observations. Third, the number of individuals in the consulting room exponentially increases the complexity. Fourth, the level of immediate hostility may be more intense in CFP than in individual contexts, since the couple and family are bringing both the problems and the individuals involved in the problems into the consulting room. Because symptoms/problems are both system maintained and system maintaining, they are often difficult to bring out into the open (Yingling, Miller, McDonald, & Galewaler, 1998).

SCOPE OF CFP ASSESSMENT METHODS

The second essential component of the assessment knowledge domain is that the CFP specialist understands the scope of evaluation methods used in CFP. The behavioral anchors for this component involve understanding the range of CFP assessment methods and knowledge of the appropriate uses and misuses of the methods.

Range of Assessment Methods

In this section we review the range of CFP assessment methods that have traditionally been classified in the following categories: informal transactional observations, self-report, clinical rating scales, and family interaction coding schemes (Bray, 1995a; Filsinger, 1983; Fredman & Sherman, 1987; Grotevant & Carlson, 1989; Touliatos, Perlmutter, Straus, & Holden, 2001; see these texts for a comprehensive review of the range of assessment methods). We briefly review the categories here.

Self-report Measures: Self-report measurement is the most common method of CFP assessment (Bray, 1995b). Self-report instruments are an important part of the assessment endeavor because they are quick to administer, provide a large amount of information in a short period of time, and provide multiple "insider" perspectives on the nature and scope of the presenting problem in the context of couples and families (Olson, 1977). In addition, self-report instruments are useful for assessment of treatment progress (e.g., the STIC®; Pinsof & Chambers, 2009) and overall outcome of treatment, since they can be administered easily throughout the course of treatment (Bray, 2004). Self-report measures are an easy way to collect baseline data of couple and family functioning, and repeated administration of the measures allows the evaluator to utilize a repeated measures case study approach to ongoing evaluation.

There are well over 1,000 CFP self-report instruments of varying quality that have been used for research and treatment purposes (Touliatos et al., 2001). If an evaluator has an interest in focusing on a specific construct, there probably is an available instrument. Unfortunately, many of the instruments lack an appropriate empirical foundation to warrant use in a clinical context. Criticisms of self-report instruments will be covered later in the chapter. Table 4.2 provides a list of the most widely used couple and family assessment instruments, along with the theoretical constructs assessed by the instrument. This list is far from complete; for a comprehensive review of self-report instruments, see Bray, 1995a; Filsinger, 1983; Fredman and Sherman, 1987; Grotevant and Carlson, 1989; Jordan, 2003; and Touliatos et al., 2001.

Observational Methods: Given some of the limitations noted about self-report instruments, observational methods are an important addition when conducting a multimodal evaluation of a couple or family. Observational methods are sometimes criticized as more subjective than self-report instruments; however, they are not as susceptible to the social

TABLE 4.2 **Common Self-Report Instruments**

SELF-REPORT INSTRUMENT	CONSTRUCTS ASSESSED
Centripetal/Centrifugal Family Style Scale (CP/CF) Kelsey-Smith & Beavers (1981)	Dependency needs; styles of adult conflict; proximity; social presentation; verbal expression of closeness; aggressive/assertive behaviors; expression of positive/negative feelings; internal scapegoating; global family style
Colorado Self-Report Measure of Family Functioning Bloom (1985)	Cohesion; expressiveness; conflict; intellectual-cultural orientation; active-recreational orientation; religious emphasis; organization; family sociability; external locus of control; family idealization; disengagement; democratic family style; laissez-faire family style; authoritarian family style; enmeshment
Conflict Tactics Scale (CTS) Straus (1979)	Conflict reasoning; verbal aggression; violence
Dyadic Adjustment Scale (DAS) Spanier (1976)	Dyadic satisfaction; dyadic cohesion; dyadic consensus; affectional expression
Enriching Relationship Issues, Communication and Happiness (ENRICH) Olson (2002)	Multiscale inventory assessing marital needs, concerns, problems
Family Adaptability and Cohesion Evaluation Scales IV (FACES-IV) Olson, Tiesel, & Gorall (1996)	Family cohesion and family adaptability
Family Assessment Measures—III (FAM-III) Skinner, Steinhauer, & Santa-Barbara (1984)	Task accomplishment; role performance; communication; affective expression; affective involvement; control; values and norms
Family Emotional Involvement and Criticism Scale (FEICS) Shields, Franks, Harp, McDaniel, & Campbell (1992)	Expressed emotion; perceived criticism; emotional involvement
Family Environment Scale (FES) Moos & Moos (1986)	Cohesion; expressiveness; conflict; independence; achievement orientation; intellectual-cultural orientation; active-recreational orientation; moral-religious emphasis; organization; control
Family Inventory of Life Events and Changes (FILE) McCubbin, Patterson, & Wilson (1987)	Intrafamily strains; marital strains; pregnancy and childbearing strains; finance and business strains; work-family transitions and strains; illness and family care strains; losses; transitions; legal strains
Global Assessment of Relational Functioning (GARF) Self-Report for Families Yingling, Miller, McDonald, & Galewaler (1998)	Problem-solving/interactional skills; family organization and structure; family attitudes of belonging
Marital Adjustment Test (MAT) Locke & Wallace (1959)	Marital satisfaction; cohesion

(Continued)

TABLE 4.2 **(Continued)**

SELF-REPORT INSTRUMENT	CONSTRUCTS ASSESSED
Marital Disaffection Scale Kayser (1996)	Loss of positive emotions toward one's spouse
Marital Satisfaction Inventory-Revised (MSI-R) Snyder (1997)	Global distress; affective communication; problem-solving communication; aggression; time together; disagreement about finances; sexual dissatisfaction; role orientation; family history of distress; dissatisfaction with children
McMaster Family Assessment Device (FAD) Epstein, Baldwin, & Bishop (1983)	Problem solving; communication; roles; affective responsiveness; affective involvement; behavior control; general functioning
Parenting Stress Index (PSI) Abidin (1983)	Child adaptability; acceptability of the child to the parent; child demandingness; child mood; child distractibility/hyperactivity; child reinforces parent; parent depression; parent attachment; restrictions imposed by the parental role; parent's sense of competence; social isolation; relationship with spouse; physical health
Personal Authority in the Family System Questionnaire (PAFS-Q) Bray, Williamson, & Malone (1984)	Spousal intimacy; spousal fusion/individuation; nuclear family triangulation; intergenerational intimacy; intergenerational intimidation; personal authority
Premarital Personal and Relationship Evaluation Program (PREPARE) Olson (2002)	Identification of needs and concerns of premarital couples
Relational Assessment Measure for Same-Sex Couples (RAM-SSC) Burgoyn (2001)	Conflict resolution; cohesion; affection; sexuality; identity; compatibility; autonomy; expressiveness; social desirability
Self-Report Family Inventory (SFI) Beavers, Hampson, & Hulgus (1985)	Family health; conflict; family communication; family cohesion; expressiveness; directive leadership
Systematic Assessment of the Family Environment (SAFE) Yingling, Miller, McDonald, & Galewaler (1998)	Organizational structure and interactional processes

desirability factor as are objective instruments. Observational methods are more varied than paper-and-pencil measures and can be grouped into several categories: informal or transactional evaluations, clinical rating scales, and observation-based coding schemes (Carlson, 1995). Observational measures can be situated across three axes with respect to formality and standardization, scientific and psychometric integrity, and depth of idiographic data obtained. On the formality axis, those observational methods that occur naturally during the course of the initial clinical interviews would have a low formality and a loosely configured structure and format.

Conversely, structured observer-rated interviews would be higher on the formality axis because of the consistency of administration and coding rules. It follows that those methods high on formality will probably be high on scientific and psychometric integrity, but lower on depth of idiographic information. Evaluation methods should be selected on the basis of the needs of the client or referral source. In some situations depth of information is preferable to scientific rigor, such as in the case of a treatment setting. Evaluations that occur in the context of treatment have the opportunity to hold the results more loosely as a working model, and hypotheses can be refined over the course of treatment as new information emerges. In contrast, a court-ordered evaluation would necessitate using evaluation methods that are scientifically supported and able to meet admissibility standards (e.g., *Daubert* or *Frye*). In the following section we review the major categories of observational methodologies and comment on the strengths and weaknesses of each category.

Some of the earliest assessment methods in CFP involved informal observation of transactions between family members. During the course of treatment, CFP specialists would observe transactions between family members to develop hypotheses about family structure, organization, hierarchy, subsystems, coalitions, alliances, and boundaries (Duffy & Chenail, 2004). According to general systems theory and the properties of living systems (e.g., interrelatedness, hierarchy, organization), dysfunctional family patterns are evident in repeated interactional and communication sequences between members of the family unit (Carlson, 1995). Those practicing CFP from a first-wave model of family therapy such as structural or strategic family therapy are likely to utilize this type of assessment method, and it has been incorporated into general specialty practice across models. Consistent with the structural and strategic school, there is no formal evaluation phase. Rather, assessment begins with the first session and continues throughout the treatment. Regardless of the type of assessment methodology used, structural/strategic observational assessment, because of its foundational link to evaluating family systems, is considered an important element of demonstrating competency in CFP assessment. Strengths of this type of evaluation method include flexibility, richness of idiographic data, and historical significance. Weaknesses include lack of standardization, interpreter bias, and low scientific integrity.

Observations may also revolve around a prescribed task, such as solving a puzzle or planning a family trip. These problem-solving tasks are used as an alternative to observing the couple or family interact naturally without parameters and may be designed to elicit conflictual interactions. Observation tasks may be informal and unstandardized, such as observing a child and adult playing with blocks. They may also be standardized and coded, such as the Philadelphia Child Guidance Clinic Family Task (Kerig & Lindahl, 2000; Rosman, 1978, cited in Grotevant & Carlson, 1989). Observational tasks can be used in routine clinical services or in highly specialized child custody evaluations (Gould, 2006).

Clinical Rating Scales: Semistructured diagnostic interviews or clinical rating scales should also be considered part of the existing knowledge base of CFP assessment. Diagnostic interviews usually are conducted at the outset of therapy, and the information obtained is compared with a preestablished set of normative data. Clinical rating scales provide a structured format for clinician evaluation of select couple or family constructs. Examples of widely known clinical rating scales include the Beavers Interactional Scales (BIS; Beavers & Hampson, 1990); the Global Assessment of Relational Functioning (GARF; American Psychiatric Association, 1994); the McMaster Model of Family Functioning (Epstein, Bishop, & Levin, 1978); and the Circumplex Model of Marital and Family Systems (Olson & Killorin, 1988). Clinical rating scales provide an "outsider's" perspective on the family interaction (Olson, 1977) and are not as vulnerable to the biases inherent in the rationally derived self-report instruments such as the social desirability bias, single-source variance, face validity, and under- or overreporting.

Family Interaction Coding Schemes: Family interaction coding schemes are a microanalytic observational method in which family researchers or clinicians apply a criterion-based code to verbal interaction or behavioral events during the course of a couple or family interaction (Gilbert & Christensen, 1985). Coding schemes are more often used in couple and family research than in clinical settings. Coding schemes offer high-yield information about family transactions, sequences of behaviors, and overall family functioning. Unfortunately, the time required to code an interactional sequence is prohibitive in a clinical setting, when cost-effective approaches to assessment are necessary. Moreover, because of the increased time required to code a transactional series, fewer transactions can be coded, and evaluation with this method is typically limited to one family session, which might not be representative of the family (Carlson, 1995). These methods offer high internal validity but may not generalize to behavior in a naturalistic setting. For more detailed descriptions on verbal interactions of family members, see Grotevant and Carlson, 1989, pp. 17–41. For reviews of coding systems that evaluate marital or family interaction in therapy, see Gilbert and Christensen, 1985; Pinsof, 1981; or Pinsof and Chambers, 2009.

MEASUREMENT AND PSYCHOMETRICS OF CFP ASSESSMENT INSTRUMENTS (A.3)

The CFP evaluator understands the theory of measurement and psychometrics of CFP assessment instruments. The behavioral anchors of this essential component include awareness or psychometric properties of CFP instruments and an understanding of the appropriate uses and misuses of CFP instruments.

Awareness of Psychometric Properties of CFP Instruments

Competency in CFP assessment includes awareness of the psychometric properties that constitute the scope of CFP assessment instruments and an understanding of the strengths and weaknesses of using the tools in diverse contexts. The *APA's Guidelines for Test User Qualifications (TFTUQ;* Turner, DeMers, Fox, & Reed, 2001) identified psychometric and measurement knowledge as a core domain for qualification to use psychological testing. The importance of this knowledge base was echoed by the Assessment Task Force at the APPIC Competencies Conference (Krishnamurthy et al., 2004). The psychometric foundation required, at a minimum, includes knowledge of descriptive statistics (central tendency, dispersion, skewness, and kurtosis); reliability (consistency); validity (evidence for a construct); normative interpretations of test scores (characteristics of a distribution, standard scores); sources of measurement error; statistical tests frequently used in psychometrics such as factor analysis, and structural equation modeling (Anastasi & Urbina, 1997; Krishnamurthy et al., 2004; Turner et al., 2001).

The psychometric properties of the more commonly used CFP assessment instruments are generally acceptable, and some of the instruments have benefited from many years of research. However, a number of criticisms have been leveled against self-report instruments. Halverson (1995) notes that self-report instruments typically solicit information from individuals within the family who endorse their perceptions of various aspects of family functioning; this represents single-source variance, and the contribution to understanding family variance is suspect. Wampler and Halverson (1993; cited in Halverson, 1995) did not find incremental validity to single-source family measures when entered into a multiple regression following entry of individual measures. It is important to note that there have been correction procedures to account for the predominance of individual variance in family assessment measures (Bray, 2009). These measures are generally based on averaging data or applying weighting systems (Cole & McPherson, 1993; Cook & Kenny, 2004, both cited in Bray, 2009).

Another important criticism by Halverson (1995) is that the majority of family self-report measures are developed on inadequate sample sizes, often including fewer research participants than the number of test items. Moreover, family self-report inventories lack relevant comparison data to account for the multiple factors that contribute to family functioning. Collecting normative data for families is much more complex than for individuals. Self-report instruments function best in relation to normative data. The task of providing an adequate normative sample is overwhelming. As an example, consider the many types of variables that affect family functioning. Would separate strata have to be created for common variables such as number of children and developmental stage of family, adults, and children? The number of possible contributing factors to any individual family constellation raises serious concerns about the representative nature of norm-referenced tests to any single family. Grotevant and Carlson (1989) also note that self-report instruments lack differential clinical validity and are often not able to discriminate between clinical and normal samples or to discriminate between various types of dysfunction within the family. Finally, self-report family measures are often inappropriate for collection of children's perceptions.

Clinical rating scales have fared comparatively well and have avoided many of the criticisms applied to self-report instruments. The three most common clinical rating scales (BIS, McMaster Model, and Circumplex Model) have a long history of research in clinical settings. These models also capture the observational spirit of early family theorists and are generally seen as more systemically pure in comparison to the self-report instruments. The BIS, McMaster Model, and Circumplex Model are psychometrically reliable and provide an evidence base for validity. One study found that the BIS and McMaster models yielded high levels of sensitivity in the ability to discriminate between clinical and nonclinical families (Drumm, Carr, & Fitzgerald, 2000). In the same study, the Circumplex model was particularly adept at identifying nonclinical cases. Accordingly, Drumm and colleagues recommend the use of one of the three instruments in all family assessments. Relatedly, Beavers and Hampson (2000) conducted a similar study evaluating the criterion-related validity of these three systems and discovered similar findings.

Uses and Misuses of CFP Assessment Methods

The CFP evaluator demonstrates understanding of the appropriate uses and recognizes the misuses of CFP assessment methods. As mentioned previously, a mismatch between the tests and the testing situation may invalidate the usual test interpretation (Turner et al., 2001). CFP evaluators should not assume that a single method of family assessment adequately captures the complexity of family functioning; accordingly, they should apply a multisource, multimethod approach to evaluation.

Most CFP assessment instruments have been theoretically derived from Western concepts of the family and "normal" family functioning (Bray, 1995b). Relatedly, the vast majority of family measures are based on European American normative data sets (Bray, 2009). Accordingly, caution should be used to denote the appropriate limitations of the assessment measure. Culturally relevant assessment studies have been conducted with several well-known instruments and clinical ratings scales, including the Self-Report Family Inventory (Shek, 1998), the Family Assessment Device (Morris, 1990; Shek, 2002), the Family Environment Scale (Negy & Snyder, 2006), and the Beavers Interactional Competence and Style Scales (Hampson, Beavers, & Hulgus, 1990).

Skills

In this section we describe the attendant skills necessary for the assessment competency. We have identified the two essential component skills as the ability to competently use multiple CFP assessment methods and the ability to use the assessment data to contribute to a case conceptualization.

COMPETENTLY USES MULTIPLE CFP ASSESSMENT METHODS

The CFP evaluator demonstrates the ability to competently use multiple assessment procedures appropriate to the assessment of couples and families. This essential component is made up of two anchors. First, the CFP evaluator demonstrates the ability to select and use common CFP assessment methods appropriate to the client's sociocultural context. Second, the CFP evaluator demonstrates the ability to appropriately apply individual assessment instruments within a couple and family assessment context.

Selection and Use of Common CFP Methods

The ability to select and apply a range of common CFP assessment methods that are appropriate to the couple or family's social context (e.g., ethnocultural or socioeconomic) is a core skill. As discussed, CFP evaluators must clearly identify the constructs of interest and select the assessment methods that are best suited to the task. According to the 2002 APA Ethics Code, psychologists base opinions and comment on psychological characteristics of examinees only after they have collected information in a manner suitable and sufficient to justify the conclusions (American Psychological Association, 2002). It follows that assessment must be conducted from a multimodal perspective (Houts, Cook, & Shadish, 1986), which proposes that social science constructs are most accurately measured from a multimodal-multimethod perspective (Halverson, 1995). Because no one method can accurately assess the complexities of a psychological construct, not to mention the reciprocal interactions with other constructs, multiple methods will better approximate the elusive systemic constructs. Wampler and Halverson (1993) summarize the need for a multimodal perspective: "In the family area we mostly deal with highly complex, abstract, 'nonvisible' constructs that must be estimated from fallible and biased measurement systems. The bias is maximized when our constructs are estimated by one measure from one source with one method at one point in time" (p. 189; cited in Halverson, 1995).

Turner and colleagues (2001) provide a thorough list of the knowledge required for the appropriate selection of tests. These include reliability, validity, test bias, normative sample and standardization group, test administration procedures, knowledge base of the test taker, difficulty level, and scoring procedures. When several normative data sets are available, the CFP evaluator should use the normative data that are most consistent with the demographic and sociocultural context of the couple or family being assessed.

When selecting CFP assessment methods, the CFP specialist must conduct a cost-benefit analysis, since there are no "gold standard" family assessment methods (Bray, 2009). In the ideal world, CFP assessment would simultaneously provide depth, breadth, scientific rigor, and flexibility. Unfortunately, this is not the case, and the CFP evaluator shares many of the same challenges faced by the research methodologist when selecting an analysis strategy. As noted previously, it is necessary to employ a multimodal assessment strategy to adequately address the referral question because some methods excel at providing idiographic depth (qualitative interviews), whereas others excel at providing reliable and valid assessments of psychological or family constructs (self-report measures). The question before the CFP specialist will dictate the type of assessment approach taken.

Selection of a CFP assessment methodology must take into consideration diversity factors, including ethnicity, race, culture, sexual orientation, gender, disability, age, spirituality, and linguistic ability. Turner et al. (2001) recommended consideration of the following when using tests with diverse groups: (a) construct equivalence, which includes consideration of motivation, attitudes, and stereotype threat on test performance; (b) orientations and values of the test takers that may alter how the definition of the constructs is assessed and interpreted; (c) the impact of testing environment on diverse groups; (d) test bias; (e) laws and public policies governing the use of tests with diverse groups; (f) differences between diverse groups and the standardization samples; and (g) differential validity with certain racial or cultural groups.

Testing individuals with disabilities presents unique challenges, such as the need to use modified tests that may deviate from standard test administration practices (Turner et al., 2001). In addition, the CFP evaluator should be familiar with the implications of testing and test interpretation in light of the Americans with Disabilities Act (ADA). For CFP evaluators who conduct assessments on individuals with disabilities, we recommend consulting the work of Ekstrom and Smith (2002), who have written a sourcebook on behalf of the Joint Committee on Testing Practices entitled *Assessing Individuals with Disabilities in Educational, Employment, and Counseling Settings.*

Application of Individual Assessment Instruments to CFP Context

One of the important contributions that CFP has made to the field of systemic assessment is to incorporate the use of a host of evidence-based methods of individual psychological assessment into CFP assessment. The CFP evaluator demonstrates the ability to apply individual psychological assessment instruments within a systemic context. There is some disagreement about the role of individual instruments in CFP assessment. Some argue that individual measures are of "limited relevance" for CFP assessment (L'Abate, 2004, p. 254); however, given that most of the couple and family self-report measures primarily capture individual variance, we believe that the addition of individual psychological measures provides an important dimension to the assessment process.

The application of individual psychological instruments to a systemic context has many benefits. First, individual measures excel at identifying areas of severe psychological problems such as Axis I and Axis II psychiatric disorders. The responsible CFP specialist cannot avoid attending to individual psychiatric problems that might need psychopharmacological intervention or hospitalization (Nurse, 1999). Second, nearly all of the individual psychological assessment instruments are concerned with how an individual interacts with his or her environment. For instance, the underlying theory of the Millon Clinical Multiaxial Inventory – 3rd Edition (MCMI-III) is relationally focused (Millon, Davis, & Millon, 1997). By definition, Axis II disorders display chronic interpersonal problems. Consider the theoretical underpinnings of the Rorschach Inkblot Method (Exner, 2002; Exner & Erdberg, 2005); individuals react in personal ways to ambiguous elements in the stimulus cards. The Rorschach Inkblot Method excels at explaining how an individual interacts with his or her environment. Finally, the Minnesota Multiphasic Personality Inventory – 2 (MMPI-2) has a host of variables that are interpreted in light of an individual's relationship with the environment. Scales 3 (hysteria) and 6 (paranoia) are excellent examples of the relationally focused nature of the MMPI-2 interpretations (Butcher, Dahlstrom, Graham, Tellegen, & Kaemmer, 2001).

Individual psychological assessment instruments have a solid empirical base when it comes to explaining and predicting how individuals will interact with other individuals or the demands of the environment. Whether identified as such, we believe that individual measures of psychological functioning capture the essence of a systemic epistemology. Individual assessment instruments are used to describe an individual's intrapersonal characteristics, explain interpersonal interactions, and predict his or her relationship to macrosystemic elements. For example, the MCMI-III provides personality information that may inform couple therapy (Nurse & Stanton, 2008; Stanton & Nurse, 2009).

We would even go so far as to suggest that many of the forensic assessment instruments contain systemic elements. Forensic psychology has recognized the need to adapt a broader epistemology for understanding complex behavior as evidenced by the distinction made between actuarial assessment (static) and structured professional judgment (dynamic). Interestingly, the static and dynamic specifiers are terms used in nonlinear dynamic systems theory. The HCR-20 (violence risk assessment; Webster, Douglas, Eaves, & Hart, 1997) and Static-99 (sex offender risk assessment; Hanson, 1997) both consider the importance of an individual's potential exposure to destabilizing events in the environment; this is a close cousin to macrosystemic assessment.

CASE CONCEPTUALIZATION

The ability to incorporate assessment findings into a conceptual framework ready for implementation and communication is a central skill to the CFP assessment competency. In Chapter 3 we covered the entire process of case conceptualization from beginning to end. Accordingly, we will briefly summarize the skills required for case conceptualization.

Case conceptualization in general is defined as "a method and process of summarizing seemingly diverse case information into a brief, coherent statement or 'map' that elucidates the client's basic pattern of behavior" (Sperry, 2005, p. 354). Case conceptualization contains three components: diagnostic formulation, clinical formulation, and treatment formulation (Sperry et al., 1992). The three behavioral anchors presented in the following section encompass the ability to arrive at a diagnostic formulation, explain the assessment data as a clinical formulation, and use the assessment data to arrive at a treatment formulation.

Problem Formulation

The CFP evaluator demonstrates the skills necessary to arrive at a problem (diagnostic) formulation of individual and systemic assets and liabilities. "Diagnostic formulations are descriptive, phenomenological, and cross-sectional in nature" (Sperry, 2005, p. 355). As mentioned previously, the prudent examiner will be simultaneously attuned to both individual and systemic strengths and weaknesses. In the assessment context, the CFP evaluator will formulate and test hypotheses about the interaction between individual factors, interpersonal relationships, and contextual factors. Many clinicians have adverse reactions to diagnoses and other labels that might predispose the evaluator to rely exclusively on a categorical or a medicalized model of human functioning. If an evaluator considers individual and couple/family assets (e.g., strengths) and liabilities (e.g., diagnoses if applicable) within a systemic epistemology, then we believe that many of the concerns related to diagnosis can be circumvented. Because CFP specialists voluntarily self-identify with the broader profession of professional psychology, we believe that it is important to work collaboratively within an imperfect system that is recognized by the majority of psychologists as routine standard practice.

A good example of how systemically oriented mental health professionals have interfaced with medical psychiatry is represented by the advancements made in relational diagnoses in the last 20 years. Relational diagnosis began in the mid-1980s with the Group for the Advancement of Psychiatry (GAP) Committee on the Family trying to work relational concepts into the diagnostic nosology of the *DSM* series (F. W. Kaslow, 1996). In addition, the Coalition on Family Diagnosis cochaired by Herta Guttman and Florence Kaslow has been a strong force in representing family diagnosis to the American Psychiatric Association. Consideration of relational diagnoses has been slow to make its way into the *DSM*, although significant advancements have been made since the pioneering efforts of the GAP and the Coalition. Some of these advancements will be reviewed.

First, the *Global Assessment of Relational Functioning (GARF;* Yingling et al., 1998) is currently the only family-oriented measure in the *DSM-IV-TR*. The GARF was developed by the collaborative work of the GAP Family Committee and the Coalition on Family Diagnosis. The original hope was that the GARF would end up as a major axis in the multiaxial system; however, the final publication of the *DSM-IV* placed it in the "Criteria Sets and Axes Provided for Further Study" (Yingling et al., 1998). Nevertheless, inclusion of the GARF within the pages of the *DSM-IV* was a major step forward in the recognition of the importance of relational assessment. According to the *DSM-IV-TR*, the GARF evaluates three areas of functioning: problem solving, organization, and emotional climate. The GARF developers used slightly different labels to represent the constructs: "(a) interactional processes, (b) organizational structure, and (c) emotional climate/developmental nurturing output of the client family system" (Yingling et al., 1998, p. 2). The GARF scale is an observer-rated measure that places the family's relational functioning on a scale from 1 to 100, similar to the Global Assessment of Functioning (GAF).

A second major contribution to relational diagnosis is the inclusion of relational problems in the V-Codes (partner relational problem and parent-child problem). Inclusion of relational problems as a focus of clinical treatment in the *DSM* "recognizes that some clinical interventions may be targeted specifically at couple and family processes" (Lawrence, Beach, & Doss, 2009, p. 165). Third, the *DSM-IV* recognizes the importance of relational processes as sources of situation-specific factors to be considered in diagnosis.

Lawrence et al. (2009) identifies three ways that relational factors could be considered in diagnosis: relational syndromes, central relational processes, and relationship specifiers. Relational syndromes are patterns of relational functioning characterized by relative intractability, persistence, and inflexibility. Regardless of the problem, couples or families with relational syndromes will respond with a limited range of problem-solving options to different stressors. Relational syndromes could be characterized by the old adage "if all you have is a hammer, the whole world looks like a nail." Central relational processes are "useful when the focus of clinical attention is on the impaired interaction pattern that may influence the longitudinal course of the disorder, the pattern of remission, or the likelihood of relapse following treatment" (Lawrence et al., 2009, p. 168). Central relational processes are destabilizing family climates such as the high expressed emotion family. Finally, relationship specifiers bring a relationally focused sensitivity to understanding the contextual factors that might play a central role in the etiology, expression, or maintenance of a disorder.

Case Formulation

Once the diagnostic formulation has been completed, the CFP specialist then goes a step beyond description and provides an explanation for understanding the etiology, system-serving functions, and system-maintaining elements of the symptoms or problematic relational patterns (Sperry, 2005). CFP specialists demonstrate the ability to organize assessment data and identify meaningful relationships between the entire corpus of client data and the assessment findings. Interpretation of the data is accomplished by making sense of the data in light of a systemic paradigm. See Chapter 3 for more information on case formulation

Treatment Formulation

CFP specialists are able to take assessment data and, in light of the problem and case formulation, specify a plan to target goals and interventions. According to Carlson (1995), "the goals of family assessment at the treatment planning phase are to specify objectives for change, analyze the contingencies maintaining the problematic behavior, identify family strengths and resources, and determine the intervention sequence and the level of change that is adequate for treatment to be terminated" (p. 24). Treatment formulation involves providing feedback to clients in a way that enhances motivation and is viewed by the client(s) as a therapeutic experience (Finn, 2007). In addition, CFP specialists invite the client(s) into a collaborative goal-setting process and, in light of the assessment, specify which areas of the problem will be tackled first and with what interventions. Finally, CFP sepcialists will monitor the progress of treatment and make adjustments to the case conceptualization and treatment as necessary. For more information on treatment planning, refer to Chapter 3.

Attitudes

In Chapter 3 we identified possessing a client-centered perspective as the core attitude of the case conceptualization competency. It follows that this attitude also characterizes the assessment competency. Accordingly, CFP specialists strive to present assessment findings in a manner that is immediately useful to clients and other professionals, to avoid using discipline-specific language, and to present the assessment results in a manner that honors the complexity and dignity of the human experience. Accordingly, CFP specialists are constantly mindful that clients are allowing the examiner to see the most vulnerable and intimate aspects of themselves and, consequently, handle this information with the deepest respect for the client's private life. In the spirit of client-centered assessment, CFP specialists consider the client's strengths as well as weaknesses.

CFP specialists also value a commitment to critical and integrative thinking during the assessment process (Krishnamurthy et al., 2004) and constantly strive for greater knowledge and skill enhancement. CFP evaluators are committed to lifelong learning and regularly pursue continuing education opportunities related to assessment and its related functions. CFP evaluators strive to keep abreast of the most current scientific evidence and evaluation procedures. Evaluators are appropriately aware of the inherent limitations in CFP assessment and always consider the relative strength of the data when offering interpretive statements and making clinical decisions. Because of the human element involved in the interpretation process, CFP specialists are committed to continually evaluating biases, values, and interpretive habits through a regular peer review process. Evaluators demonstrate appropriate humility in interpreting assessment data and are mindful of using language that indicates more certainty than reasonably exists. Finally, CFP evaluators pay particular attention to detail, take pride in the accuracy of their work, and value excellence in assessment.

Conclusion

In this chapter we have presented the knowledge, skills, and attitudes of the assessment competency. The required knowledge base for CFP specialists includes understanding the nature and scope of integration, knowledge of the strengths and limitations of instruments, and a foundation in psychometrics and test theory. The skill set required for this competency broadly included the ability to select, administer, and interpret individual and couple and family assessment methods, and to use the data to describe the client's problem, formulate a conceptual understanding of the case, and inform treatment planning. Finally, CFP specialists maintain a client-centered assessment perspective and continually strive to improve their assessment knowledge and abilities.

PART III

Functional Competency— Intervention

FIVE

Intervention Competency

The CFP specialist intervention competency is central to the professional practice of most CFP specialists. Competent provision of specialty interventions requires a foundation of knowledge about interventions and evidence-based practice that is consistent with the specialty epistemology and science, as well as skills in the selection, provision, and evaluation of interventions, and attitudes that support the intervention competency. This chapter describes the knowledge, skills, and attitudes required for specialty intervention competency, organized to parallel the categories of Table 5.1.

Intervention Knowledge

The CFP specialist demonstrates advanced knowledge of the application of a systemic epistemology to intervention, specialty evidence-based practice, common factors in specialty intervention, established specialty interventions, and the application of evidence-based practice to various presenting issues and client populations. This section describes the knowledge necessary for competency in CFP specialist interventions.

UNDERSTANDS SYSTEMIC EPISTEMOLOGY AND INTERVENTION

The adoption and use of a systemic epistemology is a distinguishing feature of the CFP specialty (see Chapter 2). The application of that epistemology and an associated paradigm, including key concepts and habits of systemic thinking, to the understanding of specialty interventions is central to CFP specialist competency. Intervention is defined as the "ability to conceptualize interventions systemically and to utilize evidence-based systemic

TABLE 5.1 Intervention Competencies: Developmental Level—Specialty Competence in Couple and Family Psychology

COMPETENCY DOMAIN AND ESSENTIAL COMPONENT	BEHAVIORAL ANCHOR	ASSESSMENT METHODS
Knowledge (A) Knowledge of CFP evidence-based practice (EBP) and specialty interventions (A.1) Knowledge of CFP interventions and application of EBP to issues and populations	(A.1.1) Understands and capably utilizes a systemic framework for specialty intervention (A.1.2) Demonstrates advanced knowledge of specialty EBP (A.1.3) Understands common factors in CFP interventions (A.1.4) Demonstrates advanced level of knowledge in the specialty interventions, including which interventions apply to particular treatment issues and/or populations	1. ABPP examination 2. Ongoing status for practice through licensure 3. Continuing education in CFP intervention 4. Peer consultation and clinical case review 5. Client feedback 6. Self-evaluation 7. Consultation or supervision feedback 8. Publication and presentation in peer reviewed venues
Skills (B) Ability to select and implement CFP interventions (B.1) Accurate selection of EBP interventions, effective implementation, and evaluation of intervention	(B.1.1) Ability to review the case conceptualization, select prioritized intervention goals, and provide a rationale for the treatment plan that is understood and accepted by the client(s) (B.1.2) Ability to select interventions appropriate to the issue and/or population (B.1.3) Ability to demonstrate CFP common factors in treatment (B.1.4) Ability to provide the intervention in a manner consistent with its theoretical and/or evidence-based formulation (B.1.5) Independently evaluates treatment progress and treatment outcomes (B.1.6) Ability to modify the intervention to meet the specific needs of the client(s) and/or emerging circumstances during treatment (B.1.7) Collaborates effectively with other service providers (B.1.8) Seeks consultation when needed to ensure treatment outcomes	
Attitudes (C) Values the role of research in intervention (C.1) Independently studies intervention research	(C.1.1) Values intervention research and lifelong learning to remain current in intervention research (C.1.2) Values self-evaluation, peer review, and client feedback in specialty practice	

Note. Adapted from the format and content of the Assessment of Competency Benchmarks Work Group (2007). This table assumes that the specialist has achieved competence in professional psychology at the three previous developmental levels, as specified in the benchmarks. The competency domains and behavioral anchors serve as the primary organizing structure for this chapter; content explaining each domain and anchor is provided in the chapter.

interventions that are targeted to specific points in the systems" (Stanton & Harway, 2007, p. 6). This suggests that the CFP specialist avoids reductionistic interventions (e.g., simple symptom reduction that misses the source of the problem) and pursues interventions that approach the complexity and reciprocity of real-life problems. The specialist considers the change mechanisms of various interventions and models to determine if they are inclusive of systemic concepts (e.g., nonlinear change dynamics, complex adaptation) and accord with systemic thinking habits (e.g., does the model represent the system in a meaningful manner?; does the model incorporate reciprocal effects in its understanding of the etiology, progression, and treatment of problems?; does the model recognize homologies and patterns?; does the model locate leverage points that facilitate significant change?).

It is insufficient to consider intervention models systemic simply because there are multiple clients involved in treatment. The key issue is the incorporation of a systemic epistemology in the intervention. In fact, interventions with an individual may be systemic if they incorporate and address systemic factors (e.g., multigenerational patterns, family-of-origin dynamics) and systemic concepts (e.g., reciprocal influences). CFP specialist "is not defined by the number of people in the consulting room, but it is a broad theoretical framework for understanding human behavior" (Nutt & Stanton, 2008, p. 521). The use of a systemic epistemology means that many CFP specialist interventions and models conceptualize presenting issues in relational terms, and they identify and treat dysfunctional relational patterns (Davis & Piercy, 2007a, 2007b; Sprenkle, Davis, & Lebow, 2009).

The systemic epistemology of CFP specialist makes it especially amenable to interventions in complex systems, including couples, families, larger social systems, and organizations. CFP specialists work in many contexts and settings and conduct interventions appropriate to those settings, including schools, primary health care, and businesses and organization (Nutt & Stanton, 2008).

KNOWLEDGE OF SPECIALTY EVIDENCE-BASED PRACTICE

Efforts to integrate science and practice in CFP specialist (see Chapter 2) are consistent with broad initiatives in psychology. There has been a significant movement to establish the importance of scientific evidence for the specification of validated practices. Early efforts found resistance from some psychologists who thought that the evidence-based practice movement did not allow sufficient consideration of various types of evidence, including the clinician's judgment. Subsequently, the APA Presidential Task Force on Evidence-Based Practices (2006) considered various perspectives on evidence-based practice and arrived at a definition that gave credence to both research and clinical experience: *"Evidence-based practice in psychology* (EBPP) is the integration of the best available research with clinical expertise in the context of patient characteristics, culture, and preferences" (APA Presidential Task Force on Evidence-Based Practices, 2006, p. 273). Subsequently, APA Task Force members clarified that "the task force designated the *use* of research evidence as a *component* of clinical expertise" and that there is not a dichotomy between clinical experience and research findings (Wampold, Goodheart, & Levant, 2007, p. 617). Bieschke et al. (2004) note that evidence-based practice is more than "merely knowing which treatments have been shown to be effective with specific disorders, evidence-based practice focuses on asking answerable clinical questions with a reliance on scientific strategies" (p. 717). Kazdin (2008) notes that researchers and clinicians are more united than it might appear when it comes to patient care that involves a family member (i.e., where the rubber meets the pragmatic road) and recommends three goals: (a) optimally develop the knowledge base; (b) provide the best information to improve patient care; and (c) materially reduce the divide between research and practice (p. 151). He suggests that direct collaboration between researchers and clinicians is needed to achieve these goals.

Evidence-Based CFP specialist Practice

The Society for Family Psychology (APA Division 43) appointed a task force in 2004 to consider the issue of evidence-based practices in the specialty. The task force was composed of clinicians, researchers, trainers, supervisors, and intervention designers. They focused on the reliability of evidence for an intervention program and the usefulness of the intervention in its context(s) (see Sexton & Coop-Gordon, 2009, for an overview of the task force process and results). The report of the task force (Sexton et al., 2007) proposes three levels of evidence: a1) evidence-informed interventions/treatments (model informed by identified research base); (b) promising interventions/treatments (initial or preliminary research support); and (c) evidence-based treatments (substantial high-quality support specified within four categories that evaluate the breadth, comparison strength, and generalizability; Sexton & Coop-Gordon, 2009). This model provides the basis for future evaluation of the research evidence for new, existing, and developing interventions.

Knowledge About Conveying Science to Practice

Sexton et al. (2010) identify two knowledge domains for the translation of science into practice: clinical intervention research and specification of clinical practices. Clinical intervention research involves direct application of research to practice; specification of practices involves levels of evidence and specific focus of treatment.

Clinical intervention research: Evidence-based practice is founded on clinical intervention research, "a variation of the research process that is specific to the work of clinical practice. Clinical intervention research is the systematic study of the relationship between identifiable clinical practice (techniques, interventions, treatment problems) and client outcomes" (Sexton, Hanes, & Kinser, 2010, p. 166). Wampold, Lichtenberg, and Waehler (2005) present the Society of Counseling Psychology principles for research into interventions: (a) utilize a broad perspective of evidence, (b) consider a range of psychological interventions, (c) emphasize the quantitative aggregate of research evidence, (d) consider various levels of specificity, and (e) recognize philosophy of science issues that impinge on the types of conclusions that can be made (p. 27). These principles are generally consistent with CFP specialist research. Ultimately, the goal of clinical intervention research is to determine specific elements regarding what works, when it works, how it works, and for whom or what it works in the real world (Minami, Wampold, & Walsh, 2008; Sexton et al., 2010; Wampold, 2001).

Liddle, Bray, Levant, and Santisteban (2002) present the term *family psychology intervention science* to denote the mix of science and practice research in the CFP specialty. They comment that "family psychology intervention science compares well to other specialties" (Liddle et al., 2002, p. 5), noting the variety of research being conducted in the specialty (e.g., process research that studies change mechanisms or processes; clinical research that seeks to connect research more thoroughly to clinical practice; and clinical research gathering effectiveness evidence for interventions).

Sexton et al. (2010) specify six types of clinical intervention research: (a) outcome studies (clinical trials or comparison studies); (b) process-to-outcome studies (research to identify specific treatment conditions to outcomes); (c) ideographic case studies; (d) qualitative research based in clinical practice; (e) transportability research (examining the implementation of evidence-based practices in real-world clinical settings); and (f) qualitative and meta-analytic research reviews (identification of mechanisms across studies). Each provides particular information (data) and informs specific clinical questions. The CFP specialist remains cognizant of these conceptual advances in the field of clinical research in order to inform the consumption and/or conduct of CFP specialist intervention research.

Specification of clinical practices: Sexton et al. (2010) propose a model for specification of clinical practices that delineates levels of scientific evidence ("extensiveness, reliability, and confidence of research support"; p. 169) and specificity in treatment ("from broad theoretical models to highly specific evidencebased treatment packages" in terms of "practice, client, and context"; p. 169). Each level builds on and/or interacts with the former and demonstrates increased levels of evidence and specificity. They suggest that psychologists need to understand the levels and what knowledge of psychological science is needed at each level in order to apply appropriate research approaches and methods to best respond to the research question and produce evidence appropriate to the method. The model begins with basic research, extends to best practices (commonly accepted professional practices), builds to evidence-based practices, and culminates in empirically based treatments. See Sexton et al. (2010) for a figure and thorough explanation of this model. CFP specialists understand contemporary models of CFP specialist evidence-based practice and apply that knowledge to the intervention competency.

Understands CFP specialist Common Factors

Knowledge of CFP specialist interventions requires understanding of the current debate regarding the relative salience of specific evidence-based models of intervention that rely on distinctive change mechanisms versus the "common factors" found across evidence-based interventions (i.e., they are common across theoretical approaches, such as client factors, therapist demographic traits, training, personality and well-being, and the nature of the therapeutic alliance) in treatment (Blow, Sprenkle, & Davis, 2007). The bottom line in the debate seems to be a fundamental disagreement about whether the treatment or the therapist is the primary factor in achieving effective outcomes.

Advocates of a moderate common factors approach (Sprenkle et al., 2009) argue that "psychotherapy works predominantly not because of the unique set of interventions (what we call the model-driven change paradigm) but rather because of a set of common factors or mechanisms of change that cuts across all effective therapies" (p. 2). From this perspective, models are the "vehicles through which common factors operate" (p. 5). This provides a counterbalance to an extreme focus on evidence-based treatments; in their opinion, evidence-based treatments should be modest about their status because the fact that they have been tested extensively does not necessarily mean that they are superior to other models with less research. They indicate that "few reputable widely practiced contemporary treatments based on sound psychosocial principles are found to be not effective when studied empirically" (Sprenkle et al., 2009, p. 172). In other words, they believe that the evidence for common factors supports the idea that use of the common factors is crucial, even to the success of model interventions. Common factor advocates value the quality of the therapeutic alliance and the allegiance of the clinician to the model practiced because allegiance invokes other common factors (e.g., clinician confidence and credibility, which evoke client hope and change expectations). Ultimately, they assert that "the qualities and capabilities of the person offering the treatment are more important than the treatment itself" (Sprenkle et al., 2009, p. 4).

Some note that what may be most important in treatment outcomes is the interplay between the therapeutic relationship and specific treatment techniques (Eisler, 2006; Gelso, 2005). This perspective recognizes the salience of both factors and the importance of the interaction between them. It focuses on how the two treatment paradigms interact to affect or hinder change processes (Eisler, 2006). We endorse this perspective.

Sexton (2007; Sexton, Ridley, & Kleiner, 2004) presents one cogent model that bridges between perspectives to create a dialectic "in which the therapeutic process is seen as a multi-layer change process including the client's change process, the relational interaction between therapist and client, the specific mechanism within a therapy, and common factors" (Sexton, 2007, p. 104). This comprehensive model recognizes the systemic complexity and reciprocity of various factors in the therapeutic process. The therapist plays an important role, but it is not simply the personal characteristics of the therapist that effect change. Instead, Sexton (2007) suggests that the therapist functions "as both an independent factor and a key link within the therapy process" (p. 106). This comprehensive understanding of the therapist's role recognizes the importance of how an individual therapist invokes the common factors, demonstrates interpersonal abilities, and adheres to evidence-based models in order to achieve positive outcomes. For instance, Sexton (2007) notes that particular manifestations of a common factor may need to vary according to the requirements of different evidence-based treatments; he reviews research on the therapeutic alliance by Robbins et al. (Robbins et al., 2006; Robbins, Turner, Alexander, & Perez, 2003) that finds such alliance is best achieved in Functional Family Therapy by a balanced relationship with the adolescent and the parents, while in Multidimensional Family Therapy it is best accomplished by a strong relationship with the parents. Subsequent research suggests that the relative importance of a balanced therapeutic relationship may vary within a particular treatment model by family ethnicity, perhaps due to different cultural expectations regarding hierarchical structure and respect for those differences in treatment (Flicker, Turner, Waldron, Brody, & Ozechowski, 2008).

Currently, the trend seems to be toward broader acceptance of a dynamic interaction between treatment models and common factors. "Just as many common factors work through models, models in turn work through therapists" (Blow et al., 2007, p. 299). "The empirical research shows that both the therapy relationship and the treatment method make consistent contributions to treatment outcome" (Norcross, 2001, p. 352). The CFP specialist cannot ignore either aspect; instead, the CFP specialist must advocate fully for each and balance them in the dynamic process of treatment. The CFP specialist needs to know the research about the reasons for the effectiveness of evidence-based interventions and provide them in a manner that reflects the specific elements of that treatment. On the other hand, the CFP specialist must link the particular needs of an individual, couple, or family to the treatment by adjusting the administration of common factors and evidencing interpersonal skills. These "therapist-offered relationship qualities" (Gelso, 2005, p. 419) remain important to the complex phenomenon of effective treatment.

KNOWLEDGE OF SPECIALTY INTERVENTIONS

The CFP specialist understands the conceptual and scientific foundations of CFP specialist interventions and applies that knowledge to achieve an understanding of interventions that accord with the specialty. Knowledge of specialty interventions includes a general awareness of the scope of recognized interventions in the specialty and knowledge about which interventions are particularly suited to specific presenting issues and client populations.

Knowledge of Recognized Interventions

CFP specialists demonstrate advanced knowledge and understanding of recognized specialty interventions and treatment models (Celano, Smith, & Kaslow, 2010). At a broad level, this involves knowledge of a list of specialty interventions that are founded on the specialty epistemology and science (Table 5.2). At the level of the specific intervention or model, this includes knowledge of the model, understanding of its primary common factor and model-specific change factors, familiarity with the sequence of the intervention (e.g., stages or phases of intervention), and awareness of projected outcomes. CFP specialists remain current in the specialty literature regarding intervention development and refinement in order to incorporate the latest research and clinical experience into their practice of an intervention or model.

TABLE 5.2 CFP Interventions

MODEL-INTERVENTION	REFERENCE CITATIONS	FOCUSED TREATMENT ISSUES	TREATMENT POPULATIONS
Attachment-Based Family Therapy	(Diamond, 2005; Diamond, Levy, Israel, & Diamond, 2009)	Depression, anxiety	Adolescents
Behavioral Couples Therapy	(Gordon, Dixon, Willett, & Hughes, 2009)	Behavioral aspects of relationship; serious mental illness	Individual, couples, families
Behavioral Couples Therapy	(Fals-Stewart, Birchler, O'Farrell, & Lam, 2009)	Alcoholism/drug abuse	Adults, couples, families
Bowen Family Systems Theory	(Hargrove, 2009)	Emotions, differentiation of self	Individuals, Couples, Parents, Families
Brief Strategic Family Therapy™	(Robbins, Szapocznik, & Horigian, 2009)	Behavior problems	Adolescents
Cognitive-behavioral	(Gordon et al., 2009)	Behavioral, cognitive, affective aspects of relationship; clinical syndromes	Individual, couples, families
Collaborative Divorce	(Nurse & Thompson, 2009)	Divorce	Couples
Collaborative Practice: Relationships and Conversations (Social Construction)	(Anderson, 2009)	Spectrum	Spectrum
Common factors in couple and family therapy	(Sprenkle, Davis, & Lebow, 2009)	Therapeutic alliance; spectrum of issues	Couples, families
Couple's treatment for Intimate Partner Violence	(Stith, McCollum, 2009)	Intimate partner violence	Couples
Couples therapy for depression	(Whisman, Whiffen, & Whiteford, 2009)	Depression	Couples
Emotionally Focused Couple Therapy	(Johnson & Bradley, 2009)	Relationship (emotional engagement)	Couples
Empirically Informed Systemic Psychotherapy	(Pinsof & Chambers, 2009)	Therapeutic alliance; treatment progress	Individuals, couples, families
Family intervention for serious mental illness	(Marsh & Lefley, 2009)	Serious mental illness (schizophrenia, bipolar disorder, etc.)	Individuals, couples, families
Family therapy for ADHD	(Wells, 2005)	Attention-deficit / hyperactivity	Children, adolescents, adults

(Continued)

TABLE 5.2 (Continued)

MODEL-INTERVENTION	REFERENCE CITATIONS	FOCUSED TREATMENT ISSUES	TREATMENT POPULATIONS
Family therapy for anorexia nervosa	(Eisler, 2009)	Eating disorders	Individuals, families
Family therapy with traumatized families	(Barnes & Figley, 2005)	Trauma	Families
Family-centered, school-based intervention	(Dishion & Stromshak, 2009)	Disruptive school behavior	Adolescents, families
Family-of-Origin treatment	(Nichols, 2003)	Multiple-generation relationships	Families
Family-school	(Carlson, Funk, & Nguyen, 2009)	Home-school relationship	Children, adolescents, families
Functional Family Therapy	(Sexton, 2009a; Sexton & Alexander, 2005)	Behavior problems	Adolescents, families
Integrative approach to health and illness in family therapy	(Pisani & McDaniel, 2005)	Health, illness	Individuals, families
Integrative Couple Therapy	(Lebow, 2006a)	Relationship issues	Couples
Integrative family therapy for high-conflict divorce	(Lebow, 2005b)	Divorce	Couples
Intensive Family-of-Origin Consultation	(Weber & Cebula, 2009)	Relational process	Individuals, couples, families, family of origin
Interventions for adult depression	(Gupta, Beach, & Coyne, 2005)	Depression	Individual, family
Multidimensional Family Therapy	(Liddle, 2009)	Drug abuse	Adolescents
Multisystemic Therapy	(Henggeler, Sheidow, & Lee, 2009)	Behavior problems	Adolescents
Personality-Guided Couples Psychology	(Nurse & Stanton, 2008; Stanton & Nurse, 2009)	Relationship adjustment, personality dysfunction	Couples
Psychodynamic family psychotherapy	(Magnavita, 2005)	Clinical syndromes, personality dysfunction, relationship factors	Individual, couples, families

Intervention/Model	Focus	Citation	Population
Psychoeducational multifamily groups for families with persons with severe mental illness	Severe mental illness	(McFarlane, 2005)	Families
Relationship Education Programs	Relationship factors, communication	(Ragan, Einhorn, Rhoades, Markman, & Stanley, 2009)	Couples, families
Solution-Focused Brief Therapy	Spectrum of issues	(Cheung, 2009b)	Children, adolescents, adults, couples, families
Stepfamily therapy	Stepfamily challenges	(Bray, 2005; Browning & Bray, 2009)	Stepfamilies
Structural Ecosystems Therapy	HIV/AIDS	(Mitrani, Robinson, & Szapocznik, 2009)	Women
Systemic Sex Therapy	Sexual issues	(Hertlein, Weeks, & Gambescia, 2009)	Couples
Systemic treatments for substance use disorders	Motivation to change; integrating self-help; relapse prevention	(Stanton, 2009c)	Individuals, couples, families, groups
Therapeutic Alliances in Couple and Family Therapy	Therapeutic alliance	(Friedlander, Escudero, & Heatherington, 2006)	Couples, families
Therapy for Families in Later Life	Geriatric issues	(Bevcar, 2005)	Individuals, couples, families
Treating Affair Couples	Affairs	(Baucom, Snyder, & Gordon, 2009; Gordon, Baucom, & Snyder, 2008)	Couples

Note. This table provides a list of models and approaches to intervention selected from recent comprehensive texts in family psychology. It is not intended to be comprehensive, but illustrative. Levels of evidence for the interventions vary significantly. A recent citation is provided that includes references to other publications regarding the intervention or model.

Knowledge of Specialty Interventions for Issues and Populations

CFP specialists refine their knowledge of specialty interventions and models through advanced understanding regarding which client issue(s) and/or population may be appropriately treated with the intervention (see Table 5.2). The specialist remains current in the literature in order to recognize when an intervention has been successfully applied to a new problem or new client population.

Intervention Skills

Intervention involves the ability to utilize the process of case conceptualization, including problem formulation (description of presenting problems), case formulation (explanation of assessment results in light of CFP specialist theory), and treatment formulation (prescription of treatment plan) (see Chapter 3), to inform treatment goals, the selection of CFP specialist interventions, effective implementation of those interventions, and evaluation of intervention outcomes. The entire intervention process is centered on the client(s) and actively incorporates client input. This section describes the skill necessary for intervention competency, including the ability to establish collaborative intervention goals, select interventions appropriate to the issue(s) and population(s), demonstrate CFP specialist common treatment factors, adhere to the intervention as designed, evaluate treatment progress and outcomes, modify the intervention in response to needs or circumstances, collaborate with other service providers, and seek consultation when needed to ensure treatment outcomes.

COLLABORATIVE INTERVENTION GOALS

The selection of intervention goals is part of the treatment formulation phase in the case conceptualization process and leads directly to intervention selection. Five tasks constitute the treatment formulation process: (a) provide feedback; (b) set collaborative goals; (c) identify interventions; (d) specify delivery format; and (e) create plan to monitor progress (see Chapter 3).

The ability to establish collaborative goals is an outgrowth of the specialty foundational competency in interpersonal interaction (see Chapter 12 for a thorough review of this competency). In a sense, development of the therapeutic alliance is an initial intervention in the system because it prepares the client(s) for collaborative goal setting and intervention selection. The therapeutic alliance in CFP specialist is complex and involves multiple perspectives and various interpersonal relations through the inclusion of various clients in couple, family, or larger social system interventions; the CFP specialist must quickly create a treatment context that incorporates multiple perspectives (Knobloch-Fedders, Pinsof, & Mann, 2007), is fair to all (van den Bos & Miedema, 2000), responds to individual concerns in a nondefensive manner (Waldron, Turner, Barton, Alexander, & Cline, 1997), and creates an effective interpersonal interaction between the CFP specialist and each client (Blow et al., 2007). Goal setting must pay attention to these same factors.

Collaborative goal setting arises out of accurate CFP specialist empathy for client issues, reflective feedback regarding those issues, and discussion of recommendations regarding potential treatment goals. CFP specialists must recognize that the client(s) contribute their own form of expertise to goal setting; Anderson (2009) suggests that the "client is an expert on themselves and their world; the family psychologist is an expert on a process and space for collaborative relationships and dialogical conversations" (p. 308). Ultimately, "Clients need to view the 'tasks' of therapy as credible, and if what the therapist is doing does not fit with their expectations, or the therapist cannot sell them on the merits of the approach, it matters little what the therapist believes" (Sprenkle & Blow, 2007, p. 111). Joint determination of treatment goals is an important aspect of the therapeutic alliance and may be evaluated as part of treatment progress research. For instance, the STIC Couple measure (Pinsof & Chambers, 2009) includes an item that allows one partner to evaluate the CFP specialist's understanding of the other partner ("The therapist understands my partner's goals for this therapy"; p. 442). Alternatively, simple CFP specialist queries to the client(s), such as, "Does this seem like the right direction to you?" or "Do we all agree on this direction for our time together?" can elicit input regarding perception of treatment goals.

TARGETED INTERVENTION SELECTION

The CFP specialist demonstrates the ability to select CFP specialist interventions appropriate to the presenting issue(s) and client population(s). This is a final aspect of the case conceptualization competency (see Chapter 3 for additional information on this skill). Selection should be based on current specialty science and the unique needs and preferences of the client(s) (Adams & Grieder, 2005). This requires knowledge of available interventions that have demonstrated some level of effectiveness and evidence (Sexton & Coop-Gordon, 2009) (see "Intervention Knowledge" section above and Table 5.2). Of course, the specialist must have the requisite education, training, and experience in the provision of the treatment to provide it in an ethical and responsible manner. Recent CFP specialist clinical research has moved away from grand schemes that address universal issues to emphasize targeted intervention models that focus on more narrow areas (Lebow, 2005c). Certain interventions were developed for particular issues (e.g., depression, substance use disorders) or populations (e.g., couples, at-risk adolescents, families), so selection should be informed by knowledge of those models and their relative fit with the presenting issue(s) and client(s). Additional factors that may influence intervention selection include diversity elements (i.e., is the intervention culturally appropriate for the particular client or clients in this case?); the mix of client strengths, skills, social supports, resources, and motivation; legal and ethical considerations (e.g., agreements about confidentiality; see Chapter 10); and the time available for treatment (many interventions are designed for 3- to 12-month delivery; Lebow, 2005a). Finally, intervention selection often involves determination of the session format(s). This can also be an ethical issue, but many CFP specialist models and specialists now vary format according to the pragmatic needs of the specific client(s) and the presenting issue(s) and may even mix formats over time when working with the same clients. Of course, this requires attention to ethical concerns (see Chapter 10), but it may enhance the effectiveness of the intervention as long as care is exercised in the format change process.

IMPLEMENT CFP SPECIALIST COMMON FACTORS

Specialists implement the common factors (see "Intervention Knowledge" section above) in a manner that enhances the therapeutic alliance (see Chapter 12) and improves intervention outcomes. This ability requires knowledge of the role of common factors in interventions and the ability to monitor the factors during the treatment intervention.

Implementation of the common factors puts an emphasis on the context in which a particular treatment is provided. It "believes such qualities as credibility, alliance, and allegiance 'surrounding' the treatment are more important than the unique aspects of treatment" (Sprenkle et al., 2009, p. 4). This means that simple treatment adherence is insufficient if it ignores elements of the common factors that have been demonstrated to be effective in the facilitation of change. In this sense, the CFP specialist activates the intervention model using skills, personality, and professional experience as a mechanism for implementation of the intervention. In fact, many intervention models were designed around principles that reflect common factors, such as the instillation of hope and an expectation of change (e.g., Functional Family Therapy is built on such a principle; Sexton, 2009a).

Specialist belief in the intervention and commitment to it is a common factor across interventions. If the CFP specialist evidences a strong dedication to an intervention based on education or personal experience in using the model, the clients perceive that commitment, and it engenders trust and hope in them that the model will be effective in addressing the presenting issue(s) (Sprenkle et al., 2009). Client factors are the single most powerful contribution to treatment outcomes (Duncan, Miller, & Sparks, 2003), so the CFP specialist knows how to recognize and utilize the client(s)' strengths and competencies in treatment. The complex therapeutic alliance with multiple clients in couple and family psychotherapy and all the factors contributing to it (see Chapter 12 for a thorough analysis) must be monitored and managed by the CFP specialist (Friedlander, Escudero, & Heatherington, 2006). Each clients' belief in the treatment, including the perception that the clinician is competent, and the hope that comes from being involved in psychotherapy is another common factor (Davis & Piercy, 2007b; Duncan et al., 2003), so it is crucial that the CFP specialist has the ability to engage the client(s) in the intervention in a way that enhances hope and the expectancy of positive outcomes. Sprenkle and colleagues (2009) specify additional factors common to couple and family psychotherapy, including conceptualizing difficulties in relational terms (most CFP specialist models move beyond the individual to understand problems as occurring between people, including cognitive, affective, and behavioral elements despite the apparent or claimed focus of a model on one or another of these; Davis & Piercy, 2007b); disrupting dysfunctional relational patterns (CFP specialist models interrupt negative relationship cycles in couples, families, and social systems; Davis & Piercy, 2007b); and expanding the direct treatment system (involvement of significant others in treatment) (pp. 35–40). CFP specialists demonstrate the ability to enact these specialty factors.

INTERVENTION MODEL ADHERENCE

It is important that CFP specialists implement intervention and treatment models in a manner that adheres to the theoretical, scientific, and clinical foundations. Specialists understand the theory of an intervention, the specific change mechanisms involved in the model, the typical progression of the intervention, and the expected outcomes (Frey, Ellis, Naar-King, Sieloff, & Frey, 2007). Model fidelity requires dissemination of the intervention in a manner consistent with its design and intent (Hogue, Liddle, Singer, & Leckrone, 2005). This cannot be assumed and must be monitored as an intervention is designed and implemented (Berzin, Thomas, & Cohen, 2007). One crucial factor in dissemination is the level of knowledge and skill of the person providing the intervention; this requires sufficient education, training, and supervised experience in the model prior to attempts at implementation. Sexton, Weeks, and Robbins (2003) reflect on large-scale dissemination efforts with Multisystemic Therapy (more than 120 sites) and Functional Family Therapy (more than 100 locations) and suggest that long-term training and processes to ensure treatment fidelity are crucial. CFP specialists have the requisite preparation and the ability to implement interventions in a manner consistent with the intervention design.

Some models attempt to facilitate thorough dissemination of the model through the use of manualized treatment (e.g., G. Diamond, Siqueland, & Diamond, 2003). Interventions are prescribed in significant detail so that the provider may follow the manual step-by-step. Manualized treatment facilitates clinical research regarding the model, but many practitioners eschew highly structured intervention manuals because they believe they are impersonal and wooden; in fact, too mechanistic an approach may limit the applicability of a model (see the section "Intervention Modification for Emerging Needs" below). However, manualized treatments may specifically target development of the therapeutic alliance (G. Diamond et al., 2003) or allow room for adjustment to specific clients (Loeb, Hirsch, Greif, & Hildebrandt, 2009; Rohrbaugh, Shoham, 2002). Proponents suggest that it is important that treatment providers faithfully implement the intervention if they want to achieve outcomes similar to the original design.

The organization and structure of an intervention model itself may be understood as a kind of common factor in effective treatment (Duncan et al., 2003). "We believe that one explanation for the potency of empirically validated models resides in their being very organized and coherent" (Sprenkle et al., 2009, p. 58). Organized models provide a clear pathway to address the presenting issue(s), increase the CFP specialist's expressed confidence as the intervention is presented, and result in improved client hope and confidence in the intervention.

MONITOR TREATMENT PROGRESS

CFP specialists monitor and evaluate the effectiveness of interventions for the presenting issue(s) and the defined client(s) during the course of treatment and at the conclusion of treatment.

During Treatment

It is common specialty practice to solicit feedback from the client(s) during clinical interviews. For example, simple questions regarding perception of treatment (e.g., Do you think we are moving in the right direction? Have you noticed improvement in the areas on which we are working?) provide a sense of client engagement and agreement with interventions. It is possible to schedule these inquiries (e.g., every four to five sessions) and to use select questions from more formal measures (see below) as part of a less formal process. The results should be charted and may inform or modify the intervention. Otherwise, client feedback is "infrequent, unsystematic, and ambiguous" (Sapyta, Riemer, & Bickman, 2005, p. 151). If these informal processes, at least, are not incorporated actively into treatment, it is likely that client concerns will be presented only when they reach a critical level; this makes it more difficult to respond constructively and/or to alter the course of treatment to accommodate the concern. However, there is evidence that even seasoned clinicians may not adequately assess therapeutic process when relying on observation and intuition alone; formal assessment can benefit evaluation (Kelley & Bickman, 2009).

More formal treatment monitoring occurs when implementing an intervention that has stage-specific goals (e.g., Functional Family Therapy). The CFP specialist monitors goal completion and progress through the stages of the intervention. Additionally, progress research is a formal means of monitoring key elements of the treatment, including development of the therapeutic alliance and collaborative creation of intervention goals. Kelley and Bickman (2009) suggest that "what is necessary for effective treatment is a measurement feedback system (MFS). A MFS is defined as a battery of comprehensive measures that are administered frequently concurrent with treatment, and provide timely and clinically useful feedback to clinicians" (p. 363). They recommend that an MFS assess treatment processes and progress toward desired outcomes with input from several reporters. Sapyta and colleagues (2005) note that the function of such feedback is to give "clinicians knowledge about how close to or far away they are from accomplishing the goal" (p. 150). Two significant models for progress evaluation and feedback are the Systemic Inventory of Change (STIC®; Pinsof & Chambers, 2009) and the System for Observing Family Therapy Alliances (SOFTA; Friedlander et al., 2006). These tools provide research-based and focused questions about the therapeutic alliance (see Chapter 12 for more detail about the use of these measures to evaluate interpersonal interaction in psychotherapy) and intervention progress. The STIC® involves input from individual clients about individual, couple, or family psychotherapy (e.g., "Some of the other members of my family and I do not feel safe with each other in this therapy"; Pinsof & Chambers, 2009, p. 443). It begins with an INITIAL STIC before the first session and proceeds to an INTERSESSION STIC (composed of the highly loading items on the INITIAL version that represent each scale so that it takes only 5 to 8 minutes) that is completed by the client(s) in the 24 hours before every subsequent session. The authors hope to have an Internet-based version available to clinicians in the near future. See Pinsof and Chambers (2009) for details about this instrument and the specific aspects of treatment it evaluates. The SOFTA includes client self-report and therapist observation measures on a variety of intervention issues (e.g., "What happens in therapy can solve our problems"; "Some members of the family don't agree with others about the goals of therapy"; Friedlander et al., 2006, p. 298). Use of measures like these that integrate CFP specialist theory, research, and clinical perspectives can greatly inform the intervention process while it is under way in order to initiate corrective measures to ensure intervention outcomes.

Conclusion of Treatment

There are a number of ways for the CFP specialist to evaluate intervention outcomes at the conclusion of treatment or subsequent to treatment. For instance, the process leading to termination of treatment should include an opportunity for the client(s) to provide feedback about perceptions of the therapeutic process. It is important that the specialist not allow this to be a surface interaction but to delve deeper for both the critiques and the compliments that clients may wish or need to express during the time prior to the conclusion of psychotherapy. This information may inform CFP specialist practices and encourage professional development in areas identified for improvement.

Less helpful, but informative, is the frequency with which the specialist receives referrals from former clients. Such recommendations to family members, friends, and associates are an indication that the clients perceived their own experience as helpful and valuable. However, there is no normative formula to compare the number or frequency of referrals with other specialists, so this is nonspecific feedback. Finally, we live in an Internet culture of ready evaluation (e.g., reader ratings and reviews on Amazon.com; faculty member ratings on RateMyProfessors.com), and there are already rating websites for mental health providers (e.g., therapistratings.com). These may provide information, but it will be skewed by the voluntary nature of the process that results in nonrandom sampling of treatment participants. However, these reviews will be readily available to potential clients and may impact public perceptions of the specialist. Proactive evaluation measures during and at the conclusion of treatment may balance these external measures.

INTERVENTION MODIFICATION FOR EMERGING NEEDS

It is important that the CFP specialist is able to modify an intervention to the particular needs and circumstances of the clients in treatment. Sometimes termed *client-centered* or *contextual* psychotherapy, this approach recognizes that an intervention cannot assume that it is uniformly applicable to all clients without any modification. The particular needs of the client(s) must be attended, and adjustments must be made to the intervention. For example, Functional Family Therapy (FFT) attends to the "unique therapeutic nature of the interaction between the family and the family psychologist as the primary mechanism of change .... to be successful FFT must be conducted in a style that is artful, personal, and relational" (Sexton, 2009a, p. 331).

Sprenkle and colleagues (2009) note that client-centered psychotherapy focuses on the client's role; it "places less importance on performing the treatment in a specific way and more on improvising to match the clients' needs and world views; and invests a stronger conviction in clients using whatever is offered in therapy for their own purposes in often unique and idiosyncratic ways" (p. 5). For example, psychotherapy that is more congruent with clients' values may be perceived as more effective (Whalley & Hyland, 2009), and interventions that evoke the clients' motivations for change, rather than imposing external motivations, are more successful (Miller & Rose, 2009).

CFP specialist interventions may need to be modified if new circumstances, issues, or needs emerge during the course of the intervention. It is not uncommon for there to be changes in interpersonal relations, employment, legal situations, and so forth, during the course of treatment. The CFP specialist must adapt to these changes or risk loss of credibility and effectiveness.

Finally, ethnicity or individual differences in and among the client(s) may require the CFP specialist to modify the intervention to meet particular cultural expectations (e.g., variations in family structure, roles, decision making; Flicker, et al., 2008). CFP specialists recognize individual and group differences and accommodate interventions in a manner sensitive to those differences (Comas-Diaz, 2006).

PROFESSIONAL COLLABORATION

CFP specialists collaborate with other professionals to meet the overall needs of the client(s). This usually requires that the specialist ensure the completion of informed consent releases for the specialist to convey information to other professionals. Common collaborations include referral of individuals to a physician for medication evaluation and case discussion with the physician; interaction with teachers about school behavior for children and adolescents; and referral to religious leaders regarding spiritual factors that intersect with treatment issues. Over time, the specialist may develop ongoing relationships with professional collaborators because of the reciprocal referral process involved in a community of professionals; this may serve the clients well because the CFP specialist is able to readily interact with other professionals who may help address aspects of the clients' needs.

INTERVENTION CONSULTATION

CFP specialists recognize the value (see below) of peer consultation in interventions and seek consultation when it is needed to ensure treatment outcomes. Specialists practice only within their scope of education, knowledge, training, and experience, but even then it is possible that certain cases will present challenges that suggest the importance of consultation with other specialists who have experience with the issues under address. Specialists observe legal and ethical standards in seeking consultation (e.g., protect the identity of the clients).

Intervention Values

CFP specialists value the role of research as it informs the intervention competency. Specialists remain current in intervention research in order to maximize their professional practice. In addition, specialists value professional practice review and regularly evaluate their own interventions and seek peer review and client feedback in order to ensure that they provide appropriate interventions.

VALUES INTERVENTION RESEARCH

CFP specialists place a high value on intervention research, consistent with their identity as psychologists and the importance of a scientific foundation for professional practice (Bieschke et al., 2004). For most specialists, this attitude is developed in graduate education (Halonen, Bosack, Clay, & McCarthy, 2003; see Chapter 9) and enhanced in predoctoral internship and postdoctoral residency. The crucial issue is the understanding and inculcation of the value that research and treatment are not two separate entities in psychology; they are closely related, and each should inform the other (Black & Lebow, 2009). Once adopted, this value leads naturally to a commitment to lifelong learning in order to remain current in the science of intervention research. Treatment models and interventions evolve over time, and research may enhance existing models or demonstrate that they are ineffective or even harmful (Lebow, 2005a). CFP specialists ensure competent intervention practices by remaining up to date in intervention research.

VALUES SELF-EVALUATION, PEER REVIEW, AND CLIENT FEEDBACK

A key value in psychology is the willingness to look critically at one's own practices and to invite peer review from other specialists when appropriate or beneficial to the clients. Peer review is a hallmark of the scientific process. This is especially true for those who develop intervention models (Olds, 2009), but also true for those who implement interventions originated or refined by others. For example, treatment fidelity is an important aspect of ensuring that providers implement the specific change mechanisms in an intervention in a manner likely to achieve the intended results, so training in that model must necessarily involve substantial supervision and peer review (Sexton, Robbins, et al., 2003). But review does not end at the completion of graduate education or postdoctoral residency. Intervention competency suggests that the CFP specialist will continue to examine her or his own interventions and that the specialist will seek peer review on a regular basis. Many psychologists demonstrate this value by regular participation in peer consultation groups; others have trusted colleagues to whom they turn in difficult cases. Of course, all peer consultation or review observes ethical standards regarding client confidentiality.

In addition, CFP specialists value and invite feedback from their clients. This may be accomplished in a structured format that incorporates feedback about recognized interventions in order to track client progress (Friedlander et al., 2006; Pinsof & Chambers, 2009; see "Skills" section above), or it may involve informal invitations for the clients to discuss perceptions of treatment or the interaction with the specialist. In either course, the CFP specialist values that input and considers it in the progression of treatment.

Conclusion

The intervention competency is at the core of professional practice for most CFP specialists. It requires knowledge, skills, and attitudes to ensure competent implementation of interventions that achieve specified outcomes by addressing specific issues and client populations. CFP specialists are aware of the competency requirements and endeavor to demonstrate competency in the provision of interventions.

PART IV

Other Functional Competencies

SIX

Consultation Competency

The consultation competency in CFP involves the application of a systemic epistemology to working with clients in a manner both similar and dissimilar to traditional psychotherapy. This chapter briefly reviews the development of the consultation competency in professional psychology; introduces a definition of CFP consultation, including a description of common consultation venues (e.g., family business consultation, school consultation, health care consultation); describes the specialty knowledge needed as a foundation for the competency; and specifies the skills and attitudes needed to function as a consultant. Table 6.1 provides an overview of the knowledge, skills, and attitudes for the CFP specialist consultation competency with specified behavioral anchors and competency assessment methods. This chapter follows the organization of that table and describes the domains and behavioral anchors in detail.

It should be noted at the outset that there is a clear overlap between this competency within CFP and the specialty of consulting psychology, which frequently references a systemic foundation. Consulting psychology has developed significantly in recent years (see below), and the CFP specialist who regularly provides consultation services may consider pursuing concurrent American Board of Professional Psychology (ABPP) board certification in consulting psychology.

Development, Definition, and Venues

DEVELOPMENT OF THE CONSULTATION COMPETENCY

Consultation was identified as an emerging core competency in professional psychology in the 1990s (Stanton, 2009a). Subsequently, various

TABLE 6.1 **Consultation: Developmental Level—Specialty Competence in Couple and Family Psychology**

COMPETENCY DOMAIN AND ESSENTIAL COMPONENT	BEHAVIORAL ANCHOR	ASSESSMENT METHODS
Knowledge (A) Knowledge of CFP consultation (A.1) Knowledge of consultation theory, research findings, roles, assessment, and methodology	(A.1.1) Understands and capably articulates the application of a systemic epistemology to consultation with individuals, groups, or organizations (A.1.2) Demonstrates theoretical and scientific knowledge of consultation models in the specialty and knowledge of the field in which the consultation is provided (A.1.3) Demonstrates understanding of the roles, assessment methodologies, and intervention methodologies for CFP consultation	1. Graduate coursework assignments and exams 2. Predoctoral and/or postdoctoral applied assignments and evaluation 3. Self-evaluation 4. Supervision feedback 5. Peer review 6. Continuing education in CFP consultation 7. Client feedback 8. Publication and presentation in scholarly venues
Skills (B) Ability to conduct effective CFP consultations (B.1) Conducts needs assessments, provides reports and recommendations, conducts effective interventions,	(B.1.1) Ability to apply systemic orientation and research to conduct a needs assessment using appropriate assessment methodologies and devices to provide focus to the referral questions (B.1.2) Ability to prepare written and verbal reports that include cogent recommendations to address the referral question and the results of the needs assessment (B.1.3) Ability to implement interventions based on organizational approval of recommendations using relationship skills, problem-solving, and implementation skills (B.1.4) Ability to demonstrate ethical and diversity competencies in consultation	
Attitudes (C) Values ethical and collaborative interaction and practice (C.1) Independently values ethical practice that is culturally competent	(C.1.1) Values and adopts the role of consultant as part of the CFP specialty (C.1.2). Values ethical and professional standards for consultation practice (C.1.3) Values collaboration between the consultant and the client (C.1.4) Values and respects individual and group diversity in consultation	

Note. Adapted from the format and content of the Assessment of Competency Benchmarks Work Group (2007). This table assumes that the specialist has achieved competence in professional psychology at the three previous developmental levels, as specified in the benchmarks. The competency domains and behavioral anchors serve as the primary organizing structure for this chapter; content explaining each domain and anchor is provided in the chapter.

organizations and entities discussed, debated, and developed definitions and standards for consultation, including the Society of Consulting Psychology (Division 13 of the American Psychological Association), the National Council of Schools and Programs of Professional Psychology (NCSPP), and the 2002 Competencies Conference (Stanton, 2009a).

The Society of Consulting Psychology advocated for cohesive models of education and training in consultation that provide systematic and structured development of the core competency (Lowman, 1998b). It created official principles for doctoral and postdoctoral education and training in consultation (American Psychological Association, 2007). Concurrently, the 1999 NCSPP Conference on Emerging Competencies and the 2005 NCSPP Self Study (Paskiewicz et al., 2006) explored the status of the consultation competency in member programs and substantiated the need to enhance education in the competency to address increased professional consultation by graduates and rising interest from students (Stanton, 2009a). The 2002 Competencies Conference included a work group on Consultation and Interprofessional Collaboration that defined the core competency and delineated the cultural awareness, knowledge, and skills needed for competency; the group suggested that generic competency in consultation may be supplemented with applications in various specialty areas (Arredondo, Shealy, Neale, & Winfrey, 2004). All the models developed share a focus on developmental progression in achievement of competency in consultation from beginner to expert (Arredondo et al., 2004). This chapter assumes achievement of the generic competency in consultation as a foundation for competency at the CFP specialist level.

DEFINITION OF CFP CONSULTATION

A number of definitions of the generic consultation competency have been developed by professional organizations or entities (Table 6.2). Several elements of the generic competency may be delineated in common across definitions, including the ideas that consultation is a planned interaction; advisory or collaborative between the consultant and individuals or organizations; focused on needs and objectives of the consultee(s); based on the science and procedures of psychology; at the individual, group, program, or organization level; for which the consultant has no direct authority for implementation of recommendations or changes.

CFP consultation competency is an extension of this generic competency, established earlier in education and training, to the specialty level.

TABLE 6.2 **Definitions of Consultation**

Society of Consulting Psychology
"Consulting psychology, a practice that focuses on consultation to, with, or for individuals and organizations at individual, group, and organizational/systemwide levels rooted in multiple areas of substantive expertise, is used here as defined in the 1999 Bylaws of the Society of Consulting Psychology (SCP), Division 13 of the American Psychological Association (APA): 'Consulting psychology, for the purposes of these By-Laws, shall be defined as the function of applying and extending the special knowledge of a psychologist, through the process of consultation, to problems involving human behavior in various areas. A consulting psychologist shall be defined as a psychologist who provides specialized technical assistance to individuals or organizations in regard to the psychological aspects of their work. Such assistance is advisory in nature and the consultant has no direct responsibility for its acceptance. Consulting psychologists may have as clients individuals, institutions, agencies, corporations or other kinds of organizations' (www.div13.org/bylaws.aspx)" (American Psychological Association, 2007, p. 980).

National Council of Schools and Programs of Professional Psychology
"Consultation refers to the planned collaborative interaction between the professional psychologist and one or more clients or colleagues, in relation to an identified problem area or program. Psychological consultation is an explicit intervention process that is based on principles and procedures found within psychology and related disciplines, in which the professional psychologist has no *direct* control of the actual change process. Psychological consultation focuses on the needs of individuals, groups, programs, or organizations" (McHolland, 1992, p. 165).

2002 Competencies Conference
"Psychological Consultation focuses on the needs of individuals, groups, programs, and organizations. It refers to planned interactions between the professional psychologist (consultant) and one or more representatives of clients, colleagues, or systems (consultees) relative to a problem, person, area, or program. Psychological consultation is based on principles and procedures found within psychology and related disciplines in which a professional psychologist applies his/her areas of expertise in response to the presenting needs and stated objectives of consultees" (Arredondo et al., 2004, p. 789).

Specialty consultation competency involves the achievement of the knowledge, skills, and attitudes indicated in Table 6.1 and applied to venues related to the specialty.

For the purposes of this text, we define the CFP consultation competency as the engagement of the CFP specialist in the provision of specialty psychological consultation services to individuals, groups, programs, or organizations (at any level of the system or subsystem) based on a systemic epistemology in order to assess needs, proffer recommendations, and engage in interventions using specialty skills and abilities to achieve desired outcomes. CFP consultants provide services in a variety of venues, including mental health; education and school-based settings; health care (e.g., behavioral health and family systems medicine); programs (e.g., couple or family programs, CFP education and training venues); and organizations, including family businesses.

CFP CONSULTATION VENUES

CFP specialists may consult in a variety of venues. In this section, we briefly note three venues for CFP consultation.

Family Business

CFP consultants are ideally prepared to provide consultation services to family businesses by virtue of their education and training in systems theory and family dynamics (Kaslow, 2006c). The discipline of family business consultation was pioneered in the 1980s and evolved to specify core competencies required for practice: "These consist of law, behavioral science, family dynamics and family systems theory…, management science, finances, and accounting" (Kaslow, 2006b, p. 404). A multidisciplinary professional organization for consultants to family businesses was created, the Family Firm Institute, that publishes a journal, *The Family Business* Review (Kaslow, 2006a). Several models were developed, including the three-circle model, the Aspen Consulting Process Model, and the Interpersonal Model for Reconciling Relationships (Kaslow, 2006b).

Kaslow (2006b) suggests that the three-circle model is frequently cited and influential. Created by Hilburt-Davis and Dyer (2006), it uses a systems perspective to propose three overlapping systems (circles) of a family business: the ownership/governance system, the business system, and the family system (p. 75). Consultants function in the interface between these three circles to create structures, develop processes, and produce policies and procedures that help manage systemic interaction between the three systems of the family business. Hilburt-Davis and Dyer (2006) delineate five levels of intervention, some of which are common to organization consultation (e.g., operations) and some distinctions that apply specifically to family business (e.g., working relationships vs. interpersonal relationships). Their consulting process has much in common with typical organization consultation processes (see below), but they note the special circumstances of intense affect in family business interaction and complications around confidentiality because of family relationships. Finally, they suggest the use of the genogram (see Chapter 4) to understand family dynamics.

The Aspen Family Business Group Process (Jaffe, Dashew, Lane, Paul, & Bork, 2006) combines family systems theory and organizational development. Aspen describes eight principles for practice (e.g., "Our work is about helping both individuals and systems move in a positive direction"; p. 54) and uses concepts from Bowen theory (e.g., individuation, undoing communication triangles; Titelman, 2008) to create trust and establish principles upon which the family business will be organized and function.

Common issues in family business include generational differences between family members (i.e., often two or three generations are involved in the business) and family conflict that leads to interpersonal wounds and relationship ruptures, especially in "power-over" (oppressive systems where particular family members have more power than others) and "disengaged" (the withdrawal of particular members from the business, sometimes jeopardizing its existence) systems (Kadis & McClendon, 2006, p. 99). McClendon and Kadis (2004) present a reconciliation model that allows a family to change negative patterns, reconcile members to one another, and rebuild family cohesion for effective collaboration in the business. New trends in family business include the increase of adult daughters entering the family business, the change in their roles within the business, and the likelihood that they will be mentored by their mothers (Kaslow, 2005).

Education and School-Based Consultation

There is significant interaction between families and schools in the socialization and education of students (Carlson, Funk, & Nguyen, 2009). CFP specialists share a foundation in systemic conceptualization with the specialty of school psychology, and there is overlap between the two specialties; dual board certification is possible and suggested for those who work actively on both sides of the family-school interaction. CFP specialists work to enhance the quality of the home-school relationship because there is evidence that parental involvement in a child's education (e.g., home discussion of school topics) and parenting style (e.g., authoritative parenting with European American and Hispanic adolescents, authoritarian with African American and Asian American) are likely to result in better education outcomes (Carlson et al., 2009). Consultation to improve home-school collaboration is recommended, and several evidence-based models have been developed. See Carlson and Christenson (2005) for an overview of these models and reference citations. For example, one model (the EcoFIT) provides a family-centered approach to parental management of student behavior and addresses the social interactions around child behavior and child mental health and achieves positive outcomes with as little as 6 hours of contact with high-risk families (Dishion & Stromshak, 2009).

Health Care Consultation

CFP specialists consult in health care in a variety of ways, including family systems medicine, behavioral health consultation or primary care psychology, and organizational consultation around teamwork and interpersonal interaction in the health care environment.

Primary care family psychology (McDaniel & LeRoux, 2007) recognizes that "research consistently demonstrates the prevalence of psychosocial and family influences on common, and uncommon, medical presentations" (Rosenberg & Watson, 2009, p. 540). Rosenberg and Watson (2009) note several pathways of family impact on health, including genetic, environmental, health behaviors, family stress, family support, and family affect management. CFP specialists "pay particular attention to the systemic processes involved in the illness experience as it impacts the family and the patient-family-healthcare system matrix" (Rosenberg & Watson, 2009, p. 542).

Primary care psychology (Bray, Frank, McDaniel, & Heldring, 2004; McDaniel & LeRoux, 2007) and behavioral health consultation (Robinson & Strosahl, 2009) integrate the psychologist into primary care as a member of the health care team. Although there is a long history of barriers to integration of mental health and medical practices, there is a strong rationale for integrated services (Kessler, Stafford, & Messier, 2009). Because psychological distress correlates with the use of medical service, brief interventions around issues like depression have been found to improve clinical outcomes in a cost-effective manner (see Robinson & Strosahl, 2009, for a thorough review of studies). Behavioral health consultation includes providing direct patient services and training medical and other providers to provide psychologically informed services that encourage health practices and free physicians from time-consuming behavioral health patients (Robinson & Strosahl, 2009). Primary care consultation by a CFP specialist involves collaboration between physicians and the specialist to address challenging issues in primary care, such as chronic illness and disability (Holleman, Bray, Davis, & Holleman, 2004), and "services provided may well extend beyond traditional psychotherapy and include brief consultation to patients and their families as well as to providers struggling to manage a behaviorally challenging family or seeking to incorporate behavioral health and systems perspectives into their medical treatment" (Rosenberg & Watson, 2009, p. 543). CFP consultants "not only assess and treat common behavioral, mental health, and relational problems that present in primary care, but also consult regarding prevention, sub-threshold disorders, referral, the functioning of primary care teams, the stresses and strains of being a primary care physician or nurse practitioner, outcome evaluation, and quality improvement" (McDaniel & LeRoux, 2007, p. 23). A training curriculum to prepare for primary care psychological practice has been created that integrates family psychology with health and pediatric psychology (McDaniel, Belar, Schroeder, Hargrove, & Freeman, 2002).

Knowledge

The central aspects of knowledge for CFP competency in consultation include understanding and capably applying a systemic epistemology to consultation, demonstration of theoretical and scientific knowledge of consultation models and knowledge of the field in which the consultation is provided, and demonstrated understanding of the roles, assessment methodologies, and intervention methodologies for CFP consultation.

SYSTEMIC EPISTEMOLOGY AND CONSULTATION

The systemic epistemology of CFP makes the specialty especially amenable to the provision of consultation at the individual, group, or larger social organizational levels (Stanton, 2009b; see Chapter 2). Kilburg (1995) notes that "modern approaches to organization development practice are primarily based on the conceptual foundations of general systems theory as it is applied to human organizations" (p. 28). Fuqua and Newman (2002) suggest "systems theory, as it relates to consulting psychology, is a very powerful set of ideas that establishes the framework for conceptualizing human systems from a wholistic perspective" (p. 103). Many psychologists, educated in programs that emphasize an individual approach, receive little instruction in systems theory; this is why the Consultation and Interprofessional Collaboration Work Group (Arredondo et al., 2004) and the consultation chapter in the updated NCSPP text on the core competencies (Stanton, 2009a) recommend course work in systems theory for all professional psychology students. CFP specialists must extend their basic knowledge of systems theory to the consultation arena by learning systemic models of organizational process in order to demonstrate competence in consultation.

Fuqua and Newman (2002) note several assumptions based on systems theory that apply to consultation in organizations, including these select items: (a) "Organizations are usefully understood as dynamic, whole systems"; (b) "Human behavior, which is constantly being dramatically influenced by organizational structure, must selectively serve to regulate the structural aspects of an organization"; (c) "Changes in any one aspect of the organization might reverberate throughout the system in unintended and unexpected ways" (p. 98). These assumptions are an important foundation for the extension of CFP practice to consultation, but they are consistent with systemic principles at the dyadic and family levels.

Fuqua and Newman (2002, pp. 80–86) also posit a systemic model of the organization that includes as subsystems the purposive (formal and informal mission and objectives of the organization), operational (the roles, power dimensions, norms, expectations, communication pathways, and rewards for performance in the organization), methodological (the functions and procedures to accomplish the mission), and psychosocial (the characteristics

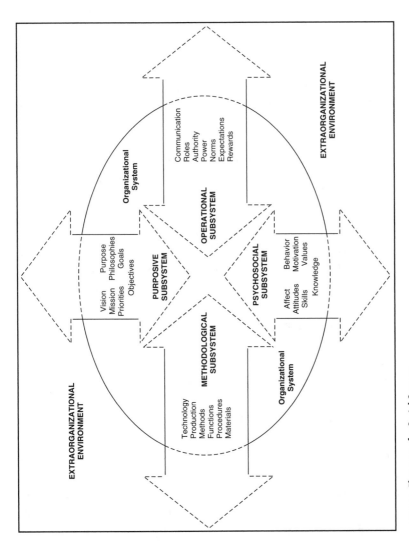

FIGURE 6.1 Elements of a Social System

This figure is reproduced from R.L. Lowman (ed.), (2002). *The California School of Organizational Studies: Handbook of organizational consulting psychology: A comprehensive guide to theory, skills, and techniques* (pp. 76–105) by permission of John Wiley & Sons.

of the individual people in the organization) arenas (Figure 6.1). Each of these subsystems is crucial to the organization and interacts reciprocally with other subsystems to constitute the whole organization. This model conveys the permeable, dynamic, and interactive elements of an open system that interrelates internally (within the organization) and externally (with the larger context or environment), and it can be applied to various levels of the system in small or large organizations. Systemic concepts, such as equifinality, dynamic equilibrium, conflict, and differentiation, operate within this model and explain its processes. The model provides a "conceptual platform" (Fuqua & Newman, 2002, p. 79) for needs assessment, conceptualization of the organization, and intervention in its delineation of crucial factors that may interact around the consultation question.

The CFP consultant may use such a framework in a manner consistent with his or her foundational education and training in systems theory, as noted by Fuqua and Newman (2002): "Systems theory equips the consulting psychologist with an expanded appreciation of the dynamics of interdependence and interconnectedness of component parts of a system that, in interaction, create an entity that is more complex and dynamic than individual components alone" (p. 103). This avoids the potential errors of simplicity and reductionism in consultation, common when psychologists shift from the provision of one-hour sessions of psychotherapy to substantial engagement with a complex organization in consultation (Levinson, 2009a). For instance, a simple cause-effect examination of reports concerning the problematic behavior of a particular manager may focus primarily on the attributes of the manager; a systemic assessment will consider how organizational norms about power and rewards may interact with current organization priorities and objectives, as well as recent methodological problems, and the characteristics of the individual manager in order to understand the situation. The behavior of the manager does not stand alone; it interacts reciprocally with a variety of other organizational factors. Understanding the complexity of the systemic dynamics will result in an improved assessment and more complete recommendations to address the consultation issue. In addition, "helping organization members expand, extend, and adapt their conceptual framework [to a systemic framework] for understanding and managing their organization is an empowering process that can continue to improve organizational performance and the quality of lifelong learning after the consultation contract is completed" (Fuqua & Kurpius, 1993, p. 607).

To be clear, a systemic framework does not ignore individual factors but includes them fully as part of the system; Stanton (2009b) notes the interplay between individual, interpersonal, and environmental-macrosystemic factors. Consequently, individual or psychodynamic factors are frequently assessed and serve as one focus of intervention in consultation (Kilburg, 1995), but systems conceptualization would argue that they not be understood as entirely separate or distinct from the system of which they are a part. Levinson (2009b) argues for a living system understanding of organizations that requires an understanding of the whole organization within a historical and contextual frame, yet he notes that organizations comprise individual, group, and larger institution behaviors, noting that a comprehensive understanding of the individual is important; from that foundation, he assumes "an underlying psychoanalytic theory of motivation" (Levinson, 2002c, p. 418). Systems theory allows for this range of conceptualization.

The mix of responsibility for change is difficult to determine between individual and organization. Fuqua and Newman (2002) propose a four-quadrant model to facilitate determination of consultation to an individual or an organization that depends on the views of the individual and the organization about the locus of responsibility at the individual or system level. CFP consultants need to understand such models to ferret out the exact manner in which to apply a systemic epistemology to a particular consultation question.

KNOWLEDGE OF MODELS AND METHODS

Fuqua and Kurpius (1993) provide an overview of conceptual models that have demonstrated usefulness in organizational consultation. These include systems theory (see above); data-based models (often used in needs assessment; see below); force field analysis (focused on change from a current problem situation to a future desired goal state); strategic planning (determination of mission, strategy to fulfill the mission, plan for action, and review processes); high-performance programming (moving from a reactive organization to responsive to proactive to high performance); organizational culture (influencing the behavioral and social patterns of an organization); organizational change cycles (helping organizations avoid decline and crisis states by facilitating renewal to the developmental stage); and paradigm shifts (helping organizations to change their conceptual framework when it fails to meet current needs; pp. 607–615). They unpack each of these models and provide principles for using them in organizations, such as the idea that "models should be carefully tailored to the perceived needs and characteristics of consultees and their organization" and "the most powerful conceptual application will involve a developmental intervention including teaching, cognitive modeling, collaboration, and feedback" (Fuqua & Kurpius, 1993, p. 616). Finally, they argue that conceptual models should be integrated, and consultants need to consider core characteristics of effective consultation.

There have been some attempts to translate traditional systemic models of psychotherapy to consultation. Matheny and Zimmerman (2001) conducted a content analysis of articles that related family systems theory to organizational consultation across three decades (1970s, 1980s, and 1990s). They found that therapists trained in systemic models of intervention do apply those models in organizational consultation, but that the detail and depth of model use varied across decades according to the relative influence of that model in the family treatment field (e.g., use of Bowen theory was greater in the 1970s than in the 1990s). Overall, however, this study illustrated the relative paucity of literature on the application of models to consultation and the lack of sophisticated research around such possible applications.

Fuqua and Newman (2009) describe the typical method or process of consulting in sequential steps: "Pre-entry, Entry, Problem exploration, Contracting, Information gathering, Problem confirmation, Goal setting, Solution searching, Intervention selection, Implementation, Evaluation, and Termination" (p. 138). The CFP specialist needs to understand these models and processes in order to implement consultation projects.

Skills

Many skills are important to the delivery of consultation services. In this section we describe briefly those that are most central to CFP consultation. These include the ability to apply a systemic epistemology and CFP research to the performance of an effective needs assessment that examines the referral question, the ability to prepare reports with recommendations to address the referral question, the ability to implement interventions using relationship skills, problem-solving skills, and implementation skills, and the ability to demonstrate ethical competency and diversity competency in consultation.

NEEDS ASSESSMENT

The critical skill for the CFP consultant is the ability to use a systemic epistemology to conceptualize the environmental scan of the organization in order to fully ascertain the circumstances of the referral questions. This requires the ability to understand the presenting question in light of the multitude of factors that might be involved and to focus on appropriate factors and the interaction between those factors: "Effective consultants, guided by systems thinking, or at least aware of its implications, learn to become skillful at identifying the most relevant interactional patterns in complex fields of interactions" (Fuqua & Newman, 2002, p. 86). It is helpful to understand and apply a systemic framework in order to fully consider the range of factors that may be involved in the consultation questions. For instance, the model by Fuqua and Newman (2002), detailed above (see "Knowledge" section above), describes the reciprocal dynamic between purposive, psychosocial, operational, and methodological subsystems of an organization. The CFP consultant may use these categories and the factors embedded in them as a framework to guide the needs assessment (data collection and analysis). This ensures thorough coverage of organization factors and awareness of the complex interactive dynamics that may contribute to the issue(s) identified by the organization. Fuqua and Kurpius (1993) describe seven stages for data processing: (a) planning; b) data collection, (c) analysis of data; (d) synthesis of data; (e) data feedback, f) follow-up; and g) taking action (pp. 609–610). Levinson (2002a) identifies four types of data in the assessment process: (a) genetic data (description of the organization); (b) structural data (demographics, policies, finances, etc.); (c) process data (communications transmission); and (d) interpretative data (how the organization perceives itself and its environment; p. 322 [abbreviated selection]) and details several important issues in assessment (e.g., "consultant as diagnostic instrument"; p. 323; "role of power in organizations"; p. 327). The assessment process often combines quantitative and qualitative research methods in order to provide sufficient data to address the issue(s). The CFP consultant may use interviews, focus groups, survey instruments, psychometric measures (e.g., assessment of individual factors), organization structure analysis, role investigation, and so forth (Levinson, 2002c), selected according to their perceived value within a systemic framework.

REPORT AND RECOMMENDATIONS

The results of the needs assessment are usually summarized in a written or oral report to the organization. At this point, the CFP consultant must demonstrate the ability to present the findings in an accurate yet concise manner that is appropriate to the organization recipients. Levinson recommends a summary "that can be read in an hour or less" (2002a, p. 339) and provides guidelines for debriefing the report (e.g., allow the client to process negative affect about the findings with the consultant). The results must be stated in an evenhanded manner because systems theory is not about locating blame for an issue; it is about understanding the issue and taking mutual responsibility to address it. Senge (2006) noted this about systems theory when he posited among the "Laws of the Fifth Discipline" that "there is no blame" and explained, "Systems thinking shows us that there is no separate 'other'; that you and the someone else are part of a single system. The cure lies in your relationship with your 'enemy'" (p. 67). Solutions are often interactive and rely on multiple contributors and dynamic processes. It is our experience that although some people would prefer reductionistic solutions that can be easily implemented, they are often open to explanations of systemic complexity and recommendations that more thoroughly address the multifaceted and interactive nature of the issues when the consultant clearly communicates those findings in a comprehensible manner and outlines a possible plan of action.

INTERVENTION SKILLS

Consultants use a variety of interventions, depending on the client(s) (e.g., individual coaching, team or group, organization). In this section, we note specific intervention skills related to these interventions that are transferable from clinical CFP practice to the consultation role. These skills underlie many interventions and facilitate administration of the intervention. These include relationship skills, problem-solving skills, and implementation skills.

Relationship skills in consultation are similar to the skills noted in the CFP relationship competency (see Chapter 12 for a review of the knowledge, skills, and attitudes of the Interpersonal Interaction competency). CFP specialists recognize and understand that professional relationships are complex because we work often with multiperson groups, but there is an added complexity when working with a larger group, especially within an organizational setting. In particular, this is because consultation relationships can blur boundaries; for instance, the consultant may provide coaching services to a director but hold a contract with the vice president to whom the director reports. It is crucial that confidentiality, boundaries, and reporting responsibilities be conducted in an ethical manner, but this still complicates the relationship and requires special skills in order to maintain an effective consulting relationship with all parties to the consultation. Second, consultation requires a more active stance by the consultant. Ulvila (2000) notes that consultants must create frequent formal and informal communication contact with consultees in order to create positive working relationships. Third, consultation involves creation of a triadic relationship (consultant, consultee, and the client or customer of the consultee organization; Newman, Robinson-Kurpius, & Fuqua, 2002).

The consultant must remain cognizant of the client's interests in order to best serve the consultee, and the client is always a factor in the consultation, even if she or he is not directly involved in the consultation. As noted by Glasser (2002), organization clients are frequently impacted by change effected by a consultation, "which means that consulting is in essence an indirect service" (p. 30). Fourth, consultants do not have direct power or control in the organization, so "the ability to quickly establish trusting relationships and to gain support of the decision makers and influencers in a given situation is crucial for a consultant" (Glasser, 2002, p. 31). The only way that consultant recommendations will be implemented in an organization is if the consultees find the consultant credible and competent (Glasser, 2002). This requires the type of relationship skills expected of CFP specialists (see Chapter 12). The Consultant Effectiveness Scale identified factors that received high ratings for interpersonal skill as "Shows Respect for the Consultee, Trustworthy, Approachable, Encouraging, Pleasant, and Positive Attitude" (Knoff, Hines, & Kromrey, 1995, n.p.)

Second, the consultant must have the skill to implement a problem-solving process in the organization. Fuqua and Newman (2009) delineate the common steps in such a process: "1. Relationship development, 2. Problem definition, 3. Convert the problem statement to goals and objectives, 4. Explore alternatives, 5. Intervention selection, 6. Implementation, 7. Evaluation, and 8. Termination" (p. 138). It should be noted that problem solving assumes establishment of an effective consulting relationship (see above) and leads to implementation (see below). It requires the consultant to ascertain whether addressing the consultation question will benefit the organization (Glasser, 2002). The Consultant Effectiveness Scale identified 14 factors relevant to problem solving and found that the factors that received the highest ratings were "Skillful, Good Facilitator, Active Listener, Effective at Establishing Rapport, Good at Problem Solving, and Astute Observer/Perceptive" (Knoff et al., 1995, n.p.).

Third, the consultant needs implementation skills to enact the organization-approved consultation action steps. This involves the ability to propose recommendations that may be effectively implemented, appraise organizational/consultee readiness to implement change, predict which recommendations are likely to be endorsed by the consultee, create consensus, and teach new abilities to organization associates (Glasser, 2002). The Consultant Effectiveness Scale identified the highest-rated consultation process and application factors as "Willing to Get Involved, Evaluates/Focuses Ideas, Active, Pursues Issues/Follows Through, and Identifies Clear Goals" (Knoff et al., 1995, n.p.).

ETHICAL COMPETENCY IN CONSULTATION

Many of the same ethical and professional standards in CFP clinical practice apply to consulting practice, such as the definition of the client and changes in definition of the client during treatment (see Chapter 10), but the frame of reference is different, and there are unique challenges to the consultant (Levinson, 2002b; Lowman, 1998a). For instance, Fuqua and Newman (2002) note that if the focus of the consultation changes from individual consultation to system responsibility for a problem, the consultant will want to reassess his or her role to determine if it is appropriate to continue with the project. At the very least, the change will need to be negotiated and the role relationships clarified in an ethical manner.

Newman and colleagues (2002) identify several common ethical issues in consultation, considered from a systemic perspective, including (a) definition of the client; (b) informed consent; (c) confidentiality; (d) dual relationships; (e) consultant competence; (f) tension between business demands and helping perspectives; (g) determination of the intervention level within the organization and systemic impacts from intervention at any level; (h) assessment issues (e.g., confidentiality, forced participation); (i) intervention issues (e.g., the role of professional opinion and evidence for intervention effectiveness); and (j) consultant responsibility for inclusion of moral and ethical discourse. Each of these has parallels to CFP clinical practice because of the systemic nature of such CFP specialty work, but they must be taken to another level when the CFP specialist practices as a consultant to groups or organizations. See Lowman (1998a) for a thorough review of ethics in consultation. The Consultant Effectiveness Scale identified the highest-rated ethical and professional practice skills as "Practices in an Ethical Manner, Maintains Confidentiality, Trustworthy, Emotionally Well-Adjusted/Stable, and Clear Sense of Identity" (Knoff et al., 1995, n.p.).

In particular, the CFP consultant should be aware that consultation may involve attention to moral and ethical issues that relate to the consultation question, especially in light of the current pervasive concern about business ethics. Fuqua and Newman (2006, 2009) note the prevalence of moral issues in human organizations and describe the quandary around the need to provide meaningful consultation to leaders who are responsible for the moral conditions in their organizations when the desire to engage in moral discourse has decreased in our society. They suggest that an organizational system must address issues of ethics in light of the purposive system (core organizational values and principles), the psychosocial system (alignment of personal ethics with organization values), the operational system (the code of conduct in the organization), and the methodological system (processes for ethical discourse and decision making, and remediation of violations; Fuqua & Newman, 2006, p. 209). They suggest that organization leaders should be exemplars of ethical behavior in their organizations ("the morality of an organization rarely rises above that of its leadership"; Fuqua & Newman, 2009, p. 136) and that consultants have a responsibility to recognize information about ethical and moral problems discovered during the needs assessment, to address those issues in recommendations to the organization, and to facilitate moral discourse during the consulting process. For instance, if consulting regarding accountability for clinical services in health care, the CFP consultant may use a systemic epistemology to help the organization focus on the interrelated factors that surround ethical problems instead of looking only at single cases; this helps the whole organization take responsibility for the complex factors that result in unethical practices (MacRae, Fox, & Slowther, 2008). Such actions require an underlying attitude of commitment to ethical process from a systems perspective.

DIVERSITY COMPETENCY IN CONSULTATION

Competency in the delivery of consultation includes the ability to interact effectively when there are individual or group diversity issues. Chapter 11 describes the knowledge, skills, and attitudes required for CFP diversity competency. Recognition and inclusion of individual and group diversity is an important part of a systemic epistemology (Stanton, 2009b). Diversity competency is part of the guidelines for consultation (American Psychological Association, 2007). In this section, we will address briefly the importance of this competency in CFP consultation.

Cooper and Leong (2008) note that "the increases in cultural, racial, and ethnic diversity rapidly taking place in most U.S. and global organizations and industries...demand significant attention from those practicing consulting psychology if they wish to practice competently and effectively" (p. 133). They cite existing literature regarding the probability of impaired consultation effectiveness if these differences are not addressed with skill. The interaction between consultants, consultees, and the organizational system increasingly involves issues of diversity (Romney, 2008).

Mullin and Cooper (2002) present a six-factor systemic model for competent consultation when diversity factors are present: (a) self-awareness in relational and environmental context; (b) professional and technical skills to consult consistent with the culture; (c) knowledge of how culture factors into the complexity of exosystems and macrosystems; (d) knowledge of consultant's personal value system as socially constructed and the flexibility to align with consultee(s); (e) recognizing variations in cultural heterogeneity/homogeneity and the complex impact on interpersonal interaction during consultation; and (f) valuing differences and developing skills to interact in a nonjudgmental manner (pp. 554–555). They suggest that the greater the difference of consultee culture from consultant culture, the more difficult the challenge. In some cases, the consultant may need to advocate for social justice in an organization by facilitating challenging discussions around diversity issues (Sue, 2008).

Of course, a variety of additional factors can contribute to differences between consultant and consultee in the workplace, including age, gender, socioeconomic status, religion, sexual orientation, and other individual characteristics (Romney, 2008). These differences enrich organizations and may provide diverse perspectives that can strengthen the organization's ability to achieve its mission and purpose. It is important that the consultant monitor these individual factors and endeavor to understand differences in perception and behavior due to differences in order to provide effective consultation.

Finally, given the increased diversity in the contemporary workplace, consultants are sometimes asked to consult regarding issues of diversity. This requires knowledge of diversity frameworks and extensive skill in facilitating effective interactions across aspects of diversity in the workplace (Mullin & Cooper, 2002). It is most likely to effect change when it is a collaborative process with internal leaders (Romney, 2008).

Attitudes

In order to provide effective CFP consultation, it is necessary for the CFP specialist to hold certain attitudes that serve as a foundation for the consultation skills. Important attitudes include valuing and adopting the role of the consultant as part of the specialty, recognizing the importance of ethical and professional standards in consultation, having positive regard for collaborative processes, and respecting individual and group diversity in consultation.

VALUING THE ROLE OF CONSULTANT

Because of the title of our specialty, many people assume that couple and family psychology is simply the delivery of clinical services to couple and families (Nutt & Stanton, 2008). However, as noted above, CFP specialist is ideally suited to extension into consultation with larger social groups and organizations because of its reliance on a systems epistemology. In order for the CFP specialist to provide consultation services, it is important that he or she appreciates the differences between psychotherapy and consultation (Levinson, 2009a) and adopts the role of the consultant when providing those services. Lippitt and Lippitt (1986) suggest that consultants fulfill several possible roles, including educator/trainer, catalyst, advocate, expert, and reflector. The CFP consultant needs to understand the differences in role enactment and select styles that meet the needs of the clients.

IMPORTANCE OF ETHICAL AND PROFESSIONAL STANDARDS

The CFP consultant must place the same type of emphasis and value on ethical and professional standards in consultation as is placed on the delivery of psychotherapeutic services (see Chapter 10). The attitudinal value takes seriously the role of the CFP consultant and the importance of holding oneself to the highest standards. This commitment underlies the skills needed for ethical and professional consultation.

POSITIVE REGARD FOR COLLABORATION

Consultation is, by definition, advisory and collaborative. It is important that the CFP consultant move away from reliance on a power-based expert stance and embrace a collaborative model that allows the expertise of the consultant and the consultee(s) to manifest itself in the consultation process. The trend toward collaboration is noted in school-based consultation through a shift in mode of professional communication from consultation to collaboration (Caplan, Caplan, & Erchul, 1995) and the trend in health care toward more patient-centered services, although that focus must counter the systemic forces in health care that would undermine a collaborative process, if the CFP consultant works in that environment (Taylor, 2009). Knowles (2009) discusses frequent barriers to collaborative communication between psychologists and primary care providers in health care and makes suggestions to improve collaboration.

RESPECT FOR INDIVIDUAL AND GROUP DIVERSITY

The foundation of diversity competency in professional psychology includes self-awareness and self-monitoring of one's own biases and prejudices in regard to professional interaction. Workplace diversity in the contemporary United States is significant, and it is important that the CFP consultant examine her or his own attitudes and behaviors toward others around issues of diversity (Mullin & Cooper, 2002).

Conclusion

CFP consultancy is an emerging competency, and more specialists are consulting in arenas related to the specialty emphases. This chapter reviewed the fundamental knowledge, skills, and attitudes involved in relating a systemic epistemology to the practice of consultation.

SEVEN

Competencies in Family Forensic Psychology

Couple and family psychology (CFP) specialists are uniquely suited to work with individuals, couples, and families involved in the court system. Some CFP specialists work with couples in distress or divorcing couples, some treat parents and children involved in a custody dispute at the behest of the court and describe their role as a treating expert, while other CFP specialists specialize in family forensic psychology. To function effectively, all CFP specialists must have some knowledge of forensic issues that face couples and families. This chapter is separated into two sections. In the first, we will distinguish between CFP specialists who provide routine clinical services to couples and families that are distressed with the parents at risk for divorce, and the forensically informed family psychologist or treating expert. In the second section we will outline specialty competencies for family forensic psychology (FFP) specialists who conduct forensic evaluations in the dependency or family courts.

Routine Clinical Services

Even if CFP specialists deliberately try to avoid court-involved families, the nature of the specialty requires a basic familiarity with the forensic world. Consider the unsuspecting CFP specialist who treats a family for a seemingly innocuous issue. Several years later the couple divorces, and the CFP specialist is asked by one of the parents to write a letter to the court describing the goodness of fit between him or her and the children in the family. CFP specialists need a basic familiarity with forensic practice so that they do not practice beyond their abilities or confuse the separate roles of therapist and evaluator. CFP specialists should be aware that forensic practice requires specialized knowledge, skills, and attitudes that are not obtained in the course of most graduate and postgraduate training programs in professional psychology. In the following sections we outline two areas where CFP specialists might find themselves in a precarious situation, both ethically and legally, if they are not forewarned. We recommend that whenever CFP specialists encounter a forensic issue in the course of providing routine clinical services that they consult with a trusted colleague or attorney before taking action.

ADVOCACY

CFP specialists are often advocates for their clients, and in many cases functioning in this role is appropriate. However, when a couple or family is involved in a contentious custody dispute, CFP specialists may overstep their role by functioning as an advocate. Once a couple/family becomes involved in the court system, their attorney becomes their advocate. At this point, the advocacy offered by a CFP therapist may actually cause harm to the clients or the legal proceeding (Shuman, S. Greenberg, Heilbrun, & Foote, 1998). A CFP specialist may inappropriately function as an advocate by drafting a letter on behalf of the client. Many well-intentioned psychotherapists cross role boundaries when they agree to provide a letter of support to the courts and offer opinions that are forensic in nature without meaning to do so. In the spirit of advocacy, a well-meaning therapist may comment on the goodness of fit between the child's needs and the client/parent's parenting abilities. The therapist may even go so far as recommending one parent over the other without ever evaluating the other parent. Once a family is involved in a court proceeding, the CFP specialist should avoid functioning as an advocate and recognize that the advocate role is best left to the family's attorney.

PROVIDING TESTIMONY

CFP specialists may be asked by the courts, their clients, or clients' attorney to provide testimony in a custody dispute about information that was obtained during couple or family psychotherapy. S. Greenberg and Shuman (1997) note that there is "an irreconcilable professional conflict of interest" between forensic services and clinical services. They do note that therapists may provide testimony on the following, assuming it is "subject to privilege, confidentiality and qualifications":

> the reported history as provided by the patient; mental status; the clinical diagnosis; the care provided to the patient and the patient's

response to it; the patient's prognosis; the mood, cognitions, or behavior of the patient; and any other relevant statements that the patient made in treatment. These matters, presented in the manner of descriptive "occurrences" and not psycholegal opinions, do not raise issues of judgment, foundation, or historical truth. Therapists do not ordinarily have the requisite database to testify appropriately about psycho legal issues of causation (i.e., the relationship of a specific act to claimant's current condition) or capacity (i.e., the relationship of diagnosis or mental status to legally defined standards of functional capacity). These matters raise problems of judgment, foundation, and historical truth that are problematic for treating experts. (S. Greenberg & Shuman, 1997, p. 56)

Providing expert testimony on information that was obtained in the course of a therapeutic context is a frequent area of danger encountered by CFP specialists as they may yield to partisan pressures or believe that they are helping their clients. We are not advancing here that therapists cannot provide expert testimony about their clients as some authors do (Shuman et al., 1998), although that would eliminate many of the potential ethical pitfalls. Rather, we are suggesting that CFP specialists must recognize when they are asked a psycholegal question by the court and respectfully decline to provide an opinion. A psycholegal question is a legally disputed question that bears directly on expert psychological opinion. Typical psycholegal questions involve recommendations about custody arrangements, parenting capacity, needs of the child and the resulting fit of one parent over another, and determining child sexual abuse. Even though CFP specialists may think that they have gathered relevant data in the course of psychotherapy, providing such an opinion violates ethical and legal boundaries. For example, providing expert opinion about psycholegal constructs that were gathered during the course of psychotherapy violates informed consent unless the purpose of the professional interaction was explained at the outset of the relationship. Moreover, expert opinions require a methodology of data collection and critical analysis that is not typically conducted in routine clinical services (S. Greenberg & Shuman, 1997). CFP specialists should be alert that they are in dangerous territory if they are offering expert knowledge of the type not reasonably obtained during the course of treatment as usual.

Recommended Resources
For those CFP specialists who frequently work with divorcing families but do not treat court-ordered children or families, we recommend a basic

forensic knowledge that will help the specialist identify potentially problematic situations before they escalate. Several good resources for the CFP specialist are available (L. Greenberg, Gould, Gould-Saltman, & Stahl, 2003; L. Greenberg, Gould-Saltman, & Gottlieb, 2009; S. Greenberg & Shuman, 1997; Shuman et al., 1998).

TREATING EXPERTS

We previously distinguished between CFP specialists who treat divorcing families and those who routinely accept court-ordered children and families in the context of custody disputes. A higher level of forensic expertise is required for those who hold themselves out as treating experts. The primary goal of the forensically informed treating expert is to provide intervention to distressed families involved in the legal system; however, the interventions may have varied reporting requirements. Treating experts should clarify the court's reporting expectations at the outset of treatment. Several excellent articles address the role of treating expert with court-involved families (L. Greenberg & Gould, 2001; L. Greenberg et al., 2003; L. Greenberg et al., 2009). The articles advanced by Greenberg and colleagues provide a thorough discussion of the higher level of forensic knowledge and skills required by treating experts. Treating experts provide a valuable service to court-involved families and are frequently relied on by dependency and family courts. Court-involved treatment should not be conducted by CFP specialists without advanced forensic training.

Family Forensic Psychology

Family forensic psychology (FFP) has been defined as "a special application of family psychology and forensic psychology that provides expert-level services to families involved with the legal system, their attorneys, and the courts" (Welsh, Greenberg, & Graham-Howard, 2009, p. 703). FFP practice is broadly conceptualized to include specialized dispute resolution functions (e.g., mediator, parent coordinator), consultation, testimony, evaluation, or research. FFP has been defined by the presence of three distinctive features: (a) FFP serves a population that involves the interaction between children, couples, and families; (b) FFP is a specialty with overlapping fields of interest between couple and family psychology, forensic psychology, and the legal system; and (c) FFP involves the application of a systemic epistemology to forensic cases (Welsh et al., 2009). The specialty practice of FFP has been applied to many areas of law, including family law, dependency law, minor law, and elder law (Grossman & Okun,

TABLE 7.1 **Potential Areas of Practice in Family Forensic Psychology**

COUPLE AND FAMILY	CHILD AND JUVENILE	ELDER
Abortion	Child abuse and neglect	Elder abuse
Adoption	Juvenile delinquency	Euthanasia
Alienation	Minor privacy rights	Legal guardianship
Alternative families		Succession planning
Child custody		Wills and trusts
Divorce mediation		
Family business planning		
Foster parenting		
Parent coordination		
Paternity		
Postnuptial arrangements		
Prenuptial arrangements		
Relocation		
Spousal abuse		
Surrogacy		
Visitation		

Note. From F. W. Kaslow 2000; Grossman and Okun 2003; Goldstein 2003.

2003; F. W. Kaslow, 2000). Accordingly, the practice of FFP is broadly practiced in diverse settings. Table 7.1 provides examples of common activities.

FFP is one specialty application of the CFP competencies. Because many CFP specialists also practice FFP, we have included a set of competencies unique to the specialty practice of FFP for those specialists who also identify with CFP. To our knowledge this has not been done previously. What makes this emerging competency area especially challenging is the broad practice that characterizes FFP and the possible range of knowledge, skills, and attitudes that encompasses FFP. In this section we propose a set of competencies specifically suited to FFP evaluations typically encountered in custody and dependency cases, although they could easily be applied to juvenile forensic evaluations as well (Table 7.2).

The knowledge base required for FFP practice is largely dependent on the work product produced by the specialist. For example, the knowledge base required for child custody evaluations is significantly different than

TABLE 7.2 Specialty Competency in Family Forensic Psychology

COMPETENCY DOMAIN AND ESSENTIAL COMPONENT	BEHAVIORAL ANCHOR	ASSESSMENT METHODS
Knowledge		1. ABPP examination
(A) Foundational family forensic knowledge	(A.1.1) Command of APA ethics code and relevant practice guidelines	2. Exemplary work products
(A.1) Knowledge of applicable ethical and legal sources of authority	(A.1.2) Knowledgeable about laws that govern specialty practice	3. Self-evaluation
	(A.2.1) Understands preparatory steps in FFP evaluations	4. Ongoing supervision and consultation
(A.2) Knowledge of forensic methodology	(A.2.2) Understands data collection methods in FFP evaluations	5. Peer consultation with family forensic psychologists and family law attorneys
(A.3) Knowledge of FFP specialty area literature	(A.2.3) Understands data interpretation procedures in FFP practice	6. Continuing education
	(A.3.1) Knowledgeable of central FFP specialty literature	7. Publication and presentation in scholarly venues
Skills	(B.1.1) Demonstrates the ability to practice ethically in the FFP context	
(B) Ability to conduct a high-quality FFP evaluation	(B.1.2) Demonstrates professional conduct in an adversarial setting	
(B.1) Demonstrates the ability to manage the adversarial nature of the FFP context	(B.1.3) Demonstrates the ability to establish initial parameters for conducting the evaluation	
	(B.2.1) Demonstrates the ability to gather data using multiple sources, including record review, clinical interview, and psychological testing	
(B.2) Demonstrates the ability to conduct an FFP evaluation	(B.2.2) Demonstrates the ability to critically evaluate the data to address the psycholegal question(s)	
(B.3) Demonstrates the ability to clearly and accurately convey psychological concepts to the retaining attorney, court, or other fact finder	(B.3.1) Demonstrates the ability to clearly and accurately communicate in the form of a written report and expert testimony	
Attitudes	(C.1.1) Demonstrates a forensic perspective that includes exemplar ethical practice, an objective mindset, critical scrutiny of data, and	
(C) Forensic perspective		
(C.1) Demonstrates a forensic perspective		

Note. Adapted from the format and content of the Assessment of Competency Benchmarks Work Group (2007). This table assumes that the specialist has achieved competence in professional psychology at the three previous developmental levels, as specified in the benchmarks. The competency domains and behavioral anchors serve as the primary organizing structure for this chapter; content explaining each domain and anchor is provided in the chapter.

the knowledge required for work in the juvenile justice system (Welsh et al., 2009). Each area of FFP practice will require a somewhat different knowledge base depending on the type of psycholegal question, functional abilities relevant to the psycholegal question, population involved in the evaluation, and the legal context where the evaluation takes place (e.g., dependency court, family court). In this chapter we focus on three broad domains of knowledge required for FFP practice. First, CFP specialists practicing FFP must understand the ethical and legal literature that governs their area of practice. Second, CFP specialists practicing FFP must possess a forensic methodology that guides the activities of the evaluation. This includes preparation, data collection methods, interpretation, and forensic communication (Heilbrun, 2001). Finally, the CFP specialist practicing FFP specialist must be knowledgeable about the theoretical and scientific literature that encompasses each area of specialty practice.

ETHICAL AND LEGAL KNOWLEDGE BASE

CFP specialists engaged in FFP practice at the intersection of forensic psychology, couple and family psychology, and the legal system. Practicing within this multidisciplinary setting can create frequent ethical conflicts if the CFP specialist does not have a solid footing in ethics and the laws governing FFP practice. The knowledge base of the CFP specialist practicing FFP includes command of the Ethical Principles of Psychologists and Code of Conduct (APA Ethics Code; APA, 2002), specialty guidelines related to FFP practice, and the law that pertains to FFP practice.

Knowledge of Ethics and Practice Guidelines
The ethical practice of FFP is governed by several sources of professional authority, including the APA Ethics Code (APA, 2002) and relevant practice guidelines. The Ethics Code is sufficiently broad to cover a wide range of activities in professional psychology and is intended to be general in nature and scope. The Ethics Code does not address any area of specialty practice in enough detail to be the only source of authority. Nevertheless, it provides the basis for ethical practice in FFP, and all specialty guidelines are used in conjunction with the APA Ethics Code. Areas of particular relevance to forensic practice include, but are not limited to, informed consent (§3.10; §9.03), privacy and confidentiality (§4), multiple relationships (§3.05), conflicts between ethics and law, regulations, or other governing legal authority (§1.02), and boundaries of competence (§2.01). There are several good overviews of the application of the Ethics Code to general forensic practice, with which FFP specialists should be familiar (Bush,

Connell, & Denney, 2006; Lipsitt, 2007; Weissman & DeBow, 2003). There are also a number of ethics articles applicable to a variety of FFP specialty evaluations, including custody and dependency cases (Greenberg, Martindale, Gould, & Gould-Saltman, 2004), child sexual abuse evaluations (Koocher, 2009), and juvenile justice (Koocher, 2006).

There are also a limited number of practice guidelines that are applicable to CFP specialty practice in FFP. Broad guidelines for forensic psychology practice exist in the form of the *Specialty Guidelines for Forensic Psychology* (SGFP; Committee on Ethical Issues for Forensic Psychologists, 1991). The SGFP is a document that was produced by the American Psychology-Law Society, APA Division 41, and endorsed by the American Academy of Forensic Psychology to "provide an aspirational model of desirable professional practice by psychologists" (Committee on Ethical Issues for Forensic Psychologists, 1991, p. 656). These guidelines apply to all forensic practice and are currently being revised; they may be downloaded at www.ap-ls.org/links/currentforensicguidelines.pdf. More specific guidelines that are uniquely applicable to FFP include the Association of Family and Conciliation Courts (AFCC) *Model Standards of Practice for Child Custody Evaluation* (AFCC, 2006) and the APA *Guidelines for Child Custody Evaluations in Divorce Proceedings* (APA, 1994). In addition, those

TABLE 7.3 **Guidelines Relevant to Practice in Family Forensic Psychology**

American Academy of Child and Adolescent Psychiatry (1997a)	Practice parameters for the forensic evaluation of children and adolescents who may have been physically or sexually abused
American Academy of Child and Adolescent Psychiatry (1997b)	Practice parameters for child custody evaluation
American Academy of Psychiatry and the Law (2005)	Ethical guidelines for the practice of forensic psychiatry
American Medical Association (1997)	Bonding programs for women prisoners and their newborn children
American Professional Society on the Abuse of Children (1996)	Psychosocial evaluations of suspected psychological maltreatment in children and adolescents
American Psychological Association (1994)	Guidelines for child custody evaluations in divorce proceedings
American Psychological Association (2002)	Ethical principles of psychologists and code of conduct
Association of Family and Conciliation Courts (2000)	Model standards of practice for divorce and family mediators
Association of Family and Conciliation Courts (2005)	Guidelines for parenting coordination
Association of Family and Conciliation Courts (2006)	Model standards of practice for child custody evaluation
Board of Professional Affairs Committee on Professional Practice and Standards, American Psychological Association (1999)	Guidelines for psychological evaluations in child protection matters
Committee on Ethical Issues for Forensic Psychologists (1991)	Specialty guidelines for forensic psychologists

CFP specialists that perform dispute resolution functions within the family law courts should be aware of the AFCC's *Model Standards of Practice for Family and Divorce Mediation* (AFCC, 2000) and the AFCC's *Guidelines for Parenting Coordination* (AFCC, 2005). CFP specialists practicing in the dependency courts should be aware of the *Guidelines for Psychological Evaluations in Child Protection Matters* (Committee on Professional Practice and Standards, 1999), and the *Psychosocial Evaluations of Suspected Psychological Maltreatment in Children and Adolescents* (American Professional Society on the Abuse of Children, 1996). Table 7.3 lists the specialty guidelines that are potentially relevant for practice in FFP.

Familiar with Laws Guiding FFP Practice

CFP specialists who practice FFP are knowledgeable about the laws and rules that govern their area of practice. "When assuming forensic roles, psychologists are or become reasonably familiar with the judicial or administrative rules governing their roles" (APA Ethics Code §2.01f). Many evaluations are statutorily defined and may differ from jurisdiction to jurisdiction. FFPs are knowledgeable about the statutes that govern their practice. For example, custody evaluators must be knowledgeable about "criteria for original determination of custody, criteria for change of custody, the use of custody evaluations, qualifications for custody evaluations, and the legal requirements of the custody evaluation process of the jurisdictions in which the evaluators will be performing their evaluations" (AFCC, 2006, pp. 9–10). In addition, FFP specialists are familiar with case law in their jurisdiction that governs their area of practice. FFP specialists may practice in several different courts (e.g., family, dependency, juvenile, probate) and should be familiar with the local rules that govern the respective court.

FORENSIC METHODOLOGY

CFP specialists that practice FFP use a method to guide forensic evaluation (Heilbrun, 2001; Martindale & Gould, 2004; Gould, 2006). They must understand the process of the forensic evaluation from beginning to end and consistently use a scientifically informed methodology that guides their professional activity. Using the same methodology across evaluations increases the reliability of the forensic evaluations (Rogers, 1995) and may increase accuracy and decrease bias. Heilbrun (2001) proposed 29 principles that guide forensic assessment across four broad steps of the evaluation process: preparation, data collection, data interpretation, and communication. Martindale and Gould (2004) also proposed a model for child custody evaluations that included seven essential components. This model has some overlap with Heilbrun's model but is specifically applicable to the work of the child custody evaluator. The essential component discussed here is arranged around Heilbrun's (2001) four broad steps of forensic mental health assessment (Table 7.4).

Knowledge of Preparatory Steps

CFP specialists who practice FFP understand the initial steps to beginning an FFP evaluation. Once a referral is received, the CFP specialist identifies

TABLE 7.4 **Principles of Forensic Mental Health Assessment**

Preparation
1. Identify relevant forensic issues
2. Accept referrals only within area of expertise
3. Decline referral when evaluator impartiality is unlikely
4. Clarify role with attorney
5. Clarify financial arrangements
6. Obtain appropriate authorization
7. Avoid dual-role relationships of therapist and forensic evaluator
8. Determine the role to be played within forensic assessment if the referral is accepted
9. Select and employ a model to guide data gathering, interpretation, and communication

Data Collection
10. Use multiple sources of information for each area being assessed
11. Use relevance and reliability (validity) as guides for seeking information and selecting data sources
12. Obtain relevant historical information
13. Assess clinical characteristics in relevant, reliable, and valid ways
14. Assess legally relevant behavior
15. Ensure that conditions for the evaluation are quiet, private, and distraction free
16. Provide appropriate notification of purpose and/or appropriate authorization before beginning
17. Determine whether the individual understands the purpose of the evaluation and the associated limits on confidentiality

Data Interpretation
18. Use third-party information in assessing response style
19. Use testing when indicated in assessing response style
20. Use case-specific (idiographic) evidence in assessing clinical condition, functional abilities, and causal connection
21. Use nomothetic evidence in assessing causal connection between clinical condition and functional abilities
22. Use scientific reasoning in assessing causal connection between clinical condition and functional abilities
23. Do not answer the ultimate legal question
24. Describe findings and limits so that they need change little under cross-examination

Communication
25. Attribute information to sources
26. Use plain language and avoid technical jargon
27. Write report in sections, according to model and procedures
28. Base testimony on the results of the properly performed Forensic Mental Health Assessment (FMHA)
29. Testify effectively

Note. Adapted from Heilbrun 2001.

the relevant psycholegal question, or series of questions, that frames the evaluation. In custody cases, the forensic issue typically involves evaluating the goodness of fit between the child's needs and the parent's abilities. In dependency cases the evaluation often centers on the behavior of parents such as whether or not a child has been neglected or abused, or whether there is foreseeable risk for abuse. In cases where termination of parental rights is before the court, the evaluation typically involves assessment of parental capacity and potential for parent remediation (i.e., unless there has been severe abuse). In juvenile justice cases, the forensic issue may be one of competency or suitability for rehabilitation. Forensic issues are often statutorily defined or specified by the referring party (e.g., court or attorney). There are also situations where a different forensic issue might emerge during the course of an evaluation. For example, in both child custody and child dependency cases, the FFP may need to evaluate domestic violence (Austin, 2000, 2001; Bancroft & Silverman, 2002a, 2002b) and child abuse and neglect (Bow, Quinnell, Zaroff, & Assemany, 2002; Kuehnle & Connell, 2008) because there are often allegations of this nature in both evaluations.

CFP specialists who practice FFP accept referrals only in areas of their expertise and decline referrals where impartiality may be compromised (AFCC, 2006; Committee on Ethical Issues for Forensic Psychologists, 1991; Heilbrun, 2001). During the preparatory steps of an FFP evaluation, the specialist clarifies the relationship with the referring party and clarifies the role that the evaluator will play in the FFP assessment (AFCC, 2006). If the referral source is an attorney, the CFP specialist must understand the difference between the role of forensic evaluator and forensic consultant (Melton, Petrila, Poythress, & Slobogin, 2007). In addition, CFP specialists practicing FFP must also be knowledgeable about the confidentiality issues surrounding attorney-client work product if the referral is initiated by the client's attorney. CFP specialists also understand the role boundary differences between functioning as a forensic evaluator and a therapist (S. Greenberg & Shuman, 1997).

Once all roles have been clarified and authorization obtained to conduct the evaluation, the CFP specialist selects a model that will guide data collection, interpretation, and communication (Heilbrun, 2001). There are several guiding models for forensic evaluations and family forensic evaluations (Benjamin, Monarch, & Gollan, 2003; Grisso, 2003; Morse, 1978a, 1978b). Grisso (2003) provides a conceptual model for assessing legal competencies that includes five components: functional, causal, interactive, judgmental, and dispositional. Grisso's model is theoretically rich and broadly applicable to assessing legal competencies, including parenting competencies addressed in divorce and dependency proceedings (Otto & Edens, 2003).

Knowledge of Data Collection

The data collection strategy is driven by the forensic issue and forensic model chosen. For example, a juvenile justice competency evaluation may limit the examination to the adolescent without evaluating the parents and may not use psychological assessment instruments to answer the referral question. Prior to the evaluation, the CFP specialist explains the nature, purpose, and procedures of the evaluation to the parties being evaluated. The evaluator also explains the limits to confidentiality, or the nonconfidential nature of the evaluation if applicable, and explains the likely uses of the evaluation. CFP specialists often document the information given to the examinee prior to the evaluation in the form of a statement of understanding that the clients sign. The CFP specialist employs a data collection strategy that is multimodal (uses multiple methods of data collection), relevant to the forensic issue, and reliable (Heilbrun, 2001). Depending on the nature of the forensic issue, CFP specialists may examine multiple sources of historical documents including, but not limited to, therapy records, medical and legal history, Child Protective Service reports, school records, and financial records. CFP specialists also frequently conduct interviews with a range of family subsystems (parent-child; siblings) and should be knowledgeable of systemic methods of assessment (see Chapter 4, "Assessment"). For example, in a child custody evaluation, observed parent-child interactions with both parents are required as part of the overall evaluation. CFP specialists should be aware of methods used to evaluate parent-child interactions and research on observation methods (Condie, 2003). CFP specialists may also need to personally interview other parties not directly involved in the case. The collateral contacts might include teachers, coaches, clergy, and employers (Gould, 2006; Heilbrun, Warren, & Picarello, 2003).

CFP specialists also understand the range of assessment instruments available to them and recognize the strengths and weaknesses when applied to a forensic context. Heilbrun (1992) provided seven recommendations for selecting, administering, and interpreting psychological tests in forensic assessment (Table 7.5). Specifically, tests should be psychometrically sound, used for the purposes for which they were created, relevant to the legal issue or related constructs, administered according to standardized procedures, appropriate for the population evaluated, and interpreted in light of an individual's unique response style. When

TABLE 7.5 **Psychological Testing: Guidelines for Use in Forensic Assessment (Heilbrun, 1992)**

Selection

1. The test is commercially available and adequately documented in two sources. First, it is accompanied by a manual describing its development, psychometric properties, and procedure for administration. Second, it is listed and reviewed in *Mental Measurements Yearbook* or some other readily available source.
2. Reliability should be considered. The use of tests with a reliability coefficient of less than .80 is not advisable. The use of less reliable tests would require an explicit justification by the psychologist.
3. The test should be relevant to the legal issue, or to a psychological construct underlying the legal issue. Whenever possible, this relevance should be supported by the availability of validation research published in refereed journals.

Administration

4. Standard administration should be used, with testing conditions as close as possible to the quiet, distraction-free ideal.

Interpretation

5. Applicability to this population and for this purpose should guide both test selection and interpretation. The results of a test (distinct from behavior observed during testing) should not be applied toward a purpose for which the test was not developed (e.g., inferring psychopathology from the results of an intelligence test). Population and situation specificity should guide interpretation. The closer the "fit" between a given individual and the population and situation of those in the validation research, the more confidence can be expressed in the applicability of the results.
6. Object tests and actuarial data combination are preferable when there are appropriate outcome data and a "formula" exists.
7. Response style should be explicitly assessed using approaches sensitive to distortion, and the results of psychological testing interpreted within the context of the individual's response style. When response style appears to be malingering, defensive, or irrelevant rather than honest/reliable, the results of psychological testing may need to be discounted or even ignored and other data sources emphasized to a greater degree.

Note. Adapted from K. Heilbrun (1992), The role of psychological testing in forensic assessment, *Law and Human Behavior*, 16, 257–272.

selecting psychological assessment instruments, FFP specialists should consider evidentiary standards (e.g., *Frye* or *Daubert*) and are knowledgeable about the scientific literature published on the instrument. Otto and Edens (2003) provide a comprehensive review of common instruments used in some FFP evaluations (e.g., custody and dependency cases). CFP specialists are also aware of normative data relevant to family forensic specialty evaluations (e.g., Bathurst, Gottfried, & Gottfried, 1997; McCann et al., 2001 cited in Gould, 2004).

Knowledge of Data Interpretation

The interpretation of data in the context of an FFP evaluation is the litmus test of expertise. More will be said about the skill of data interpretation and presenting findings later in the chapter. Heilbrun (2001) lists seven principles related to interpretation. Because of the adversarial nature of forensic evaluations, the CFP specialist should understand ways to use third-party data and measures of response style to cross-check the examinee's self-report and behavioral presentation. CFP specialists should be familiar with psychometric measures used to assess superlative responding, malingering, or the suppression of actual abilities (Rogers, 2008).

CFP specialists also understand the appropriate uses of idiographic and nomothetic data to causally link personal history, psychological data, and functional abilities to the legal construct being assessed (Grisso, 2003; Heilbrun, 2001). When interpreting data, CFP Specialists understand the range of the contextual mediator variables (e.g., ethnocultural; socioeconomic) that could change the interpretation of the data (Dana, 2005) and understand the multicultural factors that might better explain the examinee's presentation (see Chapter 11). When evaluating individuals substantially different than the standardization sample, the CFP specialist has a rationale for including the instrument in the evaluation and appropriately documents the limitations to the interpretation. Finally, when providing interpretations of data and generating opinions about the forensic issue, CFP specialists understand both sides of the "ultimate opinion" argument and understand the probative and prejudicial nature of providing such an opinion.

KNOWLEDGE OF FFP SPECIALTY LITERATURE

CFP specialists are knowledgeable about the theoretical and empirical literature that governs their area of practice. CFP specialists interact with individuals, couples, and families at all ages, and forensic opinions will typically be established in light of stage-specific factors (e.g., developmental needs of children). Accordingly, CFP evaluators must have a firm grasp of developmental literature at all stages throughout the life span, and possess knowledge of developmentally appropriate abilities, norms, and delays. In two of the most common FFP cases, child custody and child protection, the knowledge of psychological and developmental needs of the child/children is at the center of the evaluation. In addition, specialty guidelines governing child custody (AFCC, 2006; APA, 1994) and child protection (APA, 1999) specifically note that the developmental and psychological needs of the child must be considered to determine the "best interests" or "health and welfare" of the child.

FFP specialists who work with custody and dependency cases are also knowledgeable about the effects of divorce and separation, child abuse and neglect, family conflict, domestic violence, substance abuse, relocation, and alienation (Table 7.6). They should also be familiar with methods used to evaluate allegations of child abuse and domestic violence, which includes knowledge of research on interviewing children, knowledge of assessment methods, and child and spousal abuse risk assessment. The knowledge base required for work in custody and dependency cases is vast. For more specific information, the reader should consult the respective specialty

TABLE 7.6 **Knowledge of Research for FFP Evaluations**

RESEARCH DOMAIN	REFERENCES
Abusive families	Appel & Holden (1998); Belskey (1993); Belskey, Woodworth, & Crnic (1996); Berrick, Barth, & Gilbert (1997); Bousha & Twentyman (1984); Budd, Poindexter, Felix, & Naik-Polan (2001); Burrell, Thompston, & Sexton (1994); Crittenden (1988); Webster-Stratton & Herbert (1994); Zuravin, McMillen, DePanfilis, & Risley-Curtiss (1996)
Child abuse: assessment of allegations	Bow, Quinnell, Zaroff, & Assemany (2002); Bradley & Wood (1996); DeVoe & Coulborn Faller (1999); Drozd & Olesen (2004); Faller (2005); Johnston, Lee, Olesen, & Walters (2005); Kuehnle & Connell (2008); Kuehnle, Coulter, & Firestone (2000); Kuehnle & Kirkpatrick (2005); Sorensen & Snow (1990); Trocme & Bala (2005)
Child abuse: effects on children	Chaffin, Wherry, & Dykman (1997); Heim, Shugart, Craighead, & Nemeroff (2010); Spaccarelli (2004); Spaccarelli & Fuchs (1997)
Child interviewing	Lamb & Fauchier (2001); Lamb, Sternberg, & Esplin (2000); Lamb, Sternberg, & Esplin (2003); Lamb, Sternberg, Orbach, Esplin, Stewart, & Mitchell (2003); Orbach et al. (2000); Poole & Lamb (1998); Quas, Davis, Goodman, & Myers (2007); Saywitz, Goodman, & Lyon (2002)
Children's memories/testimony	Bjorklund et al. (2000); Bruck & Ceci (2009); Bruck, Ceci, & Francoeur (1999); Ceci, Bruck, & Battin (2000); Ceci (1999); Holliday, Reyna, & Hayes (2002); Krackow & Lynn (2003); London, Bruck, Ceci, & Shuman (2005); Principe & Ceci (2002);
Domestic violence: effects on children	Bancroft & Silverman (2002); Fergusson, Horwood, & Ridder (2005); Geffner, Jaffe, & Sudermann (2000); Graham-Bermann & Edleson (2001); Holden, Geffner, & Jouriles (1998); Johnston & Campbell (1993); Sternberg, Baradaran, Abbott, Lamb, & Guterman (2006a, 2006b)
Domestic violence allegations: evaluation	Austin (2000, 2001); Bow & Boxer (2003); Drozd & Olesen (2004); Drozd, Kuehnle, & Walker (2004); Dutton (2006); Geffner, Conradi, Geis, & Aranda (2009); Jaffe, Crooks, & Bala (2009)
Family dynamics, blended families, extended family relationships	Apel & Kaukinen (2008); Dunn, Davies, O'Connor, & Sturgess (2001); Furstenberg (1990); Jacob (2004); Hetherington (1989, 1999); Portie & Hill (2005); Shermerhorn, Chow, & Cummins (2010)
Interparental conflict: effects on children, adolescents, and adults	Amato (2010; 2006; 2001); Amato, Loomis, & Booth (1995); Ayoub, Deutsch, & Maraganore (1999); Booth & Amato (2001); Buchanan & Waizenhofer (2001); Cox & Brooks-Gunn (1999); Cummings & Davies (1994); Cummings & Merrilees (2010);; Goodman, Barfoot, Frye, & Belli (1999); Grych, Fincham, Jouriles, & McDonald (2000); Johnston & Roseby (1997); Kelly (1993); Kelly & Emery (2003); Roseby & Johnston (1998)

(Continued)

TABLE 7.6 (Continued)

RESEARCH DOMAIN	REFERENCES
Parental alienation: effects on children	Bruch (2001); Faller (1998); Gardner (1992, 2003); Johnston (2003, 2005); Kelly & Johnston (2001)
Parenting	Bornstein (2002a,b); Bornstein & Lansford (2010); Collins, Maccoby, Steinberg, Hetherington, & Bornstein (2000)
Parenting plans	Bauserman (2002); Lamb (2002); Lamb & Kelly (2001); Pruett, Ebling, & Insabella (2004); Wang & Amato (2000); Warshak (2000)
Parenting with mental illness	Cummings & Davies (1999); Kahng, Oyserman, Bybee, & Mowbray (2008); Mowbray, Oyserman, Bybee, & MacFarlane (2002); Ostler (2010); Wan et al (2007)
Postdivorce parenting	Bauserman (2002); Braver & Griffin (2000); Emery, Laumann-Billings, Waldron, Sbarra, & Dillon (2001); Fabricius & Braver (2006); Goodman, Barfoot, Frye, & Belli (2004)
Psychological and developmental needs of children	Bray (1991); Fields & Prinz (1997); Garber (2010); Kelly & Lamb (2000); Lamb (2002); Solomon & Biringern (2001)
Relocation: effects on children	Braver, Ellman, & Fabricius (2003); Fabricius & Hall (2000); Fabricius & Braver (2006); Wallerstein & Tanke (1996)
Separation and divorce: effects on children	Amato (2010; 2006; 2001); Amato, Loomis, & Booth (1995); Amato & Keith (1991); Buchanan (2000); Buchanan, Maccoby, & Dornbusch (1991, 1996); Chase-Lansdale, Cherlin, & Kiernan (1995); Cherlin, et al. (1991); Emery (1999); Fabricius (2003); Gunnoe & Braver (2001); Hetherington, Bridges, & Insabella (1998); Kelly & Emery (2003); Wang & Amato (2000); White & Gilbreth (2001)
Sexual orientation of parents: effects on children	Falk (1989); Farr, Forsell, & Patterson (2010); Fulcher, Sutfin, & Patterson (2008); Goldberg & Smith (2009); Patterson (2009)
Substance abuse: effects on children	Berlin & Davis (1989); Bernardi, Jones, & Tennant (1989); Chassin, Barrera, & Montgomery (1997); Famularo, Kinscherff, & Fenton (1992); Logue & Rivinus (1991); Meyer, McWey, McKendrick, & Henderson (2010); Rivinus (1991);
Visitation	Birnbaum & Alaggia (2006); Garrity & Baris (1994); Gunnoe & Braver (2001); Hauser (2005); Johnston & Roseby, (1997); Stewart (2010)

guidelines for custody and dependency evaluations (APA, 1994, AFCC, 2006; Committee on Professional Practice and Standards, 1999). Table 7.6 provides a sample of research on the expected areas of expertise necessary to competently conduct these evaluations.

Skills

Competency in FFP requires specialists to possess skills that allow them to function effectively in a highly complex adversarial setting. FFP skills cover three broad essential components. First, CFP specialists are able to manage the adversarial nature of the FFP context and are able to practice ethically and professionally in a high-conflict setting. Second, CFP specialists possess skill to consistently generate high-quality work products. To do so, CFP specialists need to be able to establish the parameters of the evaluation as specified by court order, stipulation, or referral request. They are also able to use multiple methods of data collection and have the skill to critically evaluate the data to answer the psycholegal question. Finally, they must be able to clearly communicate the process, reasoning, and findings of the evaluation in the form of a written report and be able to effectively testify to the contents of the report.

MANAGE ADVERSARIAL NATURE OF THE FFP CONTEXT

CFP specialists demonstrate the ability to manage the adversarial nature of the FFP context. Specifically, they are able to use their command of ethics, law, and the specialty guidelines to practice ethically in the FFP environment. They are also able to display continued professional conduct within the adversarial setting of FFP practice. Finally, they are able to establish parameters that will guide the rest of the forensic evaluation.

Ability to Practice Ethically

Because of the high stakes typically involved in most FFP evaluations, there are many partisan pressures that must be managed. Accordingly, CFP specialists demonstrate the ability to practice ethically in the FFP context. CFP specialists organize their practice in the form of written policies or stipulations that specifically articulate expectations regarding role boundaries, confidentiality, ex parte communication, financial arrangements, and evaluation procedures (AFCC, 2006; APA, 2002; Committee on Ethical Issues for Forensic Psychologists, 1991). In addition, they are able to recognize potential ethical conflicts and proactively manage the conflicts by clearly communicating with involved parties their commitment to the Ethics Code. CFP specialists also consult with colleagues and experts in forensic ethics when unusual ethical dilemmas arise. Professional listservs are an excellent way to get timely feedback on difficult ethical issues from some of the nation's top experts. Listservs relevant to FFP practice include those managed by the American Academy of Forensic Psychology (AAFP), AFCC, and the American Psychology-Law Society (APLS).

Professional Conduct

CFP specialists practice in a high-conflict setting where there is much at stake for the participants. Consider the potential consequences of a custody dispute or evaluating a parent's capacity to maintain parental rights. Examinees involved in FFP cases may resort to dramatic behavior, including demands, hostility, deception, or manipulation to ensure the case comes out in their favor. Because of the emotionally charged environment of FFP cases, it is essential for the specialist to maintain the highest levels of professionalism. Lapses in professional demeanor can result in errors of judgment, bias, and inaccuracy. CFP specialitsts should be able to keep calm in the midst of a high-conflict situation and should regularly utilize peer consultation and support to maintain impartiality and equanimity.

Establish Initial Parameters

The initial contacts in an FFP evaluation set the frame for the rest of the evaluation. CFP specialists in FPP demonstrate the ability to clearly establish initial parameters prior to conducting the evaluation (B.1.3). They are able to identify the relevant forensic issues after receiving a referral from a retaining attorney or court. Heilbrun (2001) defines the forensic issue as "the capacities, skills, and functional abilities that are relevant to the broader legal question that a court must decide in a given case" (p. 21). The CFP specialist must be able to clarify the forensic issue before selecting an evaluation strategy. They also recognize the limits of their competence (i.e., evidenced by specialized knowledge, skill, experience, and education; SGFP § III.A) and do not accept referrals that exceed these limits. Accordingly, CFP specialists accurately assess their own abilities and regularly participate in peer review and self-evaluation to ensure that they clearly understand the parameters of their competence. CFP specialists are reasonably able to foresee the complexities of a given case, and if it develops into one that is more complex than initially thought, the specialist seeks professional consultation or supervision. They clearly communicate the purpose and explain the procedures of the examination, convey the limitations to confidentiality, and secure the proper documentation prior to beginning the examination.

SKILL TO CONDUCT A FFP EVALUATION

The hallmark of competency in FFP is the ability to consistently produce high-quality FFP evaluations. This essential component contains two behavioral anchors. First, CFP specialists are able to collect data from multiple sources and using multiple methods. Second, they are able to critically evaluate data that lead to well-reasoned opinions.

Data Collection

CFP specialists in FFP are able to collect data from divergent sources and have the skill to use multiple methods of data collection. They identify important sources of historical records and use the information to cross-check reliability and to guide further inquiry. A related skill is to determine which data are relevant to the forensic question and not include material that has no bearing on the psycholegal issue.

CFP specialists also use diverse data-gathering procedures, including interviews with collaterals, parent-child observations, observer-rated instruments, and formal assessment instruments. They can defend their rationale for selecting an assessment battery and are able to clearly explain the limitations of the assessment instruments. When evaluating psychological and personality functioning, CFP specialists are careful to explain the findings in terms of functional abilities and limitations rather than in diagnostic terms unless a diagnostic label is relevant to the forensic issue (AFCC, 2006 §4.6c).

CFP specialists in FFP are able to accurately interpret nomothetic data and appropriately contextualize the findings in light of the examinee's idiographic data. Data must be considered in light of "other characteristics of the person being assessed, such as situational, personal, linguistic, and cultural differences, that might affect psychologists' judgments or reduce the accuracy of their interpretations" (APA Ethics Code §9.06). Because all case data yielded from evaluation methods must be scrutinized according to evidentiary standards, interpretations of the data do not go beyond the available scientific literature. CFP specialists should be wary of offering interpretations of data that are not scientifically supported unless the interpretation is the result of the analytic method or sound clinical inference. Accordingly, CFP specialists are skilled at linking data to reasoning and reasoning to conclusions. They arrive at firm conclusions only when supported by data and reasoning and do not rely exclusively on a restricted range of data.

CLEAR AND ACCURATE COMMUNICATION

The third essential component of the skill domain is the ability to clearly and accurately communicate findings from the forensic evaluation to the referral source in the form of a written report or oral expert testimony. The CFP specialist demonstrates the ability to answer the psycholegal question and supports the opinion with data-driven and scientifically reasoned explanations. Both the written report and expert testimony should clearly explain psychological concepts to the retaining attorney, court, or other fact finder with as little discipline-specific language as possible (APA Ethics Code §9.10). CFP specialists should indicate when interpretations or opinions are based on scientific research and provide the reference in the report (AFCC, 2006 §4.6b). FFP evaluators should carefully document in their report or professional notes the data used as the basis for an opinion (SGFP §IV.B; §VII E). Heilbrun (2001) highlights the importance of producing a well-organized report, "making it as clear as possible what was done, for what purpose, with what results, and leading to what conclusions" (p. 249). Finally, CFP specialists should describe the limits of the findings in the written report and in expert testimony "with respect to methodology, procedure, data collection, and data interpretation" (AFCC, 2005 §12.4). Heilbrun (2001) notes that the limitations of the findings should be described so that they "need little change under cross-examination" (p. 226).

Attitudes

The work of an FFP evaluator has the ability to cause significant harm if done carelessly. Accordingly, CFP specialists maintain the highest level of ethical commitment and competence (L. Greenberg et al., 2004). In previous chapters we discussed the importance of possessing a client-centered perspective and conducting therapeutic assessment. However, in a forensic context, the evaluator must adopt a "forensic perspective" (L. Greenberg et al., 2004) because the nature of the relationship between the FFP evaluator and client is evaluative and not therapeutic. A forensic perspective recognizes the necessity for accuracy, impartiality, critical evaluation, clearly defined boundaries, careful data collection, and strict adherence to laws, ethical standards, and specialty guidelines. Unlike a therapeutic perspective, a forensic perspective critically evaluates information that is presented by the examinees and cross-checks the validity of the information with third-party sources. The CFP specialist does not assume that the client is being honest and routinely evaluates the response style of the examinee.

FFP evaluators also consider multiple perspectives when interpreting the case data and "differentially test plausible rival hypotheses" (SGFP §IV.C). Like a scientist, they evaluate data with an objective mind-set, are aware of their own biases that might impact the findings, and strive to produce an opinion that is the result of a meticulous process of data collection and critical evaluation. CFP specialists also value honesty and integrity, and accordingly, accurately represent the strengths and weaknesses of their data, methodology, interpretation, and conclusions (AFCC, 2006).

Conclusion

In the last 20 years the quality of FFP specialty practice, training, and research has significantly improved. This chapter has proposed a set of competencies for the specialty practice of FFP organized around knowledge, skills, and attitudes to lay a foundation for further work in competency-based education and training. Because of the wide range of FFP practice, it seems necessary to produce competency benchmarks in major FFP activities to continue to enhance the quality of education, supervised training, and practice.

EIGHT

Supervision Competency in Couple and Family Psychology

Supervision is a core competency in couple and family psychology and one of the primary pedagogies used to train students to become CFP specialists. Supervision was identified as a core competency in professional psychology at the 2002 APPIC Competencies Conference, and a work group was convened to draft a preliminary statement about the supervision competency (Falender et al., 2004). The work group used the following definition of supervision offered by Bernard and Goodyear (2004):

> [Supervision is] an intervention provided by a more senior member of a profession to more junior member or members of that same profession. This relationship is evaluative, extends over time, and has the simultaneous purposes of enhancing the professional functioning of the more junior person(s), monitoring the quality of professional services offered to the client, she, he or they see, and serving as a gatekeeper of those who are to enter the particular profession. (p. 8)

The supervision work group identified the essential elements of the supervision competency across the domains of knowledge, skills, and attitudes (KSAs) and three developmental levels (see Rodolfa et al., 2005). The preliminary draft of the KSAs for the supervision competency in professional psychology was published in a consensus statement by the supervision work group (Falender et al., 2004) and in the *Revised Competency Benchmarks* (Assessment of Benchmark Competencies Workgroup, 2007).

TABLE 8.1 Supervision Competency: Developmental Level—Specialty Competence in Couple and Family Psychology

COMPETENCY DOMAIN AND ESSENTIAL COMPONENT	BEHAVIORAL ANCHOR	ASSESSMENT METHODS
Knowledge (A)		1. ABPP examination
(A.1) Knowledge of supervision in CFP specialty	(A.1.1) Knowledge of systemic concepts and theories applicable to teaching in a supervisory setting.	2. Exemplary work products
	(A.1.2) Knowledge of supervision models, theories, modalities, and research in CFP supervision	3. Self-evaluation
	(A.1.3) Knowledge of theories, research, and methods "to facilitate supervisee developmental progression in psychology competencies	4. Ongoing supervision of supervision and consultation
(A.2) Demonstrates advanced knowledge of CFP competencies	(A.2.1) Knowledge of foundational competencies, including ethics and diversity	5. Peer consultation
	(A.2.2) Knowledge of functional competencies including case conceptualization, assessment, and intervention	6. Continuing education in supervision and other CFP competencies
	(A.2.3) Knowledge of identified developmental markers and competency levels expected of supervisees at specific stages of training	7. Supervisee feedback and evaluation
		8. Publication and presentation in scholarly venues regarding supervision
Skills (B) Provides effective CFP supervision	(B.1.1) Skilled in applying systemic concepts, modalities, and research to teach systemic thinking about CFP practice	
	(B.1.2) Ability to teach CFP competencies in the context of supervision	
(B.1) Application of systemic epistemology to CFP supervision	(B.2.1) Able to form a supervisory alliance and accurately assess supervisee skills, developmental level, and training needs	
(B.2) Ability to facilitate student development through CFP supervision	(B.2.2) Provides effective feedback and monitors progress in a supportive manner	
	(B.2.3) Able to identify and remediate problems of CFP competence	
Attitudes (C) Attitudes necessary for supervision in specialty	(C.1.1) Values self-evaluation and invites peer review and supervisee feedback regarding the supervision experience	
(C.1) Commitment to growth in self and others	(C.1.2) Committed to providing an environment where supervisees can realize their professional and personal potential.	
(C.2) Commitment to professionalism	(C.2.1) Committed to displaying the highest levels of professionalism, including integrity, respect for others, and professional courtesy	
	(C.2.2) Values ethical and legal specialty practice and ensures personal and supervisee compliance with all relevant laws and ethical standards related to supervised experience.	

Note. Adapted from the format and content of the Assessment of Competency Benchmarks Work Group (2007). This table assumes that the specialist has achieved competence in professional psychology at the three previous developmental levels, as specified in the benchmarks. The competency domains and behavioral anchors serve as the primary organizing structure for this chapter; content explaining each domain and anchor is provided in the chapter.

In this chapter we apply the seminal work of Falender et al. (2004) and the Assessment of Competency Benchmarks Workgroup (2007) to the specialty area of CFP supervision. In Table 8.1 we outline the essential components of the CFP supervision competency across the three domains of competency education (KSAs).

Knowledge

In this first section, we propose two essential components of knowledge-based competency. First, CFP specialists demonstrate knowledge of supervision as it is performed across the specialty. Second, CFP specialists demonstrate knowledge of the foundational and functional competencies within the specialty. Supervision is a primary method for transferring information, praxis, and professional values to students and, as such, is a central pedagogy for delivering a competency-based education to trainees.

KNOWLEDGE OF SUPERVISION IN CFP SPECIALTY

CFP specialists demonstrate knowledge of supervision within the CFP specialty. This essential component contains two behavioral anchors. First, CFP supervisors are knowledgeable about the foundational systemic concepts and theories that can be conveyed to supervisees in the context of supervision. Second, CFP specialists are knowledgeable about supervision approaches and modalities applicable to CFP training. Third, CFP specialists understand theory, research, and methods that facilitate supervisee developmental progression in the specialty.

TABLE 8.2 **Systemic Concepts That CFP Supervisees Should Know**

SYSTEM	SUBSYSTEM	STRUCTURE	PROCESS
Organization	Positive feedback	Negative feedback	Circularity
Reciprocity	Closed boundaries	Diffuse boundaries	Open boundaries
Open system	Closed system	Enmeshing	Disengaging
Communication	Balance	Homeostasis	Parentification
Spousal subsystem	Sibling subsystem	Parent-child subsystem	Power
Triangles	Alliances	Intergenerational system	Scapegoating
Coalitions	Family of origin	Internal boundaries	Emotional cutoff
Differentiation	Hierarchy	External boundaries	
Power	Myths	Secrets	
Centripetal	Centrifugal	Complementarity	
Fusion	Vertical loyalties	Horizontal loyalties	

Note. Reprinted by permission from Lee & Everett 2004.

Knowledge of Systemic Concepts and Theories

CFP specialists must have command of the systemic concepts and theories that serve as the foundational lexicon for discussing clinical cases from a systemic perspective. Each psychological specialty has its own technical language for describing human behavior, and for effective systemic supervision to occur, the supervisor and supervisee must speak the same language. Accordingly, CFP supervisors must have a strong working knowledge of the core systemic concepts and theories of couple and family psychotherapy. Relatedly, CFP supervisors understand what these concepts look like in the context of a couple/family case. Lee and Everett (2004) identified the core systemic concepts that all beginning trainees should master (Table 8.2) and CFP supervisors should be able to explain.

Knowledge of Supervision Approaches and Modalities

CFP specialists demonstrate knowledge of diverse supervision approaches and have a clear rationale for applying a particular approach with a supervisee or particular case. Supervision approaches have been arranged into three broad categories: psychotherapy-based, developmental, and process-based (Bernard & Goodyear, 2004; Falender & Shafranske, 2004). We describe each category of supervision model and situate approaches to CFP supervision in each section.

Psychotherapy-Based Approaches.   Psychotherapy-based approaches are characterized by a master therapist teaching an apprentice to practice in the modality of the master therapist (Storm, Todd, Sprenkle, & Morgan, 2001). Supervising from a particular theoretical modality "inform[ed] the observation and selection of clinical data for discussion in supervision as well as the meanings and relevance of those data" (Falender & Shafranske, 2004, p. 9). In CFP, the early approaches to supervision were grounded in family psychotherapies associated with a particular school such as the Mental Research Institute approach. These psychotherapy-based approaches were often seen as "pure" systemic approaches and were taught to students with religious fervor by master clinicians. CFP specialists who supervise from a psychotherapy-based model need to be aware of the limitations of that particular approach to treatment (Breunlin, Rampage, & Eovaldi, 1995). For example, a structural or strategic approach to family therapy may not be appropriate for all types of problems. Moreover, there is no empirical support to suggest that one theoretical model of supervision is better than another (Storm et al., 2001).

Prior to the 1990s, this approach was the dominant method of training supervisees, and it was generally assumed that having obtained the status of master clinician automatically qualified one to supervise a trainee. However, Falender and Shafranske (2004) note that "the aims of supervision are not equivalent to those of psychotherapy, and therefore the approaches and learning strategies used in supervision must be specifically tailored to accomplish the goals of clinical oversight and clinical training" (p. 10).

Gradually, other supervision approaches emerged that were not directly tied to transmission of a specific theoretical model. CFP specialists often supervise from an integrative perspective, which is still model based to some extent; however, an integrative model generally transcends specific schools of family therapy or combines theory from several schools (Lebow, 1997). Integrative models are based on systemic principles and are generally more flexible (Lebow, 2005a). N. J. Kaslow, Celano, and Stanton (2005) recommend that CFP supervisors use an integration of diverse theoretical approaches. Integrative models, in general, can be classified into two types: assimilative and accommodative (Carere-Comes, 2001). Assimilative models of integration are characterized by maintaining fidelity to one preferred theoretical tradition and incorporating other perspectives or techniques into the dominant or preferred model (Fraenkel & Pinsof, 2001). An example of this type of integrative model is Functional Family Therapy (FFT; Alexander & Parsons, 1982). Accommodative integrative models (i.e., technical or theoretical eclecticism) are characterized by a plurality of systemic ideas and techniques that are often applied on the basis of a superordinate framework in which trainees are taught "which theoretical approach to use when and with whom" (N. J. Kaslow et al., 2005, p. 342). The Metaframeworks perspective (Breunlin et al., 1992) is an example of an accommodative integration model. Some authors have also argued that the common factors (see Chapter 5) approach to psychotherapy supervision (Morgan & Sprenkle, 2007) would also fall under the accommodative model (Carere-Comes, 2001).

Developmental Models. The developmental approach to supervision focuses training efforts on a predictable developmental sequence or trajectory that a supervisee possesses at a particular level of training. The Integrated Developmental Model (IDM; Stoltenberg, McNeil, & Delworth, 2009) is the most comprehensive model in this category. Stoltenberg and colleagues describe three levels of supervisee developmental states that are similar to the developmental levels subsequently identified in the Competency Cube Model (Rodolfa et al., 2005). Level 1 supervisees exhibit high anxiety and motivation, focus on the self more than the client, and are fearful of evaluation. Level 2 supervisees experience conflicting roles between autonomy and dependency, fluctuate between confidence and insecurity, and are generally more client oriented than in Level 1. Level 3 supervisees begin to transition to independent practice and are characterized as more confident; they understand strengths and weaknesses, are more comfortable with ambiguity, and know when to seek additional supervision. Numerous developmental models of supervision exist and are nuanced variations of the same theme. Holloway (1995) identified 18 different developmental models. Supervisors and trainees report that these models are helpful conceptually, but they are criticized for being descriptive rather than based on achieving outcomes (Falender & Shafranske, 2004).

Process-Based Approaches.   A process-based approach to supervision is atheoretical and was developed "to provide descriptions of the component roles, tasks, and processes within supervision and as a means to uniformly classify events occurring in supervision" (Falender & Shafranske, 2004, p. 17). A process-based approach is organized around predictable activities that the supervisors perform, and focus on describing what takes place in supervision (Morgan & Sprenkle, 2007). Examples of process-based approaches to supervision include Bernard's (1997) discrimination model; Holloway's (1995) systems approach to supervision (SAS); and Ladany, Friedlander, and Nelson's (2005) critical events approach.

CFP specialists also understand the range of supervision modalities and understand the strengths and weaknesses associated with each modality. Birchler categorized four broad modalities of couple and family psychotherapy supervision: (a) traditional case report and didactic discussion; (b) co-therapy; (c) direct supervision with delayed feedback (e.g., audiotaping, videotaping, and one-way mirror); and (d) direct supervision with instant feedback (e.g., live supervision with methods for communicating feedback instantly, such as "bug in the ear" or computer technology). Traditional case consultation is used with the greatest frequency because of the efficiency and ease of this modality. Supervisees recount the details of previous sessions to the supervisor. However, relying on a supervisee's report of a session is less than optimal because the account of the session(s) may be clouded by the supervisee's inexperience. When possible, CFP specialists are encouraged to use direct methods of supervision, including audio- and videotaped delayed review, co-therapy, and live observation with delayed or immediate feedback. For obvious reasons, direct observation gives the supervisor more accurate information about the supervisee's skills and training needs. Supervisees and supervisors consistently rate direct observation more highly than indirect methods of supervision

(Goodyear & Nelson, 1997; Romans, Boswell, Carlozzi, & Ferguson, 1995). In addition, direct modes of supervision increase client protection, provide the best vicarious learning experience, and increase the possibility of supervisees taking on more difficult cases (Falender & Shafranske, 2004). In addition, the Ethical Guidelines for Counseling Supervisors of the Association for Counselor Education and Supervision (1995), identified audio- and videotaped supervision as the industry standard for supervision (Falender & Shafranske, 2004), presumably because it is the only way to know for sure what happens during a psychotherapy session.

Knowledge That Facilitates Learning Competencies

The second behavioral anchor that CFP specialists must achieve is knowledge of the theory and research that identify factors that facilitate supervisee learning. "[A] supervisor empowers the supervisee to enter the profession by understanding the attitudes, skills, and knowledge demanded of the professional and by guiding the relationship strategically to facilitate the trainee's achievement of a professional standard" (Holloway, 1995, p. 7). CFP specialists are minimally aware of research on developmental theories and trainee needs, and the literature on what makes effective supervision. CFP specialists understand that supervisees progress through a fairly predictable developmental trajectory from novice to expert and at each stage require different strategies of intervention and support (Stoltenberg, McNeil, & Delworth, 2009). Broadly speaking, beginning supervisees are self-focused and concerned with performance, novice supervisees shift their focus toward their client, and advanced trainees are able to balance and integrate the two perspectives (Stoltenberg, 2005). Developmental models have been criticized by systemically oriented authors for lacking adequate empirical support of the developmental stages (Holloway, 1995; Storm et al., 2001); however, there is equally compelling literature to indicate that developmental progression does occur in supervisees (Ellis & Ladany, 1997; Stoltenberg, McNeill, & Crethar, 1994; Worthington, 1987).

CFP specialists are also familiar with the literature on the supervisory alliance and the type of relational climate that supervisees rate as supportive (Ellis & Ladany, 1997; Henderson, Cawyer, & Watkins, 1999). Relatedly, CFP specialists are aware of the literature on behaviors of supervisors that facilitate learning in supervision (Ellis & Ladany, 1997; Worthen & McNeill, 1996; Worthington, 1984). Falender and Shafranske (2004) provide an excellent summary of this literature. CFP specialists should also be aware of the literature that demonstrates how a trainee's supervision experience directly impacts the in-session behavior, including interpersonal skills, attitudes toward the client, and the implementation of treatment (Callahan, Almstrom, Swift, Borja, & Heath, 2009; Holloway & Neufeldt, 1995; Lambert & Arnold, 1987).

Advanced Knowledge of CFP Competencies: Supervision is a prominent pedagogy in CFP training because it provides the opportunity to encounter real-world clinical phenomena. Accordingly, in the context of the supervisory relationship, CFP specialists have the responsibility for conveying the knowledge, skills, and attitudes of the CFP specialty to their supervisees. It follows that knowledge of the foundational and functional competencies of the specialty are essential components for CFP supervision.

Knowledge of Foundational Competencies: CFP specialists have knowledge of the foundational competencies for practice in the specialty. The foundational competencies include reflective practice and self-assessment, scientific knowledge and methods, relationships, ethical and legal standards, individual and cultural diversity (ICD), and interdisciplinary systems (Rodolfa et al., 2005). These competencies have been covered elsewhere in this volume (Chapter 2, Chapter 10, Chapter 11, and Chapter 13); however, we will highlight aspects of the ethical, legal, and ICD competencies as they apply specifically to supervision.

CFP specialists demonstrate command of the ethical literature and laws related to CFP practice and supervision. In Chapter 10 we describe the KSAs related to the ethical and legal competency for CFP specialty practice. CFP specialists are knowledgeable of the American Psychological Association Ethical Principles of Psychologists and Code of Conduct (Ethics Code; APA, 2002), specialty guidelines, attendant ethical literature, and laws related to CFP practice and are able to apply the ethical and legal sources of authority to supervised CFP practice. CFP supervisors are knowledgeable about ethical issues related to supervision. Specifically, CFP specialists should ensure that they are competent to supervise in the area of CFP service conducted by the supervisee (Ethics Code §2.01(a)), which includes assessment, diagnosis, intervention techniques and theoretical orientations, and working with unique populations (Vasquez, 1992). Relatedly, supervisees should not be given clinical tasks that exceed their level of training (§2.05). This can be accomplished by accurately assessing supervisee abilities (Tanenbaum & Berman, 1990).

Supervisees occupy a vulnerable position in the supervisory relationship; accordingly, CFP specialists should be mindful of the power differential and handle the emotionally sensitive information that naturally arises during the course of supervision with a "special duty of care" (Koocher & Keith-Spiegel, 2008, p. 358). Historically, supervisors sometimes blurred the lines between encouraging supervisee self-awareness of personal factors that might interfere with treatment and encouraging inappropriate self-disclosure. CFP specialists are aware that they do not elicit deeply personal information from supervisees (e.g., sexual history, abuse history) without clearly disclosing this expectation prior to entering the supervisory relationship (§7.04). Given the emphasis on family-of-origin work in the specialty, some supervisors will have their trainees complete a personal genogram as part of the supervision. Although this can be a powerful training experience, supervisees need to be informed of this expectation prior to commencing supervision. We are aware of one postdoctoral CFP fellowship that notifies prospective trainees that it uses in-depth genogram work as part of the supervision process. This site uses adjunct faculty members, who do not have supervisory or evaluative responsibility, to protect the supervisee's private information and avoid potential misuse of power in the supervisory/evaluative relationship (N. J. Kaslow et al., 2005).

As discussed in Chapter 11 ("Diversity Competency"), supervision is a multicultural process (APA, 2003a). Supervision is a prominent modality for teaching the ICD competency. CFP supervisors are knowledgeable about the major sources of ICD literature, including the Guidelines on Multicultural Education, Training, Research, Practice, and Organizational Change for Psychologists (APA, 2003a); the Guidelines for Psychotherapy with Lesbian, Gay, and Bisexual Clients (APA, 2000a); the Guidelines for Psychological Practice with Older Adults (APA, 2003b); and the Guidelines for Providers of Psychological Services to Ethnic, Linguistic, and Culturally Diverse Populations (APA, 1990). In addition, they are knowledgeable about the factors that contribute to individual and societal perceptions about individual and cultural diversity factors in others. They are mindful that their perceptions might differ from those with whom they work. CFP specialists are knowledgeable about ICD elements in couples and families, including normal family cultural patterns, worldviews and values, and macrosystemic factors. CFP specialists also understand the factors that contribute to intraindividual variations between family members and their contexts, including identity models, acculturation difference, and multiple identities. Finally, the CFP specialist is knowledgeable about the major theoretical contributions for providing CFP clinical services to multicultural populations (see Chapter 11 for a review of these contributions). CFP specialists are also knowledgeable about potential iatrogenic effects of strategies and techniques employed in the course of treatment.

Knowledge of Functional Competencies: CFP specialists also are knowledgeable about the functional competencies. They specifically understand the knowledge base required for the case conceptualization, assessment, and intervention competencies, since they are the primary focus of service delivery. CFP specialists should also be knowledgeable about, and address the research, consultation, and management competencies when they arise during the course of supervision.

CFP specialists are knowledgeable about case conceptualization (see Chapter 3). Specifically, they understand the concept, purpose, and components of case conceptualization for the purposes of teaching trainees to frame cases within a systemic paradigm. CFP specialists understand that case conceptualization includes developing a problem formulation, case formulation, and treatment formulation and understand the steps at each stage of case conceptualization. CFP specialists are knowledgeable about the skills necessary for arriving at a problem formulation and have a strong working knowledge of individual and relational diagnosis. In addition, CFP specialists understand what skills are necessary for organizing and explaining data from a systemic perspective. Finally CFP specialists are knowledgeable about selecting interventions and the elements contained in a treatment formulation. CFP specialists also understand the assessment competency and the attendant KSAs (see Chapter 4). Specifically, they understand how to apply a systemic paradigm and are familiar with the differences between individual and CFP assessment. They understand the range of CFP assessment methods and are knowledgeable about the appropriate uses and misuses of CFP instruments. They also have a basic knowledge of psychometrics and the statistical foundations of common CFP assessment instruments. CFP specialists also understand the strengths and weaknesses of using CFP assessment methods in diverse contexts. Finally, CFP specialists are knowledgeable about the KSAs of the intervention competency (see Chapter 5). They understand the importance of developing a therapeutic alliance and joining with a couple/family in the intervention (see Chapter 12). CFP specialists are aware of the range of available interventions and are able to contextualize technique within a particular theory. They are also familiar with the CFP evidenced-based treatments and are knowledgeable about the research literature associated with a range of interventions appropriate to their scope of practice.

Knowledge of Developmental Markers: The ability to supervise in the CFP specialty requires the specialist to determine which knowledge, skills, and attitudes the trainee needs at the culmination of the supervision experience or training program and then is able to develop a supervision plan for how to bring the supervisee to the desired outcome. Developmental markers across various levels of training have been developed for the practice of professional psychology by two groups. First, the Assessment of Competency Benchmarks Workgroup produced a series of developmentally sensitive competency benchmarks organized around the "competency cube" (Rodolfa et al., 2005), from which the current volume on CFP specialty practice draws much of its material. Second, the National Council of Schools and Programs in Professional Psychology (NCSPP) produced a similar competencies model called the Developmental Achievement Levels (DALs; NCSPP, 2007). Both of these competency models provide competency outcomes at three different developmental levels (practicum; internship; entry-level practice). To date, no similar developmental levels have been proposed for specialty competencies. In light of the absence of any graduated developmental criterion-based outcomes for the CFP specialty, it is recommended that supervisors create competencies that fit the needs of the training environment and are based on one of the two competency models previously listed in combination with information contained in this volume.

Skills

The skills required to competently supervise in the specialty are varied and complex. As previously mentioned, the skills required to supervise are different than those required to provide clinical services. Rarely are these skills acquired in graduate training, internship, and postdoctoral training. Falender and Schafranske (2004) note:

> The technical competency required for being a supervisor is multifaceted, as it encompasses skills in multiple clinical areas, and depth in several of these areas. These skills include general experience in supervision; education and skills in the diversity components of the population of the trainee and the client; competence in a whole domain of supervision skills including trainee assessment, educational planning and intervention, laws and ethics, and evaluation; and facility in establishing the supervisory alliance. (p. 73)

The skills necessary for supervision in the CFP specialty require a special set of abilities. First, the supervisor works with the trainee to learn to think in a new way about human behavior. Second, the supervisor attends to several generations of client behavior and multiple therapist-client sub-systems. Third, the supervisor helps a novice trainee manage the often highly volatile clinical activity that occurs in a couple/family session. We have identified two essential components that broadly capture these skills. First, CFP specialists are able to apply a systemic paradigm to the process of supervision. Second, CFP specialists are able to facilitate trainee learning in the specialty.

APPLICATION OF SYSTEMIC EPISTEMOLOGY

The centerpiece of the CFP specialty is applying a systemic epistemology to all clinical activities. In kind, the central goal of the CFP supervisor is to teach students/supervisees to think recursively about clinical phenomena and to teach the CFP competencies. In Chapter 9 we extensively cover the CFP teaching competency; thus, here we focus our discussion on the skills required for training in the context of supervision. This essential component contains two behavioral anchors. First, CFP supervisors teach systemic thinking to trainees. Second, CFP specialists teach foundational and functional competencies in the context of the supervision relationship.

Teach Systemic Thinking

Lee and Everett (2004) articulated an integrative model for teaching supervisees to think systemically. The model is graduated in complexity and organized across three levels of teaching/supervision. We recommend that CFP supervisors use this or a similar model to structure the supervision goals. Each of the goals is easily operationalized and measurable. Lee and Everett's integrative supervision model has the following goals: (a) deepen trainees' basic understanding of systems theory; (b) ensure that trainees have a basic knowledge in family systems theory in order to apply it to live case situations; (c) increase trainees' sensitivity to recognize systemic principles in clinical families; (d) help trainees use systemic data to formulate assessments of families; (e) assist trainees to integrate theoretical and assessment data in order to select appropriate clinical interventions; and (f) help trainees reflect on their successes and failures to help them develop confidence to take a different approach in light of failed interventions.

Lee and Everett (2004) provide a framework for conducting systemic supervision from an integrative perspective organized within a three-level process-based approach. The first level of trainee supervision involves ensuring that trainees have a solid grasp of basic systems theory and concepts. During this phase of training, the supervision is heavily didactic, with frequent assigned readings. CFP trainees in the early stage of development need to acquire a basic systemic vocabulary before more advanced training can occur. Table 8.2 lists common systemic concepts that trainees should master. More important, trainees need to move beyond knowledge of concepts to the inculcation of systemic thinking habits (see Chapter 2). Providing supervision at this level requires supervisors to draw on the teaching competency. CFP specialists review systemic concepts and theory with the trainee and give examples so that the trainee can recognize systemic concepts in case material.

The goal of Level 2 training is to integrate systemic concepts with live clinical assessment. During this stage of training supervisees are taught to recognize systemic concepts in the clinical data of their couple/family cases. Trainees are taught to recognize family structure (subsystems, boundaries, triangles), individual and family symptomatology and the interaction between these symptoms and family functioning, family life cycle events, macrosystemic factors, and intergenerational influences graphically represented in a genogram (Lee and Everett, 2004). CFP supervisors must be able to help the supervisee recognize patterns, identify systemic concepts in the case information, and model systemic case formulation. Perhaps most important, CFP supervisors help supervisees identify family strengths with less emphasis on pathology. The ability to think systemically about assessment is a crucial outcome competency for this level (see Chapter 2).

The final stage of supervision, Level 3, teaches the supervisee to integrate theory and assessment with the selection of interventions. The supervisee is taught to organize the data into meaningful patterns and select interventions that target the most pressing couple/family need (Breunlin, Karrer, McGuire, & Cimmarusti, 1988; Lee and Everett, 2004). Once interventions have been selected, the CFP supervisor is able to explain the intervention or model it through role-playing or co-therapy. For supervisees without much experience with couple/family psychotherapy, it is advised that supervisors judiciously select cases for the trainee that are developmentally appropriate to the supervisee's level of training and experience. During subsequent supervision sessions, the CFP specialist regularly reviews cases and frequently uses direct methods of supervision (audio- and videotaping, live observation, and co-therapy).

Teach CFP Competencies

CFP specialists demonstrate the ability to teach and model the CFP specialty competencies in the context of supervision. In this section we will briefly review the skills necessary to teach the foundational ethical and diversity competencies and the functional conceptualization, assessment, and intervention competencies. Supervision affords the opportunity to teach ethical CFP practice to trainees and to inculcate the value of habitual ethical reasoning and decision making in the supervisee. Working with couples/families presents unique ethical challenges that are part of every case. CFP specialists should be able to explain the ethical expectations about working with couples and families such as issues related to identifying the client, informed consent, confidentiality, change of format (Gottlieb, 1995), and other ethical challenges that are involved in multi-person therapies (see Chapter 10). They are able to consider ethical conflicts and dilemmas by articulating a decision-making model and working through the ethical conflict in the presence of the supervisee. They are also able to foresee ethical problems and teach the supervisee indicators of possible ethical conflicts before they emerge. In addition, working with couples and families provides the opportunity to consider ethical issues related to family life such as divorce, custody, domestic violence, and end-of-life decisions (N. J. Kaslow et al., 2005).

CFP specialists also model a culture-centered supervision perspective and incorporate diversity factors into all aspects of the supervision. CFP specialists are able to teach trainees how to develop a therapeutic alliance with diverse families and alert the trainee to differences in communication styles, the difference between establishing respect versus rapport, and acknowledging culturally embedded family values (e.g., hierarchy, worldview, religious beliefs). CFP supervisors are aware of the moderator variables (e.g., acculturation; proficiency in English) that may contribute to misinterpretations and misunderstandings during the assessment process (Dana, 2005); accordingly, they have the responsibility to teach supervisees to habitually consider these variables. CFP specialists should also convey to supervisees the importance of considering contextual factors when interpreting clients' problems. For example, the effects of racism and poverty should be considered before case formulation occurs.

CFP specialists are able to recognize and address issues of individual diversity in the supervisor-supervisee relationship. CFP specialists can model a culturally centered perspective by discussing multicultural issues between the supervisor and supervisee. The supervisor's comfort with discussing ICD factors in the supervisory relationship can help the supervisee become more comfortable with these discussions.

FACILITATE STUDENT SKILL DEVELOPMENT IN CFP

The second essential component of the skills domain is the ability to facilitate skill development in the trainee. This essential component has three behavioral anchors. First, CFP specialists are able to establish a productive supervisory alliance and conduct an accurate skills assessment. Second, CFP specialists regularly monitor progress and provide formative feedback to the supervisee. Finally, CFP supervisors are able to identify and develop a remediation plan for improving skills deficits.

Supervisory Alliance and Skill Assessment

As previously noted under the knowledge domain, research on supervision practices has identified characteristics of effective supervisors. After reviewing the available research on supervision, Falender and Shafranske (2004) provided a list of important skills that competent supervisors possess. Accordingly, CFP specialists are able to form a strong supervisory alliance with supervisees, they are adaptable and flexible, and they demonstrate openness to the process of self-evaluation and avail themselves to evaluation by supervisees and peers (Falender & Shafranske, 2004). CFP supervisors are also able to enhance the self-confidence of the trainee through providing support, appropriate autonomy, and encouragement. They are able to model equanimity, calmness, and humor in the face of challenge and crisis, and to model appropriate self-reflection and self-disclosure.

CFP specialists are capable of accurately assessing the supervisee's developmental level (Stoltenberg, McNeil & Delworth, 2009) and areas of professional strength and weakness, and are able to target and articulate training needs and goals appropriate to the training setting. Falender and Shafranske (2004) recommend constructing a self-report measure that operationalizes the competencies that will be evaluated during the training experience. The supervisor and supervisee collaboratively identify the training goals and complete the criteria for a self-report measure at the beginning of training. We also recommend that supervisors directly observe their supervisee in order to corroborate the trainee's self-report. Following the assessment, CFP specialists collaboratively set training goals with the supervisee and clearly establish a supervision contract that is developmentally appropriate, outcome driven, and measurable. As training commences, both the supervisor and the supervisee should be clear about the competency expectations for training.

Feedback and Monitoring

CFP specialists provide regular formative feedback in light of the supervision plan established at the beginning of training. CFP specialists demonstrate excellent communication abilities, give feedback in a frequent and constructive manner, and balance evaluation with support. CFP specialists are able to foresee potential conflicts or areas of discomfort (Falender & Shafranske, 2004) and are skilled at introducing these issues with the supervisee in a manner that encourages openness and nondefensive reflection and invites productive dialogue. CFP specialists are knowledgeable about and use multiple formats of supervision modalities. Given the benefits of direct supervision, CFP supervisors should, when possible, provide feedback on information that was obtained through direct methods of observation (e.g., audio- and videotaping, live supervision, co-therapy). In addition to providing regular informal verbal feedback about the supervisee's progress toward achieving the minimal competency benchmarks, the CFP supervisor should provide regular formal written formative feedback. If there are serious problems of competence, the CFP supervisor should initiate a written remediation plan as early as is feasible.

Identify and Remediate Problems of CFP Competence

In an ideal world, all trainees would be able to satisfactorily meet the competency benchmarks laid out at the beginning of the training relationship. Unfortunately, this is not always the case, and some trainees fail to achieve minimal levels of competence. Problems of competence occur at all levels of training and must be remediated before the supervisee advances to higher levels of training and eventual independence. Kaslow and colleagues (2007) articulated eight recommendations for assessing and remediating problems of competence. We have compiled these recommendations in

TABLE 8.3 **Eight Recommendations for Recognizing, Assessing, and Intervening With Problems of Professional Competence**

1. When assessing competence problems, define key terms, establish benchmarks for performance, and develop a categorization schema.
2. When assessing competence problems, prepare the system so that policies are in place that permit decision makers to undertake assessment processes and make and communicate assessment decisions.
3. When assessing competence problems, evaluate and, when necessary, bolster self-assessment capacity for learning and responding to feedback for the purpose of identifying and addressing competence challenges and preventing competence problems.
4. When assessing competence problems, remediation strategies for enhancing performance should be based upon a systematic evaluation that is balanced in terms of reliability and fidelity and designed to maximize learning, expand on self-assessment capacity, and utilize gatekeeping functions when indicated.
5. When assessing competence problems, consider the impact of beliefs, values, and attitudes about individual and cultural differences on decisions regarding problem identification, assessment, and intervention.
6. When assessing competence problems, communicate across levels of training, professional organizations, and credentialing boards as appropriate.
7. When assessing competence problems, maximize transparency through the identification and communication of limitations to the individual's rights to privacy and confidentiality.
8. When assessing competence problems, ethical, regulatory, and legal implications must be considered.

Note. Adapted from Kaslow et al. (2007).

Table 8.3; however, this article should be required reading for all supervisors and supervisors in training.

When assessing and evaluating problems of competence, the "law of no surprises" reigns supreme. As previously mentioned, full disclosure at the beginning of the supervisory experience is required. If serious problems exist, a remediation plan should be initiated following a systematic evaluation. The remediation plan clearly identifies the competency deficit, provides the program expectation, outlines training methods to achieve the expectation, explains the performance indicator, and describes the assessment methods and time line (N. J. Kaslow et al., 2007).

Attitudes

CFP supervisors play a pivotal role in the lives of trainees and should take this responsibility seriously. A positive supervision experience can literally change the course of a student's career. Supervisors have multiple roles, including teacher, mentor, coach, and evaluator. As such, they are in a unique position to convey the attitudes of the CFP specialty. Supervisors socialize CFP trainees into the specialty by the way they conduct themselves personally and professionally. There are two broad essential attitudes that CFP supervisors possess. First, they value and are committed to personal and professional growth in self and others. Second, CFP supervisors value and are committed to the highest level of professionalism.

COMMITMENT TO GROWTH IN SELF AND OTHERS

CFP supervisors are committed to lifelong professional and personal growth in themselves and encourage and facilitate this in those whom they supervise. CFP supervisors demonstrate openness by valuing self-evaluation and regularly inviting peer review and supervisee feedback regarding the supervision experience. By modeling an attitude of openness to personal and professional growth, supervisees are also encouraged to nondefensively evaluate their own professional competence. CFP specialists are also committed to providing an environment where supervisees can realize their professional and personal potential. Schon (1983) states that "learning all forms of professional artistry depends, at least in part, on…freedom to learn by doing in a setting relatively low in risk, with access to coaches who initiate students into the 'traditions of the calling' and help them, by 'the right kind of telling' to see on their own behalf and in their own way what they need most to see" (p. 17, cited in Holloway, 1995, p. 2).

COMMITMENT TO PROFESSIONALISM

CFP specialists are committed to ever-increasing levels of professionalism, including honesty, integrity, respect for others, cooperation, and professional courtesy. Professionalism is communicated by attention to the routine aspects of life as a psychologist. For example, CFP supervisors model respectful dialogue and cooperation with colleagues and supervisees, discuss client difficulties with respect and compassion, and model reliable fidelity to significant, as well as insignificant, tasks. CFP supervisors also value ethical and legal specialty practice and ensure personal and supervisee compliance with all relevant laws and ethical standards related to supervised experience. CFP supervisors routinely discuss ethical and legal matters in daily CFP practice.

Conclusion

In this chapter we have articulated and discussed the knowledge, skills, and attitudes of the CFP supervision competency. We highlighted the important role that CFP supervisors play in training supervisees in foundational and functional CFP competencies and described the knowledge base that the specialist should possess. We also described the skills that CFP supervisors need to teach in order for trainees to learn how to think systemically and improve their abilities in CFP practice. Finally, we explained how the role of CFP supervisor is a powerful way to convey important attitudes needed in the specialty.

NINE

Teaching Competency in Couple and Family Psychology

The continuation and expansion of the specialty of couple and family psychology depend on the ability of CFP specialists to educate psychology students in elements of the specialty knowledge, skills, and attitudes across the specialty competencies. This chapter focuses on higher education (undergraduate to postdoctoral, including professional continuing education) teaching in the specialty field. We describe the knowledge, skills, and attitudes needed to function effectively as an educator (Table 9.1). In addition, we address specialty psychoeducation to client populations as a component of this competency. The relevant sections of this chapter describe the content underlying the table items.

Knowledge for Teaching CFP

Effective CFP instruction requires the demonstration of an acquired foundation of knowledge regarding the theoretical and applied methods of teaching a systemic epistemology, an advanced level of scientific knowledge in the specialty, knowledge of specialty curriculum design and teaching methods and advanced understanding of the CFP competencies and intervention models.

THEORETICAL AND APPLIED METHODS FOR TEACHING A SYSTEMIC EPISTEMOLOGY

There is limited research on teaching a systemic epistemology or systems thinking in higher education. We know that systems theory and systemic concepts are often taught in undergraduate and graduate CFP courses (e.g.,

TABLE 9.1 Teaching: Developmental Leve —Specialty Competence in Couple and Family Psychology

COMPETENCY DOMAIN AND ESSENTIAL COMPONENT	BEHAVIORAL ANCHOR	ASSESSMENT METHODS
Knowledge		1. ABPP examination
(A) Knowledge of teaching-learning in CFP	(A.1.1) Understands theoretical and applied methods of teaching a systemic epistemology, including critiques and variations on a systemic orientation;	2. Ongoing status for practice through licensure
(A.1) Knowledge of teaching-learning theory, methodology, and assessment in the specialty	(A.1.2) Demonstrates advanced level of scientific knowledge and current evidence-based models of CFP as a foundation for teaching others	3. Evaluation of critical systemic thinking
		4. Comprehensive evaluation of teaching for full-time faculty
	(A.1.3) Demonstrates advanced level of knowledge of specialty curriculum	5. Student/client feedback and evaluations
	(A.1.4) Demonstrates advanced level of understanding of CFP competencies	6. Peer teacher observation, consultation, or review
		7. Self-evaluation
Skills		8. Consultation or supervisory feedback
(B) Education ability	(B.1.1) Ability to facilitate understanding and adoption of a systemic orientation and specialty scientific methods	9. Publication and presentation in peer-reviewed venues
(B.1) Understanding, implementation, and evaluation of teaching-learning methodologies	(B.1.2) Ability to conceptualize and/or create comprehensive specialty curriculum	10. Completion of continuing education in specialty research and teaching methods and practices
	(B.1.3) Ability to develop a course in a specialty content area that reflects current specialty research and methods and fits within a comprehensive CFP curriculum	
	(B.1.4) Ability to apply teaching-learning methods appropriate to the specialty in instructional venues	
	(B.1.5) Ability to teach specialty content in professional and applied publications and presentations	
Attitudes		
(C) Values lifelong learning and teaching	(C.1.1) Independently identifies, reviews, and incorporates new specialty research and literature into teaching	
(C.1) Independently values ongoing learning and quality instruction of others	(C.1.2) Conducts self-evaluation and invites peer review and student feedback regarding the teaching-learning experience	

Note. Adapted from the format and content of the Assessment of Competency Benchmarks Work Group (2007). This table assumes that the specialist has achieved competence in professional psychology at the three previous developmental levels, as specified in the benchmarks. The competency domains and behavioral anchors serve as the primary organizing structure for this chapter; content explaining each domain and anchor is provided in the chapter.

family development, couples therapy, family psychology; Stanton, Harway, & Vetere, 2009). Professional psychology programs vary in their inclusion of CFP-related courses and may be divided into those that offer only one or two CFP courses, often as electives, those that provide a track (three to four courses, often elective), and those that provide a prespecialty emphasis of several courses and clinical training in CFP (Stanton, Harway, & Eaton, 2006). The APA Commission for the Recognition of Specialties and Proficiencies in Professional Psychology (CRSPPP) has recently posited four categories of specialty education: (a) exposure (one to two courses); (b) experience (one to two courses and practicum in the specialty); (c) emphasis (four courses and two practica in the specialty); and (d) major area of study (2 to 3 years of didactic education, supervised experience, and research or dissertation in the specialty (Massoth, Rozensky, Kelly, Carlson, & Rehm, 2009). Individuals who did not receive education in systems theory within their doctoral program in psychology usually secure it in predoctoral internships, postdoctoral residencies, or postdoctoral institutes en route to identification as a CFP specialist (Stanton & Nurse, 2005; see Chapter 14). Peterson (1996) conducted a study comparing practitioners who graduated 3 to 10 years previously from one of two programs (one with a strong systems orientation, the other without) regarding their ability to think systemically when presented with a videotaped family treatment session using the Family Therapy Assessment Exercise (Breunlin, Schwartz, Krause, & Selby, 1983). He found that systemic education predicted systemic thinking ability. However, no sophisticated models exist today to evaluate psychology education and training effectiveness in achieving increased systemic thinking or a systemic epistemology.

The research that is available focuses primarily on K-12 education in systems thinking; however, it is conceptually precise (i.e., it zeroes in on key concepts that apply across systems) and may extend to higher education applications in preparing psychologists. Research is needed to substantiate such extension, but the fact that teachers have been included in some of the K-12 education studies provides an initial foundation for extension of the research models (Sweeney & Sterman, 2003, 2007). One of the key findings of this research is that some children are capable of equivalent or more advanced systemic conceptualization than their teachers, suggesting that age and education are not the necessary correlates of developing systems thinking (Sweeney & Sterman, 2007). Some suggest that a Cartesian-based education system may actually stunt the natural inclination to think systemically (Sweeney & Sterman, 2007). In fact,

> The limits of traditional age-appropriate instruction have been challenged and replaced with a new view of what is developmentally

appropriate. Students actively depict and analyze trends, connect existing knowledge to novel settings and consider other points of view in addition to their own perspectives. (Benson, 2007, p. 3)

Such achievements challenge beliefs about learning capabilities and have encouraged a number of K-12 school-based initiatives around systems thinking in order to prepare what Richmond (2000) called *systems citizens*, those who "view themselves as members of a global community. They understand the complexities of today's worldly systems and have the capability to face into problems with knowledge and skill" (Benson, 2007, p. 5). This outcome ability to understand and address life problems is parallel to that needed for effective CFP practice.

An assertion by Benson (2007) regarding K-12 education is equally applicable to higher education: "The challenge facing educators is not only to develop ways to teach these skills, but also to measure the impact of such courses on students' ability to think dynamically and systemically" (p. 2). Sweeney and Sterman (2003, 2007) developed an inventory of brief tasks created to assess specific systemic concepts (e.g., systemic feedback processes and complexity; homological reasoning; underlying dynamics; complex policy thinking; see below for details) in order to ascertain how people learn systems thinking, what skills are needed, which concepts may be learned readily, and which are more difficult to comprehend. For example, they designed several social and natural system scenarios that were intended to raise thoughts about complex cause-and-effect interactions (e.g., hunger and eating; births and population growth; teacher perception and student achievement or self-esteem [2007, p. 289]). They found that participants rarely recognize feedback processes related to complexity when it is presented in situations (e.g., the positive feedback loop between teacher expectations and student achievement), and most participants did not extend beyond the boundaries of the immediate scenario to include other factors not directly mentioned (e.g., availability of food as a factor in hunger and eating; this is an ability important to systems thinking). In the homology queries (i.e., "How might this scenario be similar to another scenario in a different setting?" [p. 290]), participants focused on power, affect, and categorization issues that are more concrete and direct (e.g., power: "They're the same because they both have someone telling you what to do," or taxonomic: "They are both mammals"; Sweeney & Sterman, 2007, p. 294) rather than seeing complex feedback structures. Related to time dimensions, they found that most participants did not volunteer time perspectives in situations created to evoke that factor in systemic analysis (e.g., the time delay in feeling full after eating). Related to stock and flow (the dynamic interaction between rates of inflow-outflow and change in stock, such as the idea that the amount of money in the bank is related to the amount deposited and amount withdrawn), they found that recognition and understanding of these dynamics is poor, with participants not considering all factors or making naive assumptions about rates. Participants were better at recognizing differences in feedback structures when presented with diagrams that represented structures drawn from the interview scenarios, perhaps due to learning from the earlier feedback process section, or they benefited from the use of diagrams. Homologous reasoning (i.e., recognition of similar underlying structures despite different surface characteristics) was more apparent within domains but less apparent for distinct domains (e.g., many could extend an understanding of the wolves-rabbits predator-prey interaction to human overfishing that may result in extinction of the fish and less food for humans, but not to a nonanimal situation). Of course, this ability is central to the ability to make sense of complex phenomena and extend solutions across domains. Finally, when asked about complex issues that impact policy decisions (e.g., adding a highway lane to reduce traffic), many participants noted some unanticipated consequences, and some suggested meaningful solutions. Overall, the measure demonstrated its utility in assessing systemic thinking and may serve as a model for conceptualizing and developing measures at the higher education level in psychology.

The remaining literature on teaching methods is primarily theoretical and anecdotal. Benson (2007) reflects on her work to build systems thinking capacity and suggests:

> Borrowing from learning theories that reinforce the importance of learning styles, experiential learning, and multiple intelligences, systems thinking training is most effective when visual, linguistic, and kinesthetic modalities are utilized....The ability to express complex thinking, insights, and new ideas orally and in writing is integral to systems thinking learning. Speaking and listening skills include dialogue, discussion, inquiry and advocacy. (p. 4)

Sweeney (n.d.) notes three "core learning capabilities" (Understanding Living Systems, Making Systems Visible, and Talking About Systems) and the need to activate them in the teaching-learning process. Lucas and Bernstein (2005) provide an overview of basic principles for teaching psychology, practical suggestions about course and syllabus development, pragmatics of class management, options related to teaching style, learning evaluation methods, management of student-faculty interaction, the use of technology, and the evaluation of teaching. These general ideas provide a foundation for more specific specialty teaching.

SCIENTIFIC KNOWLEDGE AND EVIDENCE-BASED PRACTICE

In order to teach effectively, the CFP educator must understand the theory and the science of family psychology, including its research methodology. As Snyder and Kazak (2005) note, "The science of family psychology— ranging from acquiring understanding of basic developmental processes within the family milieu to developing and testing interventions with various family systems across the range of cultural contexts—comprises a particularly diverse discipline" (p. 3). The CFP educator needs to fully understand the primary theories and research methods in order to base instruction on those theories and methods, as well as to explain them to students. Most education in research and research about research education has focused on research as a contribution to knowledge (Bieschke, 2006). More emphasis is needed on the application of research to practice. Halonen, Bosack, Clay, and McCarthy (2003) propose eight domains of scientific inquiry (descriptive skills; conceptualization skills; problem-solving skills; ethical reasoning; scientific values and attitudes; communication skills; collaboration skills; and self-assessment) and delineate developmental proficiency levels in these domains at the advanced undergraduate and professional graduate levels and beyond. CFP educators may adopt this broad rubric and its focus on proficiencies to assess student proficiency and inform educational offerings. Eisler and Dare (1992) suggest that a prominent place must be given in our graduate education programs to teaching research in a manner that enables students to fully comprehend that research and treatment are not two disparate disciplines; they are integrally interactive. Black and Lebow (2009) echo this theme and provide a rationale for a both/and approach. L. W. Green (2008) suggests that the typical recommendation that improving communication of evidence-based practices to clinicians is shortsighted and will not solve the problem. He provides a more systemic analysis of the research pipeline and recommends more practice-based approaches to research in order to increase relevance to clinicians. CFP educators may engage students in clinical research in order to establish this foundation. Silverstein and Auerbach (2009) and Levant (2004) argue that qualitative research, in particular, is useful to link research and practice and to ensure that evidence-based practices are culturally competent. Liddle (2003) challenges graduate programs and CFP faculty to determine the value they will place on education in the interaction between research and practice, arguing for a comprehensive curriculum in the area. For a review of CFP theory and scientific methods, see Chapter 2 of this volume, the 2005 special issue of the *Journal of Family Psychology* on methodology in family science (Snyder & Kazak, 2005), the *Wiley-Blackwell Handbook of Family Psychology* (Bray & Stanton, 2009), and *Family Psychology: Science-Based Interventions* (Liddle, Santisteban, Levant, & Bray, 2002).

In a similar fashion, the CFP educator needs advanced knowledge of the evidence-based practices in the specialty (see Chapter 5). This includes understanding a conceptual model of evidence-based practice that delineates the levels of evidence to support an intervention (Sexton & Coop-Gordon, 2009), as well as the scope of evidence-based models in the specialty (Bray & Stanton, 2009; Liddle et al., 2002) and interventions for particular population issues (Lebow, 2005b). Because there is clear evidence for the role of the therapeutic relationship in CFP interventions (see Chapter 13) and for process feedback mechanisms that inform treatment using clinical evidence (Friedlander, Escudero, & Heatherington, 2006; Pinsof & Chambers, 2009), they should be part of the CFP educator's knowledge base, as well. Stanton (2005b) notes that "family psychology intervention science is one current trend that needs to be further inculcated into graduate education in family psychology (p. 12). CFP educators must commit to provide current information on effective interventions.

KNOWLEDGE OF SPECIALTY CURRICULUM

CFP educators remain current in the literature on specialty education. Recent CFP education articles or chapters have been published in a variety of venues, including *Professional Psychology: Research and Practice* (Nutt & Stanton, 2008), *Family Process* (N. J. Kaslow et al., 2005), the *Wiley-Blackwell Handbook of Family Psychology* (Stanton et al., 2009), and *The Family Psychologist* (TFP). In fact, TFP has been the predominant venue recently for professional dialogue regarding the enhancement of education and training in the specialty. Specialty education has been featured in several issues over the last 5 years, and there is a regular column on CFP education. However, one limitation of the articles in TFP is that they are not listed in PsycINFO, the primary APA database; however, they are available as full-text versions in PsycEXTRA, the APA gray database, and the Society of Family Psychology maintains an archive of issues dating back to 2002 on its website. General articles on education in professional psychology are available in *Training and Education in Professional Psychology* and *Teaching of Psychology,* the APA Society for the Teaching of Psychology publication.

The CFP educator knows the national models for specialty education, including the Recommendations for Doctoral Education and Training in Family Psychology (Stanton & Harway, 2007). These recommendations provide a framework for doctoral education in the specialty that was approved by the Family Psychology Specialty Council, the Society for Family Psychology (APA Division 43), the American Board of Couple and Family Psychology (an ABPP board), and the Academy of Couple and Family Psychology. They are based on the standards and framework of the Guidelines and Principles for Accreditation of Programs in Professional Psychology of the Commission on Accreditation (APA, 2008). Programs with a prespecialty emphasis or track in CFP may also use these guidelines to inform their curriculum and clinical training, establish student outcome expectations, and consider faculty qualifications in the specialty. There is also a Model for the Development of Postdoctoral Programs in Family Psychology (see Grossman, 2005).

In addition, it is important for the CFP educator to be cognizant of exemplary programs with strong CFP content. These may be found at the prespecialty level in clinical, counseling, and school psychology programs through a CFP emphasis or track (R.-J. Green, 1992, 2005a; Nutt, 2005; Stanton, 2005b, 2005c; Stanton et al., 2006). N. J. Kaslow and colleagues (2005) did a 2004 survey of the inclusion of couple and family rotations in Association of Psychology Postdoctoral Internship Centers (APPIC) and found predoctoral internship rotations (31% major rotation in family, 61% minor; 13% major rotation in couples, 42% minor) and postdoctoral residencies (62% provide family treatment; 54% provide couples training). In addition, there are a number of postdoctoral institutes in the specialty. Dobbins (2005) did a program type review of APPIC training sites and found that the majority of CFP training sites specialized in child and adolescent populations and provide couple and family collateral treatment; these were augmented by major rotations in family intervention at community mental health centers and minor rotations in VA Medical Centers. The Society for Family Psychology maintains information about programs with specialty content on its website: www.apa.org/divisions/div43/.

The CFP educator should also understand the challenges facing education in the specialty. Green (2005b) notes the "gap between American society's need for highly trained family psychologists and the current status of family psychology training in the U.S." (p. 8). Although some programs include CFP content, most programs, internships, and postdoctoral residencies provide minimal coverage of CFP. R.-J. Green (2005b) questions if this deficit of coverage in an area of significant need is ethical or morally acceptable in professional psychology and proposes increased coverage of CFP in doctoral course work, field placements, and research training. Student authors (Joseph & Tavegia, 2005) agree that it is difficult to secure extensive CFP internship training, suggesting that the emphasis on particular individual evidence-based treatments for symptom reduction (e.g., cognitive-behavioral therapy for posttraumatic stress disorder without addressing family factors) and pragmatic factors (e.g., lack of supervisors with expertise in CFP and the fact that CFP models require more skill from the student and more time from the supervisor) may lessen opportunities. They recommend proactive measures (e.g., asking questions during the interview) to determine the actual level of CFP education in internship sites during the application process and seeking mentors to enhance specialty education.

The most challenging issue for specialty education today involves APA accreditation. It is not currently possible to receive APA accreditation in the specialty at the doctoral level. The APA Commission on Accreditation (CoA) created the category Developed Practice Areas, and it may be possible for family psychology to fulfill the requirements for recognition in that category. The Family Psychology Specialty Council is considering actions toward that goal. Nutt (2007a) believes that the specialty can meet the CoA requirements, and she challenges doctoral programs to consider pursuit of APA accreditation in the specialty or combined with another specialty (e.g., clinical, counseling, or school joint programs). R.-J. Green (2005b) suggests that perhaps programs should rise to meet the need without the immediate pursuit of APA accreditation, letting accreditation follow. However, the strong national recognition of APA accreditation, the circular process between program accreditation and student receipt of APA-accredited predoctoral internships, and the bias toward the three traditional specialties by internship and residency training directors in selection of interns present challenging hurdles for doctoral accreditation in the specialty.

Finally, specialty educators may provide postdoctoral education, often in the form of continuing education in the specialty. Given the paucity of CFP education in many professional psychology doctoral programs, this is one avenue for psychologists to gain the education necessary for CFP specialization (Stanton & Nurse, 2005). To be effective, continuing education must be based on the same specialty foundations in systemic orientation, specialty scientific knowledge and evidence-based practices, and CFP outcome competencies as doctoral education and training in CFP. The primary intent of continuing education is twofold: to provide specialty education not included in one's doctoral education, and to ensure continuing competency through education in recent research and practice advances. Methods for specialty continuing education include face-to-face education and distance education using technological delivery methods or literature review and examination.

KNOWLEDGE OF PSYCHOEDUCATION SPECIALTY CURRICULUM

CFP specialists may also function as educators when providing psychoeducation directly to the public. This requires knowledge of the effectiveness of psychoeducation, knowledge of specialty curriculum for psychoeducation, and understanding of the characteristics of psychoeducation, as distinct from psychotherapy.

Effectiveness Research

Research suggests that relationship education, often focused on marriage and family interaction, demonstrates positive effects on communication skills and overall relationship quality (Halford, Markman, & Stanley, 2008; Hawkins, Blanchard, Baldwin, & Fawcett, 2008). Although there are benefits for some individuals in leaving a relationship, there are substantial negative consequences for many adults and their children; relationship education can help people develop healthy, fulfilling relationships that are associated with health factors, improved financial conditions, and advantages for children (Halford et al., 2008). Stanley, Amato, Johnson, and Markman (2006) conducted a study with a large random sample across four U.S. states and found that premarital education was related to increased relationship commitment and satisfaction and lower relationship conflict and divorce across racial groups, income levels, and educational status. Blanchard, Hawkins, Baldwin, and Fawcett (2009) conducted a meta-analysis of 97 research studies of marital and relationship education and found some evidence that there is a universal prevention effect (by enhancing relationships already functioning well) and a selective prevention effect (by enhancing relationships at risk or currently evidencing low-level relationship problems). This suggests that the field may extend beyond the current emphasis on nondistressed relationships and move toward the inclusion of more at-risk couples and families, although further research is needed, especially including long-term assessment (2 to 3 years after the education program; Blanchard et al., 2009).

Relationship education has now achieved public policy support accompanied by federal and state funding to provide services that enhance marriage in low-income families in order to improve child welfare and reduce poverty (Hawkins et al., 2008). However, rigorous research on education outcomes in low-income and diverse ethnic populations is scarce. Halford et al. (2008) suggest that current funding provides an important opportunity for focused research regarding the effectiveness of relationship education in high-risk, diverse populations.

Psychoeducation Curriculum

Typical relationship psychoeducation includes knowledge, skills, and attitudes important to relationship health (Markman et al., 2005); satisfaction; and commitment (Halford et al., 2008). This involves didactic instruction (e.g., information regarding factors that enhance relationship quality, such as shared expectations, commitment, forgiveness, and financial management) and skill development and practice (e.g., problem-solving communication techniques and conflict management; Hawkins et al., 2008). Programs typically provide 9 to 20 hours of education (Blanchard et al., 2009), although there is some indication that there is limited benefit beyond 12 hours and unnecessary additional hours may add pointless costs (Halford et al., 2008). Ragan, Einhorn, Rhoades, Markman, & Stanley (2009) review evidence-based relationship education programs and provide a summary of program characteristics. Relationship education originated in premarital education and extended to marriage enrichment, transition to parenthood, and stepfamily transition training in a variety of settings, such as churches, education organizations, military services, jails, and health care organizations (Halford et al., 2008).

Some relationship education includes assessment of relationship factors using devices developed to evaluate relative strength or weakness in certain categories. Halford and colleagues (2008) note several instruments, including PREPARE-ENRICH, FOCUS, and RELATE, but suggest that there is currently limited research on outcome effects.

Education Is Not Psychotherapy

Most relationship psychoeducation is distinctly different than psychotherapy in that it does not entail intensive address of problems specific to one couple or family; instead, it focuses on general issues identified as important and is conducted in a group setting with multiple couples or families "before problems become too serious and entrenched" (Hawkins et al., 2008, p. 723). Some programs have extended relationship psychoeducation to at-risk or low-level-distress relationships; this type of prevention comes closest to psychotherapy, but it still has distinct differences and outcomes (Blanchard et al., 2009). There are efforts to tailor programs to specific issues or the life cycle stage relevant to those entering the program, but this requires more sophisticated assessment practices and development of program modules that may be selected based on the assessment (Halford et al., 2008). It may be that relationship education will come closer to psychotherapy as it develops further and refines its ability to target specific issues and individual relationships.

KNOWLEDGE OF CFP COMPETENCIES

In order to be an effective CFP educator, one must have an advanced understanding of the CFP professional competencies (N. J. Kaslow et al., 2005; Stanton & Welsh, 2011). Knowledge of the framework of competencies and the particular knowledge, skills, and attitudes involved in each competency inform the creation of CFP curriculum, the design of CFP courses, and the processes of instruction and evaluation of CFP students. The CFP educator will assess the developmental level of the student and provide an educational experience that advances competency in defined areas. Courses will target particular competencies, noting the desired progression in the syllabus, and assess that progression through outcome evaluation measures that effectively measure elements of the competency (Roberts, Borden, Christiansen, & Lopez, 2005).

In particular, the CFP educator pays attention to the diversity competency and the manner in which it informs all other competencies. Nutt (2007b) suggests that increasing globalization mandates advanced knowledge and education in cross-cultural or multicultural issues and that systemic thinking is needed to enhance education, practice, and research in collectivistic cultures. Hong (2007) reminds us that the APA *Ethical Principles* and the APA *Guidelines on Multicultural Education, Training, Research, Practice, and Organizational Change* inform our specialty education and that their recommendations cannot be fulfilled in a single course. R.-J. Green (2002) indicates that sensitization, personal interaction, didactic education, supervised practice, and consultation are interactive elements of education to learn to provide professional services within cultural groups and notes the particular need for CFP education on lesbian, gay, and bisexual issues. Ivey and Conoley (1994) investigated gender bias in family assessment and family psychotherapy; they concluded that "training and experience may influence how individuals evaluate parent functioning" (p. 344) and that research is needed to determine how education may best reduce gender bias. CFP educators recognize the importance of teaching knowledge, skills, and attitudes to develop diversity competency in students. Cultural competence is assessed across all competency domains (Roberts et al., 2005).

Skills for Teaching CFP

In addition to the foundation of knowledge needed for effective education in the specialty, CFP specialists need particular skills to provide instruction. These include the ability to facilitate understanding and adoption of a systemic orientation and specialty scientific methods; the ability to conceptualize and create comprehensive specialty curriculum; the ability to develop a course in a specialty content area; the ability to apply teaching-learning methods appropriate to the specialty; and the ability to teach via professional and applied presentations and publications.

FACILITATE SYSTEMIC ORIENTATION AND SCIENTIFIC PRACTICE

Systemic Orientation

CFP educators know how to facilitate adoption of a systemic orientation. Sweeney and Sterman (2007) begin instruction in a systemic orientation with an assessment of current ability to conceptualize complex problems using ideas from systems theory. In fact, they note that assessment may even facilitate enhanced systemic conceptualization, as their research suggests that some people may learn from the queries in the assessment, although this has not yet been empirically demonstrated. Regardless, it seems reasonable that the CFP educator will want to know the current level of systemic conceptualization as a foundation for the further development of a systemic orientation. There is currently no psychometric instrument for the measurement of systemic thinking, but the models reviewed above (see "Knowledge for Teaching" section) may be extrapolated from childhood education to adult learning environments to provide some evaluation of ability to use systemic thinking in addressing complex problems.

At the anecdotal level, a number of CFP educators suggest that it is somewhat apparent when a student "gets it." Even informal discussion of complex topics reveals the epistemological framework one is using to organize information and understand the problem; many people socialized in the United States were educated in the Cartesian method and now use it automatically, with little or no conscious awareness that they are following a formal method. This is evidenced by linear thinking, reductionism, and extreme objectivism (Stanton, 2009b). Those who recognize reciprocity, complexity, and the social construction of knowledge stand out in contrast to solely Cartesian thinkers. In our experience teaching a course in systems theory, we regularly find

> that students entering a doctoral program in psychology have not thought about how they think. They automatically utilize

the Cartesian methodology to understand concepts and issues with little or no awareness that the methodology influences their thoughts and conclusions. As we trace the history of thought and methodologies from ancient times to the scientific revolution to contemporary society, many students struggle with the differences in underlying epistemological assumptions between ancient, modern, and post-modern philosophies. (Stanton, 2005a, p. 26)

The CFP educator needs to create an environment or context in which reductionistic thinking is demonstrated to be inadequate for the realities of contemporary life and use methods that facilitate adoption of systemic thinking. Shifts in one's epistemological framework require a process that includes experiencing some level of dissatisfaction or discomfort with one's existing conceptualization and presentation of another means of conceptualization that seems plausible and proves over time to enable the solution of real problems (Gregoire, 2003; Sandoval, 1996). Stanton (2005a) describes this process:

It is sometimes necessary to use Cartesian methods to help students understand systemic thinking, but that is usually not enough to effect a transformation in their personal thought process. I have had the most success with inculcation of systems thinking when the complexity of a case example disallows reductionistic solutions; students shift from nodding "no" to nodding "yes" in the midst of the discussion as they begin to see the system at work.... many students experience frustration and irritation.... It is disconcerting for them to encounter arguments and illustrations that evidence systemic properties of complexity and nonlinear causality. (p. 26)

Mary Catherine Bateson terms this an "epistemological shock" that undercuts one's normal way of thinking (cited in Bloom, n.d.). Because this can be quite unsettling, the CFP educator needs to provide a supportive environment as the individual relinquishes long-held ways of thinking and experiments with new conceptualization (Gregoire, 2003). Stanton (2009b) refers to the entire process as an "epistemological transformation" (p. 8) and notes, "Once the transformation takes place, it is impossible to see things in the old way" (p. 10).

One important aspect in the adoption of a systemic epistemology is the use of a conceptual paradigm that captures the dynamic nature of the systemic interaction between individual, interpersonal, and environmental or macrosystemic factors over time (Stanton, 2009b; see Chapter 2).

A systemic paradigm functions as a framework for CFP case conceptualization, assessment, understanding, and intervention (Stanton, 2009b). The CFP educator can facilitate adoption of systemic thinking by helping individuals inculcate a systemic paradigm.

The CFP educator may use a variety of methods to facilitate an epistemological transformation. Gregory Bateson (1972) used ecological illustrations and literary conversations (termed *metalogues*) to stimulate new thinking. Analogies and metaphors identified in a group discussion that illustrate systemic properties can enhance the adoption of systemic thinking (Duit, Roth, Komorek, & Wilbers, 2001). Auerswald (1990) recommends exercises that challenge objectified, reductionistic categories with personal experience. For instance, he asks students to describe their own family; most begin with descriptions of their family structure, but he pushes them to extend to descriptions of their relationships and interaction within the family so that they see that the family is more than a "thing" as he moves toward a systemic epistemology. Similarly, Whitchurch (2005) notes that she committed the common error of trying to teach systems theory in a linear fashion for years until she shifted to an inductive model that begins with student observation of families in a social context (e.g., shopping malls) and proceeds to unpack systemic concepts related to their observations of families. She reports, "I see them developing systems thinking: They develop a complex understanding of family relationships as systemic rather than cause and effect, and they also think systemically about families at macro levels" (Whitchurch, 2005, p. 574).

Group exercises that require the analysis of contemporary issues or ideas and the delineation of the multitude of factors involved in them establish the importance of a systemic framework. Descriptions of the evolution of psychological concepts, such as the shift from understanding attachment as the unidirectional influence of the mother on the child to a complex interaction within the mother-father-child-environment system, evidence the value of systemic thinking in psychology (Schermerhorn, Cummings, & Davies, 2008; Stanton, 2009b). Explication of systemic concepts (e.g., self-organization, change, reciprocity) and applied illustrations of those concepts can provide knowledge that facilitates a shift in thinking. Examples of complex clinical cases that disallow simple or reductionistic analysis interest psychology students and practitioners and demonstrate the value of systemic conceptualization (Stanton, 2005a). Carlson (2003) describes the practical application of this process:

> As a school psychology faculty member, teaching systems thinking
> permits me to challenge the bias toward individual child pathology

that permeates a curriculum that comprehensively trains students to evaluate and intervene with *every* imaginable aspect of child functioning (cognitive, behavioral, socio-emotional, psycho-educational, and neuropsychological). (p. 4)

These methods allow individuals to shift "from looking primarily for intra-psychic explanations for human behavior and from understanding inter-personal interactions in a linear, cause-effect manner to recognition of the complex factors that interact in reciprocal fashion to shape human life" (Stanton, 2005a, p. 26).

Scientific Methods

In addition to providing standard courses in research methods, CFP educators may demonstrate their own reliance upon scientific methods to encourage student adoption and use of the methods (Black & Lebow, 2009). Consistent citation of sources and explanation of relevant research methods and findings by educators in CFP courses facilitate student recognition of the importance of those methods to CFP practice. Friedberg, Gorman, and Beidel (2009) suggest that skepticism about the value of research evidence in practice is an obstacle that impedes adoption of evidence-based models and that it is important for educators to provide a foundation of understanding about the role of evidence in practice. Course assignments that require critical thinking and the review of research reinforce the adoption of specialty scientific methods. Mattson and Johnson (2007) suggest that CFP educators must prepare students to consume primary and secondary research resources by teaching research design and methodologies that are capable of capturing the complex nature of interpersonal processes through didactic and applied experiences and integrating them into clinical coursework as well as research courses and the dissertation process.

Scientific Interventions

Using the framework of levels of evidence (Sexton & Coop-Gordon, 2009) for CFP interventions, the educator may reinforce the importance of consistently considering the degree to which a particular intervention is supported. Syllabus notation of models may include some designation of the current level of support for that model. Alternatively, students may be challenged in an assignment to research popular models to determine the research literature around the model and/or to debate those findings in class relative to the assignment of a level of support designation.

CFP educators develop effective means to teach important intervention models. Sexton and Alexander (2003) note the importance of thorough model dissemination processes that ensure that evidence-based models are taught and reinforced in such a way that the treatment delivered remains true to the model. They suggest that "without model fidelity and therapist model adherence the demonstrated outcomes of evidence-based approaches cannot be replicated in community settings" (p. 344). They recommend a protocol that includes "three assumptions: (a) model fidelity must be measured from different perspectives (therapist, client, and outside consultant); (b) fidelity and adherence information should be readily available to therapists, supervisors, and program administrators for daily use; and (c) attention to fidelity and adherence should be a central part of clinical practice and supervision" (p. 344) and they created a web-based monitoring system for data collection and ready review. The CFP educator must make certain that students understand the importance of using evidence-based models in the way they were designed and teach mechanisms to reinforce model adherence.

CONCEPTUALIZE AND CREATE COMPREHENSIVE SPECIALTY CURRICULUM

Crucial factors related to the skill to conceptualize and create a comprehensive specialty curriculum include (a) knowledge of the APA CoA *Guidelines and Principles for Accreditation* (APA, 2008); (b) knowledge of the Recommendations for Doctoral Education and Training in Family Psychology (Stanton & Harway, 2007); (c) the ability to determine the level of specialty training desired (track, emphasis, or doctoral specialty; Stanton et al., 2006); and (d) the ability to select the relevant content appropriate to the chosen level of emphasis.

The CFP educator must be able to take the recommendations and use them to inform the development of a comprehensive specialty curriculum. It is important that a track, for instance, include sufficient specialty knowledge, skills, and attitudes to provide a minimal foundation for future pursuit of the remaining specialty education. This requires instruction in theory as well as clinical content, and initial professional identification with CFP. It is insufficient to simply offer disjointed courses in couple therapy and family therapy. The CFP educator must know specialty education well and select the specific elements appropriate to the outcome goals intended for the program.

In some ways, an emphasis within a doctoral program is easier to design because there is more unit allocation to allow reasonable coverage of the crucial prespecialty dimensions of CFP. The resultant curriculum should evidence thoughtful consideration of which content domains and competency factors are included to prepare students at the prespecialty level; it should reflect best practices in established programs with a CFP emphasis. Remaining elements may be achieved during internship, postdoctoral residency, or continuing education. A doctoral program in the specialty would follow the guidelines more thoroughly.

DEVELOP A SPECIALTY COURSE

CFP educators must have the skill to design a course in a specialty content area that fits within the specialty curriculum and reflects current specialty research findings and specialty competency education. The most common courses in a track or emphasis include (a) systems theory; (b) couple and/or family assessment; (c) couple therapy; and (d) family therapy (Stanton et al., 2006). Additional courses that are often considered part of the specialty include child psychology, adolescent psychology, human sexuality or sex therapy, gerontology, and CFP practicum. Family violence and family forensic psychology courses are becoming increasingly common as those areas require education and training for basic competency in practice. Consultation, based on a systemic epistemology, is an area of increased CFP practice that requires education (see Chapter 6).

The process for developing a course includes review of exemplar syllabi created by other CFP specialists (see the curriculum compendium hosted by the Society for Family Psychology at http://www.apa.org/divisions/div43/Discussion/Syllabi.html); creation of a course description that details the central elements of the course (new faculty members, however, should be aware that established course descriptions at most institutions may not be changed by the individual faculty member without review and approval through established faculty governance processes); delineation of the student outcome competencies that the course will seek to develop; selection of a textbook and/or assigned readings that reflect current scholarship and best practices in the specialty; specification of topics and development of teaching-learning activities that will cover those topics; and development of student learning assessments and grading standards (Lucas & Bernstein, 2005; Vande Kemp, 1981).

If the course in question is for continuing education, the CFP educator must work with an organization that is approved by the American Psychological Association to offer approved continuing education. It will be necessary to complete a syllabus for the course, similar to the graduate education model above, noting student learning objectives and providing an assessment to evaluate student outcomes.

For psychoeducation, there are no formal standards unless the program is offered under the auspices of an organization. However, the CFP educator will want to follow a pattern similar to those above for graduate and continuing education to ensure that there are clear student outcome objectives and measures to assess learning.

ADOPT CFP EDUCATION METHODS

CFP educators use a variety of methods to effectively teach specialty knowledge and skills. Most CFP educators do not receive formal education in pedagogy but may find examples and illustrations of helpful techniques in the literature. Benson (2007) reminds us that learning theory suggests that teaching should accommodate "various learning styles, experiential learning, and multiple intelligences" (p. 4). Campbell, Draper, and Huffington (1991) refer to a process they term a "co-evolving system" between teachers and participants, in which the participants are "learning about systemic thinking and family therapy, and we are learning about teaching systemic thinking" (p. 13). Florence Kaslow (1987) reminds us that CFP education "should be rigorous, theoretical, grounded in extant research on family structures and processes and therapy process and outcome, and conducive to new basic and applied research" (p. 80). Storm et al. (2003) suggest that education methods must take into account the feminization of CFP as greater percentages of women than men are entering the field and the increasing globalization of practice (due to information sharing and migration) to ensure that we meet current needs.

Common techniques include the use of video segments to facilitate analysis of differing perspectives between theoretical orientations and intervention models; lectures, demonstrations, experiments, discussions, and simulations; student personal family-of-origin analysis; provision of thorough literature reviews of complicated issues; and application of course material to students' personal lives. Some literature notes the possible negative aspects of particular teaching techniques (e.g., use of movies or overreliance on technology) to assist the CFP educator in making critical evaluations of those methods (Hudock & Warden, 2001; Lucas & Bernstein, 2005). Table 9.2 provides an overview of competency areas, illustrative techniques, and reference citations that describe the use of those techniques to develop the desired competency.

Some specialty material may require adherence to prescribed content and teaching techniques in order to enhance thorough dissemination of the model and student adherence to the model as designed and determined to be an evidence-based intervention. For instance, Functional Family Therapy has determined the importance of therapist adherence to

TABLE 9.2 **CFP Education Methods**

CFP COMPETENCY	TEACHING-LEARNING METHOD	REFERENCES
All competencies	Lectures, demonstrations, asking and answering questions, leading discussions	(Lucas & Bernstein, 2005)
Conceptual foundation All competencies	Critical examination of strengths and weaknesses of concepts and models	(Laszloffy, 2002)
Conceptual foundation	Methods to make systems visible: graphs, archetypes, causal loop diagrams	(Sweeney, n.d.)
Conceptual foundation Scientific foundations	Visual, linguistic, and kinesthetic learning for different learning styles	(Benson, 2007)
Conceptual foundation Scientific foundations	Student-written metaphors	(Taber, 2007)
Conceptual foundation Scientific foundations	Questions that require the learner to declare his or her association to new ideas	(Taber, 2007)
Conceptual foundation Scientific foundations	Videos and graphic illustrations	(Benson, 2007) (Taber, 2007)
Conceptual foundation Therapeutic alliance	DVD that combines pictures, text, video, and audio	(Bledsoe, 2006)
Conceptual foundation Case formulation	Student analysis of family interaction video using different theoretical models to illustrate perspectives	(Laszloffy, 2002)
Research	Early student involvement in research activities	(Eisler & Dare, 1992)
Interpersonal interaction	Modeling and role-play of complex interactions; instruction in process assessment of therapeutic alliance	Chapter 12, this volume
Assessment Intervention	Student connection to personal family life and/or family of origin	(Laszloffy, 2002; Tonti, 1991)
Assessment Intervention	Feature movies that illustrate assessment domains or intervention models	(Stinchfield, 2006)
Intervention	Model transformative conversations	(Anderson & Levin, 1998)
Intervention	Video review that springboards to treatment planning	(R.-J. Green, 2002)
Intervention	Un-learning individualistic models; service learning experiential exercises	(Murray, Lampinen, & Kelley-Soderholm, 2006)
Diversity	Annotated literature reviews; experience with nonclinical group representatives	(R.-J. Green, 2002)
Consultation	Examples of organizations as systems; needs assessment exercises; consultation report preparation	(Stanton, 2009a); Chapter 6, this volume

the established model (Sexton, 2007). Systemic Family Development has specified an entire framework, including material for the syllabus, session specifications, exercises, teaching techniques, and assignment examples (Laszloffy, 2002). Some psychoeducation models, such as the Prevention and Relationship Enhancement Program (PREP), have highly defined goals, session structure, and teaching techniques (Ragan et al., 2009). In these cases, the CFP educator must be careful to use the prescribed format and instruction methods to ensure similar outcomes.

When addressing diversity issues in specialty education, R.-J. Green (2002) uses illustrations from teaching about lesbian and gay family psychology and recommends providing a foundation of knowledge in the literature through assigned readings. This requires the CFP educator to develop an annotated literature review that provides an introduction to the particular population. In addition, he indicates that educators cannot assume student familiarity with ordinary family life in minority groups; therefore, he suggests the use of video that depicts normal life in the population (not treatment video that focuses on dysfunction) and interview assignments that provide opportunities for direct contact in order to decrease prejudice. Finally, he provides an exercise for the creation of a treatment plan based on a video segment that can lead to classroom discussion and evaluation.

Some methods may be adapted from K-12 education to the graduate level. For instance, see segments on such topics as "Systems Thinking: What and Why" and "Habits of a Systems Thinker" at WebEd: http://www. watersfoundation.org/webed/.

TEACH IN PROFESSIONAL AND APPLIED VENUES

CFP educators teach specialty content in professional and applied venues. CFP educators regularly function in higher education (e.g., graduate/ doctoral education and training, predoctoral internship or postdoctoral residency education, and postdoctoral continuing education), as well as in applied venues (e.g., psychoeducation, organizational training within the consultant role, family life education). This wide range of audiences requires the CFP educator to understand the differences in student preparation and foundation of knowledge, as well as differences in expected learning outcomes, based on the education venue. The ability needed involves assessment of student developmental level and application of education content and methods that will communicate effectively with students at that level and promote additional learning outcomes.

Attitudes for CFP Education

The crucial CFP educator attitudes that underlie provision of specialty education focus on valuing lifelong learning as an essential element of teaching and a commitment to the provision of quality education. These attitudes are demonstrated in behaviors around independent review and incorporation of new research into teaching and the performance of evaluation processes regarding the quality of teaching provided.

REVIEW AND INCORPORATE NEW RESEARCH

CFP educators regularly identify, review, and incorporate new specialty research and literature into their teaching. The fundamental attitude required for this competency is a high value for continued learning and reliance upon recent research findings for one's teaching. F. W. Kaslow (1987) recommended that CFP educators must not only found their teaching on extant knowledge, but remain open to new research. This requires that the specialist seek out new literature related to course topics. This is often accomplished through subscriptions to the primary specialty publications and awareness of new books in the field; however, the easy availability of electronic databases such as PsycINFO and PsycARTICLES that provide full-text publications enables the educator to readily research her or his topic to include recent advances in the field. This ongoing pursuit of knowledge models active learning for students.

CONDUCT EVALUATIONS OF TEACHING

CFP educators value quality of instruction and make efforts to evaluate their performance as educators. This may include self-evaluation, peer review, and student feedback about the teaching-learning experience. Lucas and Bernstein (2005) emphasize the value of creating a continuous process of evaluation to ensure quality instruction over time. Self-evaluation may include assessment of one's energy and interest in teaching, currency in the specialty literature, and critical reflection on student learning outcomes. Some institutions may facilitate videotaping the educator in the teaching process; this is often done at the beginning of one's career if one completed a pedagogy course, but it may not have been done recently. Videotaping can help the individual identify effective techniques and teaching strategies, as well as poor habits or techniques for correction. Peer review is a common institutional review process that can be effective if it is conducted in a positive environment and framed as professional development, not employment evaluation. Another form of peer involvement is observation of recognized master teachers; this can be inspiring and motivating. Student feedback is an important final element. Some educators devalue student evaluation ratings or comments because of the inevitable odd comment or unreasonable rating. However, it is important to consider if there is value in even the harshest evaluations, as they may reveal areas for growth and professional development (although, to be fair, this may come only after a few days of discounting or ignoring the feedback). Ultimately, student accomplishment of learning outcomes or competency enhancement is the most important measure of teaching. Assignments or examinations that measure student learning or development of particular competencies provide compelling evidence of effective specialty education.

Conclusion

Specialty education is crucial to the progress of CFP within professional psychology. CFP educators must have the necessary knowledge, skills, and attitudes to provide effective specialty education in the public arena, clinical settings, organizational contexts, and higher education.

PART V

Foundational Competencies

TEN

Ethical and Legal Competency

The number of ethical challenges confronted by a professional psychologist grows exponentially when couples and families are treated (O'Shea & Jessee, 1982). In addition, the scope of laws that govern the practice of psychology also expands when working with families. This chapter will move from the general to the specific as we cover law and ethics in couple and family psychology. First, we will review legal and ethical standards as a foundational competency; second, we will propose ethical and legal competencies unique to the specialty practice of CFP; and third we will discuss several common legal and ethical challenges that are unique to the specialty practice of CFP.

Legal and Ethical Competency

In this first section, we provide a context for the development of the "ethics–legal standards–policy" competency (ethics competency), as defined by the Assessment of Competency Benchmarks Workgroup (2007) as an "application of ethical concepts and awareness of legal issues regarding professional activities with individuals, groups, and organizations" (p. 25). During the 2002 APPIC Competencies Conference, Workgroup 2, led by Cynthia de las Fuentes, was given the broad charge to "address issues related to ethical, legal, public policy/advocacy, and professional issues" (APPIC Competency Conference Workgroup Summary, 2002, p. 5). The workgroup conceptualized the ethics competency as "interwoven in all areas of practice and all activities" (p. 5) and was later described, along with diversity, as a "crosscutting competency" (N. J. Kaslow et al., 2004). The initial findings of the ethics workgroup may be reviewed at http://www.appic.org/news/3_1_news_Competencies.htm. The work group's recommendations

TABLE 10.1 Ethical and Legal Competency: Developmental Level—Specialty Competence in Couple and Family Psychology

COMPETENCY DOMAIN AND ESSENTIAL COMPONENT	BEHAVIORAL ANCHOR	ASSESSMENT METHODS
Knowledge (A) Ethical and legal knowledge (A.1) Command of ethical and legal knowledge related to CFP	(A.1.1) Understands the APA code of ethics as applicable to the practice of CFP, with awareness of the limitations of the code when applied to work with couples and families (A.1.2) Understands the attendant ethics literature and applicable guidelines applicable to the practice of CFP (A.1.3) Awareness of the scope of family law relating to CFP in the specialist's area of practice (A.1.4) Understands common legal and ethical issues in the specialty and demonstrates advanced knowledge of the literature regarding management of those issues	1. ABPP examination 2. Ongoing status for practice through licensure 3. Successful record of navigating ethical conflicts 4. Self-evaluation 5. Student reviews 6. Peer consultation 7. Client feedback 8. Continuing education in legal and ethical issues in CFP 9. Publication and presentation in scholarly venues regarding legal and ethical issues 10. Participation in consultation groups or ongoing supervision 11. Service as ABPP examiner 12. Ethics consultation to other practitioners
Skill (B) Awareness and application of ethical decision-making model (B.1) Intentional inclusion of relevant ethical and legal principles in all aspects of professional activity in CFP	(B.1.1) Ability to articulate the ethical decision-making model used to reason through ethical dilemmas (B.1.2) Ability to reasonably foresee ethical and legal conflicts that present with some regularity in the practice of couple and family psychology (B.1.3) Able to identify, analyze, and proactively address legal and ethical conflicts that arise during the course of providing couple and family psychology services (B.1.4) Professional writings, presentations, research, teaching, supervision, intervention, and consultation will represent efforts to include ethical principles and standards related to couple and family psychology	
Attitudes (C) Commitment to ethical and legal development (C.1) Strives to continually improve in the competency	(C.1.1) Evidence of continued development in the competency (C.1.2) Would be characterized as managing rather than avoiding risk (C.1.3) Takes responsibility for continuing professional development of knowledge, skills, and attitudes in relation to ethical-legal-standards and policies relevant to couple and family psychology	

Note. Adapted from the format and content of the Assessment of Competency Benchmarks Work Group (2007). This table assumes that the specialist has achieved competence in professional psychology at the three previous developmental levels, as specified in the benchmarks. The competency domains and behavioral anchors serve as the primary organizing structure for this chapter; content explaining each domain and anchor is provided in the chapter.

were also published in a subsequent article (de las Fuentes, Willmuth, & Yarrow, 2005). Following the work of the APPIC Competencies Conference, the ethics competency has been further codified in the report of the Assessment of Competency Benchmarks Workgroup (2007). The foundational ethics competency in professional psychology was outlined by the Benchmarks Workgroup according to requisite knowledge, skills, and attitudes (Knowledge, Awareness and Application of Ethical Decision Making Model, and Ethical Conduct) across three developmental levels (readiness for practicum; readiness for internship; readiness for entry-level practice).

In this section we propose a set of ethical and legal competencies for the advanced specialty of CFP. We have tried to remain closely aligned in format and concept to the original Benchmark Competencies. Accordingly, we have specified three competency domains (knowledge; awareness and application of ethical decision-making model; and ethical conduct), a guiding essential component for each domain, and behavioral anchors to illustrate what competency looks like when it is obtained (Table 10.1).

Knowledge

The knowledge domain is the base of ethical and legal knowledge that a CFP sepcialist must possess to be competent to practice in the specialty. The essential component of this domain requires that CFP specialists have command of ethical and legal knowledge related to the practice of CFP. The essential component includes four requisite areas of knowledge: (a) APA Ethical Principles and Standards related to the practice of CFP; (b) specialty guidelines applicable to CFP and the attendant ethical literature related to CFP; (c) law related to the practice of CFP; and (d) policy issues and advocacy relevant to CFP.

ETHICS CODE

The CFP specialist understands the APA Ethical Principles and Code of Conduct (Ethics Code; APA, 2002) as applicable to the practice of CFP, with awareness of the limitations of the code when applied to work with couples and families. Training for specialty practice assumes that competency has been attained as a professional psychologist. It is further assumed that the specialist trainee has a command of the Ethics Code as it applies to the practice of professional psychology. The Ethics Code is sufficiently broad in order to apply to most areas of practice in psychology and only briefly refers to specialty practice. For example, the closest that the 2002 Ethics

Code comes to directly addressing the practice of CFP is Standard 10.02, Therapy Involving Couples or Families.

> When psychologists agree to provide services to several persons who have a relationship (such as spouses, significant others or parents and children), they take reasonable steps to clarify at the outset (1) which of the individuals are clients/patients and (2) the relation the psychologist will have with each person. This clarification includes the psychologist's role and the probable uses of the service provided or the information obtained. (APA, 2002, pp. 1072–1073)

Expansion of the Ethics Code to include work with couples and families is a welcome addition; however, it does little more than draw attention to the difference between working with individuals and multiple persons when providing psychological services. Because more than one individual is participating in therapy or assessment, complexities surrounding privilege, privacy, confidentiality, and recording keeping need to be understood by the specialist. Several authors have identified the unique ethical and legal considerations in working with multiple persons in psychological treatment (Lakin, 1986, 1994; Margolin, 1982; O'Shea & Jessee, 1982). These authors suggest that the fundamental difficulty in multiperson therapy is the competing needs and preferences between the various parties (including the therapist). We address common ethical and legal issues surrounding privilege and confidentiality later in this chapter.

ETHICAL LITERATURE AND GUIDELINES

CFP specialists do not make decisions about practice in a vacuum but instead rely on documents that are time-tested and considered as authoritative sources for ethical decision making by the vast majority of professionals in the field of psychology. We identify two sources of attendant ethical literature related to the practice of CFP: (a) *Specialty Guidelines for the Delivery of Services by Family Psychologists* (Specialty Guidelines; Division 43, 2003); and (b) scholarly publications about ethical issues in CFP. The Specialty Guidelines were developed by the Society for Family Psychology to provide guidance to CFP specialists and improve the quality of services offered by those practicing the specialty. Like all other guidelines in professional psychology, the Specialty Guidelines are compatible with the APA Ethics Code and more specifically address areas of practice unique to CFP that are not covered by the more general APA code. The Specialty Guidelines are applicable to all professional psychologists who practice couple and family psychology. They specify typical areas of proficiency, the requisite knowledge base, and ethical practices unique to systems work with couples, families, and organizations. The Specialty Guidelines may be downloaded at www.apa.org/divisions/div43. Other practice guidelines, as listed in the Specialty Guidelines §C.3 and § C.4, are also relevant for the practice of CFP with particular populations (e.g., *Guidelines for Psychotherapy with Lesbian, Gay, and Bisexual Clients* [APA, 2000a], the *APA Guidelines on Multicultural Education, Training, Research, Practice, and Organizational Change for Psychologists* [APA, 2003a]), and guidance for clarifying elements of practice (e.g., *Record Keeping Guidelines* [APA, 1993]).

Ethical decision making does not stop with the corpus of ethical literature specifically published by institutional psychology. According to the 2002 APA Ethics Code, "Psychologists may consider other materials and guidelines that have been adopted or endorsed by scientific and professional psychological organizations." Because CFP specialists practice in diverse areas, the ethics codes and specialty guidelines of closely related disciplines are relevant. Bush, Connell, and Denney (2006) state that practitioners "must consider guidelines promulgated within their areas of specialty" (p. 22). Examples of related ethics codes include the American Association of Marriage and Family Therapists (AAMFT, 1991) and the American Association of Sexuality Educators, Counselors and Therapists (AASECT, 2008). A second type of attendant knowledge includes scholarly articles written by well-respected representatives of the field of couple and family psychology. Citations used in this chapter should be consulted as authoritative sources of ethical issues pertaining to CFP.

GOVERNING LAW

CFP specialists must be familiar with the law that governs their practice, including state, federal administrative, and common law (a.k.a. landmark cases). Federal administrative law are those laws that the president or administrative designee drafts, such as the Health Insurance Portability and Accountability Act (HIPAA, 1996), and the Americans with Disabilities Act (ADA, 1990). State law includes legislation that might be relevant to CFP practice in the specialist's state. State law is typically written in a legislative code such as the Business, Penal, or Family Codes. Examples of state legislation governing practice would include the child and elder abuse reporting laws, licensure requirements, and recording-keeping requirements. There are likely to be substantial differences between states on laws governing CFP. One example is the conditions under which minors may consent to treatment. Finally, the third type of law that governs practice is common law or "judge-made" law. These "landmark" cases set a precedent for how states will interpret legal questions that have not been codified or sufficiently interpreted in legislation. Each state will have a series of landmark cases that define parameters of practice; those that are relevant to CFP specialists should be included in the requisite knowledge base for a specialist. An example of a landmark case that CFP specialists are likely to be aware of is *Tarasoff v. Regents of the University of California* (1974/1976).

UNDERSTANDS COMMON ETHICAL AND LEGAL CHALLENGES TO CFP

We now turn our attention to three issues that deserve focused treatment given the frequency with which they arise in the daily practice of CFP. First, we will address the importance of competency in providing CFP specialty services. Second, we will cover the issues surrounding privilege, confidentiality, and informed consent. Finally, we will discuss the challenges of "change of format" in CFP (Margolin, 1982; Gottlieb, 1995).

Competency in CFP

We begin the discussion on focused ethical topics within CFP with the issue of competency. Many professional psychologists believe that a license to practice psychology is synonymous with competence to treat couples and families. The large number of psychologists in private practice who treat couples and families without the requisite knowledge, skill, experience, or training highlights the importance of drawing attention to the competence to practice CFP (R.-J. Green, 2005b).

Standard 2.01(a) of the APA Ethics Code (2002) states that "psychologists provide services, teach, and conduct research with populations and in areas only within the boundaries of their competence, based on their education, training, supervised experience, consultation, study, or professional experience" (APA, 2002, p. 1063). Interestingly, this definition of competence in the Ethics Code is similar to the definition of an expert according to Rule 702 of the Federal Rules of Evidence (FRE), which states that "a witness qualified as an expert by knowledge, skill, experience, training, or education, may testify thereto in the form of an opinion or otherwise" (FRE, 1975). The difference between an expert and lay witness (FRE Rule 701) states that the expert possesses specialized knowledge. Another way to think about competency in professional psychology is that the practitioner has obtained specialized knowledge and experience about the treatment or population with whom he or she works.

CFP is a recognized specialty within the broader field of psychology. As evidenced in this book, professional psychologists must possess a set of competencies before they are considered competent to practice in the specialty of CFP. The nature and scope of knowledge, skills, and attitudes associated with CFP are separate but related to other practice-oriented specialties that are currently recognized by the American Psychological Association. For example, basic interviewing skills are central to most specialties. Although historically seen as a "modality" in professional psychology, the field of CFP has advanced to the point of specialty status. Nevertheless, there are many practitioners who are trained in a clinical or counseling psychology program without an emphasis in CFP who frequently treat couples and families. In fact, the vast majority (78%) of those who belong to Division 29 (Psychotherapy) conduct marital or couples therapy, and 38% conduct family therapy (Norcross, Hedges, & Castle, 2002). In contrast, the modal number of courses in CFP in graduate training is one (R.-J. Green, 2005b). It is doubtful that professional psychologists would consider themselves competent to practice psychoanalysis with only one three-unit course in object relations. It is dismaying that so many professional psychologists would do the same with the specialty practice of CFP. We agree that there is much overlap between the transferrable skills of the broad and general education in professional psychology and couple and family therapy; however, CFP is a distinct specialty and is not synonymous with the modality of marital and family therapy.

CFP is a major paradigm change in the field of professional psychology. Interestingly, when applying for specialty status with the Commission on the Recognition of Specialties and Proficiencies in Professional Psychology (CRSPPP), the commission recommended that the specialty should be identified as "systems psychology" (Patterson, 2009). This title captures the distinctive difference of the subsequently labeled family psychology specialty, where there continues to be significant confusion about the differences between family therapists and CFP specialists.

As aptly noted by Patterson (2009) in a chapter on competence in CFP, there is much inconsistency in the distinctions drawn in professions that practice couple and family therapy. The list of those individuals who practice couple and family therapy extends beyond psychology and marriage and family therapy into medicine, nursing, social work, and professional counseling. Accordingly, for psychologists to be competent to practice CFP they need to establish and demonstrate competence in this specialty area. Currently, board certification offered by the American Board of Couple and Family Psychology (ABCFP), a specialty board of the American Board of

Professional Psychology (ABPP), is the only recognized competency certification to practice in the field of CFP. However, board certification in CFP recognizes advanced specialty competence, and no other guidelines have been available for qualifying minimal competency to practice in CFP.

Recently, Patterson (2009) proposed a three-tiered set of standards for establishing competence in couple and family psychology (Table 10.2). The highest level (Level A) of competence would apply to those individuals who self-identify as couple and family psychologists or therapists. The training required to identify oneself as a couple and family psychologist would minimally include relevant predoctoral coursework and supervision, and postgraduate supervision and continuing education sufficient to qualify for board certification by the ABCFP, an AAMFT-approved supervisor, or state-certified family or couple therapist. The second-highest level (Level B) would designate those clinicians who "regularly see couples or families conjointly" (p. 195). To qualify for this level of competence, practitioners would be required to have graduate coursework in the field and obtain 12 hours of continuing education in couples and family psychology or therapy within each licensure renewal cycle. The lowest level of competence (Level C), or what might be considered minimally acceptable competence, is for those practitioners who occasionally see couples and families conjointly and who obtain "some" continuing education within each license renewal cycle and obtain consultation as necessary to practice. These individuals would have had "some graduate level training in the field" (p. 195).

Patterson's attempt to codify competency levels is a good initial attempt at establishing standards in the specialty of CFP. One potential revision

TABLE 10.2 **A Three-Tiered Set of Standards for Competency in Couple and Family Psychology**

LEVEL	QUALIFICATIONS
A.	Specialists who identify as couple and family therapists or psychologists with relevant graduate coursework and supervised experience, and have a significant amount of postgraduate training and supervision in the field that would be equivalent to specialty designation either as an ABPP, AAMFT-approved supervisor, or certification as a family or couple therapist by state licensing boards. Continuing education would include concentrated advanced training in the field.
B	Clinicians who regularly see couples or families conjointly and, in addition to graduate coursework in the field, obtain at least 12 hours of continuing education courses and obtain consultation specifically focused in this area each renewal period.
C	Practitioners who occasionally see couples or families conjointly for relatively common problems and short duration, obtain some continuing education each licensure renewal period and in focused consultation as needed, and have some graduate-level training in the field.

Note. Adapted from Patterson 2009.

to Patterson's guidelines might be to further demarcate Levels B and C as they are not easily distinguishable. The frequency with which a psychologist treats couples or families is not associated with competency. For example, an inadequately trained psychologist could not competently conduct even one child custody evaluation. Perhaps collapsing Patterson's typology into two levels might solve this problem: specialists/experts in CFP and psychologists competent to treat couples and families. Clearly, more work needs to be done in defining initial competence to practice; however, we hope that this text provides clear direction on the competency required to practice as a specialist in CFP.

Privacy, Confidentiality, and Privilege with Couples and Families

The issues of privacy, confidentiality, and privilege with couples and families (Margolin, 1982; O'Shea & Jessee, 1982) are central to the core ethical and legal challenges that confront CFP specialists. Privacy, confidentiality, and privilege are closely related concepts, and there is frequent confusion over definitions. Privacy, rooted in the ethical principle of autonomy, is an implied constitutional right to be "let alone" by the government and to decide when, where, and how to share information about one's property, thoughts, feelings, and other personal information (Koocher & Keith-Spiegel, 2008). Relatedly, confidentiality is the duty owed the client to safeguard private information. Confidentiality is defined as "a general standard of professional conduct that obliges a professional not to discuss information about a client with anyone" (Koocher & Keith-Spiegel, 2008, p. 194). Civil lawsuits are based on the breach of the duty of confidentiality that is owed to the client resulting in harm. The closely related concept of privilege (or privileged communication) refers to "certain types of relationships that enjoy protection from disclosure in legal proceedings" (Koocher & Keith-Spiegel, 2008, p. 195). Privileged communication between the psychotherapist and his or her patient was first clearly articulated by the California case *In re Lifschutz* (1970), which established that the patient, not the therapist, owned the privilege. After *Lifschutz*, privileged communication was generally understood with individual psychotherapy clients, but adding clients to the therapy room raised new questions about privilege that were not previously asked. We now turn to some of the issues that involve all three of the aforementioned concepts of privacy, confidentiality, and privilege.

Confidentiality and Informed Consent   The 2002 APA Ethics Code requires those working with couples and families to determine who the client is at the outset of treatment. A favorite maxim of the CFP is that "the system is the client." If this is indeed the case, the therapist needs to outline exactly what members of a particular family are seen as the system. Does the therapist believe that anyone who steps into the therapy room is a client and part of the system? For those practitioners who frequently utilize extended family or other support systems, the number of clients to whom they owe a duty could become unwieldy. In a later section we discuss the informed consent requirements for those CFP specialists who routinely change formats. Relatedly, there are now many treatments that were originally tailored to individuals—treatment for depression, eating disorder, substance abuse—that are now empirically validated for systemic interventions. In this case, the identified patient is the target of the outcome of the intervention even though the "system" is still being treated. It is misleading to not inform the identified patient that he or she is the subject of treatment (Margolin, 1982).

Secrets   One of the early conflicts observed by couple and family therapists was the policy around secrets (Margolin, 1982). Usually a secrets policy is discussed in terms of treating couples, and it should apply to family or larger system treatment. This dilemma revolves around what to do with information that was entrusted to the therapist by one individual and not disclosed in the multiperson session. For example, what should a CFP specialist do if the wife discloses to the therapist that she is having an affair but does not want her husband to know? Several interesting questions emerge from this dilemma. Should the therapist disclose this information to the husband, since it is likely a key element in the couple's treatment? Is it a violation of confidentiality to tell the husband, or does confidentiality operate differently in a couples scenario?

A significant change was made to the 2002 Ethics Code in light of some of the difficulties represented by this brief vignette. The revised code included several important enforceable standards that apply in this situation. Standard 10.02a requires that a psychologist clarify (a) who the patient is (e.g., the couple, the system, or the identified patient only) and (b) the relationship that each individual will have with the psychologist. All these issues need to be contained in the informed consent. Standard 10.02a clearly implies that the psychologist should have thought through the ramifications of these issues beforehand and included it in his or her informed consent. Arguably, "clarifying the relationship" should include statements and discussions about how secrets are shared, and whether there should be a presumption of confidentiality if private information is shared by an individual client. There are varied opinions about a secrets policy, but regardless of the stance taken by the CFP specialist, a "law of no surprises" approach should be practiced with respect to setting the parameters of couple and family therapy during the informed consent process and as a matter of ongoing communication with the clients. The CFP specialist who discloses secrets without permission assumes great risk.

Disputed Privilege CFP specialists have the potential to work with clients where there is a high risk of requests for disclosure of privileged information. For those cases where some type of court proceeding is likely (e.g., divorce, pending child custody dispute), the CFP specialist needs to be aware of what may be called disputed privilege. For instance, what is the response of the CFP specialist when one party in a divorce resolution or child custody case wants to release confidential information that was obtained in the course of conjoint treatment and the other does not? The answer is that it depends on the state in which one practices. Some state codes do not distinguish between individuals and couples, so when this situation arises, it is often dealt with through litigation and the appeals process. Other states deal with this potential conflict through established legislation that covers couples privilege and have a marriage and family counselor privilege. In New Jersey, for example, the issue of disputed privilege is dealt with by legislation in the Evidence Code that specifically addresses this conflict through a marriage and family therapist privilege which states "that one party may not force disclosure of communications made by another party at a time when both parties were engaged in common therapy" (N.J. R. Evid. 505). Relatedly, the California Evidence Code 912 states that

> a waiver of the right to a particular joint holder of the privilege to claim the privilege does not affect the right of another joint holder to claim the privilege. In the case of the privilege provided by Section 980 (confidential marital communications), a waiver of the right of one spouse to claim the privilege does not affect the right of the other spouse to claim the privilege.

Some would argue that privilege is held by the couple and that both members of the couple need to give a waiver of privilege to release confidential information in a family law proceeding (e.g., New Jersey and California), whereas others would advocate that the "third-party rule" applies and negates privilege. This rule holds that information that is disclosed in front of a third party is typically viewed by the courts as not privileged, since it was made in public (not just to the doctor but with the husband or wife present). Margolin (1982) cited a case of a psychiatrist in Virginia where the trial judge denied protection of privilege to the psychiatrist who had seen a couple and was compelled to testify without mutual waiver. The judge ruled that "when a husband and wife are in a counseling session with a psychiatrist…there is no confidentiality because statements were made not in private to a doctor, but in the presence of the spouse" (Herrington, 1979, p. l, cited in Margolin, 1982, p. 793). Interestingly, several states (e.g., California, Colorado, Kansas, New Jersey, and Minnesota) have also provided legislation for privilege to extend to group therapy (Lewis, 2001). Group therapy and couples and family therapy share some of the same concerns for privacy, confidentiality, and privilege.

Given the variability of state laws related to privileged communication between family members in therapy, we offer a few recommendations for the CFP specialists. First, they should be familiar with the state privileging laws that govern their practice. Second, CFP specialists should inform couples and families about the specific laws governing privilege for multiperson therapies so that they can make an informed choice about what to share in the context of therapy. For states that do not grant privilege to couples and families, we advise that CFP specialists explicitly state this in their informed consent and explain it to the couple in understandable language. The couple needs to be aware that information shared in a conjoint session could be used in later court proceedings. For those states that do grant privilege to couples and families, CFP specialists should inform their clients that privilege is not absolute and that safety is usually an exception to privilege. For example, if the physical and emotional safety of a child is central to a child custody determination, then information obtained in a conjoint session may not be covered by privilege. Finally, we propose that CFP specialists involved in policy making would advocate for more states to adopt a specific privilege granted to couples and families in therapy.

Change of Format   One of the unique contributions offered to psychotherapy by the early systems theorists was a change in who was seen as the client. Family therapists typically treated the family system regardless of whether the presenting client was an individual or a family. In the course of treatment it was not uncommon to move from treating the index client in a one-on-one format to treating various subsystems of the family or the entire family. Conversely, when treating couples or a family, the family therapist would sometimes change the format of psychotherapy from con-joint to individual sessions. As Margolin (1982) aptly noted, the practice of CFP is characterized by diverse formats of treatment, but those mod-els that routinely change formats may be exposed to some unique ethical challenges.

Change of format was initially addressed as an ethical issue by Margolin (1982) but was not dealt with in any detail until Gottlieb (1995). Gottlieb (1995) defined change of format as "a circumstance in which the formal definition of the client changes after the initiation of treatment such that the responsibility of the therapist is altered" (p. 562). In change of format situations, the CFP should keep a separate record for each format.

According to Gottlieb, three ethical issues are central to a change of for-mat in psychotherapy: confidentiality, responsibility, and specific iatrogenic risk issues. One of the more difficult challenges of working within a change of format setting is what to do with confidential information that was dis-covered in an individual session. This dilemma closely parallels the previ-ous discussion on secrets. Depending on the modality of the CFP specialist, some may practice change of format more than others. The central issue that should be considered if change of format is instituted is how to prepare clients prior to the change of format. If the change of format goes from individual to conjoint, the CFP specialist should have a discussion with the client prior to the conjoint session to explore if there is private information that was obtained in the individual session that the client does not want introduced in the couple session. The CFP specialist should document this discussion and inquire about any potentially sensitive issues that came up during the individual sessions. Examples could include prior sexual history, substance abuse, and past relationships. Informed consent should be seen as an ongoing process, and if CFP specialists are going to practice in a change of format modality, then informed consent needs to be revisited prior to any change. When a format changes from couples to individual, the discus-sion of how to handle private information obtained during the individual session needs to be addressed with the couple prior to the change in format. When individual sessions are conducted, it is advisable to maintain indi-vidual records that are separate from the conjoint case file.

Skills

The essential component of the skill domain of the ethical and legal com-petency is demonstrating the awareness and application of an ethical decision-making model. The essential component contains four behavioral anchors. First, CFP specialists will be familiar with an ethical decision-making model that they routinely use to solve ethical dilemmas. Second, they will demonstrate the ability to foresee ethical dilemmas that occur with some regularity in CFP practice. A third, and somewhat related, behavioral anchor involves the ability to accurately identify, analyze, and proactively take steps to resolve the ethical conflict or dilemma. Finally, all activities conducted by the CFP specialist will include deliberate attempts to integrate ethical principles. These activities include all of the functional competencies. We will discuss this domain in two parts. The first will cover those behavioral anchors related to ethical decision-making and its application; the second will present attempts to integrate ethical principles into all aspects of CFP practice.

ETHICAL DECISION MAKING AND ITS APPLICATION

Ethical decision-making is not just adhering to a list of "don'ts." A CFP specialist should aspire to ever-increasing ethical and moral behavior. Accordingly, we shape our discussion around a process that will move a specialist from merely following standards to reaching one's highest ethical potential (Handelsman, Knapp, & Gottlieb, 2002).

Most of the legal and ethical sources of information (Ethics Code, Specialty Guidelines) articulate principles that can be applied to ethical conflicts and dilemmas. For ethical conflicts that are straightforward, few experienced practitioners have difficulty recognizing the right course of action. However, most ethical dilemmas are complicated and require methodical analysis. Ethical principles and standards exist to inform decision-making; however, there are more steps in ethical reasoning than just applying the principle to the problem. Accordingly, we advocate the necessity of a working familiarity with an ethical decision-making model that a specialist routinely uses to make decisions as a benchmark of competency.

Several ethical decision-making models have been proposed over the years (Kitchener, 2000; Knapp & VandeCreek, 2003; Koocher & Keith-Spiegel, 2008). All these models approach ethical decision making from similar vantage points. We recommend the eight-step ethical decision-making model proposed by Bush and colleagues (2006), who added three components to the five-step model articulated by Knapp and VandeCreek (2003). Unfortunately, many ethical violations are committed because of ignorance, inadequate moral sensitivities, or willful disregard. Of these, ignorance is the easiest to remediate. Sometimes practitioners will not realize that there is an ethical conflict until they are knee deep and on the verge of trouble. As ethical sensitivities develop and specialists enhance their ethical reasoning abilities, they begin to achieve competence in being able to foresee and proactively intervene early in the ethical dilemma. The eight steps for ethical decision making, according to Bush and colleagues (2006) are "(a) identify the problem, (b) consider the significance of the context and setting, (c) identify and use ethical and legal resources, (d) consider personal beliefs and values, (e) develop possible solutions to the problem, (f) consider the potential consequences of various solutions, (g) choose and implement a course of action, and (h) assess the outcome and implement changes as needed" (p. 28).

Attitudes

The third domain of the ethical and legal competency for CFP might be characterized as perennial ethical development. We believe that a specialist demonstrates an exemplary pursuit of higher ethical standards. To "attain" competence in the attitude domain is somewhat misleading, since we propose that specialists continue to pursue higher ethical levels. Handelsman and colleagues (2002) distinguish between positive and negative ethics. These authors observe that a "negative" approach to ethics focuses on adherence to rules, avoiding misconduct, and an ethics education that focuses on learning the codes of conduct. In contrast, positive ethics presents a "more balanced and integrative approach that includes encouraging psychologists to aspire to their highest ethical potential" (p. 731).

Conclusion

This chapter provides a working model of the ethical and legal competency for CFP specialists and covers several ethical and legal issues that CFP specialists frequently encounter. The CFP ethical and legal competency articulated in this chapter presented the knowledge, skills, and attitudes that CFP specialists should demonstrate.

ELEVEN

Diversity Competency

The Individual and Cultural Diversity (ICD) competency recognizes that we live in a multicultural world (Daniel, Roysicar, Abeles, & Boyd, 2004). Plato in the *Sophist* argued that difference is the basis of relationality. Unfortunately, in the United States and much of the world, difference has been the basis of dominance, oppression, and widespread injustice. Even in professional psychology, the vast majority of our clinical services and research has been guided by an individually oriented Eurocentric psychology. In the last two decades, the professional psychology community has recognized that multiculturalism is not just one component of psychology but rather a "defining feature of psychological practice" (D. W. Sue, Bingham, Porche-Burke, & Vasquez, 1999, p. 1061).

The Association of Multicultural Counseling and Development (AMCD), a subdivision of the American Counseling Association (ACA), was the first specialty organization to operationalize the construct of multicultural competencies (Arredondo & Perez, 2006). In a document produced by the AMCD, 31 multicultural counseling competencies were presented with 119 explanatory statements (Arredondo et al., 1996). In 1998, Sue et al. added three competencies relating to organizational change to bring the total number of multicultural counseling competencies to 34 (Arredondo & Perez, 2006). Following the publication of the 34 multicultural counseling competencies in the book *Multicultural Counseling Competencies: Individual and Organizational Development* (MCC; Sue et al., 1998), Divisions 17 and 45 combined to form a task force to develop the Guidelines on Multicultural Education, Training, Research, Practice, and Organizational Change for Psychologists (APA, 2003a). This document was approved by the APA Council of Representatives and now stands as the standard for multicultural competency. in this chapter we draw from several other authoritative sources to create the CFP ICD competencies. These include Ethical Principles of Psychologists and Code of Conduct (Ethics Code; APA, 2002), Guidelines for Psychotherapy With Lesbian, Gay and Bisexual Clients (LGB Guidelines; APA, 2000a); Guidelines for Psychological Practice With Older Adults (Geropsychology Guidelines; APA, 2003b), Guidelines for Providers of Psychological Services to Ethnic, Linguistic, and Culturally Diverse Populations (APA, 1990), and the Resolution on Poverty and Socioeconomic Status (APA, 2000b).

CFP and Individual and Cultural Diversity

Couple and family psychology began as a scientific critique of Cartesian approaches to psychiatry and psychology. John Weakland and Gregory Bateson, two of the pioneers of family systems theory, were trained as cultural anthropologists and brought a much needed macrosystemic lens to the highly individualized and pathology-focused mental health profession (R.-J. Green, 2002). The early framers of CFP were interested in multiculturalism even before the passage of the Civil Rights Act of 1964. Ackerman (one of the CFP pioneers) and Jahoda (1950), as one example, wrote a book that analyzed anti-Semitism from a psychological perspective that proposed that prejudice was the result of unconscious projective defenses against hostility and inadequacy directed toward a disadvantaged group. These concepts were later developed into the family process construct of scapegoating (R.-J. Green, 2002).

In spite of the patriarchal and Eurocentric criticisms leveled against some of the early pioneers of CFP (Hare-Mustin, 1978; McGoldrick & Hardy, 2008a), the field maintained its systemic emphasis on the reciprocal interaction of individual, interpersonal, and contextual factors. Since the formation of Division 43 (Society for Family Psychology), the body of professionals who identify with the specialty practice of CFP have been at the table in advancing multicultural concerns in professional psychology. For example, in 1999, Division 43 was a charter member of the Committee of Eight at the National Multicultural Conference and Summit held in Newport Beach, California (D. W. Sue et al., 1999). The Committee of Eight was represented by eight APA divisions (9, 17, 27, 35, 43, 44, 45, and 48), all of which pledged to take the lead in diversifying the field of psychology. The major goals of the Committee of Eight included (a) collaborating and creating the agenda for advancing social justice within and outside the profession of psychology; (b) empowering and supporting APA public interest activities; and

TABLE 11.1 Individual and Cultural Diversity (ICD): Developmental Level—Specialty Competence in Couple and Family Psychology

COMPETENCY DOMAIN AND ESSENTIAL COMPONENT	BEHAVIORAL ANCHOR	ASSESSMENT METHODS
Knowledge		1. Continuing education in ICD
(A) Self and others shaped by ICD and context	(A.1.1) Knowledge of factors that contribute to individual and societal perceptions about individual and cultural diversity factors in others.	2. ABPP examination
(A.1) Understands the individual, interpersonal, and contextual factors that shape one's perception of ICD factors in others	(A.1.2) Awareness through cultural self-assessment about the CFP specialists' perceptions of others that are different from their own	3. Self-assessment
(A.2) Understands the factors that shape the cultural experiences of others.	(A.2.1) Knowledge of cultural diversity elements in couples and families, including normal family cultural patterns, worldviews and values, and macrosystemic factors	4. Peer consultation
(A.3) Knowledge of the CFP literature for working with multicultural clients	(A.2.2) Knowledge of factors that contribute to intracultural variations between family members and their contexts, including identity models, acculturation difference, and multiple identities.	5. Supervision or consultation feedback
	(A.3.1) Knowledge of the major theoretical and empirical contributions to providing CFP clinical services to multicultural populations.	6. Client feedback and/or student feedback
		7. Ability to retain multicultural clients
Skill		8. Scholarly publications and presentations regarding ICD
(B) Perform culturally centered CFP functions	(B.1.1) Conducts culturally centered CFP assessment	9. Research program inclusive of ICD
(B.1) Ability to provide culturally centered CFP clinical services	(B.1.2) Conducts culturally centered CFP intervention	10. Evidence of clinical work with underprivileged
	(B.1.3) Provides cultural centered CFP consultation	11. Actively participating in social change in tangible ways
(B.2) Ability to provide culturally centered CFP training	(B.2.1) Provides culturally centered CFP teaching	
	(B.2.2) Provides culturally centered CFP supervision	
	(B.2.3) Conducts culturally centered CFP research	
Attitudes		
(C) Culturally centered attitude and commitment	(C.1.1) Commitment to perennial development	
(C.1) Strives to develop and maintain a culturally centered perspective	(C.1.2) Promotes multiculturalism within CFP	
(C.2) Demonstrates commitment to social justice	(C.2.1) Commitment to serving marginalized couples and families	
	(C.2.2) Commitment to advocate for policies that promote equity for marginalized	
	(C.2.3) Commitment to intervene in oppressive macrosystems	

Note. Adapted from the format and content of the Assessment of Competency Benchmarks Work Group (2007). This table assumes that the specialist has achieved competence in professional psychology at the three previous developmental levels, as specified in the benchmarks. The competency domains and behavioral anchors serve as the primary organizing structure for this chapter; content explaining each domain and anchor is provided in the chapter.

(c) overcoming barriers in valuing diversity at the individual, family, community, and societal levels (D.W. Sue et al., 1999, p. 1062).

In this chapter we propose a framework for understanding the ICD competency in terms of knowledge, skills, and attitudes as they apply to the work of the CFP specialist (Table 11.1). ICD was defined by the APPIC work group as "persons who may experience discrimination based on race and ethnicity, age, sexual orientation, gender identity, disability, religion, language, and social class" (Daniel et al., 2004, p. 756). The ICD competency is also defined similarly in the Revised APPIC Competency Benchmarks (2009). In this chapter we use multiculturalism synonymously with the ICD competency, with recognition of the more narrowly defined Multicultural Guidelines (APA, 2003a) that restricted the definition of multiculturalism to those individuals from ethnic and racial minority groups. We also use the term *culture-centered* (Pedersen & Ivey, 1993) to refer to a habitual orientation toward seeing all behavior as influenced by culture and perceived by the CFP specialist through socially constructed filters.

Knowledge

Because of the deeply personal nature of this competency, we believe that it is important to draw attention to the difference between having knowledge (filling information gaps and containing the pertinent facts about a culture) and awareness (personal and emotional understanding of culturally learned assumptions, values, and biases; D. W. Sue et al., 1998). Accordingly, the knowledge domain of the ICD competency consists of three essential components. First, CFP specialists will have knowledge, awareness, and understanding of how they have been shaped by ICD factors. Second, CFP specialists will have knowledge, awareness, and understanding of the range of reciprocally determined individual, interpersonal, and macrosystemic factors that shape the experience of individuals, couples, families, and the nature of organizations. Third, the CFP specialist will have knowledge of the major theoretical and empirical contributions to providing CFP clinical services to multicultural populations. Knowledge of self and knowledge of others as cultural beings are the first two guidelines listed in the Guidelines on Multicultural Education, Training, Research, Practice, and Organizational Change for Psychologists (APA, 2003a).

SELF SHAPED BY ICD FACTORS

The first essential component of the knowledge domain contains two behavioral anchors. First, CFP specialists possess knowledge of factors that contribute to systems of privilege. If CFP specialists do not have this foundational knowledge, they arguably will not be able to recognize barriers to increased self-awareness. Second, CFP specialists develop personal awareness through self-assessment of how they have been shaped by their culture. These two behavioral anchors are consistent with Multicultural Guideline 1, which states that "psychologists are encouraged to recognize that, as cultural beings, they may hold attitudes and beliefs that can detrimentally influence their perceptions of and interactions with individuals who are racially and ethnically different from themselves" (APA, 2003a, p. 382).

The first behavioral anchor to achieving specialty level competency in CFP is to understand the factors that contribute to systems of privilege and to appreciate how a system of privilege adversely impacts individuals, couples, and families that are not part of the dominant system. Knowledge of privilege and the factors that contribute to the development and maintenance of the dominant system is central to self-awareness. Through a process of self-assessment, the CFP specialist evaluates which biases, stereotypes, and prejudices may have influenced him or her. Without such self-knowledge, the CFP specialist may unknowingly behave in ways that further marginalize underprivileged clients. Stereotypes, prejudices, and biases held, often unconsciously, by the dominant group constitute systems of privilege that exert oppressive forces on the underprivileged in the form of "isms" (e.g., racism, ableism, ageism, heterosexism, classism, and colonialism; Hays, 2008). For CFP specialists to demonstrate competency in the ICD domain, they need to preliminarily understand the mechanisms that create and maintain systems of privilege. A system of privilege uses stereotypes, prejudice, and bias to maintain power and control over less privileged groups (Fiske, 1993). A core characteristic of possessing privileged status is a lack of awareness of having privilege. According to Hays (2008), "Society does not socialize powerful groups to perceive the rules and barriers separating the unprivileged because they do not need to; oppressed groups have little impact on their daily lives." (p. 14)

ICD-competent CFP specialists understand the sources of bias, stereotypes, and prejudice and how these perceptions and behaviors function to keep the underprivileged in a nondominant role. Bias, stereotypes, and prejudice derive from internal (individual) sources and external (contextual) sources. CFP specialists should be familiar with the internal sources of influence, including social categorization theory (Allport, 1954), in-groups and out-groups (Brewer & Brown, 1998), in-group affiliation (Tajfel, 1981), and social cognitive processes of categorization and generalization (Fiske,

1998). External sources of bias, stereotypes, and prejudice include cultural heritage, socioeconomic status, family of origin, ethnic and racial identity development, gender socialization, and dominant culture worldview and values (APA, 2003a). As specialists come to understand the many sources of individual and contextual influences on multicultural perception and behavior, they may begin to understand how these influences are manifest in their own perception and behavior through self-assessment.

The second behavioral anchor in the knowledge domain of the ICD competency is the awareness of the CFP specialists' own ICD factors. L.Smith (2009) aptly notes that "not only are we in the system, the system is within us" (p. 85). CFP specialists routinely engage in their own family-of-origin work (N. J. Kaslow et al., 2005), and this self-assessment process can easily be extended to a cultural self-assessment. Like the clients with whom they work, CFP specialists are situated within a social ecology (Bronfenbrenner, 1977, 1979) that perpetuates inaccurate perceptions and oppressive interactions with groups that are different from themselves. The CFP specialist's family of origin is a powerful source for transmission of prejudices, stereotypes, and biases against out-groups (Roysicar, 2004). Much of what is learned about nondominant groups is knowingly or unknowingly communicated through a multigenerational socialization process. CFP specialists are also socialized by their peer groups, local communities, religious organizations, socioeconomic experiences, culture of origin, and circumscribed experiences with different groups. In addition, CFP specialists are nested within a broader macrosystem of politics, cultural ideology, worldview, and values. Through this social ecology of cultural development, CFP specialists are socialized with often inaccurate perceptions about culture, gender, age, class, sexual orientation, disability, spirituality, and ethnicity. Several cultural self-assessment methods are available for the CFP specialist.

Family-of-origin self-assessments are typically conducted through the use of a genogram. As noted in Chapter 4 ("Assessment"), the genogram is a graphical assessment technique that provides basic demographic information about an index patient or, in this case, a CFP specialist (McGoldrick et al., 2008). The cultural genogram is an effective tool for CFP specialists to develop an appreciation of their multicultural heritage across three generations (Hardy & Laszloffy, 1995; Keiley et al., 2002). It graphically represents country of origin, assimilation, dominance and submission patterns, religion, and ethnic identification of the CFP specialist (Shellenberger et al., 2007). By developing a deeper appreciation and awareness of their own culture, CFP specialists are able to more capably appreciate the cultural complexities of others different than themselves. CFP specialists need to understand how their understanding of "normal" with respect to couples and families has been formed by their own family of origin and be aware of the extent to which their perceptions are a product of being a member of the dominant culture. For example, if a CFP specialist grew up in a family that believed that individuals are poor because they choose to be, then the specialist will need to be aware of impinging meritocratic perceptions and behaviors when working with low-income clients.

OTHERS SHAPED BY ICD FACTORS

The second essential component of the knowledge domain for the ICD competency is the awareness and understanding that others are shaped by multicultural factors. This component consists of two behavioral anchors. First, CFP specialists understand the array of ICD elements in couples and families, including normal family cultural patterns, worldviews and values, and other macrosystemic factors. Second, The CFP specialist understands the factors that lead to intracultural variations within family members and their contexts, including identity models, acculturation differences, and multiple identities.

Knowledge of normal cultural patterns in ethnic/racial minority groups is an important starting point for competently working with these families. The CFP specialist is mindful of cultural patterns of normal family functioning but is also aware that normative patterns can lead to stereotyping and misunderstanding. Boyd-Franklin (2003) recommends starting with knowledge of cultural patterns as working hypotheses but carefully assessing the cultural pattern with each individual family. As an example, Boyd-Franklin lists features that are common to many African American families such as kinship and extended family networks, forced immigration (slavery), and experiences with racism and discrimination. Knowledge of cultural patterns can actually help to establish rapport when CFP specialists ask culturally informed questions (Hays, 2008; S. Sue, 1998). When CFP specialists do not have specific knowledge of a minority group's culture, they will gather information about the general patterns of the culture and consult with professionals knowledgeable about the minority group. Gathering knowledge about the culture of the minority group is incumbent on the CFP specialist; it is not the role of clients to teach the specialist about their culture (Hays, 2008). CFP specialists are also aware of the stigmatizing aspects of belonging to a marginalized group and the negative experiences that are associated with being in a devalued group (APA, 2003a). All members of devalued groups will experience discrimination in the form of obvious behaviors or more subtle microaggressions (D. W. Sue et al., 2007).

CFP specialists possess knowledge of diverse worldviews and values that are held by members of multicultural groups with whom they work. The knowledge base for understanding worldviews and value orientations of diverse cultural groups is vast. However, some constructs are especially relevant to the work of the CFP specialist. At a rudimentary level, the CFP specialist needs to understand the broad differences between individualistic and collectivistic worldviews and values. Individualistic cultures are associated with Euro-American or Western beliefs and values, whereas collectivistic cultures are associated with non-Western beliefs and values. Pedersen, Crethar, and Carlson (2008) differentiate between these two worldviews by stating that "individualism describes societies in which the connections between individuals are loose and each individual is expected to look after her- or himself, whereas collectivism describes societies in which people are part of strong cohesive ingroups that protect them in exchange for unquestioned lifetime loyalty" (p. 25). Relatedly, CFP specialists need to know how these general orientations toward life impact important couple and family constructs, including, but not limited to, the relation of the individual to the family, normal culturally embedded family interactions, relational hierarchies, conflict expression and negotiation, bases of self-perception and self-esteem, and relationship of the child to the parent. Moreover, CFP specialists need to understand the traditional routes of help-seeking behavior and understand how CFP services would be perceived by non-Western cultures. For example, within a given culture, would it be more typical to seek help from a religious leader or a physician? Additionally, it is important to understand how couples and families from nondominant groups conceptualize their presenting problems.

Finally, it is important for the CFP specialist to understand the macrosystemic factors that shape the cultural experience of minority groups. As noted in the commentary on Guideline 2 of the Multicultural Guidelines (APA, 2003a):

> "Psychologists are encouraged to become knowledgeable about how history has been different for the major U.S. cultural groups. Past experiences in relation to the dominant culture, including slavery, Asian concentration camps, the American Indian holocaust, and the colonization of the major Latino groups on their previous Southwest homelands, contribute to some of the sociopolitical dynamics influencing worldview. (p. 385)

CFP specialists need to understand cultural histories of minority groups, which may include knowledge of major immigrations to the United States, major political events involving minority groups (e.g., immigration policies), and relevant legislation and public policy. A recent example of legislation that should be considered in working with LGBT couples is the legalization of same-sex marriage in some states and its prohibition in others. Knowledge of historical factors related to minority groups has profound relevance on the groups' functioning in society. R.-J. Green (2002) reviewed the work of a prominent educational anthropologist at the University of California, Berkeley (Ogbu, 1989) to illustrate how voluntary versus involuntary immigration strongly determined an individual's academic success in a given culture. Ogbu (1989) found that minority groups that were colonized or coerced into immigrating (through slavery) did worse academically than their ethnically matched counterparts in other countries where immigration was voluntary. Ogbu concluded that

> a minority group's historical pattern of incorporation within a given society and the current level of discrimination it faces within that society are more important to its academic success than are its pre-immigration intra-cultural patterns, language differences, or other cultural discrepancies from the majority. (cited in R-J Green, 2002, p. 230)

The second behavioral anchor necessary for CFP specialists to demonstrate is knowledge of the factors that contribute to intracultural variations between family members and their contexts. CFP specialists recognize that individuals in culturally disenfranchised groups possess varying degrees of identification with their cultural group. Speaking about the African American experience with identity, Cross, Parham, and Helms (1991) stated that "psychologically speaking, the social history of African Americans has been dominated by two compelling processes: deracination, or the attempt to erase Black consciousness, and nigrescence, or the struggle for Black self-awareness" (p. 4). A number of identity models have been developed for members of culturally devalued groups, all of which have in common a unique struggle of reconciling the tension of existing between two cultures: a dominant Western privileged culture and membership in a group that is devalued by the dominant culture. CFP specialists recognize the individual struggle of cultural identity and are aware that individuals within the same family may have markedly different cultural identities, which may be a significant source of tension.

Relatedly, CFP specialists are aware of how acculturation and varying degrees of acculturation within the same family may be a source of family stress. *Acculturation* refers to a process of contact between individuals or groups from a dissimilar source culture with a different receiving culture (Berry, 1997). Berry's acculturation model situates individuals across two dimensions (receiving-culture acquisition and heritage-culture retention). CFP specialists are aware of the tensions that may result within a family based on conflict-laden intergenerational acculturation differences (Szapocznik & Kurtines, 1993). The research of Szapocznik and Kurtines (1993) is illustrative of the tensions that exist between children and parents negotiating autonomy and connectedness. CFP specialists are aware of the stress placed on a family that is negotiating adherence to cultural values, worldview, language, and rituals while attempting to assimilate into a multicultural environment with a dominant American (largely European) worldview.

Finally, CFP specialists should be aware that individual members of couples and families may have multiple identities. Every individual has multiple identities across multiple dimensions. One model that encourages professional psychologists to consider multiple identities for every individual is the Hays (2008) ADDRESSING model. Hays's model considers **a**ge and generational influences; **d**evelopmental disabilities; **d**isabilities acquired later in life; **r**eligion and spiritual orientation; **e**thnic and racial identity; **s**ocioeconomic status; **s**exual orientation; **i**ndigenous heritage; **n**ational origin; and **g**ender" (p. 4). ICD factors are often treated as individual entities and not considered from a systems perspective. Silverstein (2006) proposed that professional psychologists consider multicultural identities from a "complexity paradigm" where multiple identities are considered in light of their influence on one another. Yakushko, Davidson, and Williams (2009) used Bronfenbrenner's social ecology model to develop an "identity salience model" that conceptualizes the reciprocal relationship between multiple identities and the various ecological levels of social contexts in which they occur. Once again the work of Szapocznik and Kurtines (1993) provide a good example of how multiple identities of family members are considered in assessment, intervention, and research.

KNOWLEDGE OF CFP LITERATURE WITH MULTICULTURAL POPULATIONS

CFP specialists also demonstrate knowledge of the relevant literature for working with multicultural populations. In addition to the information cited throughout this chapter, we recommend that CFP specialists become minimally aware of resources for working with ethnic/racial minority groups

(Boyd-Franklin, 2003; Demo, Allen, & Fine, 2000; Falicov, 2000; Hong, 2009; McGoldrick, Giordano, & Garcia-Preto, 2005; McGoldrick & Hardy, 2008b), GLBT populations (Goldberg, 2009; Laird & Green, 1996); gender (Silverstein & Goodrich, 2003); religion and spirituality (Walsh, 2009a, 2009b); disability/illness (McDaniel, Hepworth, & Doherty, 1992; Olkin, 1999; Rolland, 1994); aging (Becvar, 2005); and class (Aponte, 1994).

Skills

As with all competencies, knowledge is never enough. Knowledge of the CFP specialist's own attitudes, biases, and perceptions is the starting point for offering culturally centered CFP services; as noted in the Multicultural Guidelines, however, the knowledge "must be brought to bear on interactions [the CFP specialists] have with others" (APA, 2003a, p. 384). In this section we discuss the skills domain of the ICD competency as it applies to the CFP specialty. We offer two broadly defined essential components: offering culturally centered clinical services and offering culturally centered education. As previously noted, a culturally centered perspective habitually recognizes that multiculturalism is the central paradigm for CFP specialists and that, at a broader metatheory level, multiculturalism is encompassed by a systemic epistemology.

CULTURALLY CENTERED CFP CLINICAL SERVICES

The first essential component of the skill domain is that CFP specialists are able to provide culturally centered CFP clinical services. For the purpose of this competency, CFP clinical services will encompass assessment and intervention broadly, and central behavioral anchors will be articulated under the broader headings of ability to develop a therapeutic alliance with diverse families, culturally centered assessment, and culturally centered intervention.

Ability to Develop an Alliance With Diverse Families

Culturally centered CFP specialists are able to develop a therapeutic alliance with diverse families. The ability to connect with families is the cornerstone of assessment and intervention (see Chapter 12, "Interpersonal Interactions"). However, most of the training offered in graduate school and clinical practica teaches basic clinical skills from a Western perspective (A. E.Ivey, Ivey, & Simek-Morgan, 1993). Trainees are taught to maintain good eye contact, provide reflective listening, and exhibit nonverbal behavior that demonstrates an empathic stance (Hays, 2008). CFP specialists need to be aware of differences in communication styles with diverse families and should minimally be familiar with the ethnic/racial minority groups most commonly seen in one's local community. For example, in many cultures, such as African American and Latino, it is important to establish a connection first before embarking on an assessment process that may be seen as intrusive or threatening (Hays, 2008). Another example, is given by Boyd-Franklin (2003) who recommends delaying the assessment process for several sessions until a relationship has been formed.

Many cultural groups form connections on the basis of respect more than rapport, such as African Americans (Boyd-Franklin, 2003), Latinos (Falicov, 2000), and Asians (Iwamasa, Hsia, & Hinton, 2006). Respect can be demonstrated by using formal greetings, acknowledging family hierarchy, having knowledge about a culture's value orientation and worldview, openly acknowledging a history of prejudice and discrimination when appropriate, acknowledging strengths, or adopting a "one-down" position. Directly addressing the difference between the culture of the therapist and the client may be useful in certain circumstances. As Roysicar (2004) notes, "Culturally self-aware therapists show skills when they can openly discuss human diversity factors in therapy, including knowing when not to refer to salient cultural differences of the client" (p. 658). Relatedly, CFP specialists are also encouraged to be mindful of family hierarchy and, when possible, to work within the family's value system (Hays, 2008). For example, in working with a family that values filial piety, it would be important to recognize the hierarchy and not directly confront it in the early stages of assessment or therapy. It is common for diverse groups to have different values than the CFP specialist. The ICD-competent CFP specialist is capable of managing the values conflict and appreciating the couple or family's value system as meaningful. A sign of multicultural competency is when the CFP specialist is able to discern when the value conflicts are too discrepant to work ethically with the clients. For example, if a religiously conservative family brought their gay-bisexual questioning (GBQ) adolescent for "conversion therapy," the CFP specialist would be compelled to confront the values discrepancy directly with the family and disclose his or her values as part of the informed consent process.

Culturally Centered CFP Assessment

CFP specialists also demonstrate skills that indicate the CFP assessment is performed from a culturally centered perspective (see Chapter 4, "Assessment"). CFP specialists are aware of the moderator variables (Dana, 1993) that may result in misinterpreting and misidentifying problems in a couple or family. These variables should be factored in prior to arriving at an individual or relational diagnosis, problem identification, and intervention strategy. Moderating variables include, but are not limited to, immigration-related stressors (i.e., culture shock, immigration trauma), acculturation level, poverty and socioeconomic status, differential validity of assessment instruments, consideration of culture-bound syndromes, and worldview and values orientation (Comas-Diaz, 1996; Comas-Diaz & Grenier, 1998; Dana, 1993; Frisby, 1998; Geisinger, 1998).

CFP specialists also take into consideration contextual factors when formulating a diagnosis or treatment plan. According to the Multicultural Guidelines, "Culturally centered practitioners are encouraged to take into account how contextual factors may affect the client worldview (behavior, thoughts, or feelings)" (APA, 2003a, p. 391). In assessing a couple or family's problem, it is important to determine if institutional or societal racism or any other experience of prejudice may better explain the presenting problem(s). By considering cultural oppression first in a couple or family that belongs to a marginalized group, the CFP specialist will avoid

TABLE 11.2 **Contextual Assessment Areas**

1. Ethnocultural heritage
2. Racial and ethnocultural identities
3. Gender and sexual orientation
4. Socioeconomic status
5. Physical appearance, ability, or disability
6. Religion when being raised and what now practicing, spiritual beliefs
7. Biological factors (genetic predisposition to certain illness, etc.)
8. Historical era, age cohort
9. Marital status, sexual history
10. History of (im)migration and generations from (im)migrations
11. Acculturation and transcultural levels
12. Family-of-origin and multigenerational history
13. Family scripts (roles of women and men, prescriptions for success or failure, etc.)
14. Individual and family life-cycle development and stages
15. Client's languages and those spoken by family of origin
16. History of individual abuse and trauma (physical; emotional; sexual; political including torture, oppression, and repression)
17. History of collective trauma (slavery, colonization, Holocaust)
18. Gender-specific issues such as battered wife syndrome*
19. Recreations and hobbies, avocations, and special social roles
20. Historical and geopolitical reality of ethnic group and relationship with dominant group (including wars, political conflict, terrorist activity**)

Adapted from Comas-Diaz 1996. Adapted with permission by John Wiley & Sons, Inc.
* We recognize the controversy surrounding the nature of a syndrome and do not take a position in this manuscript
** Not included in original table.

misunderstanding the nature of the problems (APA, 2003a; Helms & Cook, 1999). A more complete list of contextual factors that should be considered by the CFP specialist is listed in Table 11.2 (Comas-Diaz, 1996). It should be noted that a contextual assessment should be conducted on all cases and not just those clients that appear different from the CFP specialist.

Culturally Centered CFP Interventions

Couple and family therapy is well suited to working with multicultural populations. The interventions offered by CFP specialists should be culturally centered and efficacious for the couple or family seeking services. Celano and N. Kaslow (2000) list four features that must be present for family interventions to be culturally competent and efficacious:

> 1) recognize the effects of their own culture(s) on the therapy; 2) acknowledge that family therapy theories and techniques reflect the culture within which they have been developed; 3) attend to the dynamic interplay of the cultural influences that affect the individual's and family's functioning; and (4) devise and implement problem-resolution strategies that are culturally acceptable. (p. 217)

The CFP specialist recognizes that providing couple and family interventions to marginalized groups may require a different therapeutic frame than with interventions offered to clients in the dominant culture. For example, ethnic/racial minorities may involve the use of a translator, which may necessitate longer sessions (Celano & Kaslow, 2000). Interventions offered to an aging or disabled population may require therapy to be offered in the homes of the clients. CFP interventions with cultural groups with an extended kinship network that involves clergy or other community leaders may need to be conducted in an alternate setting such as the client's home, church, community center, or school setting (Boyd-Franklin & Bry, 2000). Relatedly, CFP specialists should be aware of local community resources that will be immediately helpful for diverse couples and family, such as support networks for nontraditional families, disability services, religious and spiritual resources, culturally recognized healers, community leaders, and options for alternative culturally based services through the clients' insurance provider.

CFP specialists may also need to alter how they think about time-honored family therapy constructs such as boundaries, role definition, triangles, enactments, and differentiation, some of which may not be appropriate for a multicultural application. For example, in African American families, the executive subsystem may extend across multiple generations and may not even involve blood relatives (Boyd-Franklin, 2003). Family interventions should be time-limited, active, solution-focused, empowerment-focused, strength-based, and immediately relevant (Boyd-Franklin, 2003; Celano & Kaslow, 2000; McGoldrick et al., 2005). When appropriate, CFP should adopt culturally specific strategies for service delivery such as incorporating an influential leader (e.g., tribal healer) or member of extended kinship network (e.g., aunt's boyfriend).

CULTURALLY CENTERED CFP TRAINING

The second essential component of the skill domain for the ICD competency is that CFP specialists demonstrate the ability to provide culturally centered CFP training to students and professionals seeking the CFP specialization. Training offered by CFP specialists includes, teaching, supervision, and research. The culturally competent CFP trainer educates and supervises from a culturally centered perspective.

Culturally Centered Teaching

Culturally centered, or multicultural, teaching recognizes the use of multiple pedagogies and is cognizant of multiple student learning styles. The dominant Western or Eurocentric pedagogy emphasizes a traditional "banking" of knowledge where students are the passive receptacles of the experts' knowledge (Friere, 1970). In contrast, multicultural education usually includes integration of multicultural content, techniques to reduce prejudice, equity- or justice-focused pedagogies, critical review of dominant assumptions that support the "traditional canon and hidden curriculum," and providing an educational milieu that empowers rather than dominates (Banks, 2000, cited in Enns & Forrest, 2005, p. 4). The CFP specialist recognizes that the majority of psychological science and research and theory on couples and family therapy reflects an ethnocentric monoculturalism, which characterizes "a belief in the superiority of one's own group and the inferiority of another's group and the use of power to impose one's values on the less powerful group" (APA, 2003a, p. 386). The CFP specialist also recognizes that multicultural education has numerous benefits to students, including enhancing commitment to understand racial differences, improving self-awareness, and increasing therapeutic competence (American Council on Education & American Association of University Professors, 2000; APA, 2003a; Brown, Parham, & Yonker, 1996). It should be noted at this point that breaking stride from the traditional Western pedagogy may not be immediately accepted by students habitually trained in this model. We find a similar difficulty in trying to teach students to think systemically rather than linearly. Because of the deeply personal and potentially threatening shift to a multicultural paradigm, CFP educators should be aware that multicultural professors modeling self-disclosure, amiability, leadership, enthusiasm, and a nonjudgmental attitude were judged in positive terms (i.e., encouraging, role model) by their students (Lenington-Lara, 1999, cited in APA, 2003a). Finally, CFP specialists who conduct continuing education for professional growth or provide CFP-related seminars to the public present a culture-centered curriculum that is sensitive to the diverse learning styles of the participants and accurately reflects the underrepresentation of disenfranchised groups in the corpus of psychological literature.

Culturally Centered Supervision

CFP specialists provide culturally centered supervision to trainees (see Chapter 8, "Supervision"). CFP specialists recognize that supervision is a multicultural process that considers many of the elements listed above when providing clinical services. CFP specialists recognize that supervision is one of the primary modalities for teaching the ICD competency to students (Cook, 1994) and should strive to convey to students that multicultural competency is central to becoming a CFP specialist. Even if both the supervisor and the supervisee are from the privileged dominant culture, the CFP specialist can model a culturally centered perspective by drawing attention to the multicultural aspects between the two participants in the supervision process. If the CFP supervisor avoids discussion of multicultural factors in the supervision process, this may communicate to the supervisee that ICD factors are not important, and this attitude may be transmitted to the supervisee's client. CFP specialists are always mindful of the power imbalance between supervisor and supervisee and have the opportunity to provide an empowering experience for the supervisee, especially one who is from an underprivileged group. During the supervision process, the supervisor and supervisee can practice having discussions about ICD factors so that the supervisee becomes more comfortable with such discussions.

Attitude

Much has been said already in this chapter about the attitude of the CFP specialist with respect to ICD factors. In this section we attend in greater detail to the ongoing development of a culturally centered attitude and its natural expression in displaying a commitment to social justice in the functions of CFP.

CULTURALLY CENTERED PERSPECTIVE

The CFP specialist strives to develop and maintain a culturally centered perspective. Becoming culturally competent is a perennial process. A CFP specialist can always become more aware, more open, and more culturally relevant. We believe that the model of an expert student learner captures the essence of the culturally centered attitude. Nevertheless, in a competency-based model, CFP specialists eventually arrive at a place where they can be considered "competent." Two behavioral anchors that reflect competence in ICD factors are a commitment to perennial development and promoting multiculturalism in CFP.

CFP specialists demonstrate a commitment to perennial development of a culturally centered attitude. Demonstration of this commitment can be seen in CFP specialists' constant openness to cultural self-awareness and openness to the differences in others. CFP specialists regularly avail themselves of supervision, consultation, and training in multicultural issues. Further evidence of this competency is seen when CFP specialists actively control automatic biases (Fiske, 1998) and reduce prejudice through frequent contact and cooperation with colleagues of an underprivileged group (APA, 2003a; Brewer & Miller, 1988).

CFP specialists also advance multiculturalism within the field through training, advocacy, and leadership within the specialty discipline. Those specialists who are involved in teaching, curriculum development, or administration in undergraduate and graduate psychology programs can have direct influence in advancing multiculturalism by advocating that multiculturalism become an integrative element throughout the curriculum rather than being taught as one or two classes in the curriculum (APA, 2003a). R.-J. Green (2002) noted that most of what has been accomplished for multiculturalism in family therapy has been a first-order change. A second-order change "would seem to require that matters of race, ethnicity, social class, and prejudice become a fundamental, continual, and visible focus in the work of a majority of family therapists and researchers, including white European American family therapists and researchers" (p. 98).

COMMITMENT TO SOCIAL JUSTICE

A second essential feature of the ICD competency is the commitment to social justice in the work of CFP. This essential component contains three behavioral anchors: serving marginalized groups, advocating equity, and intervening in oppressive macrosystems. D. W. Sue, Arredondo, and McDavis (1992) in their landmark work on MCC argued that "what needs to occur is a philosophical change in the premise of counseling that incorporates a movement toward inclusiveness, altruism, community, care, and justice" (p. 481). CFP specialists are uniquely suited to address issues of social justice because they are trained to see beyond the individual and consider the reciprocal influences of multiple social ecological systems. CFP specialists routinely consider the macrosystemic context and consider intervention within an oppressive macrosystem as the domain of CFP. A psychology that does social justice "rejects the artificial separation of individual well-being from sociocultural forces" (L. Smith, 2009, p. 85).

CFP specialists can demonstrate a commitment to social justice by working with underprivileged couples and families. This can occur in the context of a private practice, community mental health center, state hospital, or prison. Relatedly, CFP specialists can routinely advocate for their underprivileged clients by helping them navigate complex social service systems, serving as liaisons to a supportive community, or giving them a positive experience of the dominant culture.

Finally, CFP specialists can demonstrate commitment to social justice by intervening with oppressive macrosystems. According to the Multicultural Guidelines:

> Psychologists are in a position to provide leadership as agents of prosocial change, advocacy, and social justice, thereby promoting societal understanding, affirmation, and appreciation of multiculturalism against the damaging effects of individual, institutional, and societal racism, prejudice, and all forms of oppression based on stereotyping and discrimination. (APA, 2003a, p. 382)

Conclusion

In this chapter we have outlined the knowledge, skills, and abilities that CFP specialists should have in order to demonstrate advanced competency in Individual and Cultural Diversity. CFP specialists possess knowledge of themselves and others as multicultural beings and provide culturally centered clinical services to couples and families and education to students and trainees. CFP specialists are encouraged to promote multiculturalism within the field of professional psychology and function as agents of social justice in the broader macrosystemic context.

TWELVE

Interpersonal Interaction Competency

Unlike some psychologists who work primarily or exclusively with individuals, CFP specialists interact regularly in professional contexts with multiple individuals in conjoint treatment interaction. It is crucial that the CFP specialist manifest the competency to relate effectively in order to create a therapeutic alliance with individuals, couples or dyads, families, groups, and larger social systems. This chapter defines interpersonal competency, specifies the specialty knowledge base and values necessary for competency, and details specialty-level skills and abilities in interpersonal interactions. See Table 12.1 for an overview of these factors.

Definition of Interpersonal Interaction Competency

Competent interpersonal interaction in CFP entails the ability to establish and maintain an effective therapeutic relationship with individuals, couples, families, and larger social systems. Effective therapeutic relations are based on knowledge of systems theory, specific interpersonal theory, and research regarding therapeutic relationships, as well as attitudes that inform the therapeutic process. Interpersonal skills reflect the application of the attitudes and knowledge to specific abilities and techniques within the treatment interaction.

Effective interpersonal interaction may be understood as a foundational competency because it plays a role in all the functional competencies. It is especially significant in the intervention competency because it interacts with treatment model implementation to affect treatment outcomes (Sexton, 2007; see below). In addition, because CFP specialty practice often

TABLE 12.1 **Interpersonal Interactions: Developmental Level — Specialty Competence in Couple and Family Psychology**

COMPETENCY DOMAIN AND ESSENTIAL COMPONENT	BEHAVIORAL ANCHOR	ASSESSMENT METHODS
Knowledge (A) Knowledge of interpersonal relations (A.1) Knowledge of systems, relationship, group, conflict, and communication theory	(A.1.1) Understands, conceptualizes, and evaluates interpersonal interaction from systemic perspective (A.1.2) Understands and capably articulates key concepts of relationship, couple, family, group, conflict, and communication theory (A.1.3) Demonstrates knowledge regarding the complex nature of CFP role in interpersonal interactions in treatment	1. ABPP examination 2. Publication and presentation regarding interpersonal interaction in scholarly venues 3. Peer consultation 4. Self-evaluation 5. Supervision or consultation feedback 6. Client feedback regarding therapeutic alliance; ability to retain clients 7. ABPP examination 8. Continuing education in CFP; interpersonal factors
Skills (B) Interpersonal, affective, and expressive skills (B.1) Creates and maintains effective relationships with clients, including the ability to manage interpersonal conflict and model effective communication	(B.1.1) Ability to create therapeutic relationships with the range of clients in CFP (individuals, couples, families, and larger social organizations), including multigenerational systems (B.1.2) Ability to manage conflict, complexity, and multiple perspectives with equity in professional interactions (B.1.3) Ability to communicate clearly and effectively in professional interactions (B.1.4) Ability to monitor interpersonal interactions in vivo and correct problems (B.1.5) Ability to facilitate treatment termination effectively	
Attitudes (C) Values constructive relations (C.1) Commitment to facilitating positive interpersonal relations	(C.1.1) Aware of differences in perspective and tolerant of differences (C.1.2) Comfortable with ambiguity in interpersonal relations (C.1.3) Values each person in professional relationships and is committed to equitable treatment (C.1.4) Personally receptive to feedback	

Note. Adapted from the format and content of the Assessment of Competency Benchmarks Work Group (2007). This table assumes that the specialist has achieved competence in professional psychology at the three previous developmental levels, as specified in the benchmarks. The competency domains and behavioral anchors serve as the primary organizing structure for this chapter; content explaining each domain and anchor is provided in the chapter.

incorporates multiple individuals in the treatment room, this competency also includes the ability to model effective interpersonal relations for the clients; this constitutes a type of intervention because it can impact treatment goals that focus on improving client relationships (see Chapter 5).

Interpersonal Knowledge

Effective interpersonal treatment skills are built on a foundation of theoretical knowledge and research findings about therapeutic interaction. The ability to relate effectively is not inherent in the clinician; relationship skills develop from knowledge about the nature of interpersonal relationships within a treatment context and supervised experience in professional practice (N. J. Kaslow, Celano, & Stanton, 2005).

FOUNDATION IN SYSTEMS THEORY

CFP advocates a systemic epistemology (Robbins, Mayorga, & Szapocznik, 2003; Stanton, 2009b; see Chapter 2) that includes knowledge about key systemic concepts (e.g., complexity, reciprocity, adaptation) and informs the psychological treatment of individuals in systemic context. The CFP specialist understands these systemic dynamics and acts in treatment in a manner consistent with that awareness. The CFP specialist conceptualizes interpersonal interaction that establishes a therapeutic alliance within a systemic framework that recognizes that multiple persons contribute to and are influenced by the developing alliance. In addition, the CFP specialist understands that particular systemic models of treatment define the interactional position of the specialist differently (e.g., from nondirective and collaborative to hierarchical and directive), so the specialist must attend to the particular treatment intervention utilized (Rait, 2000; see below). There may be different perceptions of the alliance by different individuals in treatment, and there is now evidence that gender differences in perception of alliance can exist in couple therapy that inform likely treatment outcomes (Knobloch-Fedders, Pinsof, & Mann, 2007). In addition, relationship distress between individuals in treatment and individual family-of-origin distress (poor quality of family functioning experienced as a child) predict the nature of the therapeutic alliance (Knobloch-Fedders, Pinsof, & Mann, 2004).

In that framework, the definition and manifestation of therapeutic alliance in CFP are different than in individual psychotherapy. Consistent with systems theory, the alliance is much more complex and interactive. For instance, not only might there be individual differences in alliance, but those alliances may vary subtly over time in treatment, and even the perception of another participant's alliance may impact outcomes. Knobloch-Fedders and colleagues (2007) found that women's evaluation of their partners' treatment alliance provided an additional element toward outcomes beyond her own therapeutic alliance. In addition, it is not unusual for participation in treatment by members of the system to vary over time; the alliance may change when a new person is present or someone is missing at a session. CFP recognizes the multifaceted nature of the therapeutic alliance in systemic treatment.

Systemic models of therapeutic alliance pay attention to cultural and individual differences. This is demonstrated in a multicultural understanding of empathy in the therapeutic environment (Pedersen, Crethar, & Carlson, 2008). This model distinguishes between a convergent definition of empathy that focuses primarily on understanding an individual apart from the person's context and a divergent definition that focuses on the person in the cultural context (Chung & Bemak, 2002); traditional individualistic psychology has emphasized the former, while systemic models of psychology rely on the latter (see Chapter 11 for diversity elements to consider in establishing the therapeutic alliance).

Finally, systems theory recognizes that when a CFP specialist is invited to join a social system to assist in system functioning, the specialist becomes part of that social system, at least for a time (Brooks, 2001; Stinchfield, 2004), with important treatment outcome implications. For example, the CFP specialist must establish and maintain appropriate boundaries: "The psychologist, while a part of the interaction in family sessions, should try to avoid siding with family members and colluding with the targeting of the identified patient...these methods help create a healthy therapeutic boundary" (Thoburn, Hoffman-Robinson, Shelly, & Hagen, 2009, p. 206). The CFP specialist must understand the nature of the role and act responsibly within the system; this requires skills that grow out of an understanding of systemic functioning.

CONCEPTUAL MODELS

Knowledge of systems theory is enhanced by specific awareness of relationship functioning at particular systemic levels (e.g., couple, family, and group) and in certain social circumstances (e.g., conflict). For instance, familiarity with attachment theory (Ainsworth, Blehar, Waters, & Wall, 1978; Bowlby, 1988; George, 2009) and its relevance to CFP populations may alert the CFP specialist to client limitations in developing a therapeutic alliance and/or explain client behaviors in response to clinician-initiated interpersonal interactions (Obegi, 2008). While such knowledge is the foundation for particular CFP interventions, such as Emotionally Focused Couple Therapy (Johnson & Bradley, 2009), it also informs the evolution of the therapeutic alliance (Obegi, 2008).

Knowledge of communication theory in professional settings (e.g., communication accommodation theory; Watson & Gallois, 1998) ensures that the CFP specialist understands the nature of intergroup and interpersonal communication, recognizing the barriers to accurate conveyance of information or ideas (session dynamics; Mahaffey, Lewis, Walz, Bleuer, & Yep, 2008) that may impede a therapeutic alliance. Knowledge of group process theory and research on group therapy (Yalom & Leszcz, 2005) informs CFP specialist interpersonal interaction at the group or larger social systems levels. Knowledge of conflict theory (Ma, Lee, & Yu, 2008) and models of conflict style (Rahim & Magner, 1995; Thomas & Kilmann, 1978) enables the practitioner to understand interpersonal conflict, recognize conflict styles (including the style of the specialist), and enhance one's ability to manage conflict in the treatment process. Understanding conflict is especially relevant to the practice of couple therapy (Mackey, Diemer, & O'Brien, 2000) and practice in family business or organizations (see Chapter 6). The CFP specialist demonstrates an advanced level of knowledge and the ability to apply these theories to treatment populations.

EVIDENCE-BASED RELATIONSHIPS

There is now research evidence that recognizes the importance of effective interpersonal relations in treatment (Norcross, 2001). Early attempts to identify evidence-based practices minimized the role of the psychologist and focused instead on procedures prescribed by treatment manuals in a manner that appeared to suggest that the person of the psychologist was relatively unimportant to treatment outcomes (Norcross, 2001). As Lebow (2006b) indicates, "Too often researchers regard the skills, personality, and experience of the therapist as side issues, features to control to ensure that different groups receive comparable interventions" (p. 132). Subsequent models of evaluation of evidence for intervention outcomes have given increased attention to clinical judgment and the interpersonal skills of the psychologist (Levant, 2004). Norcross (2001), detailing the results of an APA Division 29 (Psychotherapy) Task Force on Empirically Supported Therapy Relationships, notes that most clinicians experience treatment as an extremely interpersonal and affective interaction. He suggests that we cannot ignore that the "therapist as a person is a central agent of change," and "multiple and converging sources of evidence indicate that the *person* of the psychotherapist is inextricably intertwined with the outcome of psychotherapy" at a level similar to the effect of a particular treatment (Norcross, 2001, p. 346).

The APA Presidential Task Force on Evidence-Based Practices (2006) considered the various perspectives on evidence-based practice and arrived at a definition that gave credence to research and clinical experience: "*Evidence-based practice in psychology* (EBPP) is the integration of the best available research with clinical expertise in the context of patient characteristics, culture, and preferences" (p. 273). Subsequently, APA Task Force members clarified that "the task force designated the *use* of research evidence as a *component* of clinical expertise" and that there is no dichotomy between clinical experience and research findings (Wampold, Goodheart, & Levant, 2007, p. 617). Among the components of clinical expertise delineated by the Task Force is interpersonal expertise. The Task Force members suggest that clinical expertise is manifested in a variety of clinical activities, including the formation of a therapeutic alliance (APA Presidential Task Force on Evidence-Based Practices, 2006).

However, debate continues regarding the relative salience of specific evidence-based models of intervention that rely on distinctive change mechanisms versus the "common factors" found across evidence-based interventions (Blow, Sprenkle, & Davis, 2007; see Chapter 5 for an overview of this issue). Evidence suggests that common factors play a significant role in the development and maintenance of the therapeutic alliance (Sprenkle, Davis, & Lebow, 2009). A comprehensive understanding of the therapist's role recognizes the importance of how an individual therapist invokes the common factors, demonstrates interpersonal abilities, and adheres to evidence-based models to achieve positive outcomes. For example, Robbins and colleagues (Robbins et al., 2006; Robbins, Turner, Alexander, & Perez, 2003) found that in Functional Family Therapy the alliance is best achieved by a balanced relationship with the adolescent and the parents, whereas in Multidimensional Family Therapy it is best accomplished by a strong relationship with the parents. Additional research suggests that the relative importance of a balanced therapeutic relationship may vary within a particular treatment model by family ethnicity, perhaps due to different cultural expectations regarding hierarchical structure and respect for those differences in treatment (Flicker, Turner, Waldron, Brody, & Ozechowski, 2008). We suggest the recognition of a dynamic interaction between treatment models and common factors. "Just as many common factors work through models, models in turn work through therapists" (Blow et al., 2007, p. 299). The CFP specialist understands and implements common factors in light of intervention models in order to develop and maintain the therapeutic alliance.

Models for the measurement of the therapeutic alliance, such as the Systemic Inventory of Change (STIC®) that includes as subscales the Integrative Psychotherapy Alliance Scales (Pinsof & Chambers, 2009), including the Individual, Couple Therapeutic Alliance Scale-Revised (Knobloch-Fedders et al., 2007) and Family versions, allow progress reports to the CFP specialist about the nature of the alliance. This model evaluates alliance in two domains, Content (tasks, goals, and bonds) and Interpersonal System (self, other, group; Pinsof & Chambers, 2009). The Interpersonal System evaluation allows the clinician to distinguish different perceptions of alliance between the various levels of the system because they contribute to treatment continuation and progress (Pinsof & Chambers, 2009).

Alternatively, the System for Observing Family Therapy Alliances (SOFTA) model (Friedlander, Escudero, & Heatherington, 2006), based on systems theory, allows the clinician to collect evidence about the alliance by monitoring specific elements of the alliance, including engagement, emotional connection, safety, and shared perception of purpose, noting both patient and therapist behaviors. SOFTA research indicates that differentiation of self, a systemic concept evident in Bowen theory, has been demonstrated to predict a patient's perception of the treatment alliance (J. E. Lambert & Friedlander, 2008).

Interpersonal Attitudes

The primary specialty attitude for the interpersonal interaction competency is a commitment to facilitating positive and constructive therapeutic relationships. Several aspects contribute to this attitude in an interactive fashion (i.e., they are not discrete attitudes or behaviors; they evidence reciprocal influence on each other), including awareness of differences in perspective between participants in CFP treatment and clinician tolerance of differences; CFP specialist expectation and comfort with the ambiguity that exists in interpersonal interactions; clinician professional attitude to value each person in professional interaction and commitment to equitable treatment; and specialist willingness to receive and respond professionally to patient feedback.

Awareness and tolerance of differences in treatment are crucial to developing a therapeutic alliance with individuals who are different than the clinician in race, ethnicity, socioeconomic status, age, gender, sexual orientation, spirituality, physical features, primary language, national origin, and other characteristics (see Chapter 11). Comas-Diaz (2006) adopts this broad definition of culture (i.e., extending ethnicity and race to include multiple individual difference factors and the dynamic interaction between these factors) and notes the importance of the therapeutic relationship in multicultural treatment. Cultural competence begins with a basic commitment to recognize and accept individual differences in the process of establishing a therapeutic relationship. This often requires self-reflection and exploration by the clinician of past experience, personal bias, and individual values (Constantine, Fuertes, Roysircar, Kindaichi, & Walsh, 2008; Hays, 2008). This is more complicated in CFP practice than in individual treatment because there are likely to be a variety of differences within and across the multiple individuals in treatment that may elicit therapist bias; consideration of personal development from a cultural perspective may assist the CFP specialist in developing positive attitudes toward difference (Bobes & Bobes, 2005; McGoldrick, Giordano, & Garcia-Preto, 2005).

Tolerance of ambiguity is an important characteristic for CFP practitioners. "Tolerance for ambiguity implies that one is able to deal with uncertainty and/or multideterminacy.... Ambiguity-tolerant people are comfortable with the shades of gray in life" (Beitel, Ferrer, & Cecero, 2004, p. 569). Tolerance of ambiguity refers to the fact that interpersonal interaction often results in vague, imprecise, or uncertain meanings. In fact, when interacting with multiple individuals, there are often multiple interpretations of what has occurred. CFP specialists need to be able to understand and hold several perspectives at once in order to create an effective alliance with couples, families, or larger groups. This is consistent with a constructivist perspective that suggests that meaning is socially constructed (Gergen, 1985) through dialogue. Gelatt (1989) presents a "decision and counseling framework that helps clients deal with change and ambiguity, accept uncertainty and inconsistency" (p. 252) in the face of increasing ambiguity today. This model is consistent with a systemic epistemology. Termed *positive uncertainty* (Gelatt, 1989, p. 252) because Gelatt suggests that it is possible to be comfortable with the ambiguity we face regularly in interpersonal interactions, the model provides three guidelines for organizing information to determine a course of action: (a) information: information is more readily available today than before, but some level of uncertainty is beneficial because information is often ambiguous and changing; (b) process: goals may be discovered in the process of considering information to achieve decisions instead of setting goals and deciding how to get there; and (c) choice: therapists must reconsider excessive reliance on rational thought processes in decision making to embrace intuitive thinking and encourage the flexibility to both create change and respond to it (Gelatt, 1989, pp. 254–255). The CFP practitioner must be comfortable enough with ambiguity to facilitate this process. Pedersen et al. (2008) indicate that becoming comfortable with ambiguity is one element in developing multicultural empathy.

A professional commitment to equitable treatment that values each person in the treatment interaction is essential for CFP practice. For instance, a frequent concern in couple therapy involves gender equity; does the CFP specialist make stereotyped attributions based on gender, or does the CFP practitioner evaluate the cause for relationship events differentially based on gender? (Stabb, Cox, & Harber, 1997). Social psychology tells us that fairness is a common human value and that procedural fairness (the manner in which people are treated) results in a fair process effect (perceived fairness positively impacts future reactions) that positively influences future relations (van den Bos & Miedema, 2000). Procedural fairness concerns may arise when one person dominates the treatment session, when it appears that one person is being blamed for couple issues, or when individual differences between a patient and the CFP practitioner seem to result in clinician behavior that devalues one person. The CFP specialist may anticipate potential concerns regarding inequitable treatment by raising the issue at the onset of treatment, especially if it appears that some such perception may be present and may inhibit development of a therapeutic alliance. The practitioner may well establish practice norms and communicate them when treating multiple individuals (e.g., couples, families, groups). For example, when initiating couple therapy, the specialist may inform the partners that he or she makes every effort to be fair to both partners, but that a particular session may appear to focus more on one person or the other. Or the practitioner may make a comment that one partner could understand as unfair and invite each partner to express any concerns about inequitable treatment in session. At that point, specialist openness to patient feedback is important.

Practitioner willingness to receive and respond professionally to patient feedback can help establish the therapeutic alliance and avoid disruption of it. If a patient raises a concern about the professional behavior of the clinician, it is important that the specialist not react defensively. Defensiveness in CFP practice has been conceptualized as reciprocal and circular, so that therapist defensiveness engenders a defensive response from patients in a manner that undermines the therapeutic relationship; in addition, therapist defensiveness has been found to result in poorer outcomes for couple therapy (Waldron et al., 1997). Consequently, the critical attitude involves openness, equality, and responsiveness instead of dogmatism, superiority, and control over the relationship (Waldron et al., 1997). A nondefensive response that reflects accurate empathy and understanding for the concern raised and clarifies the specialist's intent in the questioned situation may resolve the difficulty or allow continued dialogue about the concern. Willingness to provide a referral to another clinician may be necessary (e.g., if the specialist is male, and a female patient has questioned gender bias, a referral may be made to a female specialist); this offer can demonstrate genuine concern to address the issue in a manner that may allow further discussion and possible resolution of the issue with the original clinician. Some CFP specialists or treatment clinics routinely use client satisfaction surveys to ensure frequent feedback from patients (Fischer & Valley, 2000; Pinsof & Chambers, 2009).

Interpersonal Interaction Skills

A variety of clinician-offered relationship qualities have been identified in CFP literature relative to creating and maintaining effective therapeutic relationships with clients. This section will review these interpersonal skills in light of the comprehensive and complex model noted above that includes speciaist manifestation of the common factors, interpersonal relationship abilities, and adherence to evidence-based models. It may not be assumed that particular manifestations of common factors will uniformly impact treatment in a positive fashion because the interpersonal skills should align with the specific treatment model used (Sexton, 2007). In addition, certain skills may be more important for some treatment than for others (e.g., managing conflict and providing safety may be more important for high-conflict couples or families experiencing physical abuse). In this section, we will describe interpersonal interaction skills at the onset of treatment, during treatment, and at termination of treatment.

INTERPERSONAL INTERACTION SKILLS AT ONSET OF TREATMENT

The literature on the role of interpersonal interaction between the clinician and the clients clearly identifies the importance of establishing a therapeutic alliance quickly in treatment. For example, in a study about couple therapy, Knobloch-Fedders et al. (2007) found that "the therapeutic alliance formed quickly, and remained relatively stable from the first session to the eighth session of treatment. It appears that couples' immediate perceptions of their therapists (formed during the first session) remain well established, at least as the therapy moves into the mid-treatment phase" (p. 255). They suggest that developing the therapeutic alliance is among the most critical tasks of the initial couple session.

Rapid establishment of a positive therapeutic alliance requires specialist characteristics and skills that will engage the clients, such as interpersonal warmth, empathy and caring, conveying expertise, appreciation of client expertise, and ability to establish an appropriate balance in alignment with different members engaged in couple, family, or larger group treatment.

Interpersonal Warmth, Empathy, and Caring

Therapist-offered factors frequently mentioned as important in establishing a therapeutic alliance include various aspects of friendliness, interpersonal warmth, and genuineness, often demonstrated as empathy and caring in treatment. This is noted by Blow and colleagues (2007), "Regarding therapeutic style, therapist positivity/friendliness is consistently associated with good outcome, and criticism/hostility has the opposite impact" (p. 304). The CFP clinician must develop the skills to communicate interpersonal acceptance, friendliness, and warmth quickly and clearly to the new clients. When clients are troubled or facing difficult challenges, most want to know that the person helping them both accurately understands their situation and cares about helping them. Obegi (2008), drawing on attachment theory, indicates that "clients seek therapists because doing so is expected to alleviate distress" (p. 433). Friedlander et al. (2006) suggest the importance of this dimension through the inclusion of the dimension "emotional connection" between therapist and client(s) in their SOFTA model of therapeutic alliance, indicating that it is "based on affiliation, trust, caring, and concern; that the therapist genuinely cares and 'is there' for the client" (p. 88). They note that "clients value therapists who are warm, active, down-to-earth, informal, trustworthy, optimistic, secure, humorous, caring and understanding" (Friedlander et al., 2006, p. 90) and indicate that clients who do not find these characteristics in the therapist may not contribute important information early in treatment, inhibiting assessment and treatment.

The desired outcome at the end of the first session is the client perception of a positive therapeutic alliance with the CFP specialist because it contributes significantly to change and treatment outcomes (Blow et al., 2007; Knobloch-Fedders et al., 2004). The early alliance has a strong impact on the continuing alliance (Knobloch-Fedders et al., 2007).

One demonstration of specialist empathy and caring is the skill of adapting one's style of interaction to the expectations and desires of the clients

(Blow et al., 2007). It is possible to vary one's style of interaction according to the needs of the moment in order to maintain the conditions that facilitate change. Another is skill in demonstrating respect for clients' cultures and aligning interventions with cultural values and beliefs; Muir, Schwartz, and Szapocznik (2004) term these *culturally syntonic interventions* because they are in tune with the clients.

Finally, it is important for the clinician to know how the clients perceive the therapeutic interaction. This requires the interpersonal skill of questioning the perception of the relationship in a friendly and caring manner. For instance, it is our practice to ask the clients at the end of the first session about their perception of the therapeutic alliance (e.g., "How do you feel about working with me on these issues?" or "Do you feel like you can talk openly with me about your problems?"). This allows the CFP specialist to process initial perceptions of the therapeutic alliance before the end of the first session, discussing any difficulties and/or correcting any mispercep-tions. Alternatively, a client feedback survey may elicit similar information after the session (see case examples in Pinsof & Chambers, 2009).

Conveying Expertise

The ability to convey professional expertise is a skill that requires careful attention to avoid the errors of arrogance and condescension, on the one hand, or self-effacing humility that undermines the clients' confidence in the specialist, on the other hand. When individuals seek treatment in the midst of challenging circumstances, it is crucial that they perceive that the clinician is capable of working with them to address their concerns.

This does not require a directive or "expert" style; it may be accomplished by accurate understanding of the presenting issues and clear communication that the specialist has a procedure to address those issues. It often involves the instillation of the perception that the presenting issue(s) did not shock, offend, or rise above the education, training, and experience of the clinician (Blow et al., 2007). The desire is to create an awareness of specialist experience with similar issues ("I've been around this block before") and a perception of specialist competence to work with the clients on them in therapy ("I have some ideas about how we can work on this"). It should be possible for the clinician to summarize the presenting issues and to discuss or negotiate initial therapeutic goals by the end of the first session. This provides a concrete sense of direction to the clients and conveys the capability of the specialist to help facilitate change, enhancing "engagement in the therapeutic process" (Friedlander et al., 2006, p. 72).

There is some confound in the research about the role of the level of experience in achieving treatment outcomes (perhaps because expertise has not been determined by clear competency measures, such as ABPP examination, in the research), but it has been suggested that it may be most significant when treating challenging clients and complex problems (Blow et al., 2007). In our practice, we have found that it is beneficial to ask the clients at the end of the first session (after the synopsis of presenting issues and suggested treatment plan, noted above) if they believe this is a place where they can find the assistance they desired when they called for an appointment. As Sprenkle and Blow (2007) note, "Clients need to view the 'tasks' of therapy as credible, and if what the therapist is doing does not fit with their expectations, or the therapist cannot sell them on the merits of the approach, it matters little what the therapist believes" (p. 111). In a manner similar to feedback on the perception of personal characteristics, this allows the clients to express their perception about the potential effectiveness of the specialist and the proposed plan of action, and it provides an opportunity for the specialist to respond by modifying and/or clarifying the plan.

Appreciation of Client Expertise

Anderson (2009), practicing from a constructivist approach, advances the idea that both the clinician and the clients contribute expertise to the therapeutic engagement. He suggests that the "client is an expert on themselves and their world; the family psychologist is an expert on a process and space for collaborative relationships and dialogical conversations" (Anderson, 2009, p. 308). This is especially important in CFP practice because of the complexity of multiple perspectives and compound information. The specialist must develop the skill of conveying respect and appreciation for the expertise of the clients because "it calls our attention to the client's wealth of know-how on his or her life and cautions us not to value, privilege, and worship the family psychologist as a better knower than the client" (Anderson, 2009, p. 308). So, for instance, the clinician may invite the clients to correct any specialist misperceptions about the clients and the relative fit of session interaction to their circumstances to establish a truly collaborative process.

Establish Balanced Alignment

A final critical skill in early treatment is the ability to establish a balanced therapeutic alignment with the various individuals, dyads, or subsystems in treatment. The exact nature of the alignment should reflect the

specifications of the treatment model (Sexton, 2007) and the particular needs of the social system in treatment (Blow et al., 2007) in order to
achieve the evidence-based outcome, so the specialist must monitor treatment adherence. In addition, it requires a careful assessment of system
dynamics by the CFP specialist and the ability to accommodate the needs
of the system instead of a rigid adherence to one's own preferences or ten-
dencies. For example, certain ethnic or cultural expectations may need to
be accommodated (Flicker et al., 2008). The clinician needs the skill to
listen carefully and observe body language or other signs of feedback from
the clients about the alignment (e.g., disengagement, arguing with the specialist), and the skill to adjust the balance of the alignment as needed over
the course of treatment, using alliance techniques. We have found that it is
sometimes helpful to bring perceptions of change in the therapeutic alliance into the session in order to discuss specialist perception of the change
and to allow the clients to clarify their perceptions so that adjustments can
be considered (see below).

INTERPERSONAL INTERACTION SKILLS DURING TREATMENT

The CFP specialist needs to evidence advanced interpersonal interaction
skills during treatment. Skills needed include the ability to continue and
enhance the therapeutic alliance, advanced proficiency in communication,
skills for handling complexity, and conflict management abilities.

Skills to Continue Development of Therapeutic Alliance

Thoburn et al. (2009) indicate that the "development of the therapeutic
alliance, both with individual family members and with the family as a
whole, is an important initial process that begins during assessment and
continues throughout treatment" (p. 206). This means that the practitioner must monitor interpersonal interaction in vivo in order to notice
any degradation of the therapeutic alliance and/or any opportunities to
enhance it and respond appropriately. Monitoring interpersonal relations
is a skill developed in training that involves learning how to interact with
and simultaneously analyze the nature and patterns of that interaction. In
other words, the specialist cannot simply relate to the clients; the specialist
must mentally observe the interaction from another level in order to gauge
the effectiveness of the interpersonal dynamics and record any indicators
from the clients of changing perceptions of the alliance. "Thus, when a
family member indicates that the therapy is not useful, implies that the
process is blocked, or shows indifference to what is being discussed or proposed, the therapist must recognize the threat to the alliance and redirect

his or her efforts" (Friedlander et al., 2006, p. 73). This is more complex in CFP practice because multiple individuals may be present in the treatment room. Live supervision (see Chapter 8), review of session video recordings, and/or co-therapy may enhance the clinician's skill in this area (Celano, Smith, & Kaslow, 2010).

Responsiveness, which is the skill of appropriate reaction to clients' concerns about the treatment alliance, has been shown to positively impact treatment outcomes. Knobloch-Fedders et al. (2007) found "that subtle shifts in the alliance through mid-treatment are associated with treatment responsiveness, at least for women. Women's alliance scores at mid-treatment made a unique contribution to the prediction of improvement in marital distress, over and above their early treatment alliance scores" (p. 255). They indicate that this implies that the clinician must demonstrate attention to the alliance and ensure that positive engagement continues throughout treatment.

Communication Skills

Competent communication in CFP treatment involves the ability to listen, demonstrate understanding, and send clear and direct messages to multiple individuals concurrently, recognizing that communication can be misinterpreted or perceived differently by various individuals in the room. These skills are most often honed in supervised experience of CFP practice with couples, families, and groups. Verbal reinforcement, a behavioral technique, and motivational language may be especially helpful when dealing with difficult problems like substance abuse (J. E. Smith & Meyers, 2004). Measures to evaluate the therapeutic alliance, such as the SOFTA self-report version (Friedlander et al., 2006), include items such as "The therapist understands me" and "The therapy sessions help me open up" or "It is hard for me to discuss with the therapist what we should work on in therapy" (p. 298) to evaluate communication proficiency. The STIC therapeutic alliance scales (Pinsof & Chambers, 2009) includes similar items (e.g., "The therapist does not understand me" [p. 443]) to examine how the clients interpret the alliance. These items relate to specialist ability to convey understanding through communication skills.

Skills to Manage Complexity

Because a systemic epistemology recognizes the salience of multiple factors in treatment and because there are often two or more clients in conjoint, family, or group treatment, the CFP specialist must be able to manage complexity. This involves monitoring all system factors, screening information for salience to the treatment goals, and holding multiple client perspectives concurrently.

The basic skill needed to monitor system factors involves clinician internalization of a multifactor paradigm (Stanton, 2009b; see Chapter 2) that allows the specialist to consider all possible individual, interpersonal, and environmental aspects that may be important in a particular case and readily categorize that information for organization and retention. The next skill involves screening the wealth of possibly important information to determine which factors are most salient to the treatment goals. This requires prioritization methods based on the knowledge and experience of the specialist and understanding of the clients' prioritization. In our experience with complex cases, the organization and screening of factors is itself helpful to clients in determining more exactly the issues they want to address in treatment. This skill facilitates joint determination of treatment goals, an important aspect of the therapeutic alliance (Pinsof & Chambers, 2009).

The ability to hold multiple client perspectives simultaneously requires the specialist to understand the tenets of social constructivism and apply them to an ongoing treatment. It involves the ability to demonstrate accurate empathy and understanding to each person in treatment, even when that person's perspective differs significantly from that of others in treatment. CFP practice includes the ability to move treatment toward addressing all perspectives and all goals. In some cases, it may be possible to bring disparate perspectives into greater alignment by helping each person to understand the role of perception and negotiating shared perceptions. It is always important to consider the treatment goals of every involved client. For instance, the STIC model includes both a "Self" dimension that measures individual alliance to the clinician and an "Other" dimension that measures each person's perception of the alliance between the clinician and other key people in the client's life (Pinsof & Chambers, 2009). For example, the Couple form includes the item "The therapist understands my partner's goals for this therapy" (p. 442). Multicultural competency skills (Comas-Diaz, 2006) are relevant here as they parallel CFP practice; the CFP specialist must often interact across cultures in multiple ways even in a particular couple or family (e.g., interracial marriage, differences between first- and second-generation immigrants in a family, different religious identities).

Conflict Management Skills

A final aspect of interpersonal interaction that impacts the therapeutic alliance is the ability of the specialist to handle interpersonal conflict in a manner that creates the perception of safety by the clients. Flicker et al. (2008) note that an important part of the therapeutic alliance requires clinicians to "simultaneously establish and manage relationships with multiple family members who are often in conflict with each other" (p. 167). Celano et al. (2010) suggest that techniques such as "diffusing hostile exchanges, minimizing blaming attributions among family members, and promoting a relational or systemic view of the problem behavior" (p. 37) are important to the alliance. Friedlander et al. (2006) connect client feelings of safety to trust in the therapist and the specific actions the therapist takes to ensure safety, noting especially that "therapeutic handling of intrafamilial hostility is undoubtedly the most important factor in creating safety" (p. 111). This means that the specialist must be able to tolerate a necessary level of interclient conflict (i.e., the specialist may not be conflict avoidant, shifting focus away from existing tension) and have the skill to manage levels of conflict in the session in a manner that allows conflict to surface without escalating to inappropriate verbal or physical behavior ("contain and conrol the conflict"; Friedlander et al., 2006, p. 119). The clinician must monitor nonverbal and verbal behaviors for signs that signal that one or more of the clients feels unsafe and then intervene in a timely fashion to establish safety. The STIC includes an item on the Family scale that assesses the perception of safety, "Some of the other members of my family and I do not feel safe with each other in this therapy" (Pinsof & Chambers, 2009, p. 443), while the SOFTA measure of therapeutic alliance includes a 12-item scale on safety in the treatment system (Friedlander et al., 2006, p. 273).

Blow et al. (2007) indicate that

> another consistent finding is the importance of therapists utilizing a sufficiently high level of activity /directiveness to prevent couples and families from simply replaying their dysfunctional patterns; and giving the session enough structure to encourage family members to face their behavioral, emotional, and cognitive issues. (p. 305)

Part of structure includes ensuring the equitable treatment of all parties in conflict situations, including fair allocation of time in the session, monitoring and managing perceived power differentials, disallowing interruptions, and teaching accurate empathy to replace hostile attacks. An adequate therapeutic alliance must include the establishment of a safe environment for exploration of interpersonal conflict.

INTERPERSONAL INTERACTION SKILLS AT TERMINATION OF TREATMENT

After some level of success in achieving the treatment goals, it is appropriate for the CFP specialist to consider how to facilitate treatment termination. The therapeutic alliance remains central to that process. If, as some studies suggest, the creation of a therapeutic alliance means that the clinician has become a quasi family member (Friedlander et al., 2006), termination requires appropriate attention to client feelings about ending an active phase of that relationship. It is likely that the clients will experience some mix of loss, sadness, and joy at the prospect. If the treatment alliance is conceptualized as a form of attachment and part of the process involves internalizing a positive therapeutic alliance (Obegi, 2008), it may be possible to consider termination as achievement of the final treatment goal. In our experience, it is not unusual for long-term clients to mention "hearing your voice" when encountering situations discussed in treatment, so the effects of the therapeutic relationship may continue after termination as the clients continue to pursue the issues addressed in treatment.

Termination requires an extension of the same skills used to establish and maintain the therapeutic alliance. Empathy, caring, and genuineness must be evident in order to process the clients' affect and determine a satisfactory plan for treatment termination. The CFP specialist will establish clear boundaries regarding possible reengagement in treatment and clarify policies about providing other forms of treatment than the one being concluded (e.g., individual psychotherapy after family treatment).

Conclusion

The ability to create and maintain a positive therapeutic alliance in a variety of treatment modalities is an essential aspect of CFP practice. This requires fundamental knowledge about interpersonal interaction, as well as attitudes, skills, and abilities to enact the alliance.

THIRTEEN

Professional Identity as a Couple and Family Psychologist

Professional identity as a couple and family psychologist grows out of a developmental process that entails progressive achievement of the knowledge, skills, and competencies of the specialty (N. J. Kaslow et al., 2005; Nutt & Stanton, 2008; Stanton, 2005a). This typically occurs in stages of development, from doctoral education to internship to postdoctoral training or residency to continuing competency as psychologists "gain, maintain, and enhance competency throughout their professional careers" (Rodolfa et al., 2005, p. 352). This chapter describes the evolution of the specialty designation and the pathways to specialty identification, participation in specialty organization, board certification in the specialty, and continuing competency in the specialty through lifelong education and practice, providing direction for the individual psychologist.

Evolution and Pathways to Specialty Identification

Historically, couple and family psychology was initially an add-on to the individual focus of professional psychology. The popularity of the family therapy movement in the 1970s and 1980s influenced the field of psychology in general, and many psychologists pursued continuing education in family therapy and/or adopted family therapy techniques (Goldenberg & Goldenberg, 2009). Some of these psychologists attended family therapy institutes for concentrated or one-year residencies. Others attended workshops and read the seminal books in the movement. As the family therapy movement grew, it fostered the American Association for Marital and

TABLE 13.1 **Professional Identity: Developmental Level—Specialty Competence in Couple and Family Psychology**

COMPETENCY DOMAIN AND ESSENTIAL COMPONENT	BEHAVIORAL ANCHOR	ASSESSMENT METHODS
Knowledge (A) Knowledge of the specialty of CFP (A.1) Command of specialty knowledge	(A.1.1) Understands and capably articulates advanced specialty knowledge in the foundational competencies (A.1.2) Understands and capably articulates advanced specialty knowledge in the functional competencies	1. Completion of doctoral degree with emphasis or track in CFP 2. Completion of predoctoral internship with CFP rotation(s) 3. Completion of postdoctoral residency with CFP rotation(s) 4. Continuing education in CFP 5. Publication and presentation in CFP in scholarly venues 6. ABPP examination 7. Membership in CFP organizations 8. ABPP examination 9. Leadership in doctoral programs, predoctoral internships, or residency programs in CFP 10. Continuing education
Skills (B) Evidence specialty skills (B.1) Command of skills and techniques in the CFP	(B.1.1) Ability to demonstrate advanced specialty skills in the foundational competencies (B.1.2) Ability to demonstrate advanced specialty skills in the functional competencies (B.1.3) Ability to present and publish in the specialty (B.1.4) Ability to teach or supervise CFP	
Attitudes (C) Identification as a CFP (C.1) Identifies as a CFP based upon demonstration of competence	(C.1.1) Aware of the ethical requirements for identification as a CFP (C.1.2) Independently pursues involvement in specialty organizations (C.1.3) Completes ABPP examination in the specialty (C.1.4) Develops or leads education and training programs in the specialty (C.1.5). Pursues CFP continuing education	

Note. Adapted from the format and content of the Assessment of Competency Benchmarks Work Group (2007). This table assumes that the specialist has achieved competence in professional psychology at the three previous developmental levels, as specified in the benchmarks. The competency domains and behavioral anchors serve as the primary organizing structure for this chapter; content explaining each domain and anchor is provided in the chapter.

Family Therapy (AAMFT), and that organization instituted an approved supervisor title for individuals who met the qualification to be designated as mentors to marriage and family training supervisees; a number of psychologists joined the AAMFT and pursued the approved supervisor designation (Goldenberg & Goldenberg, 2009; Patterson, 2009).

Over time, as systemic conceptualization and couple or family interventions became more well known in psychology circles, family psychology

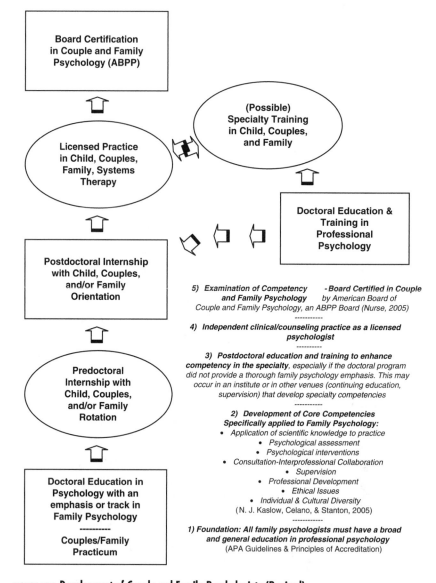

FIGURE 13.1 **Development of Couple and Family Psychologists (Revised)**

and family therapy evolved as separate guilds, although some family psychologists maintain membership in both guilds (see Goldenberg and Goldenberg, 2009, for an account of the historical progression). Family psychology recognized the importance of a broad and general education in the science of psychology, the value of psychological assessment, and a commitment to the requirement of a doctoral degree as the foundation for professional practice in psychology (Stanton, Harway, & Vetere, 2009). Couple and family psychology organizations were established (see below) and developed the standards and processes for professional identification with the specialty.

There are now established pathways to receive the education and training necessary for professional identification as a couple and family psychologist. Figure 13.1 is an updated version of a flowchart by Stanton and Nurse (2005) that depicts the routes one may take to specialty

Stanton and Nurse (2005) introduce the flowchart in this manner: "The flowchart is intended to indicate that labeling oneself as a [couple and] family psychologist requires formal education and training that develops the competencies needed for professional practice with individuals, couples, and families from a systemic perspective" (p. 4). Patterson (2009) argues strongly that it is unethical and professionally irresponsible to identify oneself as a CFP specialist in the absence of sufficient education, training, and supervised experience in the provision of psychological services to couples and families. The key issue is the demonstration of competence in the specialty. He proposes the need to identify levels of competence and a mechanism for identification that accurately conveys a psychologist's current level of competence in order to satisfy the APA Ethical Principles (APA, 2002). Professional identification as a CFP specialist must accord with these principles (see Chapter 10 for more detail on ethical issues in identification as a CFP specialist).

Participation in Couple and Family Psychology Organizations

Identification as a CFP specialist involves awareness of and participation in the specialty organizations. The specialty is composed of several organizations that constitute a central organization known as the Family Psychology Specialty Council (FPSC). These organizations facilitate education, clinical training, research, professional practice, board certification, and professional identity in the specialty of family psychology (Nutt & Stanton, 2008). Each organization has a specific purpose, and collectively they provide a network to support the growth and development of the specialty.

FAMILY PSYCHOLOGY SPECIALTY COUNCIL

The central or umbrella organization is the Family Psychology Specialty Council, created in 1992 as a synergy and currently composed of the Society for Family Psychology (SFP), the American Board of Couple and Family Psychology (ABCFP), the Academy of Couple and Family Psychology, the Council of Doctoral Programs for Family Psychology, and the Council of

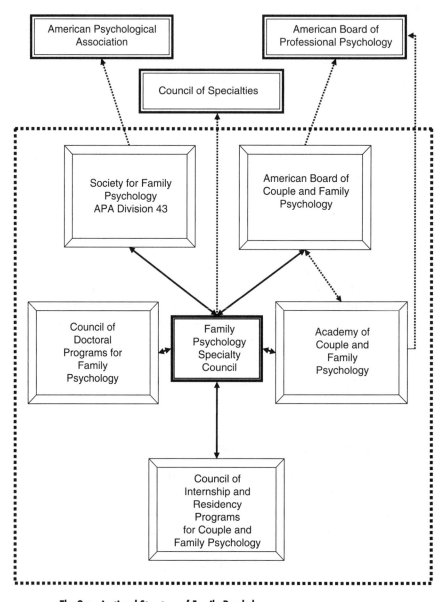

FIGURE 13.2 **The Organizational Structure of Family Psychology**

Internship and Residency Programs for Couple and Family Psychology. Figure 13.2 illustrates the interrelationship of these organizations and their relationship to higher-level, national boards that comprise diverse interests or specialties in professional psychology.

The FPSC is composed of elected or appointed representatives from each of the five constituent groups. The purpose of the FPSC is to

> 1) facilitate communication and development of coherence and consistency of policies and procedures within Family Psychology; 2) promote quality assurance of education, training, credentialing, and practice in Family Psychology; and 3) represent the specialty of Family Psychology to the Commission on Accreditation (CoA) and the Council of Specialties in Professional Psychology (CoS). (Family Psychology Specialty Council, 2001, p. 125)

The FPSC is responsible for maintaining the specialty status of family psychology through completion of the Petition for Renewal of Recognition of a Specialty in Professional Psychology to the APA Commission for the Recognition of Specialties and Proficiencies in Professional Psychology (CRSPPP) on the schedule determined by the CRSPPP. It also is responsible for the coordination and development of documents pertaining to education and training that are required by the CoA for accreditation of doctoral programs or predoctoral internships as a "developed practice area" (APA, 2008, p. 4) or postdoctoral residencies in the specialty. As an umbrella organization, the FPSC draws on the resources of the constituent organizations for the development of these documents, and each organization certifies the documents as a recommendation for overall certification to the FPSC.

SOCIETY FOR FAMILY PSYCHOLOGY

The SFP, founded in 1984, is Division 43 of the American Psychological Association. The Society delineates its purpose: "The Society's mission is to expand both the study and the practice of Family Psychology, through education, research, and clinical practice. The Society goes about fulfilling its mission through the application of systems theory to the ever-changing family unit" (Society for Family Psychology, 2009). This is further clarified in the bylaws of the Society: "Family Psychology integrates the understanding of individuals, couples, families and their wider contexts. The Society for Family Psychology seeks to promote human welfare through the development, dissemination, and application of knowledge about the dynamics, structure and functioning of families" (Society for Family Psychology, 2008, p. 88).

Membership is open to APA members in good standing, psychology doctoral students, and professionals with a doctoral degree or equivalent; in 2009, membership numbered approximately 2,100 (including almost 500 student members). The Society officers include the president (current, elect, and past), secretary, treasurer, council representative(s), student representative, and vice presidents for education, practice, public interest and diversity, and science. The Society elects representatives to the APA Council of Representatives, maintaining a voice for the specialty in APA governance. The Society founded the *Journal of Family Psychology* and developed it until it became an official APA journal (Nutt & Stanton, 2008). The Society currently publishes *The Family Psychologist,* a bulletin that includes articles and columns on the specialty, as well as Society news and announcements. An archive of past issues is posted on the Society website (http://www.apa.org/divisions/div43/mag.html); articles may be easily accessed for use in education and practice. The Society and the Journals Program of the American Psychological Association launched a new peer-reviewed journal titled *Couple and Family Psychology: Research and Practice* in 2011. The Society sponsors family psychology programs on research and professional practice during the APA annual convention and coordinates ongoing activities in international family psychology, graduate education in the specialty, family violence, and diversity.

AMERICAN BOARD OF COUPLE AND FAMILY PSYCHOLOGY

The American Board of Professional Psychology (ABPP) recognized the American Board of Family Psychology as a constituent specialty board in 1990. The board name was formally changed to the American Board of Couple and Family Psychology in 2007 in order to denote specialty competencies in working with couples as well as families. The ABCFP is responsible for establishing the qualifications for specialty board eligibility, the specifications for the practice sample to be submitted by candidates for board certification (assessment sample, intervention sample, and supporting materials), and the criteria for the assessment of the specialty competency domains. In addition, the ABCFP coordinates the screening of applicant qualifications, the review of the practice sample, and the conduct of examinations (see the description of the board certification process below). The ABCFP elects a representative to the ABPP Board of Trustees and participates in ABPP determination of macrosystemic policy issues and national advocacy efforts.

ACADEMY OF COUPLE AND FAMILY PSYCHOLOGY

Successful completion of all requirements for board certification in CFP automatically qualifies one for membership in the Academy of Couple and Family Psychology (Academy). The Academy's purpose is to

> a) support research and expansion of the database of Couple and Family Psychology; b) enhance communications among its members; c) provide continuing education programs; d) disseminate information to the public about the specialty of Couple and Family Psychology; e) support the functions of the American Board of Couple and Family Psychology as an affiliated board of the American Board of Professional Psychology; f) provide a voice for the specialty of Couple and Family Psychology within the overall profession of psychology; and g) make and implement policy decisions within the specialty. (Academy of Couple and Family Psychology, 2008, p. 1)

The Academy provides continuing education in the specialty, recruits applicants for board certification, mentors applicants during the qualification and examination processes, and publishes a newsletter to maintain communication among board-certified specialists.

COUNCIL OF DOCTORAL PROGRAMS FOR FAMILY PSYCHOLOGY

The provision of doctoral education in the specialty of family psychology is an important aspect of maintaining the specialty in professional psychology. Historically, the specialty evolved from primarily continuing education and postdoctoral education (i.e., a residency completed after a traditional doctoral degree) to increased inclusion of the specialty in doctoral degrees. A 2006 survey of doctoral programs with family psychology content found three categories: (a) programs with an emphasis (strong content in the specialty, including courses and practica); (b) programs with a track (usually three to four courses, often elective); and (c) programs with one or two courses in the specialty (Stanton, Harway, & Eaton, 2006). The programs with an emphasis provide substantial education in the specialty and satisfy most of the requirements to qualify for board certification (Stanton et al., 2009). Therefore, the ABCFP Manual for Board Certification (American Board of Couple and Family Psychology, 2008) now includes a qualification category specifically for such individuals, promoting rapid progress toward board certification in the specialty.

There has been a loose affiliation of the doctoral programs with an emphasis or track. Beginning in 2002, representatives from these programs conducted an annual meeting during the APA convention and constituted a special interest group within the Society for Family Psychology. APA convention programming has been regularly presented on graduate education and training in the specialty. In 2009, the FPSC voted to formalize the group into the Council of Doctoral Programs for Family Psychology. This is part of continued recognition of the specialty and facilitates movement toward CoA recognition as a developed practice area (APA, 2008). Stanton and Harway (2007) developed formal recommendations for doctoral education in the specialty that were endorsed by all the constituent organizations and approved by the Council of Specialties (the council composed of elected representatives from all approved specialties in professional psychology).

COUNCIL OF INTERNSHIP AND RESIDENCY PROGRAMS FOR COUPLE AND FAMILY PSYCHOLOGY

In a manner similar to doctoral programs in the specialty, internships and residencies that include specialty training have often functioned autonomously. Although a review of Association of Psychology Postdoctoral and Internship Centers indicates that many sites provide a major or minor rotation in couple and/or family psychotherapy (13–62% range), there is significant variation in content inclusion and specialty competency development (N. J. Kaslow et al., 2005).

Efforts were made in 2006–2010 to identify internship and residency programs that include a genuine emphasis in the specialty. In 2009 the FPSC voted to create a formal council of CFP internship and residency programs in order to formalize recognition of such programs in the specialty.

Board Certification in Couple and Family Psychology

ABPP board certification "provides peer and public recognition of demonstrated competence in an approved specialty area in professional psychology" (American Board of Professional Psychology, 2009, n.p.). It is a national standard of excellence.

The three-stage process of board certification in CFP and further details regarding the process as noted here are detailed on the ABPP website (http://www.abpp.org). Stage I involves submission of a completed application and review by the ABPP Executive Office for satisfaction of generic degree and licensure requirements (e.g., doctoral degree from an APA-accredited program and/or credentialing in the National Register and/or holding the Certificate of Professional Qualification in Psychology and licensed as a psychologist for independent practice at the doctoral level). Applicants who meet the generic requirements are then "reviewed by the specialty board credentials committee for compliance with the specialty's specific doctoral and post-doctoral education, training, and experience requirements" (American Board of Couple and Family Psychology, 2008, p. 6). There are three eligibility tracks: Track 1 generally applies to individuals who completed a doctoral degree with an emphasis or track in CFP; Track 2 applies to individuals who took some required courses (or equivalent) and completed a postdoctoral residency in the specialty; Track 3 is the senior track and applies to individuals who have 15 or more years of postdoctoral experience in the practice of the specialty and who evidence substantial contributions to the discipline (criteria for senior track eligibility are provided on the ABPP website).

Stage II requires the completion of a practice sample that includes a current curriculum vita, a professional statement depicting the applicant's identification with CFP (including a challenging ethical dilemma), and video recordings of assessment and intervention practice samples (accompanied by a transcript of each recording). The practice sample is reviewed by the specialty board to determine if the candidate may proceed to Stage III, an oral examination. During Stage III an examination chairperson is appointed, and a committee of examiners is chosen. They review all materials and coordinate the schedule for the examination with the applicant (the exam requires approximately 4 hours). The examination covers the following domains: (a) Specialty Knowledge; (b) Assessment; (c) Intervention; (d) Relationship; (e) Ethics and Legal Standards and Behavior; and (f) Professional Identification with the Specialty.

The ABCFP is committed to conducting exams "in a courteous, professional and collegial manner," recognizing that "the candidate has already passed many requirements and has demonstrated expertise in the specialty in order to be seated for the oral exam" (American Board of Couple and Family Psychology, 2008, pp. 21–22). The ABPP Executive Office notifies applicants of all decisions at each stage of the process.

Continuing Competency in the Specialty

The specialty recognizes that competency is not something achieved once and for all; rather, competency entails an ongoing commitment to remain current in the specialty research and evidence-based practices that apply to one's professional practice. The most common method to maintain competency is through the completion of continuing education in the specialty. Because many states require continuing education for renewal of licensure, this requirement may be met readily by completing continuing education in CFP. The Society for Family Psychology sponsors programs within the APA annual convention, many of which qualify for continuing education. In addition, it is expected that specialists will contribute to and/or read the journals, bulletins, and newsletters published by the specialty organizations (e.g., the *Journal of Family Psychology, Couple and Family Psychology: Research and Practice, The Family Psychologist,* and the Academy of Couple and Family Psychology newsletter).

Finally, couple and family psychologists maintain competency by active involvement in the specialty organizations. Service on boards, committees, task forces, and special interest groups allows the specialist to contribute meaningfully to the field and shape the growth of the specialty.

Conclusion

Professional identity as a CFP specialist is not simply a matter of self-designation; it is based on the evidence of specialty competencies designated by the organizations that constitute the specialty. Education, training, supervised experience, and board certification in the specialty provide a clear pathway for those who want to identify with the specialty. Participation in specialty organizations demonstrates continuing identification with the specialty and professional contribution to the specialty.

REFERENCES

Academy of Couple and Family Psychology. (2008). Constitution and By-Laws of the Academy of Couple and Family Psychology. Unpublished.

Ackerman, N. W., & Jahoda, M. (1950). *Antisemitism and emotional disorders: A psychoanalytic interpretation.* New York: Harper.

Adams, N., & Grieder, D. M. (2005). *Treatment planning for person-centered care.* Burlington, MA: Elsevier Academic Press.

Adams, N., Hiller, J., Wood, H., & Bolton, W. (2006). Systemic therapy techniques for sexual difficulties. In J. Hiller, H. Wood, H. & W. Bolton (Eds.), *Sex, mind, and emotion: Innovation in psychological theory and practice* (pp. 209–227). London, UK: Karnac Books.

Ainsworth, M. S., Blehar, M. C., Waters, E., & Wall, S. (1978). *Patterns of attachment: A psychological study of the strange situation.* Oxford, England: Erlbaum.

Alexander, J. F., & Parsons, B. V. (1982). *Functional family therapy: Principles and procedures.* Carmel, CA: Brooks/Cole.

Allen, J. G. (1981). The clinical psychologist as a diagnostic consultant. *Bulletin of the Menninger Clinic, 45,* 247–258.

Allport, G. (1954). *The nature of prejudice.* Reading, MA: Addison-Wesley.

Amato, P. R. (2001). Children of divorce in the 1990s: An update of the Amato and Keith (1991) meta-analysis. *Journal of Family Psychology, 15,* 355–370.

Amato, P. R. (2006). Marital discord, divorce, and children's well-being: Results from a 20-year longitudinal study of two generations. In A. Clark-Stewart & J. Dunn (Eds.), *Families count: Effects on child and adolescent development* (pp. 179–202). New York, NY: Cambridge University Press.

Amato, P. R. (2010). Research on divorce: Continuing trends and new developments. *Journal of Marriage and Family, 72,* 650–666.

Amato, P. R., & Keith, B. (1995). Parental divorce and the well-being of children: A meta-analysis. *Psychological Bulletin, 110,* 26–46.

Amato, P. R., Loomis, L. S., & Booth, L. A. (1995). Parental divorce, marital conflict, and offspring well-being in early adulthood. *Journal of Social Forces, 73,* 895–915.

American Academy of Child and Adolescent Psychiatry. (1997). Practice parameters for child custody evaluation. *Journal of the American Academy of Child and Adolescent Psychiatry, 36,* 57S–68S.

American Association of Marriage and Family Therapy. (1991). *AAMFT code of ethics.* Washington, DC: Author.

American Association of Sexuality Educators, Counselors, and Therapists (AASECT) Code of Ethics Committee. (2008). *American Association of Sexuality Educators, Counselors, and Therapists (AASECT) Code of Ethics.* Ashland, VA: Author.

American Board of Couple and Family Psychology. (2008). Manual for obtaining board certification. Retrieved December 12, 2009 from http://www.abpp.org/files/page-specific/3359%20ABCFP%20Couple%20&%20Family/10_Examination_Manual.pdf.

American Board of Professional Psychology. (2008). Specialty certification in couple and family psychology. Retrieved April 26, 2009, from http://www.abpp.org/brochures/1-09/Couple%20and%20Family%20Brochure.pdf

American Board of Professional Psychology. (2009). Value statement. Retrieved April 25, 2009, from http://www.abpp.org/

American Council on Education & American Association of University Professors. (2000). *Does diversity make a difference? Three research studies on diversity in college classrooms.* Washington, DC: Authors.

American Professional Society on the Abuse of Children. (1996). Psychosocial evaluations of suspected psychological maltreatment in children and adolescents. *Cultic Studies Journal, 13,* 153–170.

American Psychiatric Association. (1994). *Diagnostic and statistical manual of mental disorders* (4th ed.). Washington, DC: Author

American Psychiatric Association (2000). *Diagnostic and statistical manual of mental disorders: fourth edition – text revision* DSM-IV-TR. Washington, D.C.: Author.

American Psychological Association. (1990). Guidelines for providers of psychological services to ethnic, linguistic, and culturally diverse populations.

American Psychological Association. (1993). Record keeping guidelines. *American Psychologist, 48,* 984–986.

American Psychological Association. (1994). Guidelines for child custody evaluations in divorce proceedings. *American Psychologist, 47,* 1597–1611.

American Psychological Association. (2000a). Guidelines for psychotherapy with lesbian, gay, and bisexual clients. *American Psychologist, 55,* 1440–1451.

American Psychological Association. (2000b). *Resolution on poverty and socioeconomic status.* Retrieved August 2, 2009, from http://www.apa.org/pi/urban/povres.html

American Psychological Association. (2002). Ethical principles of psychologists and code of conduct. *American Psychologist, 57,* 1060–1073.

American Psychological Association. (2003a). Guidelines on multicultural education, training, research, practice, and organizational change for psychologists. *American Psychologist, 58,* 377–402.

American Psychological Association. (2003b). Guidelines for psychological practice with older adults. *American Psychologist, 59,* 236–260.

American Psychological Association. (2007). Guidelines for education and training at the doctoral and postdoctoral level in consulting psychology/organizational consulting psychology. *American Psychologist, 62,* 980–992.

American Psychological Association. (2008). *Guidelines and principles for accreditation of programs in professional psychology.* Washington, DC: Author.

Anastasi, A., & Urbina, S. (1997). *Psychological testing* (7th ed.). Upper Saddle River, NJ: Prentice Hall.

Andersen, S. M., Thorpe, J. S., & Kooij, C. S. (2007). Character in context: The relational self and transference. In Y. Shoda, D. Cervone, & G. Downey (Eds.), *Persons in context: Building a science of the individual* (pp. 169–200). New York: Guilford Press.

Anderson, H. (2009). Collaborative practice: Relationships and conversations that make a difference. In J. H. Bray & M. Stanton (Eds.), *The Wiley Blackwell handbook of family psychology* (pp. 300–313). Oxford, UK: Wiley-Blackwell.

Anderson, H., & Levin, S. B. (1998). Generative conversations: A postmodern approach to conceptualizing and working with human systems. In M. F. Hoyt (Ed.), *The handbook of constructive therapies: Innovative approaches from leading practitioners* (pp. 46–67). San Francisco: Jossey-Bass.

APA Presidential Task Force on Evidence-Based Practices. (2006). Evidence-based practice in psychology. *American Psychologist, 61,* 271–285.

Apel, R., & Kaukinen, C. (2008). On the relationship between family structure and anti-social behavior: Parental cohabitation and blended households. *Criminology: An Interdisciplinary Journal, 46,* 35–69.

Aponte, H. J. (1994). *Bread and spirit: Therapy with the new poor: Diversity of race, culture, and values.* New York: W.W. Norton & Co.

Appel, A. E., & Holden, G. W. (1998). The co-occurrence of spouse and physical child abuse: A review and appraisal. *Journal of Family Psychology, 12,* 578–599.

APPIC (2002). 2002 Competencies: Future Directions in Education & Credentialing in Professional Psychology. Retrieved from http://www.appic.org/news/3_1_news_Competencies.html

Arredondo, P., & Perez, P. (2006). Historical perspectives on the multicultural guidelines and contemporary applications. *Professional Psychology: Research and Practice, 37,* 1–5.

Arredondo, P., Shealy, C., Neale, M., & Winfrey, L. L. (2004). Consultation and interprofessional collaboration: Modeling for the future. *Journal of Clinical Psychology, 60,* 787–800.

Arredondo, P., Toporek, R., Brown, S. P., Jones, J., Locke, D. C., Sanchez, J., & Sadler, H. (1996). Operationalization of the multicultural counseling competencies. *Journal of Multicultural Counseling and Development, 24,* 42–78.

Assessment of Competency Benchmarks Work Group. (2007). *Assessment of competency benchmarks work group: A developmental model for the defining and measuring competence in professional psychology.* APA Board of Educational Affairs in collaboration with the Council of Chairs of Training Councils. Washington, DC

Association for Counselor Education and Supervision. (1995). Ethical guidelines for counseling supervisors. *Counseling Education and Supervision, 34,* 270–276.

Association of Family and Conciliation Courts. (2000). *Model standards of practice for family and divorce mediation.* Madison, WI: Author.

Association of Family and Conciliation Courts. (2005). *Guidelines for parenting coordination.* Madison, WI: Author.

Association of Family and Conciliation Courts. (2006). *Model standards of practice for child custody evaluation.* Madison, WI: Author.

Atkins, D. C. (2005). Using multilevel models to analyze couple and family treatment data: Basic and advanced issues. *Journal of Family Psychology, 19,* 98–110.

Auerswald, E. H. (1990). Toward epistemological transformation in the education and training of family therapists. In M. P. Mirkin (Ed.), *The social and political contexts of family therapy* (pp. 19–50). Needham Heights, MA: Allyn & Bacon.

Austin, W. G. (2000). Assessing credibility in allegations of marital violence in the high conflict child custody case. *Family Court Review, 38,* 462–477.

Ayoub, C. C., Deutsch, R. M., & Maraganore, A. (1999). Emotional distress in children of high-conflict divorce: The impact of marital conflict and violence. *Family Court Review: An Interdisciplinary Journal, 37,* 297–315.

Bancroft, L., & Silverman, J. G. (2002a). The batterer as parent: Assessing the impact of domestic violence on family dynamics. *Psychiatry, Psychology & Law, 9,* 284–285.

Bancroft, L., & Silverman, J. G. (2002b). *The batterer as parent: The impact of domestic violence on family dynamics.* Thousand Oaks, CA: Sage.

Banks, J. A. (2000). Multicultural education: Characteristics and goals. In J. A. Banks & C. A. M. Banks (Eds.), *Multicultural education: Issues and perspectives* (4th ed., pp. 3–30). New York: Wiley.

Barnes, M., & Figley, C. R. (2005). Family therapy: Working with traumatized families. In J. L. Lebow (Ed.), *Handbook of clinical family therapy* (pp. 309–326). Hoboken, NJ: Wiley.

Barton, J., & Haslett, T. (2007). Analysis, synthesis, systems thinking and the scientific method: Rediscovering the importance of open systems. *Systems Research & Behavioral Science, 24,* 143–155.

Bateson, G. (1972). *Steps to an ecology of mind.* New York: Ballantine.

Bathurst, K., Gottfried, A. W., & Gottfried, A. E. (1997). Normative data for the MMPI-2 in child custody litigation. *Psychological Assessment, 9,* 205–211.

Baucom, D. H., Snyder, D. K., & Gordon, K. C. (2009). *Helping couples get past the affair: A clinician's guide.* New York: Guilford Press.

Bauserman, R. (2002). Child adjustment in joint-custody versus sole arrangements: A meta-analytic review. *Journal of Family Psychology, 16,* 91–102.

Beavers, W. R., & Hampson, R. B. (1990). *Successful families: Assessment and intervention.* New York: Norton.

Beavers, W. R., & Hampson, R. B. (2000). The Beavers systems model of family functioning. *Journal of Family Therapy, 22,* 128–143.

Beavers, W. R. & Hampson, R. B. (2003). Measuring family competence: The Beavers systems model. In F. Walsh (Ed.), Normal family processes (3rd ed.). New York: Guilford Press

Becvar, D. S. (2005). Families in later life: Issues, challenges, and therapeutic responses. In J. L. Lebow (Ed.), *Handbook of clinical family therapy* (pp. 591–609). Hoboken, NJ: Wiley.

Beitel, M., Ferrer, E., & Cecero, J. J. (2004). Psychological mindedness and cognitive style. *Journal of Clinical Psychology, 60,* 567–582.

Belsky, J. (1993). Etiology of child maltreatment: A developmental–ecological analysis. *Psychological Bulletin, 114,* 413–434.

Belsky, J., Woodworth, S., & Crnic, K. (1996). Troubled family interaction during toddlerhood. *Development and Psychopathology, 8,* 477–495.

Benjamin, G. A. H., Monarch, K. K., & Gollan, J. K. (2003). *Family evaluation in custody litigation: Reducing risks of ethical infractions and malpractice.* Washington, DC: American Psychological Association.

Benson, T. A. (2007). Developing a systems thinking capacity in learners of all ages. Retrieved July 3, 2009, from http://www.watersfoundation.org/webed/library/articles/Developing-ST-capacity.pdf

Berlin, R., & Davis, R. B. (1989). Children from alcoholic families: Vulnerability and resilience. In T. F. Dugan & R. Coles (Eds.), *The child in our times: Studies in the development of resiliency* (pp. 81–105). Philadelphia, PA: Brunner/Mazel.

Bernard, J. M. (1997). The discrimination model. In C. E. Watkins (Ed.), *Handbook of psychotherapy supervision* (pp. 310–327). New York: Wiley.

Bernard, J. M., & Goodyear, R. K. (2009). *Fundamentals of clinical supervision* (4th ed.). Boston: Allyn & Bacon.

Bernardi, E., Jones, M., & Tennant, C. (1997). Quality of parenting in alcoholics and narcotic addicts. *British Journal of Psychiatry, 154,* 667–682.

Berrick, J. D., Barth, R., & Gilbert, N. (Eds.). (1997). *Welfare research review* (Vol. 2). Columbia, NY: Columbia University Press.

Berry, J. W. (1997). Immigration, acculturation, and adaptation. *Applied Psychology: An International Review, 46,* 5–34.

Berzin, S. C., Thomas, K. L., & Cohen, E. (2007). Assessing model fidelity in two family group decision-making programs: Is this child welfare intervention being implemented as intended? *Journal of Social Service Research, 34,* 55–71.

Bieschke, K. J. (2006). Research self-efficacy beliefs and research outcome expectations: Implications for developing scientifically minded psychologists. *Journal of Career Assessment, 14*(1), 77–91.

Bieschke, K. J., Fouad, N. A., Collins, F. L., Jr., & Halonen, J. S. (2004). The scientifically-minded psychologist: Science as a core competency. *Journal of Clinical Psychology, 60,* 713–723.

Birchler, G. R. (1975). Live supervision and instant feedback in marriage and family therapy. *Journal of Marriage and Family Therapy, 14,* 331–342.

Birnbaum, R., & Alaggia, R. (2006). Supervised visitation: A call for a second generation of research. *Family Court Review: An Interdisciplinary Journal, 44,* 119–134.

Bjorklund, D. F., Cassel, W. S., Bjorklund, B. R., Douglas-Brown, R., Park, C. L., Ernst, K., et al. (2000). Social demand characteristics in children's and adults' eyewitness memory and suggestibility: the effect of different interviewers on free recall and recognition. *Applied Cognitive Psychology, 14,* 421–433.

Black, D. A., & Lebow, J. (2009). Systemic research controversies and challenges. In J. H. Bray & M. Stanton (Eds.), *The Wiley Blackwell handbook of family psychology* (pp. 100–111). Oxford, UK: Wiley-Blackwell.

Blanchard, V. L., Hawkins, A. J., Baldwin, S. A., & Fawcett, E. B. (2009). Investigating the effects of marriage and relationship education on couples' communication skills: A meta-analytic study. *Journal of Family Psychology, 23,* 203–214.

Bledsoe, T. S. (2006). *A multimedia/DVD approach to training clinicians in two psychotherapy modalities.* Ann Arbor, MI: ProQuest Information & Learning.

Bloom, B. L. (1985). A factor analysis of self-report measures of family functioning. *Family Process, 24,* 225–239.

Bloom, J. (n.d.). Bateson @ 100: Multiple versions of the world. Retrieved from http://www.ccaerasig.com/papers/05/BatesonConference.pdf

Blow, A. J., Sprenkle, D. H., & Davis, S. D. (2007). Is who delivers the treatment more important than the treatment itself? The role of the therapist in common factors. *Journal of Marital & Family Therapy, 33,* 298–317.

Board of Professional Affairs Committee on Professional Practice and Standards, Practice Directorate, American Psychological Association. (1999). Guidelines for psychological evaluations in child protection matters. *American Psychologist, 54,* 586–593.

Bobes, T., & Bobes, N. S. (2005). *The couple is telling you what you need to know: Couple-directed therapy in a multicultural context.* New York: Norton.

Booth, A., & Amato, P. R. (2001). Parental predivorce relations and offspring postdivorce well-being. *Journal of Marriage and Family, 63,* 197–212.

Bornstein, M. H. (2002a). *Handbook of parenting: Vol.4: Social conditions and applied parenting* (2nd ed.). Mahwah, NJ: Lawrence Erlbaum Associates.

Bornstein, M. H. (2002b). *Handbook of parenting: Vol.5: Practical Issues in parenting* (2nd ed.). Mahwah, NJ: Lawrence Erlbaum Associates.

Bornstein, M. H., & Lansford, J. E. (2010). Parenting. In M. H. Bornstein (Ed.), *Handbook of cultural developmental science* (pp. 259–277). New York, NY: Psychology Press.

Bousha, D. M., & Twentyman, C. T. (1984). Mother-child interactional style in abuse, neglect, and control groups: Naturalistic observations in the home. *Journal of Abnormal Psychology, 93,* 106–114.

Bow, J. N., & Boxer, P. (2003). Assessing allegations of domestic violence in child custody evaluations. *Journal of Interpersonal Violence, 18,* 1394–1410.

Bow, J. N., Quinnell, F. A., Zaroff, M., & Assemany, A. (2002). Assessment of sexual abuse allegations in child custody cases. *Professional Psychology: Research and Practice, 33,* 566–575.

Bowlby, J. (1988). *A secure base: Parent-child attachment and healthy human development.* New York: Basic Books.

Boyd-Franklin, N. (2003). *Black families in therapy: Understanding the African American experience.* New York: Guilford Press.

Boyd-Franklin, N., & Bry, B. H. (2000). *Reaching out in family therapy: Home-based, school, and community interventions.* New York: Guilford Press.

Bradley, A. R., & Wood, J. M. (1996). How do children tell? The disclosure process in child sexual abuse. *Child Abuse and Neglect, 20,* 881–891.

Braver, S. L., Ellman, I. M., & Fabricius, W. V. (2003). Relocation of children after divorce and children's best interests: New evidence and legal considerations. *Journal of Family Psychology, 17,* 206–219.

Braver, S. L., & Griffin, W. A. (2000). Engaging fathers in the post-divorce family. *Marriage and Family Review, 29,* 247–267.

Bray, J. H. (1991). Psychosocial factors affecting custodial and visitation arrangements. *Behavioral Sciences and the Law, 9,* 419–437.

Bray, J. H. (1995a). Assessing family health and distress: An intergenerational-systemic perspective. In J. C. Conoley & E. Werth (Eds.), *Family assessment* (pp. 67–102). Lincoln, NE: Buros Institute of Mental Measurement.

Bray, J. H. (1995b). Family assessment: Current issues in evaluating families. *Family Relations, 44,* 469–477.

Bray, J. H. (2004). Models and issues in couple and family assessment. In L. Sperry (Ed.), *Assessment of couples and families: Contemporary and cutting-edge strategies* (pp. 13–29). New York: Taylor & Francis.

Bray, J. H. (2005). Family therapy with stepfamilies. In J. L. Lebow (Ed.), *Handbook of clinical family therapy* (pp. 497–515). Hoboken, NJ: Wiley.

Bray, J. H. (2009). Couple and family assessment. In J. H. Bray & M. Stanton (Eds.), *The Wiley Blackwell handbook of family psychology* (pp. 151–163). Oxford, UK: Wiley-Blackwell.

Bray, J. H., Frank, R. G., McDaniel, S. H., & Heldring, M. (2004). Education, practice, and research opportunities for psychologists in primary care. In R. G. Frank, S. H. McDaniel, J. H. Bray & M. Heldring (Eds.), *Primary care psychology.* (pp. 3–21). Washington, DC: American Psychological Association.

Bray, J. H., & Stanton, M. (Eds.). (2009). *The Wiley Blackwell handbook of family psychology.* Oxford, UK: Wiley-Blackwell.

Breunlin, D. C., Karrer, B. M., McGuire, D. E., & Cimmarusti, R. A. (1988). Cybernetics of videotape supervision. In H. A. Liddle, D. C. Breunlin, & R. C. Schwartz (Eds.), *Handbook of family therapy training and supervision* (pp. 194–206). New York: Guilford Press.

Breunlin, D. C., Rampage, C., & Eovaldi, M. L. (1995). Family therapy supervision: Toward an integrative perspective. In R. H. Mikesell, D. D. Lusterman, & S. H. McDaniel (Eds.), *Integrating family therapy: Handbook of family psychology and systems theory* (pp. 547–560). Washington, DC: American Psychological Association.

Breunlin, D. C., Schwartz, R. C., & Karrer, B. M. (1992). *Metaframeworks: Transcending the models of family therapy.* San Francisco: Jossey-Bass.

Breunlin, D. C., Schwartz, R. C., Krause, M. S., & Selby, L. M. (1983). Evaluating family therapy training: The development of an instrument. *Journal of Marital & Family Therapy, 9,* 37–47.

Brewer, M. B., & Brown, R. J. (1998). Intergroup relations. In D. T. Gilbert, S. T. Fiske, & G. Lindsey (Eds.), *The handbook of social psychology.* New York: McGraw Hill.

Brewer, M. B., & Miller, N. (1988). Contact and cooperation: When do they work? In P. A. Katz & D. A. Taylor (Eds.), *Eliminating racism: Profiles in controversy* (pp. 315–326). New York: Plenum Press.

Bronfenbrenner, U. (1977). Toward an experimental ecology of human development. *American Psychologist, 32,* 513–531.

Bronfenbrenner, U. (1979). *The ecology of human development.* Cambridge, MA: Harvard University Press.

Bronfenbrenner, U. (1986). Ecology of the family as a context for human development: Research perspectives. *Developmental Psychology, 22,* 723–742.

Brooks, G. R. (2001). Developing gender awareness: When therapist growth promotes family growth. In S. H. McDaniel, D.-D. Lusterman, & C. L. Philpot (Eds.), *Casebook for integrating family therapy: An ecosystemic approach.* (pp. 265–274). Washington, DC: American Psychological Association.

Brown, S. P., Parham, T. A., & Yonker, R. (1996). Influence of a cross-cultural training on racial identity attitudes of White women and men. *Journal of Counseling and Development, 74,* 510–516.

Browning, S., & Bray, J. H. (2009). Treating stepfamilies: A subsystems-based approach. In J. H. Bray & M. Stanton (Eds.), *The Wiley Blackwell handbook of family psychology* (pp. 487–498). Oxford, UK: Wiley-Blackwell.

Bruch, C. S. (2001). Parental alienation syndrome and parental alienation: Getting it wrong in child custody cases. *Family Law Quarterly, 35,* 527–552.

Bruck, M., & Ceci, S. J. (2009). Reliability of child witnesses' reports. In K. S. Douglas, J. L. Skeem, & S. O. Lilienfeld (Eds.), *Psychological science in the courtroom: Consensus and controversy* (pp. 149–171). New York, NY: Guilford Press.

Bruck, M., Ceci, S. J., & Francoeur, E. (1999). The accuracy of mothers' memories of conversations with their preschool children. *Journal of Experimental Psychology: Applied, 5,* 89–106.

Buchanan, C. M., Maccoby, E. E., & Dornbusch, S. M. (1991). Caught between parents: Adolescents' experience in divorced homes. *Child Development, 62,* 1008–1029.

Buchanan, C. M., & Waizenhofer, R. (2001). The impact of interparental conflict on adolescent children: Considerations of family systems and family structure. In A. Booth, A. C. Crouter, & M. Clements (Eds.), *Couples in conflict* (pp. 149–160). Mahwah, NJ:Erlbaum.

Budd, K. S., Poindexter, L. M., Felix, E. D., & Naik-Polan, A. T. (2001). Clinical assessment of parents in child protection cases: An empirical analysis. *Law and Human Behavior, 25,* 93–108.

Burrell, B., Thompson, B., & Sexton, D. (1994). Predicting child abuse potential across family types. *Child Abuse and Neglect, 18,* 1039–1049.

Bush, S. S., Connell, M. A., & Denney, R. L. (2006). *Ethical practice in forensic psychology: A systematic model for decision making.* Washington, DC: American Psychological Association.

Butcher, J. N., Dahlstrom, W. G., Graham, J. R., Tellegen, A., & Kaemmer, B. (2001). *Minnesota Multiphasic Personality Inventory-2 (MMPI-2) manual for administration and scoring.* Minneapolis, MN: University of Minnesota Press.

Cabrera, D., Colosi, L., & Lobdell, C. (2008). Systems thinking. *Evaluation and Program Planning, 31,* 299–310.

Callahan, J. L., Almstrom, C. M., Swift, J. K., Borja, S. E., & Heath, C. J. (2009). Exploring the contribution of supervisors to intervention outcomes. *Training and Education in Professional Psychology, 3,* 72–77.

Campbell, D., Draper, R., & Huffington, C. (Eds.). (1991). *Teaching systemic thinking.* London, UK: Karnac Books.

Caplan, G., Caplan, R. B., & Erchul, W. P. (1995). A contemporary view of mental health consultation: Comments on "Types of mental health consultation" by Gerald Caplan (1963). *Journal of Educational & Psychological Consultation, 6*(1), 23–30.

Capra, F. (1983). *The turning point.* Toronto: Bantam.

Capra, F. (1996). *The web of life.* New York: Anchor Books.

Capra, F. (2002). *The hidden connections: A science for sustainable living.* New York: Anchor Books.

Carere-Comes, T. (2001). Assimilative and accommodative integration: The basic dialectics. *Journal of Psychotherapy Integration, 11,* 105–115.

Carlson, C. I. (1995). Families as the focus of assessment: Theoretical and practical issues. In J. C. Conoley & E. Werth (Eds.), *Family assessment* (pp. 19–63). Lincoln, NE: Buros Institute of Mental Measurement.

Carlson, C. I. (2003). What is systems thinking, and why is it important? *The Family Psychologist, 19*(1), 4–5.

Carlson, C. I., & Christenson, S. (2005). Evidence-based parent and family interventions in school psychology: Overview and procedures. *School Psychology Quarterly, 20,* 345–351.

Carlson, C. I., Funk, C. L., & Nguyen, K. H. (2009). Families and schools. In J. H. Bray & M. Stanton (Eds.), *The Wiley Blackwell handbook of family psychology* (pp. 515–526). Oxford, UK: Wiley-Blackwell.

Ceci, S. J. (1999). *Jeopardy in the courtroom: A scientific analysis of children's testimony.* Washington, DC: American Psychological Association.

Ceci, S. J., Bruck, M., & Battin, D. B. (2000). The suggestibility of children's testimony. In D. F. Bjorklund (Ed.), *False-memory creation in children and adults: Theory, research, and implications* (pp. 169–201). Mahwah, NJ: Lawrence Erlbaum Associates.

Celano, M. P., & Kaslow, N. J. (2000). Culturally competent family interventions: Review and case illustrations. *American Journal of Family Therapy, 28,* 217–228.

Celano, M. P., Smith, C. O., & Kaslow, N. J. (2010). The couple and family therapy competency. *Psychotherapy.*

Chaffin, M., Wherry, J. N., & Dykman, R. (1997). School age children's coping with sexual abuse: Abuse stresses and symptoms associated with four coping strategies. *Child Abuse and Neglect, 21,* 227–240.

Chase-Lansdale, P. L., Cherlin, A. J., & Kiernan, K. K. (1995). The long-term effects of parental divorce on the mental health of young adults: A developmental perspective. *Child Development, 66,* 1614–1634.

Chassin, L., Barrera, M., & Montgomery, H. (1997). Parental alcoholism as a risk factor. In S. A. Wolchik, & I. N. Sandler (Eds.), *Handbook of children's coping: Linking theory and intervention* (pp. 101–129). New York, NY: Plenum Press.

Cherlin, A. J., Furstenberg, F. F., Chase-Lansdale, P. L., Kiernan, K. E., Robins, P. K., Morrison, D. R., et al. (1991). Longitudinal studies of effects of divorce on children in Great Britain and the United States. *Science, 252,* 1386–1389.

Cheung, S. (2009a). Asian American immigrant mental health: Current status and future directions. In J. L. Chin (Ed.), *Diversity in mind and action (Vol. 1). Multiple faces of identity* (pp. 86–104). Santa Barbara, CA: Praeger.

Cheung, S. (2009b). Solution-focused brief therapy. In J. H. Bray & M. Stanton (Eds.), *The Wiley-Blackwell handbook of family psychology* (pp. 212–225). Oxford, UK: Wiley-Blackwell.

Chung, R. C.-Y., & Bemak, F. (2002). The relationship of culture and empathy in cross-cultural counseling. *Journal of Counseling & Development, 80,* 154–159.

Cicchetti, D., Toth, S., Bush, M., & Gillespie, J. (1988). Stage-salient issues: A transactional model of intervention. *New Directions in Child Development, 39,* 123–145.

Cole, D. A., & Jordan, A. E. (1993). Relation of family subsystems to adolescent depression: Implementing a new family assessment strategy. *Journal of Family Psychology, 7,* 119–133.

Cole, D. A., & McPherson, A. E. (1993) Relation of family subsystems to adolescent depression: Implementing a new family assessment strategy. *Journal of Family Psychology, 7,* 119–133.

Collins, W. A., Maccoby, E. E., Steinberg, L., Heterington, E. M., & Bornstein, M. H. (2000). Contemporary research on parenting: The case for nature and nurture. *American Psychologist, 55,* 218–232.

Comas-Diaz, L. (1996). Cultural considerations in diagnosis. In F. W. Kaslow (Ed.), *Handbook on relational diagnosis and dysfunctional family patterns* (pp. 152–168). New York: Wiley.

Comas-Diaz, L. (2006). Cultural variation in the therapeutic relationship. In C. D. Goodheart, A. E. Kazdin, & R. J. Sternberg (Eds.), *Evidence-based psychotherapy: Where practice and research meet* (pp. 81–105). Washington, DC: American Psychological Association.

Comas-Diaz, L., & Grenier, J. R. (1998). Migration and acculturation. In J. Sandoval, C. L. Frisby, K. F. Geisinger, S. D. Scheuneman, & J. R. Grinier (Eds.), *Testing interpretation and diversity: Achieving equity in assessment* (pp. 213–240). Washington, DC: American Psychological Association.

Commission for the Recognition of Specialties and Proficiencies in Professional Psychology. (n.d.). Archival description of family psychology. Retrieved April 26, 2009, URL: http://www.apa.org/ed/graduate/specialize/family.aspx.

Committee on Ethical Issues for Forensic Psychologists. (1991). Specialty guidelines for forensic psychologists. *Law and Human Behavior, 15,* 655–665.

Committee on Professional Practice and Standards. (1999). *Guidelines for psychological evaluations in child protection matters.* Washington, DC: American Psychological Association.

Condie, L. (2003). *Parenting evaluations for the court: Care and protection matters.* New York: Kluwer Academic.

Constantine, M. G., Fuertes, J. N., Roysircar, G., Kindaichi, M. M., & Walsh, W. B. (2008). Multicultural competence: Clinical practice, training and supervision, and research. In *Biennial review of counseling psychology: Volume 1,2008* (pp. 97–127). New York: Routledge/Taylor & Francis Group.

Cook, D. A. (1994). Racial identity in supervision. *Counselor Education and Supervision, 34,* 132–141.

Cook, W. L., & Kenny, D. A. (2004). Application of the social relations model to family assessment. *Journal of Family Psychology, 18,* 361–371.

Cooper, S., & Leong, F. T. L. (2008). Introduction to the special issue on culture, race, and ethnicity in organizational consulting psychology. *Consulting Psychology Journal: Practice and Research, 60,* 133–138.

Cox, M. J., & Brooks-Gunn, J. (1999). *Conflict and cohesion in families: Causes and Consequences.* Mahwah, NJ: Lawrence Erlbaum Associates.

Crittenden, P. M. (1988). Relationships at risk. In J. Belsky & T. Nezworski (Eds.), *Clinical implications of attachment* (pp. 136–167). Hillsdale, NJ: Lawrence Erlbaum Associates.

Cross, W. E., Parham, T. A., & Helms, J. E. (1991). The states of Black identity development: Nigrescence models. In Jones, R. L. (ed.), *Black psychology* (3rd edition) (pp. 319–338).

Council of Specialties in Professional Psychology. (2009). Family psychology: Formal specialty definition. Retrieved April 26, 2009, from http://cospp.org/specialties/family-psychology

Cummings, M. E., & Davies, P. (1994). *Children and marital conflict: The impact of family dispute and resolution.* New York, NY: Guilford Press.

Cummings, M. E., & Merrilees, C. E. (2010). Identifying the dynamic processes underlying links between marital conflict and child adjustment. In M. S. Schulz, M. K. Pruett, P. K. Kerig, & R. D. Parke (Eds.), *Strengthening couple relationships for optimal child development: Lessons from research and intervention* (pp. 27–40). Washington, DC: American Psychological Association.

Dana, R. H. (1993). *Multicultural assessment perspectives for professional psychology.* Needham Heights, MA: Allyn and Bacon.

Dana, R. H. (2005). *Multicultural assessment: Principles, applications, and examples.* Mahwah, NJ: Erlbaum.

Daniel, J. H., Roysicar, G., Abeles, N., & Boyd, C. (2004). Individual and cultural-diversity competency: Focus on the therapist. *Journal of Clinical Psychology, 60,* 755–770.

Daubert v. Merrell Dow Pharmaceuticals (92–102), 509 U.S. 579 (1993).

Davis, S. D., & Piercy, F. P. (2007a). What clients of couple therapy model developers and their former students say about change, part I: Model-dependent common factors across three models. *Journal of Marital & Family Therapy, 33,* 318–343.

Davis, S. D., & Piercy, F. P. (2007b). What clients of couple therapy model developers and their former students say about change, part II: Model-independent common factors and an integrative framework. *Journal of Marital & Family Therapy, 33,* 344–363.

De La Cour, A. T. (1986). Use of the focus in brief psychotherapy. *Psychotherapy: Theory, Research, and Practice, 23,* 133–139.

de las Fuentes, C., Willmuth, M. E., & Yarrow, C. (2005). Competency training in ethics education and practice. *Professional Psychology: Research and Practice, 36,* 362–366.

Demo, D. H., Allen, K. R., & Fine, M. A. (2000). *Handbook of family diversity.* New York: Oxford University Press

Descartes, R. T. (1999). *Discourse on method and meditations on first philosophy* (D. A. Cress, Trans). Indianapolis, IN: Hackett. (Original work published 1637)

DeVoe, E. R., & Faller, K. C. (1999). The characteristics of disclosure among children who may have been sexually abused. *Child Maltreatment, 4,* 217–227.

Diamond, G., Siqueland, L., & Diamond, G. M. (2003). Attachment-based family therapy for depressed adolescents: Programmatic treatment development. *Clinical Child and Family Psychology Review, 6,* 107–127.

Diamond, G. S. (2005). Attachment-based family therapy for depressed and anxious adolescents. In J. L. Lebow (Ed.), *Handbook of clinical family therapy* (pp. 17–41). Hoboken, NJ: Wiley.

Diamond, G. S., Levy, S. A., Israel, P., & Diamond, G. M. (2009). Attachment-based family therapy for depressed adolescents. In C. Essau (Ed.), *Treatments for adolescent depression: Theory and practice* (pp. 215–237). New York: Oxford University Press.

Dishion, T. J., & Stromshak, E. (2009). A family-centered intervention strategy for public middle schools. In J. H. Bray & M. Stanton (Eds.), *The Wiley Blackwell handbook of family psychology* (pp. 499–514). Oxford, UK: Wiley-Blackwell.

Division 43. (2003). *Specialty guidelines for the delivery of services by family psychologists.* Washington, DC: Author.

Dobbins, J. (2005). Education and training in family psychology: Development, issues, and trends. *The Family Psychologist, 21*(1), 15–18.

Drozd, L., Kuehnle, K., & Walker, L. E. A. (2004). Safety first: Understanding the impact of domestic violence in child custody disputes. *Journal of Child Custody, 2,* 75–103.

Drozd, L. M., & Olesen, N. W. (2004). Is it abuse, alienation, and/or estrangement? A decision tree. *Journal of Child Custody: Research, Issues, and Practices, 1,* 65–106.

Drumm, M., Carr, A., & Fitzgerald, M. (2000). The Beavers, McMaster and Circumplex clinical rating scales: A study of their sensitivity, specificity and discriminant validity. *Journal of Family Therapy, 22,* 225–238.

Duffy, M., & Chenail, R. J. (2004). Qualitative strategies in couple and family assessment. In L. Sperry (Ed.), *Assessment of couples and families: Contemporary and cutting-edge strategies* (pp. 33–63). New York: Taylor & Francis.

Duit, R., Roth, W.-M., Komorek, M., & Wilbers, J. (2001). Fostering conceptual change by analogies—between Scylla and Charybdis. *Learning and Instruction, 11,* 283–303.

Duncan, B. L., Miller, S. D., & Sparks, J. A. (2003). Interactional and solution-focused brief therapies: Evolving concepts of change. In T. L. Sexton, G. R. Weeks, & M. S. Robbins (Eds.), *Handbook of family therapy: The science and practice of working with families and couples* (pp. 101–123). New York: Brunner-Routledge.

Dunn, J., Davies, L. C., O'Connor, T. G., & Sturgess, W. (2001). Family lives and friendships: The perspectives of children in step-, single-parent, and nonstep families. *Journal of Family Psychology, 15,* 272–287.

Dutton, D. G. (2006). Domestic abuse assessment in child custody disputes: Beware the domestic violence research paradigm. *Journal of Child Custody: Research, Issues, and Practices, 2*, 23–42.

Eells, T. D. (2007). *Handbook of psychotherapy formulation* (2nd ed.). New York: Guilford Press.

Einhäuser, W., Martin, K. A. C., & König, P. (2004). Are switches in perception of the Necker cube related to eye position? *European Journal of Neuroscience, 20*, 2811–2818.

Eisler, I. (2006). Editorial: The heart of the matter—A conversation across continents. *Journal of Family Therapy, 28*, 329–333.

Eisler, I. (2009). Anorexia nervosa and the family. In J. H. Bray & M. Stanton (Eds.), *The Wiley Blackwell handbook of family psychology* (pp. 551–563). Oxford, UK: Wiley-Blackwell.

Eisler, I., & Dare, C. (1992). You can't teach an old dog new tricks: Teaching research to family therapy trainees. *Journal of Family Psychology, 5*, 418–431.

Ekstrom, R. B., & Smith, D. K. (2002). *Assessing individuals with disabilities in educational, employment, and counseling settings*. Washington, DC: American Psychological Association.

Ellis, M. V., & Ladany, M. (1997). Inferences concerning supervisees and clients in clinical supervision: An integrative review. In C. E. Watkins Jr. (Ed.), *Handbook of psychotherapy supervision* (pp. 447–507). New York: Wiley.

Emery, R. E. (1999). *Marriage, divorce, and children's adjustment* (2nd ed). Thousand Oaks, CA: Sage Publications.

Emery, R. E., Laumann-Billings, L., Waldron, M. C., Sbarra, D. A., & Dillon, P. (2001). *Journal of Consulting and Clinical Psychology, 69*, 323–332.

Enns, C. Z., & Forrest, L. M. (2005). Toward defining and integrating multicultural and feminist pedagogies. In C. Z. Enns & A. L. Sinacore (Eds.), *Teaching and social justice: Integrating multicultural and feminist theories in the classroom* (pp. 3–24). Washington, DC: American Psychological Association.

Epstein, N. B., Bishop, D. S., & Levin, S. (1978). The McMaster model of family functioning. *Journal of Marriage and Family Counseling, 4*, 19–31.

Epstein, N. B., Ryan, C. E., Bishop, D. S., Miller, I. W., & Keitner, G. I (2002). The McMaster model: A view of healthy family functioning. In F. Walsh (Ed.), *Normal family processes: Growing diversity and complexity* (3rd ed., pp. 515–539). New York: Guilford Press.

Epstein, R. M., & Hundert, E. M. (2002). Defining and assessing professional competence. *JAMA: Journal of the American Medical Association, 287*, 226–235.

Exner, J. E. (2002). *The Rorschach: Basic foundations and principles of interpretation* (Vol. 1). New York: Wiley

Exner, J. E., & Erdberg, P. (2005). *The Rorschach: Advanced interpretation*. New York: Wiley.

Fabricius, W. V. (2003). Listening to children of divorce: New findings that diverge from Wallerstein, Lewis, and Blakeslee. *Family Relations, 52*, 385–396.

Fabricius, W. V., & Braver, S. L. (2006). Relocation, parent conflict, and domestic violence: Independent risk factors for children of divorce. *Journal of Child Custody: Research, Issues, and Practices, 3*, 7–24.

Fabricius, W. V., & Hall, J. A. (2000). Young adults' perspectives on divorce: Living arrangements. *Family and Conciliation Courts Review, 38*, 446–461.

Falender, C. A., Erickson Cornish, J. A., Goodyear, R., Hatcher, R., Kaslow, N. J., Leventhal, G., et al. (2004). Defining competencies in psychology supervision: A consensus statement. *Journal of Clinical Psychology, 60*, 771–785.

Falender, C. A., & Shafranske, E. P. (2004). *Clinical supervision: A competency-based approach*. Washington, DC: American Psychological Association.

Falicov, C. J. (2000). *Latino families in therapy: A guide to multicultural practice.* New York: Guilford Press.

Faller, K. C. (1998). the Parental Alienation Syndrome: What is it and what data support it? *Child Maltreatment, 3,* 100–115.

Faller, K. C. (2005). False accusations of child maltreatment: A contested issue. *Child Abuse and Neglect, 29,* 1327–1331.

Fals-Stewart, W., Birchler, G., O'Farrell, T., & Lam, K. K. (2009). Learning sobriety together: Behavioral couples therapy for alcoholism and substance abuse. In J. H. Bray & M. Stanton (Eds.), *The Wiley Blackwell handbook of family psychology* (pp. 388–401) Oxford, UK: Wiley-Blackwell.

Family Psychology Specialty Council. (2001). By-laws. Unpublished.

Family Psychology Specialty Council. (2009). Petition for the recognition of a specialty in professional psychology. Unpublished.

Famularo, R., Kinscherff, R., & Fenton, T. (1992). Parental substance abuse and the nature of child maltreatment. *Child Abuse and Neglect, 16,* 475–483.

Farr, R. H., Forsell, S. L., & Patterson, C. J. (2010). Parenting and child development in adoptive families: Does parental sexual orientation matter? *Applied Developmental Science, 14,* 164–178.

Federal Rules of Evidence for United States Courts and Magistrates. (1975). St. Paul, MN: West.

Fergusson, D. M., Horwood, L. J., & Ridder, E. M. (2005). Partner violence and mental health outcomes in a New Zealand birth cohort. *Journal of Marriage and Family, 67,* 1103–1119.

Fields, L., & Prinz, R. J. (1997). Coping and adjustment during childhood and adolescence. *Clinical Psychology Review, 17,* 937–976.

Fiese, B. H., & Spagnola, M. (2005). Narratives in and about families: An examination of coding schemes and a guide for family researchers. *Journal of Family Psychology, 19,* 51–61.

Fiese, B. H., & Winter, M. A. (2009). Family stories and rituals. In J. H. Bray & M. Stanton (Eds.), *The Wiley Blackwell handbook of family psychology* (pp. 625–636). Oxford, UK: Wiley-Blackwell.

Filsinger, E. E. (Ed.). (1983). *Marriage and family assessment.* Beverly Hills, CA: Sage.

Finn, S. E. (2007). *In our client's shoes: Theories and techniques of therapeutic assessment.* Mahwah, NJ: Erlbaum

Finn, S. E., & Tonsager, M. E. (1997). Information-gathering and therapeutic models of assessment: Complementary paradigms. *Psychological Assessment, 9,* 374–385.

First, M. B., Bell, C. C., Cuthbert, B., Krystal, J. H., Malison, R., Offord, D. R., et al. (2002). Personality disorders and relational disorders: A research agenda for addressing crucial gaps in DSM. In D. J. Kupfer, M. B. First, & D. A. Regier (Eds.), *A research agenda for DSM-V* (pp. 123–199). Washington, DC: American Psychiatric Association.

Fischer, R. L., & Valley, C. (2000). Monitoring the benefits of family counseling: Using satisfaction surveys to assess the client's perspective. *Smith College Studies in Social Work, 70,* 271–286.

Fishman, D. B. (1999). *The case for pragmatic psychology.* New York: New York University Press.

Fiske, S. T. (1993). Controlling other people: The impact of power on stereotyping. *American Psychologist, 48,* 621–628.

Fiske, S. T. (1998). Stereotyping, prejudice, and discrimination. In D. T. Gilbert & S. T.Fiske (Eds.), *The handbook of social psychology* (4th ed.), *Vol. 2,* (pp. 357–411). New York: McGraw-Hill.

Flicker, S. M., Turner, C. W., Waldron, H. B., Brody, J. L., & Ozechowski, T. J. (2008). Ethnic background, therapeutic alliance, and treatment retention in functional family therapy with adolescents who abuse substances. *Journal of Family Psychology, 22,* 167–170.

Fraenkel, P., & Pinsof, W. M. (2001). Teaching family therapy-centered integration: Assimilation and beyond. *Journal of Psychotherapy Integration, 11,* 59–85.

Fredman, N., & Sherman, R. (1987). *Handbook of measurements for marriage and family therapy.* New York: Brunner-Mazel

Frey, M. A., Ellis, D. A., & Naar-King, S. (2007). Testing nursing theory with intervention research: The congruency between King's conceptual system and multisystemic therapy. In C. Sieloff & M. Frey (Eds.), *Middle range theory development using King's conceptual system* (pp. 273–286). New York: Springer.

Friedberg, R. D., Gorman, A. A., & Beidel, D. C. (2009). Training and dissemination efforts in varying contexts: Navigating the yellow brick road. *Behavior Modification, 33*(1), 3–6.

Friedlander, M. L., Escudero, V., & Heatherington, L. (2006). *Therapeutic alliances in couple and family therapy: An empirically informed guide to practice.* Washington, DC: American Psychological Association.

Friere, P. (1970). *Pedagogy of the oppressed* (M. B. Ramos, Trans.). New York: Seabury Press.

Frye v. United States, 293 F. 1013 (D.C. Cir. 1923).

Frisby, C. L. (1998). Poverty and socioeconomic status. In J. Sandoval, C. L. Frisby, K. F. Geisinger, S. D. Scheuneman, & J. R. Griener (Eds.), *Test interpretation and diversity: Achieving equity in assessment* (pp. 241–270). Washington, DC: American Psychological Association.

Fulcher, M., Sutfin, E. L., & Patterson, C. J. (2008). Individual differences in gender development: Associations with parental sexual orientation, attitudes, and division of labor. *Sex Roles, 58,* 330–341.

Fuqua, D. R., & Kurpius, D. J. (1993). Conceptual models in organizational consultation. *Journal of Counseling & Development, 71,* 607–618.

Fuqua, D. R., & Newman, J. L. (2002). The role of systems theory in consulting psychology. In R. L. Lowman (Ed.), *The California School of Organizational Studies: Handbook of organizational consulting psychology: A comprehensive guide to theory, skills, and techniques* (pp. 76–105). San Francisco, CA: Jossey-Bass.

Fuqua, D. R., & Newman, J. L. (2006). Moral and ethical issues in human systems. *Consulting Psychology Journal: Practice and Research, 58,* 206–215.

Fuqua, D. R., & Newman, J. L. (2009). Consultation as a moral process. *Consulting Psychology Journal: Practice and Research, 61,* 136–146.

Furstenberg, F. F. (1990). Divorce and the American family. *Annual Review of Sociology, 16,* 379–403.

Garber, B. D. (2010). *Developmental psychology for family law professionals: Theory, application and the best interests of the child.* New York, NY: Springer Publishing.

Gardner, R. A. (1992). *The Parental Alienation Syndrome.* Creskill, NJ: Creative Therapeutics.

Gardner, R. A. (2003). The judiciary's role in the etiology, symptom development, and treatment of the Parental Alienation Syndrome (PAS). *American Journal of Forensic Psychology, 21,* 39–64.

Geffner, R. A., Jaffee, P. G., & Sudermann, M. (Eds.). (2000). *Children exposed to domestic violence: Current issues in research, intervention, prevention, and policy development.* New York, NY: Routledge.

Geffner, R., Conradi, L., Geis, K., & Aranda, B. M. (2009). Conducting child custody evaluations in the context of family violence allegations: Practical techniques and suggestions for ethical practice. *Journal of Child Custody: Research, Issues, and Practices, 6*, 189–218.

Geisinger, K. F. (1998). Psychometric issues in test interpretation. In J. Sandoval, C. L. Frisby, K. F. Geisinger, S. D. Scheuneman, & J. R. Griener (Eds.), *Test interpretation and diversity: Achieving equity in assessment* (pp. 17–30). Washington, DC: American Psychological Association.

Gelatt, H. B. (1989). Positive uncertainty: A new decision-making framework for counseling. *Journal of Counseling Psychology, 36*, 252–256.

Gelso, C. J. (2005). Introduction to special issue. *Psychotherapy: Theory, Research, Practice, Training, 42*, 419–420.

George, C. (2009). Couple relationships and the family system: Commentary from a behavioral systems perspective. *Attachment & Human Development, 11*(1), 103–110.

Gergen, K. J. (1985). The social constructionist movement in modern psychology. *American Psychologist, 40*, 266–275.

Gilbert, R., & Christensen, A. (1985). Observational assessment of marital and family interaction: Methodological considerations. In L. L'Abate (Ed.), *Handbook of family psychology and therapy* (Vol. 2, pp. 961–988). Homewood, IL: Dorsey Press.

Gilgun, J. (2005). Qualitative research and family psychology. *Journal of Family Psychology, 19*, 40–50.

Gilgun, J. (2009). Qualitative research and family psychology. In J. H. Bray & M. Stanton (Eds.), *The Wiley Blackwell handbook of family psychology* (pp. 85–99). Oxford, UK: Wiley-Blackwell.

Glasser, J. K. (2002). Factors related to consultant credibility. *Consulting Psychology Journal: Practice and Research, 54*, 28–42.

Goldberg, A. E. (2009). Lesbian, gay, and bisexual family psychology: A systemic, life-cycle perspective. In J. H. Bray & M. Stanton (Eds.), *The Wiley Blackwell handbook of family psychology* (pp. 576–587). Oxford, UK: Wiley-Blackwell.

Goldberg, A. E., & Smith, J. Z. (2009). Perceived parenting skill across the transition to adoptive parenthood among lesbian, gay, and heterosexual couples. *Journal of Family Psychology, 23*, 861–870.

Goldenberg, H., & Goldenberg, I. (2009). The revolution and evolution of family therapy and family psychology. In J. H. Bray & M. Stanton (Eds.), *The Wiley Blackwell handbook of family psychology* (pp. 21–36). Oxford, UK: Wiley-Blackwell.

Goldner, V. (1998). The treatment of violence and victimization in intimate relationships. *Family Process, 37*, 263–286.

Goldner, V. (1999). Morality and multiplicity: Perspectives on the treatment of violence in intimate life. *Journal of Marital & Family Therapy, 25*, 325–336.

Goldstein, A. M. (2003). *Handbook of psychology: Volume 11. Forensic psychology.* Hoboken, NJ: Wiley.

Goodheart, C. D., Kazdin, A. E., & Sternberg, R. J. (2006). *Evidence-based psychotherapy: Where practice and research meet.* Washington, DC: American Psychological Association.

Goodman, L. A., Liang, B., Helms, J. E., Latta, R. E., Sparks, E., & Weintraub, S. (2004). Training counseling psychologists as social justice agents: Feminist and multicultural perspectives. *The Counseling Psychologist, 32*, 793–837.

Goodman, M., Bonds, D., Sandler, I., & Braver, S. (2004). Parent psychoeducational programs and reducing the negative effects of interparental conflict following divorce. *Family Court Review: An Interdisciplinary Journal, 42*, 263–279.

Goodman, S. H., Barfoot, B., Frye, A. A., & Belli, A. M. (1999). Dimensions of marital conflict and children's social problem-solving skills. *Journal of Family Psychology, 13*, 33–45.

Goodyear, R. K., & Nelson, M. L. (1997). The major formats of psychotherapy supervision. In C. E. Watkins Jr. (Ed.), *Handbook of psychotherapy supervision* (pp. 328–344). New York: Wiley.

Gordon, K. C., Baucom, D. H., & Snyder, D. K. (2008). Optimal strategies in couple therapy: Treating couples dealing with the trauma of infidelity. *Journal of Contemporary Psychotherapy, 38,* 151–160.

Gordon, K. C., Dixon, L. J., Willett, J. M., & Hughes, F. M. (2009). Behavioral and cognitive-behavioral therapies. In J. H. Bray & M. Stanton (Eds.), *The Wiley Blackwell handbook of family psychology* (pp. 226–239). Oxford, UK: Wiley-Blackwell.

Gottlieb, M. C. (1995). Ethical dilemmas in change of format and live supervision. In R. H. Mikesell, D. D. Lusterman, & S. H. McDaniel (Eds.), *Integrating family therapy: Handbook of family psychology and systems theory* (pp. 561–570). Washington, DC: American Psychological Association.

Gottman, J. M (1994). *What predicts divorce? The relationship between marital processes and marital outcomes.* Hillsdale, NJ: Erlbaum.

Gould, J. (2004). Evaluating the probative value of child custody evaluations: A guide for forensic mental health professionals. *Journal of Child Custody, 1,* 77–96.

Gould, J. W. (2006). *Conducting scientifically crafted child custody evaluations* (2nd ed.). Sarasota, FL: Professional Resource Press.

Green, L. W. (2008). Making research relevant: If it is an evidenced-based practice, where's the practice-based evidence? *Family Practice, 25,* i20–i24.

Green, R.-J. (1992). Doctoral training in family psychology: A home in the professional schools? *Journal of Family Psychology, 5,* 403–417.

Green, R.-J. (2002). Lesbians, gays, and family psychology: Resources for teaching and practice. In E. Davis-Russell (Ed.), *The California School of Professional Psychology handbook of multicultural education, research, intervention, and training* (pp. 88–105). San Francisco: Jossey-Bass.

Green, R.-J. (2005a). The family/child emphasis in the clinical psychology PhD and PsyD programs: California School of Professional Psychology, Alliant International University–San Francisco. *The Family Psychologist, 21*(1), 4–5.

Green, R.-J. (2005b). The shallowness and narrowness of graduate education in family psychology: Are we providing ethical training and supervision? *The Family Psychologist, 21,* 8–45.

Greenberg, L., & Gould, J. W. (2001). The treating expert: A hybrid role with firm boundaries. *Professional Psychology: Research and Practice, 32,* 469–478.

Greenberg, L. R., Gould, J., Gould-Saltman, D., & Stahl, P. (2003). Is the child's therapist part of the problem? What judges, attorneys and mental health professionals need to know about court-related treatment for children. *Family Law Quarterly,* Summer, 39–69.

Greenberg, L. R., Gould-Saltman, D. J., & Gottlieb, M. C. (2009). Playing in their sandbox: Obligations of mental health professionals in custody cases. *Journal of Child Custody, 5,* 192–216.

Greenberg, L. R., Martindale, D. A., Gould, J. W., & Gould-Saltman, D. J. (2004). Ethical issues in child custody and dependency cases: Enduring principles and emerging challenges. *Journal of Child Custody, 1,* 7–30.

Greenberg, S. A., & Shuman, D. W. (1997). Irreconcilable conflict between therapeutic and forensic roles. *Professional Psychology: Research and Practice, 28,* 50–57.

Gregoire, M. (2003). *Effects of augmented activation, refutational text, efficacy beliefs, epistemological beliefs, and systematic processing on conceptual change.* Unpublished doctoral dissertation, University of Florida.

Grisso, T. (2003). *Evaluating competencies: Forensic assessments and instruments* (2nd ed.). New York: Kluwer Academic.

Grossman, N. S. (2005). Education and training in family psychology: Looking at the past to move into the future. *The Family Psychologist, 21*(1), 9–11.

Grossman, N. S., & Okun, B. F. (2003). Family psychology and family law: Introduction to the special issue. *Journal of Family Psychology, 17,* 163–168.

Grotevant, H. D., & Carlson, C. I. (Eds.) (1989). *Family assessment: A guide to methods and measures.* New York: Guilford Press.

Grych, J. H., Fincham, F. D., Jouriles, E. N., & McDonald, R. (2000). Interparental conflict and child adjustment: Testing the meditational role of appraisals in the cognitive-contextual framework. *Child Development, 71,* 1648–1661.

Gunnoe, M. L., & Braver, S. L. (2001). The effects of joint legal custody on mothers, fathers, and children controlling for factors that predispose a sole maternal versus joint legal award. *Law and Human Behavior, 25,* 25–43.

Gupta, M., Beach, S. R. H., & Coyne, J. C. (2005). Optimizing couple and parenting interventions to address adult depression. In J. L. Lebow (Ed.), *Handbook of clinical family therapy* (pp. 228–250). Hoboken, NJ: Wiley.

Halford, W. K., Markman, H. J., & Stanley, S. (2008). Strengthening couples' relationships with education: Social policy and public health perspectives. *Journal of Family Psychology, 22,* 497–505.

Halverson, C. F. (1995). Measurement beyond the individual. In J. C. Conoley & E. B. Werth (Eds.), *Family assessment* (pp. 3–18). Lincoln, NE: Buros Institute of Mental Measurements.

Halonen, J. S., Bosack, T., Clay, S., & McCarthy, M. (2003). A rubric for learning, teaching, and assessing scientific inquiry in psychology. *Teaching of Psychology, 30,* 196–207.

Hampson, R. B., Beavers, W. R., & Hulgus, Y. (1990). Cross-ethnic family differences: Interactional assessment of White, Black, and Mexican American families. *Journal of Marital and Family Therapy, 16,* 307–319.

Handelsman, M., Knapp, S., & Gottlieb, M. (2002). Positive ethics. In R. Snyder & S. Lopez (Eds.), *Handbook of positive psychology* (pp. 731–744). New York: Oxford University Press.

Hanson, R. K. (1997). *The development of a brief actuarial scale for sexual offense recidivism (User report 97–04).* Ottawa: Department of the Solicitor General of Canada.

Hardy, K. V., & Laszloffy, T. A. (1995). The cultural genogram: Key to training culturally competent family therapists. *Journal of Marital and Family Therapy, 21,* 227–237.

Hare-Mustin, R. (1978). A feminist approach to family therapy. *Family Process, 17,* 181–194.

Hargrove, D. S. (2009). Bowen family systems theory. In J. H. Bray & M. Stanton (Eds.), *The Wiley Blackwell handbook of family psychology* (pp. 286–299). Oxford, UK: Wiley-Blackwell.

Harkness, A. R., & Lilienfeld, S. O. (1997). Individual differences science for treatment planning: Personality traits. *Psychological Assessment, 9,* 349–360.

Harway, M. (2003). What is systems thinking and why is it important? *The Family Psychologist, 19*(1), 4–5.

Hauser, B. B. (2005). Visitation in high-conflict families: The impact on a child's inner life. In L. Gunsberg & P. Hymowitz (Eds.), *A handbook of divorce and custody: Forensic, developmental, and clinical perspectives* (pp. 281–289). New York, NY: The Analytic Press/Taylor & Francis Group.

Hawkins, A. J., Blanchard, V. L., Baldwin, S. A., & Fawcett, E. B. (2008). Does marriage and relationship education work? A meta-analytic study. *Journal of Consulting and Clinical Psychology, 76,* 723–734.

Hays, P. A. (2008). *Addressing cultural complexities in practice: Assessment, diagnosis, and therapy* (2nd ed.). Washington, DC: American Psychological Association.

Health Insurance Portability and Accountability Act (HIPAA) of 1996, P.L. 104–191, 119 Stat. 1936.

Health Insurance Portability and Accountability Act of 1996. (1996). Retrieved January 7, 2011, from U.S. Department of Health and Human Services, Office for Civil Rights Web site: http://www.hhs.gov/ocr/hipaa

Heilbrun, K. (1992). The role of psychological testing in forensic assessment. *Law and Human Behavior, 16,* 257–272.

Heilbrun, K. (2001). *Principles of forensic mental health assessment.* New York: Kluwer Academic.

Heilbrun, K., Warren, J., & Picarello, K. (2003). Third party information in forensic assessment. In A. M. Goldstein (ed.), *Handbook of psychology: Volume 11. Forensic psychology* (pp. 69–86). Hoboken, NJ: Wiley.

Heim, C., Shugart, M., Craighead, E. W., & Nemeroff, C. B. (2010). Neurological and psychiatric consequences of child abuse and neglect. *Developmental Psychobiology, 52,* 671–690.

Helms, J. E., & Cook, D. A. (1999). *Using race and culture in counseling and psychotherapy: Theory and process.* Boston: Allyn & Bacon.

Henderson, C. E., Cawyer, C. S., & Watkins, C. E., Jr. (1999). A comparison of student and supervisor perceptions of effective practicum supervision. *The Clinical Supervisor, 18,* 47–74.

Henggeler, S. W., Sheidow, A. J., & Lee, T. (2009). Multisystemic therapy. In J. H. Bray & M. Stanton (Eds.) *The Wiley Blackwell handbook of family psychology* (pp. 370–387). Oxford, UK: Wiley-Blackwell.

Hertlein, K. M., Weeks, G. R., & Gambescia, N. (2009). *Systemic sex therapy.* New York: Routledge/Taylor & Francis Group.

Hertlein, K. M., Weeks, G. R., & Sendak, S. K. (2009). *A clinician's guide to systemic sex therapy.* New York: Routledge/Taylor & Francis Group.

Hetherington, E. M. (1999). Family functioning and the adjustment of adolescent siblings in diverse types of families. *Monographs of the Society for Research in Child Development, 64,* 1–25.

Hetherington, E. M., Bridges, M., & Insabella, G. (1998). What matters? What does not? five perspectives on the association between marital transitions and children's adjustment. *American Psychologist, 53,* 167–184.

Hilburt-Davis, J., & Dyer, W. G., Jr. (2006). Hilburt-Davis/Dyer consulting model. In F. W. Kaslow (Ed.), *Handbook of family business and family business consultation: A global perspective* (pp. 73–93). New York: Haworth Press.

Hird, J. S., Cavalieri, C. E., Dulko, J. P., Felice, A. A. D., & Ho, T. A. (2001). Visions and realities: Supervisee perspectives of multicultural supervision. *Journal of Multicultural Counseling and Development, 29,* 114–130.

Holleman, W. L., Bray, J. H., Davis, L., & Holleman, M. C. (2004). Innovative ways to address the mental health and medical needs of marginalized patients: Collaborations between family physicians, family therapists, and family psychologists. *American Journal of Orthopsychiatry, 74,* 242–252.

Holliday, R. E., Reyna, V. F., & Hayes, B. K. (2002). Memory processes underlying misinformation effects in child witnesses. *Developmental Review, 22,* 37–77.

Holloway, E. L. (1995). *Clinical supervision: A systems approach.* Thousand Oaks, CA: Sage.

Holloway, E. L., & Neufeldt, S. A. (1995). Supervision: Its contributions to treatment efficacy. *Journal of Consulting and Clinical Psychology, 63,* 207–213.

Hong, G. K. (2007). Diversity and graduate training in family psychology. *The Family Psychologist, 23*(3), 22–23.

Hong, G. K. (2009). Family diversity. In J. H. Bray & M. Stanton (Eds.), *The Wiley Blackwell handbook of family psychology* (pp. 68–84). Oxford, UK: Wiley-Blackwell

Houts, A. C., Cook, T. D., & Shadish, W. R., Jr. (1986). The person-situation debate: A critical multiplist perspective. *Journal of Personality, 54*, 52–105.

Hudock, A. M., Jr., & Warden, S. A. G. (2001). Using movies to teach family systems concepts. *The Family Journal, 9*(2), 116–121.

In re Lifschutz, 2 Cal.3d 415 (1970).

Ivey, A. E., Ivey, M. B., & Simek-Morgan, L. (1993). *Counseling and psychotherapy: A multicultural perspective.* Needham Heights, MA: Simon & Schuster.

Ivey, D. C., & Conoley, C. W. (1994). Influence of gender in family evaluations: A comparison of trained and untrained observer perceptions of matriarchal and patriarchal family interviews. *Journal of Family Psychology, 8*, 336–346.

Iwamasa, G. Y., Hsia, C., & Hinton, D. (2006). Cognitive-behavioral therapy with Asian Americans. In P. A. Hays & G. Y Iwamasa (Eds.), *Culturally responsive cognitive-behavioral therapy: Assessment, practice, and supervision* (pp. 267–281). Washington, DC: American Psychological Association.

Jacob, L. C. (2004). Mediating with blended families. In J. Folberg, A. L. Milne, & P. Salem (Eds.), *Divorce and family mediation: Models, techniques, and applications* (pp. 336–350). New York, NY: Guilford Publications.

Jaffe, D. T., Dashew, L., Lane, S., Paul, J., & Bork, D. (2006). The Aspen family business group consulting process: A model for deep structural change and relationship shift in complex multigenerational enterprising family systems. In F. W. Kaslow (Ed.), *Handbook of family business and family business consultation: A global perspective* (pp. 47–72). New York: Haworth Press.

Jaffe, P. G., Crooks, C. V., & Bala, N. (2009). A framework for addressing allegations of domestic violence in child custody disputes. *Journal of Child Custody: Research, Issues, and Practices, 6*, 169–188.

Johnson, S., & Bradley, B. (2009). Emotionally focused couple therapy: Creating loving relationships. In J. H. Bray & M. Stanton (Eds.), *The Wiley Blackwell handbook of family psychology* (pp. 267–281). Oxford, UK: Wiley-Blackwell.

Johnston, J. R. (2003). Parental alignments and rejection: An empirical study of alienation in children of divorce. *Journal of the American Academy of Psychiatry and the Law, 31*, 158–170.

Johnston, J. R., Lee, S., Olesen, N. W., & Walters, M. G. (2005). Allegations and substantiations of abuse in custody-disputing families. *Family Court Review: An Interdisciplinary Journal, 43*, 283–294.

Johnston, J. R., & Roseby, V. (1997). *In the name of the child: A developmental approach to understanding and helping children of conflicted and violent divorce.* New York: The Free Press.

Jordan, K. (2003). *Handbook of couple and family assessment.* Hauppauge, NY: Nova Science.

Joseph, D., & Tavegia, B. (2005). The challenges of couple and family training. *The Family Psychologist, 21*(4), 14.

Kadis, L. B., & McClendon, R. (2006). Preserving the family business: An interpersonal model for reconciling relationships. In F. W. Kaslow (Ed.), *Handbook of family business and family business consultation: A global perspective* (pp. 95–111). New York: Haworth Press.

Kahng, S. K., Oyserman, D., Bybee, D., & Mowbray, C. (2008). Mothers with serious mental illness: When symptoms decline does parenting improve? *Journal of Family Psychology, 22*, 162–166.

Kaslow, F. W. (1987). Trends in family psychology. *Journal of Family Psychology, 1*, 77–90.

Kaslow, F. W. (Ed.). (1996). *Handbook of relational diagnosis and dysfunctional family patterns*. New York: Wiley.

Kaslow, F. W. (2000). *Handbook of couple and family forensics: A sourcebook for mental health and legal professionals*. Hoboken, NJ: Wiley.

Kaslow, F. W. (2005). Maternal mentoring: A relatively new phenomenon in family businesses. *Journal of Family Psychotherapy, 16*(3), 11–18.

Kaslow, F. W. (2006a). Brief history of the family firm institute. In F. W. Kaslow (Ed.), *Handbook of family business and family business consultation: A global perspective* (pp. 3–24). New York: Haworth Press.

Kaslow, F. W. (Eds.). (2006b). *Handbook of family business and family business consultation: A global perspective*. New York: Haworth Press.

Kaslow, F. W. (2006c). Themes, reflections, comparisons, and contrasts. In F. W. Kaslow (Ed.), *Handbook of family business and family business consultation: A global perspective* (pp. 403–418). New York: Haworth Press.

Kaslow, N. J. (2004). Competencies in professional psychology. *American Psychologist, 59*, 774–781.

Kaslow, N. J., Borden, K. A., Collins, F. L., Jr., Forrest, L., Illfelder-Kaye, J., Nelson, P. D., et al. (2004). Competencies conference: Future directions in education and credentialing in professional psychology. *Journal of Clinical Psychology, 60*, 699–712.

Kaslow, N. J., Celano, M., & Stanton, M. (2005). Training in family psychology: A competencies-based approach. *Family Process, 44*, 337–353.

Kaslow, N. J., & Ingram, M. V. (2009). Board certification: A competency-based perspective. In C. M. Nezu, A. J. Finch & N. P. Simon (Eds.), *Becoming board certified by the American Board of Professional Psychology (ABPP)*. New York: Oxford University Press.

Kaslow, N. J., Rubin, N. J., Bebeau, M. J., Leigh, I. W., Lichtenberg, J. W., Nelson, P. D., et al. (2007). Guiding principles and recommendations for the assessment of competence. *Professional Psychology: Research and Practice, 38*, 441–451.

Kazdin, A. E. (2008). Evidence-based treatment and practice: New opportunities to bridge clinical research and practice, enhance the knowledge base, and improve patient care. *American Psychologist, 63*, 146–159.

Keiley, M. K., Dolbin, M., Hill, J., Karuppaswamy, N., Liu, T., & Natrajan, R., et al. (2002). The cultural genogram: Experiences from within a marriage and family therapy training program. *Journal of Marital and Family Therapy, 28*, 165–178.

Kelly, J. B. (1993). Current research on children's postdivorce adjustment: No simple answers. *Family and Conciliation Courts Review, 31*, 29–49.

Kelly, J. B., & Emery, R. E. (2003). Children's adjustment following divorce: Risk and resilience perspectives. *Family Relations, 52*, 352–362.

Kelly, J. B., & Johnston, J. R. (2001). The alienated child: A reformulation of Parental Alienation Syndrome. *Family Court Review, 39*, 249–266.

Kelly, J. B., & Lamb, M. E. (2000). Using child development research to make appropriate custody and access decisions for young children. *Family and Conciliation Courts Review, 38*, 297–311.

Kelley, S. D., & Bickman, L. (2009). Beyond outcomes monitoring: Measurement feedback systems in child and adolescent clinical practice. *Current Opinion in Psychiatry, 22*, 363–368.

Kelsey-Smith, M., & Beavers, W. R. (1981). Family assessment: Centripetal and centrifugal family systems. *American Journal of Family Therapy, 9*, 3–12.

Kendjelic, E. M., & Eells, T. D. (2007). Generic psychotherapy case formulation training improves formulation quality. *Psychotherapy: Theory, Research, Practice, Training, 44*, 66–77.

Kerig, K., & Lindahl, K. M. (2000). *Family observational coding systems: Resources for systemic research*. Mahwah, NJ: Erlbaum.

Kessler, R., Stafford, D., & Messier, R. (2009). The problem of integrating behavioral health in the medical home and the questions it leads to. *Journal of Clinical Psychology in Medical Settings, 16*(1), 4–12.

Kilburg, R. R. (1995). Integrating psychodynamic and systems theories in organization development practice. *Consulting Psychology Journal: Practice and Research, 47*, 28–55.

Kitchener, K. S. (2000). *Foundations of ethical practice, research, and teaching*. Mahwah, NJ: Erlbaum.

Knapp, S., & VandeCreek, L. (2003). *A guide to the 2002 revision of the American Psychological Association's Ethics Code*. Sarasota, FL: Professional Resource Press.

Knobloch-Fedders, L. M., Pinsof, W. M., & Mann, B. J. (2004). The formation of the therapeutic alliance in couple therapy. *Family Process, 43*, 425–442.

Knobloch-Fedders, L. M., Pinsof, W. M., & Mann, B. J. (2007). Therapeutic alliance and treatment progress in couple psychotherapy. *Journal of Marital & Family Therapy, 33*, 245–257.

Knoff, H. M., Hines, C. V., & Kromrey, J. D. (1995). Finalizing the consultant effectiveness scale: An analysis and validation of the characteristics of effective consultants. *School Psychology Review, 24*, 480–496.

Knowles, P. (2009). Collaborative communication between psychologists and primary care providers. *Journal of Clinical Psychology in Medical Settings, 16*(1), 72–76.

Koocher, G. P. (2006). Ethical issues in forensic assessment of children and adolescents. In S. N. Sparta & G. P. Koocher (Eds.), *Forensic mental health assessment of children and adolescents* (pp. 46–63). New York: Oxford University Press.

Koocher, G. P. (2009). Ethical issues in child sexual abuse evaluations. In K. Kuehnle & M. A. Connell (Eds.), *The evaluation of child sexual abuse allegations: A comprehensive guide to assessment and testimony* (pp. 89–100). Hoboken, NJ: Wiley.

Koocher, G. P., & Keith-Spiegel, P. (2008). *Ethics in psychology and the mental health professions: Standards and cases* (3rd ed.). New York: Oxford University Press.

Krackow, E., & Lynn, S. J. (2003). Is there touch in the game of Twister®? The effects of innocuous touch and suggestive questions on children's eyewitness memory. *Law and Human Behavior, 27*, 589–604.

Krishnamurthy, R., VandeCreek, L., Kaslow, N. J., Tazeau, Y. N., Miville, M. L., Kerns, R., et al. (2004). Achieving competency in psychological assessment: Directions for education and training. *Journal of Clinical Psychology, 60*, 725–739.

Kuehnle, K., & Connell, M. A. (2009). *The evaluation of child sexual abuse allegations: A comprehensive guide to assessment and testimony*. Hoboken, NJ: Wiley.

Kuehnle, K., Coulter, M., & Firestone, G. (2000). Child protection evaluations: The forensic stepchild. *Family Court Review, 38*, 368–391.

Kuehnle, K., & Kirkpatrick, H. D. (2005). Evaluating allegations of child sexual abuse within complex child custody cases. *Journal of Child Custody: Research, Issues, and Practices, 2*, 3–39.

L'Abate, L. (2004). Couple and family assessment: Current and future prospects. In L. Sperry (Ed.), *Assessment of couples and families: Contemporary and cutting-edge strategies* (pp. 251–274). New York: Brunner-Routledge.

Ladany, N., Friedlander, M. L., & Nelson, M. L. (2005). *Critical events in psychotherapy supervision: An interpersonal approach*. Washington, DC: American Psychological Association.

Laird, J. & Green, R-J. (1996). *Lesbian and gays in couples and families: A handbook for therapists*. San Francisco, CA: Jossey-Bass.

Lakin, M. (1986). Ethical challenges of group and dyadic psychotherapies: A comparative approach. *Professional Psychology: Research and Practice, 17,* 454–461.

Lakin, M. (1994). Morality in group and family therapies: Multiperson therapies and the 1992 ethics code. *Professional Psychology: Research and Practice, 25,* 344–348.

Lamb, M. E. (2002). Placing children's interests first: Developmentally appropriate parenting plans. *Virginia Journal of Social Policy and the Law, 10,* 98–119.

Lamb, M. E., & Fauchier, A. (2001). The effects of question type on self-contradictions by children in the course of forensic interviews. *Applied Cognitive Psychology, 15,* 483–491.

Lamb, M. E., & Kelly, J. B. (2001). Using the empirical literature to guide the development of parenting plans for young children. A rejoinder to Solomon and Biringen. *Family Court Review, 39,* 365–371.

Lamb, M. E., Sternberg, K. J., & Esplin, P. W. (1998). Conducting investigative interviews of alleged sexual abuse victims. *Child Abuse and Neglect, 22,* 813–822.

Lamb, M. E., Sternberg, K. J., & Esplin, P. W. (2003). Effects of age and delay on the amount of information provided by alleged sex abuse victims in investigative interviews. *Child Development, 71,* 1586–1596.

Lamb, M. E., Sternberg, K. J., Orbach, Y., Esplin, P. W., Stewart, H., & Mitchell, S. (2003). Age differences in young children's responses to open-ended invitations in the course of forensic interviews. *Journal of Consulting and Clinical Psychology, 71,* 926–934.

Lambert, J. E., & Friedlander, M. (2008). Relationship of differentiation of self to adult clients' perceptions of the alliance in brief family therapy. *Psychotherapy Research, 18,* 160–166.

Lambert, M. J., & Arnold, R. C. (1987). Research and the supervisory process. *Professional Psychology: Research and Practice, 18,* 217–224.

Laszloffy, T. A. (2002). Rethinking family development theory: Teaching with the systemic family development (SFD) model. *Family Relations, 51,* 206–214.

Lawrence, E., Beach, S. R. H., & Doss, B. D. (2009). Couple and family processes in DSM-V: Moving beyond relational disorders. In J. H. Bray & M. Stanton (Eds.), *The Wiley Blackwell handbook of family psychology* (pp. 165–182). Oxford, UK: Wiley-Blackwell.

Lebow, J. L. (1997). The integrative revolution in couple and family therapy. *Family Process, 36,* 1–17.

Lebow, J. L. (2002). Training in integrative/eclectic psychotherapy. In F. Kaslow (Ed.), *Comprehensive handbook of psychotherapy: Integrative/eclectic* (Vol. 4, pp. 545–556). Hoboken, NJ: Wiley.

Lebow, J. L. (2003). Integrative approaches to couple and family therapy. In T. Sexton, G. R. Weeks, & M. Robbins (Eds.), *Handbook of family therapy: The science and practice of working with families and couples* (pp. 201–225). New York: Brunner-Routledge.

Lebow, J. L. (2004). Transcending the barriers between science and practice in family psychology. *The Family Psychologist, 20,* 1–13.

Lebow, J. L. (2005a.). Family therapy at the beginning of the twenty-first century. In J. L. Lebow (Ed.), *Handbook of clinical family therapy* (pp. 1–14). New York: Wiley.

Lebow, J. L. (Ed.). (2005b). *Handbook of clinical family therapy.* Hoboken, NJ: Wiley.

Lebow, J. L. (2005c). Integrative family therapy for families experiencing high-conflict divorce. In J. L. Lebow (Ed.), *Handbook of clinical family therapy* (pp. 516–542). Hoboken, NJ: Wiley.

Lebow, J. L. (2006a). Integrative couple therapy. In G. Stricker & J. Gold (Eds.), *A casebook of psychotherapy integration* (pp. 211–223). Washington, DC: American Psychological Association.

Lebow, J. L. (2006b). *Research for the psychotherapist: From science to practice.* New York: Routledge/Taylor & Francis Group.

Lee, R. E., & Everett, C. A. (2004). *The integrative family therapy supervisor: A primer.* New York: Routledge.

Leigh, I. W., Smith, I. L., Bebeau, M. J., Lichtenberg, J. W., Nelson, P. D., Portnoy, S., et al. (2007). Competency assessment models. *Professional Psychology: Research and Practice, 38,* 463–473.

Levant, R. F. (2004). The empirically validated treatments movement: A practitioner/educator perspective. *Clinical Psychology: Science and Practice, 11,* 219–224.

Levinson, H. (2002a). Assessing organizations. In R. L. Lowman (Ed.), *The California School of Organizational Studies: Handbook of organizational consulting psychology: A comprehensive guide to theory, skills, and techniques* (pp. 315–343). San Francisco, CA: Jossey-Bass.

Levinson, H. (2002b). Ethical problems and consulting guidelines. In R. L. Lowman (Ed.), *Organizational assessment: A step-by-step guide to effective consulting* (pp. 13–39). Washington, DC: American Psychological Association.

Levinson, H. (2002c). Psychological consultation to organizations: Linking assessment and intervention. In R. L. Lowman (Ed.), *The California School of Organizational Studies: Handbook of organizational consulting psychology: A comprehensive guide to theory, skills, and techniques* (pp. 415–449). San Francisco, CA: Jossey-Bass.

Levinson, H. (2009a). How organizational consultation differs from counseling. In H. Levinson, A. M. Freedman, & K. H. Bradt (Eds.), *Consulting psychology: Selected articles by Harry Levinson* (pp. 209–210). Washington, DC: American Psychological Association.

Levinson, H. (2009b). Psychoanalytic theory in organizational behavior. In H. Levinson, A. M. Freedman, & K. H. Bradt (Eds.), *Consulting psychology: Selected articles by Harry Levinson* (pp. 11–30). Washington, DC: American Psychological Association.

Lewis, C. L. (2001). Note. The exploitation of trust: The psychotherapist-patient privilege in Alaska as applied to prison group therapy. *Alaska Law Review, 18,* 295–316.

Liddle, H. A. (2003). Graduate training: The next frontier in bridging the research-practice divide. *The Family Psychologist, 19,* 35–40.

Liddle, H. A. (2009). Multidimensional family therapy: A science-based treatment system for adolescent drug abuse. In J. H. Bray & M. Stanton (Eds.), *The Wiley Blackwell handbook of family psychology* (pp. 341–354). Oxford, UK: Wiley-Blackwell.

Liddle, H. A., Bray, J. H., Levant, R. F., & Santisteban, D. A. (2002). Family psychology intervention science: An emerging area of science and practice. In H. A. Liddle, D. A. Santisteban, R. F. Levant, & J. H. Bray (Eds.), *Family psychology: Science-based interventions* (pp. 3–15). Washington, DC: American Psychological Association.

Liddle, H. A., Santisteban, D., Levant, R., & Bray, J. (Eds.). (2002). *Family psychology: Science-based interventions.* Washington, DC: American Psychological Association.

Lippitt, G. L., & Lippitt, R. (1986). *The consulting process in action: Skill development* (2nd ed.). San Diego, CA: Pfeiffer.

Lipsitt, P. D. (2007). Ethics and forensic psychological practice. In A. M. Goldstein (Ed.), *Forensic psychology: Emerging topics and expanding roles* (pp. 171–205). Hoboken, NJ: Wiley.

Loeb, K. L., Hirsch, A. M., Greif, R., & Hildebrandt, T. B. (2009). Family-based treatment of a 17-year-old twin presenting with emerging anorexia nervosa: A case study using the "Maudsley Method." *Journal of Clinical Child and Adolescent Psychology, 38*(1), 176–183.

Logue, M. E., & Rivinus, T. M. (1991). Young children of substance-abusing parents: A developmental view of risk and resiliency. In T. M. Rivinus (Ed.), *Children of chemically dependent parents: Multiperspectives from the cutting edge* (pp. 55–73). Philadelphia, PA: Brunner/Mazel.

London, K., Bruck, M., Ceci, S. J., & Shuman, D. W. (2005). Disclosure of child sexual abuse: What does the research tell us about the ways that children tell? *Psychology, Public Policy, and Law, 11,* 194–226.

Lowman, R. (Ed.). (1998a). *The ethical practice of psychology in organizations.* Washington, DC: American Psychological Association.

Lowman, R. (1998b). New Directions for graduate training in consulting psychology. *Consulting Psychology Journal: Practice and Research, 50,* 263–270.

Lucas, S. G., & Bernstein, D. A. (2005). *Teaching psychology: A step by step guide.* Mahwah, NJ: Erlbaum.

Ma, Z., Lee, Y., & Yu, K.-H. (2008). Ten years of conflict management studies: Themes, concepts and relationships. *International Journal of Conflict Management, 19* 234–248.

MacFarlane, P. (2002). Parenting of mothers with a serious mental illness: Differential effects of diagnosis, clinical history, and other mental health variables. *Social Work Research, 26,* 225–240.

Mackey, R. A., Diemer, M. A., & O'Brien, B. A. (2000). Conflict-management styles of spouses in lasting marriages. *Psychotherapy: Theory, Research, Practice, Training, 37,* 134–148.

MacRae, S. K., Fox, E., & Slowther, A. (2008). Clinical ethics and systems thinking. In P. A. Singer & A. M. Viens (Eds.), *The Cambridge textbook of bioethics* (pp. 313–321). New York: Cambridge University Press.

Magnavita, J. (2005). *Personality-guided relational psychotherapy.* Washington, DC: American Psychological Association.

Mahaffey, B. A., Lewis, M. S. (2008). Therapeutic alliance directions in marriage, couple, and family counseling. In G. R. Walz, J. C. Bleuer, & R. K. Yep (Eds.), *Compelling counseling interventions: Celebrating VISTAS' fifth anniversary* (pp. 59–69). Ann Arbor, MI: American Counseling Association Counseling Outfitters.

Mahoney, M. (1991). *Human change processes.* New York: Basic Books.

Margolin, G. (1982). Ethical and legal considerations in marital and family therapy. *American Psychologist, 37,* 788–801.

Markman, H. J., Kline, G. H., Rea, J. G., Piper, S. S., Stanley, S. M. & J. L. Lebow (Eds.)., et al. (2005). A sampling of theoretical, methodological, and policy issues in marriage education: Implications for family psychology. In W. M. Pinsof & J. L. Lebow (Eds.), *Family psychology: The art of the science.* (pp. 115–137). New York: Oxford University Press.

Marsella, A. J. (1998). Toward a "Global-Community Psychology": Meeting the needs of a changing world. *American Psychologist, 53,* 1282–1291.

Marsh, D. T., & Lefley, H. P. (2009). Serious mental illness: Family experiences, needs, and interventions. In J. H. Bray & M. Stanton (Eds.), *The Wiley Blackwell handbook of family psychology* (pp. 742–754). Oxford, UK: Wiley-Blackwell.

Martindale, D. A., & Gould, J. W. (2004). The forensic model: Ethics and scientific methodology applied to child custody evaluations. *Journal of Child Custody, 1,* 1–22.

Matheny, A. C., & Zimmerman, T. S. (2001). The application of family systems theory to organizational consultation: A content analysis. *American Journal of Family Therapy, 29,* 421–433.

Mattson, R. E., & Johnson, M. D. (2007). Best practices for integrating research training in marriage and family graduate education. *The Family Psychologist, 23*(3), 12–14.

McBride, N. (2005). Chaos theory as a model for interpreting information systems in organizations. *Information Systems Journal, 15,* 233–254.

McCann, J. T., Flens, J. R., Campagna, V., Colman, P., Lazzaro, T., & Connor, E. (2001). The MCMI-III in child evaluations: A normative study. *Journal of Forensic Psychology Practice, 1,* 27–44.

McClendon, R., & Kadis, L. B. (2004). *Reconciling relationships and preserving the family business: Tools for success.* New York: Haworth Press.

McDaniel, S. H., Hepworth, J., & Doherty, W. J. (1992). *Medical family therapy: A biopsychosocial approach to families with health problems.* New York: Basic Books.

McFarlane, W. R. (2005). Psychoeducational multifamily groups for families with persons with severe mental illness. In J. L. Lebow (Ed.), *Handbook of clinical family therapy* (pp. 195–227). Hoboken, NJ: Wiley.

McGoldrick, M., Gerson, R., & Petry, S. (2008). *Genograms: Assessment and intervention.* New York: Norton.

McGoldrick, M., Giordano, J., & Garcia-Preto, N. (2005). *Ethnicity and family therapy* (3rd ed.). New York: Guilford Press.

McGoldrick, M., & Hardy, K. V. (2008a). Introduction: Re-visioning family therapy from a multicultural perspective. In M. McGoldrick & K. V. Hardy (Eds.), *Re-visioning family therapy: Race, culture, and gender in clinical practice* (pp. 3–24). New York: Guilford Press.

McGoldrick, M., & Hardy, K. V. (Eds.). (2008b). *Re-visioning family therapy: Race, culture, and gender in clinical practice.* New York: Guilford Press.

McHolland, J. (1992). National Council of Schools of Professional Psychology core curriculum conference resolutions. In R. L. Peterson, J. D. McHolland, R. J. Bent, E. Davis-Russell, G. E. Edwall, K. Polite, D. L. Singer, & G. Stricker (Eds.), *The core curriculum in professional psychology* (pp. 153–176). Washington, DC: American Psychological Association.

Meadows, D. H. (2008). *Thinking in systems.* White River Junction, VT: Chelsea Green Publishing.

Melton, G., Petrila, J., Poythress, N. G., & Slobogin, C. (2007). *Psychological evaluations for the courts: A handbook for mental health professionals and lawyers* (3rd ed). New York: Guilford Press.

Meyer, A. S., McWey, L. M., McKendrick, W., & Henderson, T. T. (2010). substance using parents, foster care, and termination of parental rights. The importance of risk factors for legal outcomes. *Children and Youth Services Review, 32,* 639–649.

Miller, W. R., & Rose, G. S. (2009). Toward a theory of motivational interviewing. *American Psychologist, 64,* 527–537.

Millon, T., Davis, R., & Millon, C. (1997). *Manual for the Millon Clinical Multiaxial Inventory-III (MCMI-III)* (2nd ed.). Minneapolis, MN: NCS Pearson.

Minami, T., Wampold, B. E., & Walsh, W. B. (2008). Adult psychotherapy in the real world. In *biennial review of counseling psychology: Volume 1,2008* (pp. 27–45). New York: Routledge/Taylor & Francis.

Mitrani, V. B., Robinson, C., & Szapocznik, J. (2009). Structural ecosystems therapy for women with HIV/AIDS. In J. H. Bray & M. Stanton (Eds.), *The Wiley Blackwell handbook of family psychology* (pp. 355–369). Oxford, UK: Wiley-Blackwell.

Morgan, M. M., & Sprenkle, D. H. (2007). Toward a common-factors approach to supervision. *Journal of Marital and Family Therapy, 33,* 1–17.

Morris, T. M. (1990). Culturally sensitive family assessment: An evaluation of the family assessment device used with Hawaiian-American and Japanese-American families. *Family Process, 29,* 105–116.

Morrison, J.R. (2008). *The first interview.* New York: Guilford Press.

Morse, S. (1978a). Crazy behavior, morals, and science: An analysis of mental health law. *Southern California Law Review, 51,* 527–654.

Morse, S. (1978b). Law and mental health professionals: The limits of expertise. *Professional Psychology, 9,* 389–399.

Muir, J. A., Schwartz, S. J., & Szapocznik, J. (2004). A program of research with Hispanic and African American families: Three decades of intervention development and testing influenced by the changing cultural context of Miami. *Journal of Marital & Family Therapy, 30,* 285–303.

Mullin, V., & Cooper, S. (2002). Cross-cultural issues in international organizational consulting. In R. L. Lowman (Ed.), *The California School of Organizational Studies: Handbook of organizational consulting psychology: A comprehensive guide to theory, skills, and techniques* (pp. 545–561). San Francisco: Jossey-Bass.

Murray, C. E., Lampinen, A., & Kelley-Soderholm, E. L. (2006). Teaching family systems theory through service-learning. *Counselor Education and Supervision, 46*(1), 44–58.

National Council of Schools and Programs of Professional Psychology. (2007). *Competency developmental achievement levels (DALs) of the National Council of Schools and Programs of Professional Psychology (NCSPP).* Retrieved September 6, 2009, from http://www.ncspp.info/pubs.htm

Negy, C., & Snyder, D.K. (2006). Assessing family-of-origin functioning in Mexican American adults: Retrospective evaluation of the Family Environment Scale. *Assessment, 13,* 396–405.

Newman, J. L., Robinson-Kurpius, S. E., & Fuqua, D. R. (2002). Issues in the ethical practice of consulting psychology. In R. L. Lowman (Ed.), *The California School of Organizational Studies: Handbook of organizational consulting psychology: A comprehensive guide to theory, skills, and techniques* (pp. 733–758). San Francisco: Jossey-Bass.

Nichols, W. C. (2003). Family-of-origin treatment. In T. L. Sexton, G. R. Weeks, & M. S. Robbins (Eds.), *Handbook of family therapy: The science and practice of working with families and couples* (pp. 83–100). New York: Brunner-Routledge.

Nisbett, R. E. (2007). Eastern and Western ways of perceiving the world. In Y. Shoda, D. Cervone, & G. Downey (Eds.), *Persons in context: Building a science of the individual* (pp. 62–83). New York: Guilford Press.

Norcross, J. C. (2001). Purposes, processes and products of the task force on empirically supported therapy relationships. *Psychotherapy: Theory, Research, Practice, Training, 38,* 345–356.

Norcross, J. C. (2002). Empirically supported therapy relationships. In J. C. Norcross (Ed.), *Psychotherapy relationships that work: Therapist contributions and responsiveness to patients* (pp. 3–16). New York: Oxford University Press.

Norcross, J. C., Hedges, M., & Castle, P. H. (2002). Psychologists conducting psychotherapy in 2001: A study of the Division 29 membership. *Psychotherapy: Theory, Research, Practice, Training, 39,* 97–102.

Nurse, A. R. (1999). *Family assessment: Effective uses of personality tests with couples and families.* New York: Wiley.

Nurse, A. R., & Stanton, M. (2008). Using the MCMI-III in treating couples. In T. Millon (Ed.), *The Millon Inventories: A practitioner's guide to personalized clinical assessment* (pp. 347–368). New York: Guilford Press.

Nurse, A. R., & Thompson, P. (2009). Collaborative divorce: A family-centered process. In J. H. Bray & M. Stanton (Eds.), *The Wiley Blackwell handbook of family psychology* (pp. 475–486). Oxford, UK: Wiley-Blackwell.

Nutt, R. L. (2005). Family psychology at Texas Woman's University. *The Family Psychologist, 21*(1), 5–6.

Nutt, R. L. (2007a). The final word. *The Family Psychologist, 23*(3), 34.

Nutt, R. L. (2007b). Implications of globalization for training in counseling psychology: Presidential address. *The Counseling Psychologist, 35,* 157–171.

Nutt, R. L., & Stanton, M. (2008). Family psychology specialty practice. *Professional Psychology: Research and Practice, 39,* 519–528.

Obegi, J. H. (2008). The development of the client-therapist bond through the lens of attachment theory. *Psychotherapy: Theory, Research, Practice, Training, 45,* 431–446.

Ogbu, J. U. (1989). The individual in collective adaptation. In L. Weis (Ed.), *Dropouts from schools: Issues, dilemmas and solutions* (pp. 181–204). Buffalo, NY: SUNY Press.

Olds, D. (2009). In support of disciplined passion. *Journal of Experimental Criminology, 5,* 201–214.

Olkin, R. (1999). *What psychotherapists should know about disability.* New York: Guilford Press.

Olson, D. H. (1977). Insiders' and outsiders' views of relationships: Research studies. In G. Levinger & H. Rausch (Eds.), *Close relations* (pp. 115–135). Amherst, MA: University of Massachusetts Press.

Olson, D. H. (2002). *PREPARE/ENRICH counselors manual.* Minneapolis, MN: Life Innovations, Inc.

Olson, D. H., & Gorall, D. M. (2002). Circumplex model of marital and family systems. In F. Walsh (Ed.), *Normal family processes: Growing diversity and complexity* (3rd ed., pp. 459–486). New York: Guilford Press.

Olson, D. H., & Killorin, E. (1988). *Clinical rating scale for the Circumplex model of marital and family systems.* Family Social Science, University of Minnesota.

Orbach, Y., Herskowitz, I., Lamb, M. E., Sternberg, K. J., Esplin, P. W., & Horowitz, D. (2000). Assessing the value of structured protocols for forensic interviews of alleged child abuse victims. *Child Abuse and Neglect, 24,* 733–752.

O'Shea, M., & Jessee, E. (1982). Ethical, value and professional conflicts in systems therapy. In J. C. Hansen (Ed.), *Values, ethics, legalities and the family therapist* (pp. 1–21). Rockville, MD: Aspen.

Ostler, T. (2008). *Assessment of parenting competency in mothers with mental illness.* Baltimore, MD: Brookes Publishing.

Ostler, T. (2010). Assessing parenting risk within the context of severe and persistent mental illness: Validating an observational measure for families with child protective service involvement. *Infant Mental Health Journal, 31,* 467–485.

Otto, R. K., & Edens, J. F. (2003). Parenting capacity. In T. Grisso (Ed,). *Evaluating competencies: Forensic assessments and instruments* (2nd ed., pp. 229–305). New York: Kluwer Academic.

Paskiewicz, W., Rabe, D., Adams, W., Gathercoal, K., Meyer, A., & McIlvried, J. (2006). *2005 NCSPP Self Study with Complementary Data.* Lake Las Vegas, NV: Paper presented at the National Council of Schools and Programs of Professional Psychology.

Patten, C., Barnett, T., & Houlihan, D. (1991). Ethics in marital and family therapy: A review of the literature. *Professional Psychology Research and Practice, 22,* 171–175.

Patterson, C. J. (2009). Children of lesbian and gay parents: Psychology, law, and policy. *American Psychologist, 64,* 727–736.

Patterson, T. (2009). Ethical and legal considerations in family psychology: The special issue of competence. In J. H. Bray & M. Stanton (Eds.), *The Wiley Blackwell handbook of family psychology* (pp. 183–197). Oxford, UK: Wiley-Blackwell.

Pedersen, P. B., Crethar, H. C., & Carlson, J. (2008). *Inclusive cultural empathy: Making relationships central in counseling and psychotherapy.* Washington, DC: American Psychological Association.

Pedersen, P. B., & Ivey, A. (1993). *Culture centered counseling and interviewing skills: A practical guide.* West Port, CT: Praeger Publishers.

Peterson, R. W. (1996). Can systemic thinking be taught? The effect of systems-oriented graduate training on the systemic thinking abilities of clinical child and youth care practitioners: Report on a follow-up study. *Journal of Child & Youth Care, 11*(4), 47–68.

Pinsof, W. M. (1981). Family therapy process research. In A. S. Gurman & D. P. Kniskern (Eds.), *Handbook of family therapy* (pp. 699–741). New York, NY: Brunner/Mazel.

Pinsof, W. M. (1995). *Integrative problem-centered therapy: A synthesis of family, individual, and biological approaches.* New York: Basic Books.

Pinsof, W. M., & Lebow, J. (Eds.). (2005). *Family psychology: The art of science*. New York: Oxford University Press.

Pinsof, W. M., & Chambers, A. L. (2009). Empirically informed systemic psychotherapy: Tracking client change and therapist behavior during therapy. In J. H. Bray & M. Stanton (Eds.), *The Wiley-Blackwell handbook of family psychology* (pp. 431–446). Oxford, UK: Wiley-Blackwell.

Pisani, A. R., & McDaniel, S. H. (2005). An integrative approach to health and illness in family therapy. In J. L. Lebow (Ed.), *Handbook of clinical family therapy* (pp. 569–590). Hoboken, NJ: Wiley.

Poole, D. A., & Lamb, M. E. (1998). *Investigative interviews of children: A guide for helping professionals*. Washington, DC: American Psychological Association.

Portie, T., & Hill, N. R. (2005). Blended families: A critical review of the current research. *The Family Journal, 13*, 445–451.

Principe, G. F., & Ceci, S. J. (2002). "I saw it with my own ears": The effects of peer conversations on preschoolers' reports of nonexperienced events. *Journal of Experimental Child Psychology, 83*, 1–25.

Pruett, M. K., Ebling, R., & Insabella, G. (2004). Critical aspects of parenting plans for young children: Interjecting data into the debate about overnights. *Family Court Review, 42*, 39–59.

Quas, J. A., Davis, E. L., Goodman, G. S., & Myers, J. E. B. (2007). Repeated questions, deception, and children's true and false reports of body touch. *Child Maltreatment, 12*, 60–67.

Ragan, E. P., Einhorn, L. A., Rhoades, G. K., Markman, H. J., & Stanley, S. M. (2009). Relationship education programs: Current trends and future directions. In J. H. Bray & M. Stanton (Eds.), *The Wiley-Blackwell handbook of family psychology* (pp. 450–462). Oxford, UK: Wiley-Blackwell.

Rahim, M. A., & Magner, N. R. (1995). Confirmatory factor analysis of the styles of handling interpersonal conflict: First-order factor model and its invariance across groups. *Journal of Applied Psychology, 80*, 122–132.

Rait, D. S. (2000). The therapeutic alliance in couples and family therapy. *Journal of Clinical Psychology, 56*, 211–224.

Richmond, B. (2000). *The "thinking" in systems thinking: Seven essential skills*. Waltham, MA: Pegasus Communications.

Rivinus, T. M. (Ed.). (1991). *Children of chemically dependent parents: Multiperspectives from the cutting edge*. Philadelphia, PA: Brunner/Mazel.

Robbins, M. S., Liddle, H. A., Turner, C. W., Dakof, G. A., Alexander, J. F., & Kogan, S. M. (2006). Adolescent and parent therapeutic alliances as predictors of dropout in multidimensional family therapy. *Journal of Family Psychology, 20*, 108–116.

Robbins, M. S., Mayorga, C., & Szapocznik, J. (2003). The ecosystemic "lens" to understanding family functioning. In T. Sexton, G. Weeks, & M. Robbins (Eds.), *Handbook of family therapy: The science and practice of working with families and couples* (pp. 21–36). New York: Brunner-Routledge.

Robbins, M. S., Szapocznik, J., & Horigian, V. E. (2009). Brief strategic family therapy™ for adolescents with behavior problems. In J. H. Bray & M. Stanton (Eds.), *The Wiley-Blackwell handbook of family psychology* (pp. 416–430). Oxford, UK: Wiley-Blackwell.

Robbins, M. S., Turner, C. W., Alexander, J. F., & Perez, G. A. (2003). Alliance and dropout in family therapy for adolescents with behavior problems: Individual and systemic effects. *Journal of Family Psychology, 17*, 534–544.

Roberts, M. C., Borden, K. A., Christiansen, M. D., & Lopez, S. J. (2005). Fostering a culture shift: Assessment of competence in the education and careers of professional psychologists. *Professional Psychology: Research and Practice, 36*, 355–361.

Robinson, P. J., & Strosahl, K. D. (2009). Behavioral health consultation and primary care: Lessons learned. *Journal of Clinical Psychology in Medical Settings, 16*(1), 58–71.

Rodolfa, E., Bent, R., Eisman, E., Nelson, P., Rehm, L., & Ritchie, P. (2005). A Cube model for competency development: Implications for psychology educators and regulators. *Professional Psychology: Research and Practice, 36,* 347–354.

Rogers, R. (1995). *Diagnostic and structured interviewing: A handbook for psychologists.* Odessa, FL: Psychological Assessment Resources, Inc.

Rogers, R. (2008). *Clinical assessment of malingering and deception* (3rd ed.). New York: Guilford Press.

Rohrbaugh, M. J., Shoham, V. (2002). Couple treatment for alcohol abuse: A systemic family-consultation model. In S. G. Hofmann & M. C. Tompson (Eds.), *Treating chronic and severe mental disorders: A handbook of empirically supported interventions* (pp. 277–295). New York: Guilford Press.

Rolland, J. (1994). *Families, illness, and disability: An integrative treatment model.* New York: Basic Books.

Romans, J. S. C., Boswell, D. L., Carlozzi, A. F., & Ferguson, D. B. (1995). Training and supervision practices in clinical, counseling, and school psychology programs. *Professional Psychology: Research and Practice, 26,* 407–412.

Romney, P. (2008). Consulting for diversity and social justice: Challenges and rewards. *Consulting Psychology Journal: Practice and Research, 60,* 139–156.

Roseby, V., & Johnston, J. R. (1998). Children of Armageddon: Common developmental threats in high-conflict divorcing families. *Child and Adolescent Psychiatric Clinics of North America, 7,* 295–309.

Rosenberg, T., & Watson, W. (2009). Families and health: An attachment perspective. In J. H. Bray & M. Stanton (Eds.), *The Wiley-Blackwell handbook of family psychology* (pp. 539–550). Oxford, UK: Wiley-Blackwell.

Roysicar, G. (2004). Cultural self-awareness assessment: Practice examples from psychology training. *Professional Psychology: Research and Practice, 35,* 658–666.

Rubin, N. J., Bebeau, M., Leigh, I. W., Lichtenberg, J. W., Nelson, P. D., Portnoy, S., et al. (2007). The competency movement within psychology: An historical perspective. *Professional Psychology: Research and Practice, 38,* 452–462.

Sandoval, J. (1996). Constructivism, consultee-centered consultation, and conceptual change. *Journal of Educational & Psychological Consultation, 7*(1), 89–97.

Sapyta, J., Riemer, M., & Bickman, L. (2005). Feedback to clinicians: Theory, research, and practice. *Journal of Clinical Psychology/In Session, 61,* 145–153.

Saywitz, K. J., Goodman, G. S., & Lyon, T. D. (2002). Interviewing children in and out of court: Current research and practice implications. In J. Myers, L. Berliner, J. Briere, C. T. Hendrix, C. Jenny, & T. Reid (Eds.), *The APSAC handbook on child maltreatment* (2d ed., pp. 349–377). Thousand Oaks, CA: Sage.

Schermerhorn, A. C., Chow, S., & Cummings, E. M. (2010). Developmental family processes and interparental conflict: Patterns of microlevel influences. *Developmental Psychology, 46,* 869–885.

Schermerhorn, A. C., Cummings, E. M., & Davies, P. T. (2008). Children's representations of multiple family relationships: Organizational structure and development in early childhood. *Journal of Family Psychology, 22,* 89–101.

Seligman, S. (2005). Dynamic systems theories as a metaframework for psychoanalysis. *Psychoanalytic Dialogues, 15,* 285–319.

Senge, P. M. (2006). *The fifth discipline: The art and practice of the learning organization* (Rev ed.). New York: Random House.

Sexton, T. L. (2007). The therapist as a moderator and mediator in successful therapeutic change. *Journal of Family Therapy, 29,* 104–108.

Sexton, T. L. (2009a). Functional Family Therapy: Traditional theory to evidence-based practice. In J. H. Bray & M. Stanton (Eds.), *The Wiley-Blackwell handbook of family psychology* (pp. 327–340). Oxford, UK: Wiley-Blackwell.

Sexton, T. L. (2009b). Research and practice in family psychology: Oxymoron or fundamental dialectic. *The Family Psychologist, 25,* 1–27.

Sexton, T. L., & Alexander, J. F. (2003). Functional Family Therapy: A mature clinical model for working with at-risk adolescents and their families. In T. L. Sexton, G. R. Weeks, & M. S. Robbins (Eds.), *Handbook of family therapy: The science and practice of working with families and couples* (pp. 323–348). New York: Brunner-Routledge.

Sexton, T. L., & Alexander, J. F. (2005). Functional Family Therapy for externalizing disorders in adolescents. In J. L. Lebow (Ed.), *Handbook of clinical family therapy* (pp. 164–191). Hoboken, NJ: Wiley.

Sexton, T. L., & Coop-Gordon, K. (2009). Science, practice, and evidence-based treatments in the clinical practice of family psycholoyg. In J. H. Bray & M. Stanton (Eds.), *The Wiley-Blackwell handbook of family psychology* (pp. 314–326). Oxford, UK: Wiley-Blackwell.

Sexton, T. L., Coop-Gordon, K., Gurman, A. S., Lebow, J. L., Holtzworth-Munroe, A., & Johnson, S. M. (2007). *Task force report recommendations from the Division 43: Family Psychology Task Force on Evaluating Evidence-Based Treatments in Couple and Family Psychology.* San Francisco: Division 43 (American Psychological Association).

Sexton, T. L., Hanes, C. W., & Kinser, C. J. (2010). Translating science into clinical practice. In J. C. Thomas & M. Hersen (Eds.), *Handbook of clinical psychology competencies.* New York: Springer.

Sexton, T. L., Kinser, J. C., & Hanes, C. W. (2008). Beyond a single standard: Levels of evidence approach for evaluating marriage and family therapy research and practice. *Journal of Family Therapy, 30,* 386–398.

Sexton, T. L., Ridley, C. R., & Kleiner, A. J. (2004). Beyond common factors: Multilevel-process models of therapeutic change in marriage and family therapy. *Journal of Marital & Family Therapy, 30,* 131–149.

Sexton, T. L., Robbins, M. S., Hollimon, A. S., Mease, A. L., Mayorga, C. C., & Weeks, G. R. (2003). Efficacy, effectiveness, and change mechanisms in couple and family therapy. In T. L. Sexton, M. S. Robbins, & G. R. Weeks (Eds.), *Handbook of family therapy: The science and practice of working with families and couples* (pp. 229–261). New York: Brunner-Routledge.

Sexton, T. L., Weeks, G. R., & Robbins, M. S. (2003). The future of couple and family therapy. In T. L. Sexton, G. R. Weeks, & M. S. Robbins (Eds.), *Handbook of family therapy: The science and practice of working with families and couples* (pp. 449–466). New York: Brunner-Routledge.

Shek, D. T. L. (1998). The Chinese version of the Self-Report Family Inventory: Does culture make a difference? *Research on Social Work Practice, 8,* 315–329.

Shek, D. T. L. (2002). Assessment of family functioning in Chinese adolescents: The Chinese version of the Family Assessment Device. *Research on Social Work Practice, 12,* 502–524.

Shellenberger, S., Dent, M. M., Davis-Smith, M., Seale, J. P., Weintraut, R., & Wright, T. (2007). Cultural genogram: A tool for teaching and practice. *Families, Systems, and Health, 25,* 367–381.

Shuman, D. W., Greenberg, S., Heilbrun, K., & Foote, W. E. (1998). An immodest proposal: should treating mental health professionals be barred from testifying about their patients? *Behavioral Sciences and the Law, 16,* 509–523.

Silverstein, L. B. (2006). Integrating feminism and multiculturalism: Scientific fact or science fiction? *Professional Psychology: Research and Practice, 37,* 21–28.

Silverstein, L. B., & Auerbach, C. F. (2009). Using qualitative research to develop culturally competent evidence-based practice. *American Psychologist, 64,* 274–275.

Silverstein, L. B., Auerbach, C. F., & Levant, R. F. (2006). Using qualitative research to strengthen clinical practice. *Professional Psychology: Research and Practice, 37,* 351–358.

Silverstein, L. B., & Goodrich, T. J. (2003). *Feminist family therapy: Empowerment in social context.* Washington, DC: American Psychological Association.

Smith, J. E., & Meyers, R. J. (2004). *Motivating substantce abusers to enter treatment: Working with family members.* New York: Guilford Press.

Smith, L. (2009). Enhancing training and practice in the context of poverty. *Training and Education in Professional Psychology, 3,* 84–93.

Snyder, D. K., Cavell, T. A., Heffer, R. W., & Mangrum, L. F. (1995). Marital and family assessment: A multifaceted, multilevel approach. In R. H. Mikesell, D. D. Lusterman, & S. H. McDaniel (Eds.), *Integrating family therapy: Handbook of family psychology and systems theory* (pp. 163–182). Washington, DC: American Psychological Association.

Snyder, D. K., & Kazak, A. E. (2005). Methodology in family science: Introduction to the special issue. *Journal of Family Psychology, 19,* 3–5.

Solomon, J., & Biringen, Z. (2001). Another look at the developmental research: Commentary on Kelly and Lamb's "Using child development research to make appropriate custody and access decisions." *Family Court Review, 39,* 355–364.

Sorensen, T., & Snow, B. (1990). How children tell: The process of disclosure in child sexual abuse. *Child Welfare, 70,* 3–15.

Spaccarelli, S. (2004). Stress, appraisal, and coping in child sexual abuse: A theoretical and empirical review. *Psychological Bulletin, 116,* 340–362.

Spaccarelli, S., & Fuchs, S. (1997). Variability in symptom expression among sexually abused girls: Developing multivariate models. *Journal of Clinical Child Psychology, 26,* 24–35.

Spanier, G. B. (1976). Measuring dyadic adjustment: New scales for assessing the quality of marriage and similar dyads. *Journal of Marriage and the Family, 38,* 15–28.

Society for Family Psychology. (2008). Policy and procedures manual and by-laws. Unpublished.

Society for Family Psychology. (2009). Home page: Division 43. Retrieved March 14, 2009, from http://www.apa.org/divisions/div43/

Sperry, L. (2004). *Assessment of couples and families: Contemporary and cutting-edge strategies.* New York: Brunner-Routledge.

Sperry, L. (2005). Case conceptualization: A strategy for incorporating individual, couple and family dynamics in the treatment process. *American Journal of Family Therapy, 33,* 353–364.

Sperry, L., Blackwell, B., Gudeman, J., & Faulkner, K. (1992). *Psychiatric case formulations.* Washington, D.C.: American Psychiatric Press.

Sprenkle, D. H., & Blow, A. J. (2004). Common factors and our sacred models. *Journal of Marital and Family Therapy, 30,* 113–129.

Sprenkle, D. H., & Blow, A. J. (2007). The role of the therapist as the bridge between common factors and therapeutic change: More complex than congruency with a worldview. *Journal of Family Therapy, 29,* 109–113.

Sprenkle, D. H., Davis, S. D., & Lebow, J. L. (2009). *Common factors in couple and family therapy: The overlooked foundation for effective practice.* New York: Guilford Press.

Stabb, S. D., Cox, D. L., & Harber, J. L. (1997). Gender-related therapist attributions in couples therapy: A preliminary multiple case study investigation. *Journal of Marital & Family Therapy, 23,* 335–346.

Stanley, S. M., Amato, P. R., Johnson, C. A., & Markman, H. J. (2006). Premarital education, marital quality, and marital stability: Findings from a large, random household survey. *Journal of Family Psychology, 20,* 117–126.

Stanton, M. (2005a). Developing family psychologists: Epistemological transformation. *The Family Psychologist, 21*(4), 1, 26.

Stanton, M. (2005b). The evolving state of family psychology in graduate education in psychology. *The Family Psychologist, 21*(1), 11–12.

Stanton, M. (2005c). A family psychology emphasis in clinical psychology education. *The Family Psychologist, 21*(1), 7–9.

Stanton, M. (2009a). Consultation and education competency. In M. Kenkel & R. Peterson (Eds.), *Competency-based education for professional psycholog* (pp. 143–160). Washington, DC: American Psychological Association.

Stanton, M. (2009b). The systemic epistemology of family psychology. In J. H. Bray & M. Stanton (Eds.), *The Wiley-Blackwell handbook of family psychology* (pp. 5–20).Oxford, UK: Wiley-Blackwell.

Stanton, M. (2009c). Systemic treatments for substance use disorders. In J. H. Bray & M. Stanton (Eds.), *The Wiley-Blackwell handbook of family psychology* (pp. 637–649). Oxford, UK: Wiley-Blackwell.

Stanton, M., & Harway, M. (2007). Recommendations for doctoral education and training in family psychology. *The Family Psychologist, 23*(3), 4–10.

Stanton, M., Harway, M., & Eaton, H. (2006). *Comparison of doctoral programs with an emphasis in family psychology*. Paper presented at the annual convention of the American Psychological Association.

Stanton, M., Harway, M., & Vetere, A. (2009). Education in family psychology. In J. H. Bray & M. Stanton (Eds.), *The Wiley-Blackwell handbook of family psychology* (pp. 129–146). Oxford, UK: Wiley-Blackwell.

Stanton, M., & Nurse, R. (2005). The development of family psychologists: An annotated flowchart. *The Family Psychologist, 21*(4), 4–5.

Stanton, M., & Nurse, R. (2009). Personality-guided couple psychotherapy. In J. H. Bray & M. Stanton (Eds.), *The Wiley Blackwell handbook of family psychology* (pp. 258–271). Oxford, UK: Wiley-Blackwell.

Steinberg, L., & Schwartz, R. (2000). Developmental psychology goes to court. In T. Grisso & R. Schwartz (Eds.), *Youth on trial* (pp. 9–31). Chicago: University of Chicago Press.

Stewart, S. D. (2010). Children with nonresident parents: Living arrangements, visitation, and child support. *Journal of Marriage and Family, 72*, 1078–1091.

Stinchfield, T. A. (2004). Clinical competencies specific to family-based therapy. *Counselor Education and Supervision, 43*, 286–300.

Stinchfield, T. A. (2006). Using popular films to teach systems thinking. *The Family Journal, 14*, 123–128.

Stith, S. M., McCollum, E. E. (2009). Couples treatment for psychological and physical aggression. In K. D. O'Leary & E. M. Woodin (Eds.), *Psychological and physical aggression in couples: Causes and interventions* (pp. 233–250). Washington, DC: American Psychological Association.

Stoltenberg, C. D. (2005). Enhancing professional competence through developmental approaches to supervision. *American Psychologist, 60*, 857–864.

Stoltenberg, C. D., McNeill, B. W., & Crethar, H. C. (1994). Changes in supervision as counselors and therapists gain experience: A review. *Professional Psychology: Research and Practice, 25*, 416–449.

Stoltenberg, C. D., McNeill, B. W., & Delworth, U. (1998). *IDM supervision: An integrated developmental model for supervising counselors and therapists*. San Francisco: Jossey-Bass.

Stoltenberg, C. D., McNeill, B. W., & Delworth, U. (2009). *IDM supervision: An integrated developmental model for supervising counselors and therapists*. New York: Routledge.

Storm, C. L., McDowell, T., Long. The metamorphosis of training and supervision. In T.L. Sexton, G. R. Weeks, & M. S. Robbins (Eds.), *Handbook of family therapy: The science and practice of working with families and couples* (pp. 431–446). New York: Brunner-Routledge.

Storm, C. L., Todd, T. C., Sprenkle, D. H., & Morgan, M. M. (2001). Gaps between MFT supervision assumptions and common practice: Suggested best practices. *Journal of Marital and Family Therapy, 27,* 227–239.

Straus, M. A. (1979). Measuring intrafamily conflict and violence: The Conflict Tactics (CT) Scales. *Journal of Marriage and the Family, 41,* 75–88.

Sue, D. W. (2008). Multicultural organizational consultation: A social justice perspective. *Consulting Psychology Journal: Practice and Research, 60,* 157–169.

Sue, D. W., Arredondo, P., & McDavis, R. J. (1992). Multicultural competencies and standards: A call to the profession. *Journal of Counseling and Development, 70,* 477–486.

Sue, D. W., Bingham, R. P., Porche-Burke, L., & Vasquez, M. (1999). The diversification of psychology: A multicultural revolution. *American Psychologist, 54,* 1061–1069.

Sue, D. W., Capodilupo, C. M., Torino, G. C., Bucceri, J. M., Holder, A. M. B., Nadal, K. L., & Esquilin, M. (2007). Racial microaggressions in everyday life: Implications for clinical practice. *American Psychologist, 62,* 271–286.

Sue, D. W., Carter, R. T., Casas, J .M., Fouad, N. A., Ivey, A. E., Jensen, M. et al. (1998). *Multicultural counseling competencies: Individual and organizational development.* Thousand Oaks, CA: Sage Publications.

Sue, D. W., & Sue, D. (2007). *Counseling the culturally diverse: Theory and practice* (5th ed.). New York: Wiley.

Sue, S. (1998). In search of cultural competence in psychotherapy and counseling. *American Psychologist, 53,* 400–448.

Sue, S. (2006). Cultural competency: From philosophy to research and practice. *Journal of Community Psychology, 34,* 237–245.

Sweeney, L. B. (n.d.). Thinking about systems: 12 habits of mind. Retrieved July 2, 2009, from http://www.lindaboothsweeney.net/thinking/habits

Sweeney, L. B., & Sterman, J. D. (2003). Bathtub dynamics: Initial results of a systems thinking inventory. *System Dynamics Review, 16,* 249–286.

Sweeney, L. B., & Sterman, J. D. (2007). Thinking about systems: Student and teacher conceptions of natural and social systems. *System Dynamics Review, 23*(2), 285–312.

Szapocznik, J., & Coatsworth, J. D. (1999). An ecodevelopmental framework for organizing the influences on drug abuse: An ecodevelopmental model for risk and prevention. In M. Glantz & C. R. Hertel (Eds.), Drug abuse: Origins and interventions (pp. 331–366). Washington, DC: American Psychological Association.

Szapocznik, J., & Kurtines, W. M. (1993). Family psychology and cultural diversity: Opportunities for theory, research, and application. *American Psychologist, 48,* 400–407.

Tabachnick, B. G., & Fidell, L. S. (2006). *Using multivariate statistics* (5th ed.) Upper Saddle River, NJ: Allyn & Bacon

Taber, T. D. (2007). Using metaphors to teach organization theory. *Journal of Management Education, 31,* 541–554.

Tajfel, H. (1981). *Human groups and social categories.* Cambridge: Cambridge University Press.

Tanebaum, R., & Berman, M. (1990). Ethical and legal issues in psychotherapy supervision. *Psychotherapy in Private Practice, 8,* 65–77.

Tarasoff v. Regents of the University of California, 529 P.2d 553 (Cal. 1974).

Tarasoff v. Regents of the University of California, 551 P.2d 334 (Cal. 1976).

Taylor, K. (2009). Paternalism, participation and partnership: The evolution of patient centeredness in the consultation. *Patient Education and Counseling, 74,* 150–155.

Thoburn, J., Hoffman-Robinson, G., Shelly, L. J., & Hagen, A. J. (2009). Clinical practice in family psychology. In J. H. Bray & M. Stanton (Eds.), *The Wiley Blackwell handbook of family psychology* (pp. 198–211). Oxford, UK: Wiley-Blackwell.

Thomas, K. W., & Kilmann, R. H. (1978). Comparison of four instruments measuring conflict behavior. *Psychological Reports, 42*, 1139–1145.

Titelman, P. (2008). Sibling triangles and leadership in a family business. In P. Titelman (Ed.), *Triangles: Bowen family systems theory perspectives* (pp. 357–386). New York: Haworth Press/Taylor and Francis Group.

Tonti, R. (1991). Teaching family systems therapy to social work students. *Journal of Independent Social Work, 5*(3), 41–51.

Touliatos, J., Perlmutter, B. F., Straus, M. A., & Holden, G. W. (Eds.). (2001). *Handbook of family measurement techniques* (Vols. 1–3). Thousand Oaks, CA: Sage.

Trocme, N., & Bala, N. (2005). False allegations of abuse and neglect when parents separate. *Child Abuse and Neglect, 29*, 1333–1345.

Turner, S. M., Demers, S. T., Fox, H. R., & Reed, G. M. (2001). APA's guidelines for test user qualifications: An executive summary. *American Psychologist, 56*, 1099–1113.

Ulvila, J. W. (2000). Building relationships between consultants and clients. *American Behavioral Scientist, 43*, 1667–1680.

Vande Kemp, H. (1981). Teaching psychology of the family: An experiential approach and a working bibliography. *Teaching of Psychology, 8*, 152–156.

van den Bos, K., & Miedema, J. (2000). Toward understanding why fairness matters: The influence of mortality salience on reactions to procedural fairness. *Journal of Personality and Social Psychology, 79*, 355–366.

Vasquez, M. T. (1992). Psychologist as clinical supervisor: Promoting ethical practice. *Professional Psychology: Research and Practice, 23*, 196–202.

Wadsworth, Y. (2008). Is it safe to talk about systems again yet? Self organising processes for complex living systems and the dynamics of human inquiry. *Systemic Practice and Action Research, 21*, 153–170.

Waldron, H. B., Turner, C. W., Barton, C., Alexander, J. F., & Cline, V. B. (1997). Therapist defensiveness and marital therapy process and outcome. *American Journal of Family Therapy, 25*, 233–243.

Wallerstein, J. S., & Tanke, T. J. (1996). To move or not to move: Psychological and legal considerations in the relocation of children following divorce. *Family Law Quarterly, 30*, 305–332.

Walsh, F. (2009a). Religion and spirituality in couple and family relations. In J. H. Bray & M. Stanton (Eds.), *The Wiley Blackwell handbook of family psychology* (pp. 600–612). Oxford, UK: Wiley-Blackwell.

Walsh, F. (2009b). *Spiritual resources in family therapy* (2nd ed.). New York: Norton.

Wampler, K. S., & Halverson, C. F. (1993). Quantitative measurement in family research. In P. G. Boss, W. J. Doherty, R. La Rossa, W. R. Schumm, & S. K. Steinmetz (Eds.), *Sourcebook of family theories and methods: A contextual approach* (pp. 181–194). New York: Plenum Press.

Wampold, B. E. (2001). *The great psychotherapy debate: Models, methods, and findings.* Mahwah, NJ: Erlbaum.

Wampold, B. E., Goodheart, C. D., & Levant, R. F. (2007). Clarification and elaboration on evidence-based practice in psychology. *American Psychologist, 62*, 616–618.

Wampold, B. E., Lichtenberg, J. W., & Waehler, C. A. (2005). A broader perspective: Counseling psychology's emphasis on evidence. *Journal of Contemporary Psychotherapy, 35*(1), 27–38.

Wan, M. W., Salmon, M. P., Riordan, D. M., Appleby, L., Webb, R., & Abel, K. M. (2007). What predicts poor mother-infant interaction in schizophrenia? *Psychological Medicine: A Journal of Research in Psychiatry and the Allied Sciences, 37*, 537–546.

Wang, H., & Amato, P. R. (2000). Predictors of divorce adjustment: Stressors, resources, and definitions. *Journal of Marriage and Family, 62*, 655–668.

Warshak, R. A. (2000). Blanket restrictions: Overnight contact between parents and young children. *Family and Conciliation Courts Review, 38,* 422–445.

Watkins, C. E., Campbell, V. L., Nieberding, R., & Hallmark, R. (1995). Contemporary practice of psychological assessment by clinical psychologists. *Professional Psychology: Research and Practice, 26,* 54–60.

Watson, B., & Gallois, C. (1998). Nurturing communication by health professionals toward patients: A communication accommodation theory approach. *Health Communication, 10,* 343–355.

Weber, T., & Cebula, C. (2009). Intensive family-of-origin consultation: An intergenerational approach. In J. H. Bray & M. Stanton (Eds.), *The Wiley-Blackwell handbook of family psychology* (pp. 272–285). Oxford, UK: Wiley-Blackwell.

Webster, C. D., Douglas, K. S., Eaves, D., & Hart, S. D. (1997). *HCR-20: Assessing risk for violence manual (version 2).* Lutz, FL: PAR.

Webster-Stratton, C., & Herbert, M. (1994). *Troubled families-problem children: Working with parents: A collaborative process.* New York, NY: John Wiley & Sons Inc.

Weissman, H. N. & Debow, D. M. (2003). Ethical principles and professional competencies. In A. M. Goldstein (Ed.), *Handbook of psychology: Forensic psychology* (pp. 33–53). New York: Wiley.

Wells, K. C. (2005). Family therapy for attention-deficit/hyperactivity disorder (ADHD). In J. L. Lebow (Ed.), *Handbook of clinical family therapy* (pp. 42–72). Hoboken, NJ: Wiley.

Welsh, R., Greenberg, L., & Graham-Howard, M. (2009). Family forensic psychology. In J. H. Bray & M. Stanton (Eds.), *The Wiley Blackwell handbook of family psychology* (pp. 702–716). Oxford, UK: Wiley-Blackwell.

Whalley, B., & Hyland, M. E. (2009). One size does not fit all: Motivational predictors of contextual benefits of therapy. *Psychology and Psychotherapy: Theory, Research and Practice, 82,* 291–303.

Whisman, M. A., Whiffen, V. E., & Whiteford, N. (2009). Couples therapy for depression. In J. H. Bray & M. Stanton (Eds.), *The Wiley Blackwell handbook of family psychology* (pp. 650–660). Oxford, UK: Wiley-Blackwell.

Whitchurch, G. G. (2005). Walking the walk: Teaching systems theory by doing theory. In V. L. Bengtson, A. C. Acock, K. R. Allen, P. Dilworth-Anderson, & D. M. Klein (Eds.), *Sourcebook of family theory and research* (pp. 573–574). Thousand Oaks, CA: Sage.

White, L., & Gilbreth, J. G. (2001). When children have two fathers: Effects of relationships with stepfathers and noncustodial fathers on adolescent outcomes. *Journal of Marriage and Family, 63,* 155–167.

Worthen, V. E., & McNeill, B. W. (1996). A phenomenological investigation of "good" supervision events. *Journal of Counseling Psychology, 43,* 25–34.

Worthington, E. L. (1984). Empirical investigations of supervision of counselors as they gain experience. *Journal of Counseling Psychology, 31,* 63–75.

Yakushko, O., Davidson, M. M., & Williams, E. N. (2009). Identity salience model: A paradigm for integrating multiple identities in clinical practice. *Psychotherapy Theory, Research, Practice, Training, 46,* 180–192.

Yalom, I. D., & Leszcz, M. (2005). *The theory and practice of group psychotherapy* (5th ed.). New York: Basic Books.

Yingling, L. C., Miller, W. E., McDonald, A. L., & Galewaler, S. T. (1998). *GARF assessment sourcebook: Using the DSM-IV Global Assessment of Relational Functioning.* New York: Routledge.

Zuravin, S., McMillen, C., DePanfilis, D., & Risley-Curtiss, C. (1996). The intergenerational cycle of child maltreatment: Continuity versus discontinuity. *Journal of Interpersonal Violence, 11,* 316–334.

Adaptability—individuals, couples, and families exhibit flexibility to adjust to the demands of the environment

Ambiguity—the recognition that interdependence, complexity, and reciprocity create significant uncertainty (shades of gray) regarding causation, progression, and resolution of issues and problems.

Assessment—the application of individual, couple, and family psychological assessment methods to identify the assets and liabilities of individuals, couples, and families for the purpose of problem identification, treatment planning, and intervention, or to answer a focused question related to couple or family functioning.

Cartesian—the mechanistic system of philosophy of science espoused by Rene Descartes.

Case Conceptualization—development of the overarching framework for contextualizing assessment, diagnosis, problem description, case formulation, and treatment planning.

Case Formulation—The second phase of case conceptualization involving organizing case information, providing systemic explanations, and prioritizing treatment goals.

Change of format—to move from treating the index client in a one-on-one format to treating various subsystems of the family or the entire family. Conversely, when treating couples or a family, changing the format of psychotherapy from conjoint to individual sessions.

Common factors—change mechanisms that are found in common across effective therapies. These include client factors; therapist demographic traits, training, personality and well-being; and the nature of the therapeutic alliance.

Complexity—the dynamic, interactive relationship between system levels and components that extends beyond linear cause-effect conceptualization to incorporate multifaceted aspects of issues.

Consultation—an advisory or collaborative interaction with any system or subsystem based on psychological science and a systemic epistemology to assess needs, proffer recommendations, and engage in interventions using specialty skills and attitudes to achieve the objectives of the consultee.

Contextual factors—consideration of the environment that provides the interpretive frame for understanding, individual, couple, or family problems.

Couple and family psychology—a broad and general specialty orientation to the science and practice of professional psychology that is based on a systemic epistemology. The specialty extends beyond couple or family therapy to denote a broad orientation to human behavior that occurs in the context of relationships and larger macrosystemic dynamics.

Culture-centered—habitual orientation toward seeing all behavior as influenced by culture and perceived by the CFP specialist through socially constructed filters

Developmental supervision—a supervision modality that focuses training efforts on a predictable developmental sequence or trajectory that a supervisee possesses at a particular level of training.

Disputed privilege—when one party in a divorce resolution or child custody case wants to release confidential information that was obtained in the course of conjoint treatment and the other does not.

Equifinality—several paths towards the same result may be taken, even if the starting point is different.

Equipotentiality—starting points are the same, but different results may occur.

Equitable treatment—professional commitment to value each person engaged in multi-person psychotherapy, including gender equity, procedural fairness, and responsiveness to client feedback about perceived inequity.

Evidence-based practice—the clinical expertise to combine psychological research with clinical skills and attitudes in the provision of psychological services.

Evidence-based relationships—research on the clinician factors that contribute to the formation of an effective therapeutic alliance and improve treatment outcomes

Family forensic psychology—a special application of family psychology and forensic psychology that provides expert-level services to families involved with the legal system, their attorneys, and the courts.

General Systems Theory—a meta-theoretical approach to science characterized by open systems and nonlinear causality.

Individual factors—consideration of individual aspects of a person (e.g. biological, personality) as components to understanding a broader systemic problem

Interpersonal factors—consideration of relational dynamics and family constellation when thinking about an individual, couple, or family problem.

Open system—recognition that all living organisms are nested in hierarchical networks and receive regular feedback from the environment.

Outcome measurement—applying empirical methods to provide evidence that treatment is impacting the clients' functioning.

Perpetuating factors—system-maintaining elements that keep an individual, couple, or family stuck and unable to change without some type of intervention

Perspective—alternate views of an issue or circumstance dependent on one's position in the system. One may take the perspective of another through mental flexibility and accurate empathy; this is often necessary in providing treatment to couples, families, and larger groups.

Positive ethics—the pursuit of lifelong learning and development in ethical decision making and practice, and not just adherence to a list of "do's" and "don'ts".

Positivism—a philosophy and methodology of modern science, which argues that scientific knowledge is produced by quantitatively measuring observable phenomena.

Precipitating factors—identifiable stressors that help explain why an individual, couple, or family has witnessed a decline in functioning from previous baseline levels. Precipitating factors are often situational and challenge the client(s)' existing resources.

Predisposing factors—events or individual characteristics that enhance the likelihood that an individual, couple, or family will develop problems given the right precipitating stressors.

Problem formulation—the first phase of case conceptualization and includes establishing therapeutic alliance, conducting the preliminary interview, formulating testable hypotheses, conducting the assessment, and diagnosing or describing the presenting problem.

Process-based supervision—a supervision modality that focuses on the various roles, tasks, processes, and functions of the supervisor in the supervision process.

Psychometrics—the statistical and theoretical foundation of psychological measurement.

Psychotherapy-based supervision—a supervision methodology whereby the supervisor educates the supervisee in a modality-specific psychotherapy.

Reciprocity—the simultaneous, mutual, interactive, non-sequential effects that occur between persons or circumstances in any event, situation, or interaction.

Secrets—information that was entrusted to the therapist by one individual and not disclosed in the multiperson session.

Self-organization—a core characteristic of living systems whereby random elements organize themselves into a patterned whole.

Social constructionism—considers the individual and couple/family situated in a unique life story and a particular place in history.

Supervision—a mentor-based teaching method given by a more experienced psychologist to a less experienced trainee for the purpose of increasing competence in the delivery of psychological services.

Systemic epistemology—recognition of the complex, reflexive interaction between individual, interpersonal, and macrosystemic or environmental factors over time in the understanding of human behavior. Adoption of a systemic epistemology is evidenced by habitual systemic thinking, willingness to challenge mental models, seeing the abstract system, comprehending complexity, recognizing reciprocity, considering connections, accepting ambiguity, understanding change, observing patterns and trends, considering unintended consequences, shifting perspectives, and factoring in time.

Teaching—the ability of CFP specialists to educate psychology students in knowledge, skills, and attitudes across the specialty competencies. Alternatively, the ability of CFP specialists to provide psychoeducation to the public that includes knowledge, skills, and attitudes important to relationship health, satisfaction, and commitment.

Therapeutic alliance—the working relationship between the clinician and the client that is a significant factor in positive treatment outcomes. In CFP, the alliance between the specialist and the clients is more complex and interactive than in individual psychotherapy because there may be individual differences in alliance between particular couple or family members and the clinician and the perception of another participant's alliance may impact a client and alter his or her own alliance with the clinician.

Treatment formulation—The third phase of case conceptualization where the CFP provides feedback to the couple/family, sets consensual goals, identifies the best intervention and format for delivery, and plans for monitoring progress.

ABOUT THE AUTHORS

Mark Stanton, PhD, ABPP, is acting provost and professor of psychology at Azusa Pacific University. Dr. Stanton identifies himself as a family psychologist, adopting an understanding of human behavior that recognizes the importance of individual, interpersonal, and environmental factors. He was the 2005 president of the Society for Family Psychology of the American Psychological Association and the editor of *The Family Psychologist* (2002–2007). He is inaugural editor of Couple and Family Psychology: Research and Practice (2011-2014) and the 2011–2012 president of the American Board of Couple and Family Psychology, a constituent board of the American Board of Professional Psychology. He is a licensed psychologist in the state of California and board certified in couple and family psychology with the American Board of Professional Psychology. Dr. Stanton is coeditor of the *Wiley-Blackwell Handbook of Family Psychology* (with James Bray; 2009), a 54-chapter comprehensive overview of the specialty of family psychology, and author of articles and chapters on the specialty of family psychology, graduate education in family psychology, the systemic treatment of substance abuse, and personality-guided couple therapy. He was recognized as the Family Psychologist of the Year in 2007 by the Society for Family Psychology.

Robert K. Welsh, PhD, ABPP, is an associate professor and chair of the Department of Graduate Psychology at Azusa Pacific University. He is the director of the APA-accredited PsyD program in clinical psychology with an emphasis in family psychology. Dr. Welsh is board certified in forensic psychology by the American Board of Professional Psychology and is a fellow of the American Academy of Forensic Psychology. He was chair of the APA Society for Family Psychology committee that successfully petitioned for renewal of family psychology as a specialty by the Commission for Recognition of Specialties and Proficiencies in Professional Psychology. Dr. Welsh maintains a private psychotherapy practice in couple and family psychology and provides forensic consultation to the criminal courts. He teaches research methodology, psychological assessment, and systems theory in the doctoral program and publishes in the areas of family psychology and forensic psychology.

Arthur M. Nezu, PhD, ABPP, is professor of psychology, medicine, and public health at Drexel University and special professor of forensic mental health and psychiatry at the University at Nottingham in the United Kingdom. He is a fellow of multiple professional associations, including the American Psychological Association, and board certified by the American Board of Professional Psychology in cognitive and behavioral psychology, clinical psychology, and clinical health psychology. Dr. Nezu is widely published, is incoming editor of the *Journal of Consulting and Clinical Psychology*, and has maintained a practice for three decades.

Christine Maguth Nezu, PhD, ABPP, is professor of psychology and medicine at Drexel University and special professor of forensic mental health and psychiatry at the University at Nottingham in the United Kingdom. With more than 25 years' experience in clinical private practice, consultation/liaison, research, and teaching, Dr. Maguth Nezu is board certified by the American Board of Professional Psychology in cognitive and behavioral psychology and clinical psychology. She is also a past president of ABPP. Her research has been supported by federal, private, and state-funded agencies, and she has served as a grant reviewer for the National Institutes of Health.